Educational Administration and Leadership

This volume provides diverse perspectives and paradigms in educational administration and leadership. Focusing on particular philosophical and theoretical schools of thought, it traces the contemporary history of debates in the field while also exploring emerging, non-traditional schools for insight and potential contributions to educational administration in multicultural contexts. It critically examines trends and issues in society and their impact on educational theory, and gives an overview of the scholarly study of organizations, administration, and leadership to develop introductory understandings of significant concepts and theories.

David Burgess is Associate Professor in the Department of Educational Administration at the University of Saskatchewan, CA.

Paul Newton is Associate Professor in the Department of Educational Administration at the University of Saskatchewan, CA.

Routledge Research in Educational Leadership Series

Educational Administration and Leadership

Theoretical Foundations

Edited by
David Burgess and Paul Newton

NEW YORK AND LONDON

First published 2015
by Routledge
711 Third Avenue, New York, NY 10017

and by Routledge
2 Park Square, Milton Park, Abingdon, Oxon OX14 4RN

*Routledge is an imprint of the Taylor & Francis Group,
an informa business*

© 2015 Taylor & Francis

Library of Congress Cataloging-in-Publication Data
CIP data has been applied for.

ISBN: 978-1-138-82576-5 (hbk)
ISBN: 978-1-315-73973-1 (ebk)

Typeset in Sabon
by Apex CoVantage, LLC

Contents

Figures

Tables

Acknowledgements

From inception to publication, many individuals have offered their support and guidance; we would be remiss not to briefly acknowledge their kind contributions to our scholarly work and growth as academics. Engaged and directed by our professors (and now colleagues), our early exposure to many of the ideas and debates that permeate the pages of this volume can be traced to graduate school class discussions. For these moments of enlightenment and challenge, we wish to thank Drs Patrick Renihan, Larry Sackney, Murray Scharf, Keith Walker, and Kevin Wilson.

To our contemporary colleagues and graduate students, who have suffered with good humour and generosity our many naïve and embryonic questions and frequent esoteric debates, we thank you. To our contributors, who endured delay on our part with diligence—your professionalism precedes you. Dr Izhar Oplatka, thank you for your encouragement to bring this project forward to Routledge; and to Stacy Noto and Lauren Verity at Routledge, thank you for your eminently reasonable advice, support, and—most of all—deadlines.

Teresa, Connor, and Sean; Liam and Lauren: Thank you for your patience, stability, and support throughout.

Errors found within the covers of this volume are ours and should neither be attributed to, nor reflect poorly on, our contributors.

Dave and Paul

Introduction

Paul Newton and David Burgess

Educational administration and leadership, as a field of study, has existed since at least 1875, when William Payne published his *Chapters on Supervision*. Obviously, the field has changed considerably since those early days and has been marked by periods of stagnation, revolution, and evolution. The way in which scholars and practitioners currently understand the field of study and practice is the result of a long history of diverse perspectives on what knowledge counts and what can be known about educational organisations. In an attempt to provide the student of educational administration and leadership with a robust understanding of the current state of the field, this book provides diverse historical and contemporary theoretical perspectives/paradigms in educational administration and leadership and explores their impact on the practice of administration and leadership. The variety of epistemological perspectives that have emerged in educational administration and leadership have taken place within a historical, social, and political context. It is our hope that the chapters that follow will highlight the importance of context in the development of new perspectives. The chapters in this volume highlight the influence of philosophers, theorists, and thinkers outside of the field of educational administration and leadership as well as explore how these perspectives have been further developed by scholars of educational administration and leadership. The purpose of the book is not to suggest a preferred or superior paradigm, but to expose students of educational administration and educational leadership to the diversity of paradigms and the debates that exist in the field. The organisation of this book reflects the temporality of the development of the field of study. We have ordered chapters to reflect the historical development of theory in educational administration and leadership. We do not intend to suggest that newer theories supersede or are superior to the ones that went before. Indeed, theory development in the field of study is iterative and recursive; however, we believe there is considerable value in understanding the context in which newer incarnations of theory develop and flourish.

In the first part of this book, the contributing authors explore the debates that have taken place in the field of educational administration over the past several decades. Although intellectual debates have long been a part of the study of educational administration, the field of educational administration (along with most disciplines and fields of study in the social sciences and humanities) experienced significant upheaval in the middle part of the twentieth century. During this time, philosophers such as Kuhn, Popper, Lakatos, and Feyerabend had begun to challenge and debate the very foundation of science upon which educational administration (among many of its cognates) was based. Central to this debate was the exploration of the very idea of a *social* science, and further the relationship of the social sciences to the kindred physical and natural sciences. This debate came to the forefront of scholarly activity in educational administration during the early 1970s, primarily through the revolutionary work of the Canadian scholar Thomas Barr Greenfield. His work and the work of other scholars (notably Griffiths, Hodgkinson, Willower, and Ribbins) laid a foundation for decades of heated discussions in which scholars of educational administration reflected on the nature of our field of study. Several of the contributors to this volume explore the variety of perspectives that emerged from the debates of the 1970s and 1980s. The diverse perspectives that emerged during this period included feminism, postmodernism, naturalistic coherentism, post-positivism, and critical theory, among others. The debates that took place during this era continue to this day, and centre on fundamental questions about the nature of the practice and study of educational administration.

In later chapters, the work of our contributors represents examples of the myriad ways that educational administration is currently understood and framed in contemporary research and scholarship. The intellectual traditions and philosophical orientations explored in the early chapters of this volume are evident in the diverse perspectives on offer in later chapters. It is our purpose to establish that a full understanding of contemporary theorising and scholarship in educational administration is dependent on knowledge of the historical and theoretical context in which our current approaches are grounded and formed. This holds true even in cases where current approaches propose a rejection of the received view.

In the first chapter, David Burgess and Paul Newton explore the antecedents of educational administration in the philosophy of science and in theorising about the nature of social sciences in general. This chapter explores the foundations of theorising about science from the ancient through the enlightenment and into contemporary times. The authors argue that it is necessary to take a long-term view in order to understand the context in which knowledge is generated, justified, and assessed. As Burgess and Newton explain, those who propose new ways of thinking about educational administration are themselves rooted in the dominant ways of thinking of their own era. In their chapter, it is argued that the theoretical and philosophical debates that have taken place, and continue to take place, in educational administration are situated in a broader set of debates in the social sciences. The chapter explores key concepts in the philosophy of science and sets the stage for understanding the context of the diverse traditions that make up the academic study of educational administration. Without this grounding with respect to the philosophy of science, modes of reasoning, empiricism, rationality, and so on, it is exceedingly difficult to locate and interpret not only the historical debates in the field but also the scholarly debates occurring in our own time.

In chapter two, Derek Allison explores the early developments in the foundation of the specialised field of educational administration. This chapter is adapted from a previously unpublished conference paper; however, it feels alarmingly contemporary. It was first presented at the American Educational Research Association conference in 1989. This was a time of furious scholarly activity in the field. Not only were scholars in the field charting new theoretical territory in the wake of Greenfield's seminal 1974 paper, but there were calls from some quarters of the field for educational administration to move toward a more direct relationship with the training of educational leaders (particularly in the United States). This work, focusing almost exclusively on the training needs of school principals and superintendents (as described in Allison's chapter), would eventually lead to the Interstate School Leaders Licensure Consortium (ISLLC) and a new era of administrator standards, licensing, and the accreditation of programmes in departments of educational administration in the United States—with implications for the field of educational administration in Canada, the United Kingdom, and elsewhere. What is striking about this chapter is, first, the thoroughness with which Allison describes and situates the historical development of the field, and second, the resonance of his prognostications for possible futures in the field of educational administration. In reading this chapter, one might wonder: Are we in the fifth age? Has the fifth age come and gone? Or have we not yet moved from the era of intellectual disarray into a promised fifth age?

In chapter three, Augusto Riveros engages in an exploration of the revolutionary work of Thomas Barr Greenfield, whose work set in motion years of conversations, discussions, and, in some cases, heated arguments about the nature of educational administration as a field of study. In particular, Riveros explores the way in which Greenfield questioned the very nature of organisations as meaningful entities or as the appropriate level of interest for educational researchers. He explores Greenfield's interest in meaning, subjectivity, and values as the central phenomena of life in schools. Finally, Riveros suggests that Greenfield's work and critique of positivism in educational administration remains central in contemporary educational administration—particularly at this time in history, as we are experiencing a resurgence of positivistic approaches *vis à vis* educational improvement, high stakes testing, and accountability.

Renate Kahlke provides the context for the rise of critical perspectives and critical theory in educational administration in chapter four. She begins her chapter with a description of the key ideas of the Marxist-inspired thinkers of the Frankfurt School. She follows this with a discussion of the work of Jürgen Habermas and his advancement and revision of the ideas of earlier critical theorists. Kahlke explores the manner in which critical theory perspectives have been taken up in education (e.g., the critical pedagogy of Freire) broadly, and educational administration more specifically. Particular attention is given to the groundbreaking work of William Foster and Richard Bates in the 1980s, applying critical perspectives and analysis to the study of educational organisations. She further identifies the ways in which scholars of educational administration have challenged critical theory; however, she concludes her chapter with suggestions for scholars and practitioners seeking the successful integration of critical theory into the study and practice of educational leadership.

In chapter five, Dawn Wallin presents a thorough review of the diverse perspectives within feminism and feminist scholarship in educational administration. Additionally, in this chapter, she discusses the work of the preeminent feminist scholars in educational administration and identifies the scope and breadth of the work that has been conducted using feminist approaches. Wallin states that feminist research is "risky work" and that its ultimate aim is to reconceptualise and transform existing systems and practices.

The difficult task of bringing postmodern perspectives to description is tackled by Deborah Hicks in chapter six. After discussing the work of postmodern thinkers such as Lacan, Lyotard, Derrida, among others, she explores the ways in which scholars of educational administration have adopted postmodern approaches and perspectives to interrogate educational institutions and policies. In particular, she explores the work of educational administration scholars as they have subjected educational policies to deconstruction (e.g., Fenwick English's examination of ISLLC and its associated policies). She concludes her chapter by articulating the contradictions and inherent tensions that postmodernism presents for the field of educational administration.

In chapter seven, Madeline Press describes the naturalistic coherentism proposed (primarily) by Evers and Lakomski. The work of Evers and Lakomski has been perhaps the most significant theoretical work in educational administration in the last two decades—its significance lies in the discussions it elicited. Although their work was subjected to considerable criticism, naturalistic coherentism has arguably generated more scholarly discussion than any work since Greenfield's. Press, after tracing the origins and identifying the theoretical constructs of naturalistic coherentism, explores these debates and criticisms at length. In Evers and Lakomski's attempt to provide a "theory of everything," they brought together diverse perspectives and provided a space for a robust conversation about the state of educational administration as a field of study. For that reason alone, their work is of great significance to our field.

In chapter eight, Robin Mueller speaks about critical realism, "a methodological orientation that is relatively unknown in the field of education and the discipline of educational administration." In this chapter, she describes the philosophical underpinnings of critical realism and proposes a way of doing science that is ontologically realist, attempts to establish causality, and considers the role of prediction in social science—all rather unfashionable notions in contemporary educational research. Very little has been written about critical realism in the educational administration literature. Mueller contends, however, that critical realism has much to offer the study of organisational and administrative practices in educational institutions.

Augusto Riveros explores ways in which educational organisations can be understood as cognitive systems in chapter nine. He argues that there is a long history of cognitive perspectives in organisational studies and educational administration—from Herbert Simon's work on organisations as information processing systems to professional learning communities. Along the way, Riveros examines naturalistic coherentism, situated cognition, and the learning organisation. He concludes with examples of how cognitive perspectives can be used to understand educational phenomena.

In chapter ten, Scott Eacott explores the ways in which sociological perspectives have been and might be used in educational administration and leadership scholarship. He suggests that social theory and sociological approaches have historically been on the periphery of theorising and research in the field. He proposes multiple sociological frames incorporated into a *relational* approach to the study of educational administration and leadership that has the potential "to find unexpected and surprising resources to think through leadership, management, and administration." In many faculties of education, the disciplinary lens of sociology of education is relegated to educational foundations departments or units. Eacott provides a compelling case for the centrality of sociological approaches to educational administration and leadership research.

In chapter 11, Pamela Timanson and José da Costa provide a review of the ways in which cultural perspectives have been utilised in our field. They explore the anthropological roots of cultural studies, and they discuss the ways in which culture has been understood as a property of organisations and educational institutions. They identify the variety of types of culture research that have been conducted in schools and suggest possible future directions for continued scholarship and research in culture in educational administration.

In chapter 12, Trâm Nguyễn proposes a perspective of educational leadership based upon a Daoist ontology. She suggests that a Daoist perspective on educational leadership emphasises intersubjectivity and an interconnected harmoniousness. She examines Greenfield's notion of subjectivity in educational contexts and suggests that Greenfield's subjectivity lacks an explanation of the relatedness that occurs in the social world (and in Daoist philosophy). Her work proposes an interesting problem and potential solution—how portable are Western conceptions of educational leadership, and how much are they predicated on Western individualism? Her chapter provides an interesting starting point for a discussion on the Western-centric nature of educational administration scholarship.

Gerald Fallon and Jerald Paquette undertake a rethinking of First Nations conceptions of educational leadership in chapter 13. It is their contention that existing conceptions of educational leadership privilege the dominant Western notion of leadership, followership, and social relations. They propose a non-Western paradigm of educational leadership predicated on different understandings of social relations, sustainability, power, and hierarchy.

In chapter 14, Melody Viczko explores the potential of Actor Network Theory (ANT) in the study of the administration of educational institutions. Like Critical Realism, ANT is a relatively new approach within educational administration research and scholarship. Viczko speculates about the possible usefulness of ANT for conceptualising and theorising in our field of study. As she suggests, there are considerable strengths within ANT—particularly for work that explores the global/local nature of educational policies and practices and for exploring how power and power relations play a part in educational policies and institutions.

Coral Mitchell and Larry Sackney re-examine systems theory as a means of highlighting contemporary ecological and social justice issues in educational organisations in chapter 15. In this chapter, they question the commonplace metaphorical use of systems in organisational analysis; alternatively, the authors hold that organisations are themselves living systems. In metaphorical systems, processes (usually *business processes*) are analogous to biological processes; however, in Mitchell and Sackney's view, organisations are a specific type of system in which leadership and agency are key features. Recasting systems theoretical approaches in organisational analysis from the inside out is novel and represents the corollary of the view offered by earlier generations of theorists. From this "insider" perspective, what emerges as core functions of organisation is meaning making, relationship building, and agent promotion. What the authors propose is, ultimately, a more humane view of systems.

In the final chapter, Patrick Renihan and Fred Renihan reflect on the work of the other contributors to this volume and explore the intransigent question of how to bridge theory and practice. The theories discussed in this volume are often dense and impenetrable, not the sort of thing that practitioners find easy to operationalise. Renihan and Renihan explore the path from abstract theorising to the transformation of understandings and practices at the level of school and school systems. Their contribution in this regard is significant. Whereas many scholars in educational administration are proposing "knowledge mobilisation" strategies as a mechanism to address the theory-practice gap, Renihan and Renihan challenge scholars and practitioners alike to engage in processes of mutual knowledge generation. They argue that the conception of scholars as producers and practitioners as consumers of knowledge is no longer a tenable model.

The potential implication of Renihan and Renihan's proposal for the field of study is significant. Donmoyer's (1999) well-cited discussion of the field of study as a "big tent" in which competing and often contradictory theoretical approaches and perspectives exist concurrently is an unsettling metaphor of the state of the field. Renihan and Renihan firmly locate the "study of educational administration" in relation to the field of practice and to the realm of practitioners. We suggest that their conceptualisation is better described through a metaphor of orbits around a gravitational center. The variety of theoretical orientations to the field of study are fundamentally subject to a gravitational pull from the field of practice. Some perspectives may appear to occupy more distant orbits, yet these orbits are defined by the strong central pull of the field of practice. As is the case for celestial bodies, orbiting perspectives analogously maintain a reciprocal force toward the center and toward each other. Like all metaphors, this one, too, has its limitations; yet, it appears more likely than the "big tent" metaphor to orient the scholarship in educational administration toward the field of practice. Additionally, a "re-centering" toward the field of practice has the potential to de-emphasise the epistemological divisions within the field of study. If teachers and administrators can be thought of as knowledge co-creators, then the proper place for determining what counts as knowledge and what is useful to the field occurs in the interstitial space that is created by conversations among scholars and practitioners. In this proposed future, discussions of epistemology and the justification of knowledge claims can no longer remain purely "academic" exercises.

At this point, we would like to offer a brief comment about educational administration—or is it educational leadership? Or management? The terms are often used interchangeably; however, they are used purposefully. In this volume, our purpose is one of inclusiveness. In the title to the book, the phrase *Educational Administration and Leadership* is used. This inclusive phrase appeals to us because it achieves several aims. First, the term *leadership* has come to have a certain cachet. Additionally, *educational leadership* is the term often used when a more direct connection to the field of practice is desired. Second, *administration*, as a term, (at least in the North American context) has a wealth of history behind it. It was the term used when the field of study was first founded (see Derek Allison's chapter for more on this); as such, it has a certain historicity about it. The term *management* is one commonly used in the United Kingdom and other countries, and is similar in connotation to the term *administration* in the North American context. In one of our graduate classes, we ask students to define *leadership*, *management*, and *administration*. Invariably, the responses can be summed up thusly: leadership = *sugar and spice and everything nice*; administration = *snips and snails and puppy dogs' tails*. Leadership, at least according to our graduate students, is about moral purpose and relationships; administration is about budgets and timetables. The dichotomy identified here is one that permeates this book. The leadership versus administration (or management) dichotomy can be understood as a dichotomy of types of tasks—ones that are enjoyable and ones that are not; however, a little more digging can reveal the kind of ontological/epistemological debate discussed in this book present in the way we understand the terms of administration, management, and leadership. In typical fashion, rather than determine, once and for all, which term is a more truthful reflection of the reality of the scholarship and practice of the field, we have combined them into a useful phrase without worrying too much at all about the inherent contradictions in doing so.

As a last note, much of the work in this book, and the work of the scholars we cite, assumes that the substantive content for the study and practice of educational administration is the administration of primary and secondary schooling. University departments of education, however, are now being populated by graduate students who have limited interest in the administration of schools of this type. These students are coming from diverse contexts and professional fields, and many of them have a particular interest in increasing their qualifications as university or college teachers or administrators. How might this new context reshape the way we theorise about educational administration? If we shift our focus to accommodate graduate students from nursing, medicine, engineering, and nanotechnology, must our theories change? The theoretical concepts used in educational administration are often dense and complex; however, in the past, the graduate students in our classes were all coming from a similar professional context, and at least we knew what it was we were theorising *about*.

Part I

Antecedents and Debates

1 Examining the Antecedents of Methodological Diversity in Contemporary Educational Administration

David Burgess and Paul Newton

Over the field of study dedicated to the administration, management, and leadership of educational institutions is cast the long shadow of the history of science. As progeny, appropriator, and contributor to the larger body of disciplines known as the social sciences, educational administration continues to develop understanding of itself both often in reaction to and, occasionally, in advance of (a) the contemporary context of schooling and pedagogy; (b) the social, economic, and political contexts of schools at local, regional, national, and international levels; (c) the insights of cognate disciplines and fields of study; and (d) the history of epistemological development since at least the mid-seventeenth century. Others of our colleagues have provided valuable histories of educational administration, and we do not here intend to repeat their important contributions (*cf.* Allison, 1989; Callahan & Button, 1964; Culbertson, 1981; Evers & Lakomski, 2000; Oplatka, 2009, 2010; Willower, 1979). Rather, in this modest introductory chapter, we offer a methodological and epistemological context for the wide variety of contributions made to the understanding of the administrative theory in education over the past forty years. In the paragraphs and pages that follow, we argue from the postulate that one's understanding of theoretical context is assisted by an analysis of prevailing trends in thought in the eras preceding. As such, to examine the roots of the growth in methodological diversity in our field since the mid 1970s—the bulk of the present volume—one ought to examine the space that was made for such diversity. To understand this space, one must examine the event that spawned it—on our view in this book, Thomas Barr Greenfield's presentation at the Third International Intervisitation Programme in 1974, and the point of departure as offered by Riveros in chapter three. To understand this event, which created the space for diversity, one must examine the contexts that preceded its origin and represented the foil of its critique. Thus, ours is a brief review of this final link in the chain. The contributions of our colleagues throughout this book more closely align as reviews embodied in the former two links.

Western beliefs about the practices, and expectations for the products, of (social) scientific understanding and research have their roots in Christian Europe of the 1600s. At this time, what we understand as the genesis of the "modern scientific view" had emerged as recognisable to the modern observer, and yet much of the European psyche remained anchored in a past seemingly so antithetical as to appear contradictory to that same observer. But not, it would seem, by contemporaries. The 1600s, as Dolnick (2011) has described, on the one hand, vibrated with possibility emerging from the unabashed questioning of dogmas embodied in the status quo; on the other, they were constrained by general conservatism and reluctance to break from many forces of the past. The confrontation between a questioning attitude and the inability to fully appreciate the degree to which one is influenced by the past is not a new phenomenon, and neither was it new in the 1600s. It is representative, in many ways, of the time in the study of educational administration in which the chapters of this book begin. To make this situation more clear, we believe it is helpful to explore the paradigms (as Kuhn called them in 1962) that provide the backdrop—the past(s)—questioned, and often re-questioned, by important contributors to our field, at different times within recent decades, in their pursuit of understanding social organisations and phenomena embodied in institutions of education. Additionally, such backdrops often represent concealed anchors for those who question. For our purposes, the backdrop to the backdrop (the 1600s and the origins of modern Western scientific reasoning that itself is the backdrop of the social sciences) begins at least 600 years ago.

Any review on any subject suffers under the paring knife of brevity. Ours is no exception. We see the pages that follow as a modest testament to the works of countless individuals whose efforts underlie the vignettes and discoveries we employ as markers along the path of an important, complicated, and at times disputed trail from origins to predominance in the second half of the twentieth century. Naturally, our view is limited. The history of epistemology extends well back in time beyond our starting point, and indeed it extends along lines on which we have chosen to remain silent. Further, the history of epistemology and science is nuanced and intricate and our choices are made at the expense of others. Nevertheless, it is our belief that the sections that follow represent a minimal depth of exposure to the select works of select key individuals. On our view, their influence is present in the recasting and reexaminations found in contemporary philosophical pronouncements within the study of educational organisations and their administration.

ORIGINS

Before 1450, life in Christian Europe was almost exclusively rural. Most people were born, lived, and died in the same house, rarely if ever venturing more than 10 km afield. Daily routine was immediate and attached to one's surroundings. It was rough and dirty, intimately dependent on the weather, informed by rhymes learned as children[1] and in paintings and reliefs on church walls, and lived in a state of almost perpetual-present with a past no farther back than the lived memories of familial experience. At this time, what you knew was what you or someone with whom you were familiar had personally experienced or what was written in the Bible and read to you by the parish priest. He was your link to the world beyond your domain of experience. He could read, and this was to you a mystical power. The Bible from which he read was hand copied from an earlier copy—mistakes and all—by dedicated monks whose work was itself seen as mystical and holy (Burke, 1986; Ehrman, 2005).

The odd, but requisite, procedure of not correcting mistakes in meticulously copied texts, even perhaps obvious ones, employed by monastic scribes was one example of a practice that had emerged in scholarship rooted in the intellectual philosophy of the time. Called *Scholasticism*, the influence of St Augustine of Hippo, beginning in roughly 400 CE, solidified its dominant place in the Roman Catholic view of the world. St Augustine's was a view, itself influenced by the work of the Roman philosopher Plotinus and the Neoplatonist school, focused upon *eternal ideals* or *universal forms*. In the theological and scholastic contexts of the Church, this implied an unquestioning focus on (a) the soul and afterlife as opposed to the here-and-now material order of the world—one need not bother with originality in material life since God's predetermined plan for your soul will not change as a result (Burke, 1986)—and (b) those *facts* derived from first principles and established in ancient wisdom generally, and by Aristotle in particular (Butterfield, 1965; Crombie, 1952; Dear, 2009; Dolnick, 2011). On this view, one simply did not ask questions in life, nor ought one to question eternal knowledge from the past.

The influential view originating in the teachings of Plotinus in the 200s CE and in the Neoplatonists (and itself originating in the writing of Plato) was that a dualism exists between the world as we experience it and the *real* world that rests underneath our experiences—the so-called realm of the *forms*. Neoplatonists argued that a hierarchy existed in this *real* (*form*) world based on a descending scheme of abstraction, beginning at its apex with a *singularity* or *unity* of the *good* and the *beautiful* (which Plotinus called the "*one*"—rooted in the mathematical metaphysics of Thales and in the Pythagoreans—and which has been understood in later interpretations as a Neoplatonist creator-god), descending into the metaphysical realm of the *forms*, into the realm of *souls*, and then finally descending to the world of human experience—each level being progenitor of those below. The early Church absorbed these ideas into a reading of Aristotle that suggested everything in the universe had been created by God as a unique and individual entity—never changing but eternally *interested* (in a philosophically *intentional*, almost biological, manner) in returning to its natural place in the world (fire to the heavens; rock to the Earth; humans to the realm of souls). The only distinguishing factor was found in terms of an object's value, and this was based on its placement in closer and closer proximity to the centre of the universe (read, the Neoplatonist *"one"*) (Burke, 1986). One might consider for oneself those remnants of this view that remain visible today in the artistic murals and reliefs produced to adorn the walls and altarpieces of medieval churches. For the illiterate onlooker, the size and proportion of each figure increased in proximity to God: Christ and/or Madonna are largest; smaller are apostles, archangels, the Pope, kings, bishops, priests . . . trailing down to miniscule common people.[2] Everything was hierarchical, and you knew your place within whether you could read or not. But all was not lost, as you could be rewarded in death with ascension to a realm closer to God than that from which you came.

Consistent with Neoplatonist thought, the Scholastics subscribed to the belief that knowledge (a *form*, so to speak) was separable from its representation (how we interpret the material world through our humanly senses). Representations were merely shadows of what was *real*—the real was the ideal form upon which each sensual opinion-based representation was founded. Objects of our experience, on this line of thinking, are mere opinions of the forms. Their value is miniscule in comparison to that of knowledge of the forms. The human body, for example, was simply a shadowy representation of the real soul—so too was any other body, object, or matter—thus knowledge of the world around us was at best an opinion. Focus study upon what is *real* (like God, the soul, and heaven), said St Augustine, and not on upon that which is shadow and opinion (like the material world of our experience). Scholarship—a peculiarly spiritual and introspective version of what we now understand this word to mean—of the Church followed St Augustine's edict, and Europe ran headlong into the Dark Ages.

Throughout the later Dark Ages, efforts were focused upon better reconciling and harmonising Aristotelian, Neoplatonist, and Roman Catholic Church teachings. The texts from which these scholars worked were often poor copies of poor Latin translations of copies of Greek originals. Nevertheless, the picture of the universe at which medieval science arrived throughout this reconciliation, known as the Ptolemaic system, overlapped nicely for most concerned. In almost perfect accord with Aristotle,[3] the Earth was placed at the centre of everything, surrounded by concentric invisible spheres upon which the moon, five known planets, sun, and stars travelled around the Earth in occasionally reversing directions (Burke, 1986; Dear, 2009; Kearney, 1971). This Earth-centric view was appropriate for the Church—since God had placed humans here at the universe's centre.

In the 1500s, universities dominated European intellectual life. The curriculum reflected Scholasticism, and focused on reading and writing Latin and Greek texts (Dear, 2009). Intellectual acuity was officially measured in one's knowledge of Aristotelian wisdom. Oxford University had decreed a century before that "Bachelors and Masters of Arts who do not follow Aristotle's philosophy are subject to a fine of 5 shillings for each point of divergence" (Dolnick, 2011, p. 62). Both philosophy and divergence, however, was expanding in scope on account of two important discoveries.

First, vast volumes of pre-Christian European (Archimedes', Euclid's, Hippocrates', Plato's, Ptolemy's, and those of many others) and Arab scholarship (that of al-Haytham [Alhazen] on optics and vision, al-Majusi [Haly Abbas] on medicine, and other Golden Age Islamic works) that had been preserved by the Moorish libraries were *re*-discovered following the capture of the Muslim-controlled (now Spanish) Córdoba and Toledo in the 1100s. Yet, given the relative cost of monastic book production in the intervening centuries, the ancient works found were not widely spread until 400 years later.[4] Second, in a rediscovered work by Aristotle found preserved in these libraries (the "Prior Analytics" of the *Organon*) was offered a means of expanding one's knowledge on almost any subject. Known as *syllogistic deductive reasoning*, knowledge about two premises would lead to knowledge of a previously unknown third logical conclusion. Ironically, such reasoning would in time deprecate the Aristotelian universe.

By the 1550s, print-runs of the Greek and Arab texts in translation were available across Europe. Further, scholars could produce texts accompanied by accurately replicated woodcut illustrations at such reduced cost and such increased speed that (a) books on any subject were now available to practically anyone with an interest, and (b) what was available on any subject could not only be easily read, but could also be easily verified in the emerging renewed conception of the *real* (formerly shadowy) world—and not exclusively for remnant medieval *typos*. Clearly, but slowly, literacy and science waxed; the dominance of the Roman Catholic Church over European scholarship was slowly starting to wane, both the former and latter of these particularly so in the ever-growing Protestant Northern Europe (Burke, 1986; Kearney, 1971).

REVOLUTION

Dolnick (2011) has succinctly captured the state of affairs for the common man in seventeenth-century England. Fascinating is the fact that little had changed in many respects when compared to the image offered above of life two hundred years earlier:

> Few ages could have seemed less likely than the late 1600s to start men dreaming of a world of perfect order. . . . In the tail end of Shakespeare's century, the natural and the supernatural still twined around one another. Disease was a punishment ordained by God. Astronomy had not yet broken free from astrology, and the sky was filled with omens.
>
> . . . The same barges that brought vegetables to the city from farms in the countryside returned laden with human sewage, to fertilize the fields.
>
> . . . No one bathed, from kings to peasants. The poor had no choice, and the wealthy had no desire. (Doctors explained that water opened

the pores to infection and plague. A coat of grease and grime sealed disease away.) Worms, fleas, lice, and bedbugs were near-universal afflictions. Science would soon revolutionize the world, but the minds that made the modern world were yoked to itchy, smelly, dirty bodies.

(pp. xv–xvi)

It is not an overstatement to say that these same minds were similarly yoked to beliefs held fast in a peculiarly conservative Scholasticism. Isaac Newton, whose questions—along with those of Galileo Galilei, Nicolaus Copernicus, Johannes Kepler, and Tycho Brahe—brought on the downfall of Ptolemaic cosmology, remained entwined in the Scholastic-inspired belief that all that he had discovered (including his own detailed work on optics, his invention of the calculus, universal gravitation, etc., etc.) had actually been known to the ancients and merely lost through the passage of time. So rooted in the legacy of Scholastic traditions was Newton's mind that it has been said he dedicated as much time to decoding hidden messages in the Bible as he did to his work on astrophysics (Dolnick, 2011). These were extraordinary individuals, with the sharpest of wits, but even for them the staying power of the prevailing Scholastic view was, in such examples, clearly demonstrable. They operated with great confidence in the belief that theirs was the Lord's work. For them, understanding the detailed clockworks of God's creation was a means toward a spiritual end (Dear, 2009; Shapin, 1996).

The logical techniques rediscovered in the centuries since the fall of Muslim European enclaves had, by the mid-1600s, offered more than a means of working through esoteric problems. Mathematics expanded greatly on account of the introduction of Arabic numerals (consider performing long division on the Roman variety), decimal notation, and the application of reasoning. Art and architecture, particularly in conjunction with Italian expansions on the optical analysis of al-Haytham, was now perspective-based and harmoniously proportioned. What was seen in the world could be represented and studied on the page in exacting detail; what was detailed on the page could now be studied and then represented by artisans' hands in stone, brick, wood, metal, and plaster. Studies of ballistics demonstrated how, contrary to what Aristotle had said about only heavenly objects following curved paths, one could ascribe to actions and behaviours the codified logic of parabolic mathematics (Tartaglia, 1537). Studies of patterns in nature offered mathematical sequences as a mechanism of prediction. Order, it would seem, could be found in all of God's creation—God, it was believed by some, was a mathematician (Burke, 1986; Shapin, 1996).

A significant blow to the Aristotelian view had its origins in the publication of Francis Bacon's *Novum Organum Scientiarum* in 1620. Bacon's was, simply put, a refutation of the Scholastic (*né* Aristotelian) first principles method of study in the world that originated in the Greek mathematical view of Aristotle's predecessors, Thales and Pythagoras. First principles were thought to offer the syllogistic key to knowledge about the world. For Aristotle, the search for first principles was the key task of philosophy, as these would, through syllogistic reasoning, derive true conclusions about the nature of the world. Bacon (1620/1901) viewed this deductive system as problematic, and argued that many following this method had "not . . . derived their opinion from true sources, and, hurried on by their zeal and some affection, [had] certainly exceeded due moderation" (p. 5). His retort focused on *induction*. Begin with clear observations of the world by way of the senses, uninfluenced and uncorrupted by the "continual exercise and perpetual agitation of the mind" (p. 7). Sum these observations and over time one will establish an ever larger and ever more complete picture of the state of the world. The influence of Bacon's inductive method was both (a) a radical departure from fifteen hundred years of thought, and (b) exceedingly important in the early development of the Western scientific worldview. It would be championed some decades later by a group of influential individuals—among whom rest the names Newton and Boyle—whose natural philosophy would emerge as science.

In 1660, the Royal Society in London received its Charter from Charles II. The work of its members began in earnest on the verification of Greek and Arab science and, frankly put, any other belief of folk wisdom through empirical methods. For example, Wilson (1882) noted the early Society's discussions of "Schotter's affirmation, 'that a fish suspended by a thread would turn towards the wind'" (p. 11). Robert Hooke's *Memoranda* reported on 1672 reviews related to unicorn horns generally (Henderson, 2007), and others reported on the 1660 Society-sponsored experiments pertaining to their affects—when crushed into fine powder—on the behaviour of spiders more specifically (Dolnick, 2011; Wilson, 1882). Among reports provided in the official journal of the Society, some would publicly, but politely, follow Bacon's inductive method and challenge the wisdom of Aristotle directly. Francesco Redi (1666), for example, disagreed with Aristotle's assertion (which had apparently been confirmed in the century following the death of Christ by the observations of the Roman physician Galen of Pergamon) "that the *Spittle* of a *Fasting* person kills Vipers" (p. 162, *sic*); John Wray, in his 1669 letter to the publisher of the *Philosophical Transactions*, noted his concern with the application of Aristotle's commentary on the sexes of snails; and Dr Nehemiah Grew lamented in 1673 the fact that had Aristotle provided more commentary on the nature of snow, he would not need to. These challenges aside, it is clear from the earliest *Transactions* reported by the Royal Society that much time and effort was dedicated to the spectacle of blood transfusions among dogs, the production of spheres in glass, the investigation of spiders, and 'monstrous' birth defects in all species. Natural philosophy (or what we would come to call *science*) was certainly odd by our contemporary standards; but in a world in which the wisdom of the ancients was God's truth, what better place to begin than with the Bacon-inspired inductive verification of the minutia of knowledge entwined within the calibrations of canine cardinal humours and the ætiology of arachnid aversions to alicornic dust.

AN EARLY MODERN SCIENTIFIC VIEW

Between the end of the seventeenth and the beginning of the twentieth centuries, much of what we understand to be within the domain of science took its shape. The direct influence of God in the world of science (as seen by scientists themselves) was diminishing. As the nineteenth century advanced, the motivation for the study of natural phenomena was less and less an attempt to understand God's work, and increasingly based on the practicality of those understandings that would provide demonstrable benefits. The road toward this result required much push and pull. In some cases, this jostling reflected the difficulty with which questioning the prevailing view might grow to be an accepted norm. In other cases, the back and forth reflected the debate between the self-interests of the scientists themselves and a more broadly cast interest in knowledge development for its own sake or for the sake of humanity writ large.

The first of the two above-noted types of jostlings seems reflected in the continental European reaction to Newton's publication of the *Philosophiæ Naturalis Principia Mathematica* in 1687. Within this volume, Newton offered his reader a purely rational and mathematical description of laws of physical behaviour in nature, including motion and gravitation. It is upon this work that the undergirding of classical mechanics is based. Controversial at the time was his manner of including the power of God to overcome and correct minor imperfections in the organisation of the solar system.[5] The arguments of his detractors—principally Gottfried Wilhelm Leibniz, who was himself eminently brilliant and had independently developed a version of the calculus contemporaneously to Newton—were theological: If God were needed to correct imperfections in the function of the solar system, then was Newton not saying that God himself was imperfect for not setting all perfectly in order at genesis (Dear, 2009)? Interesting that a mechanistic and mathematical view of the solar system was not, by this point, the heresy—rather, Newton's more *run-of-the-mill* heresy was the heresy.

The second of the above jostlings is demonstrable in the wrestling of natural philosophers with the most appropriate method for actually *doing* the work of Bacon's empirical science, and how one ought to know what counts as the work of science. The first of these is technological, the second epistemological—but the two are indeed linked and are embedded in much larger questions: *Who should be believed? Why should we believe their accounts?* By the late 1600s, it was growing ever more clear that neither the Church nor Aristotle had provided commentary on a great number of phenomena of interest to natural philosophers. With these authorities removed, what might act as replacement arbiter of fact and fiction? And to this end, what exactly was an *authority* and how would we recognise one if we saw one? Shapin and Schaffer (1985) examined this very issue in great detail through the work of Roberts Boyle and Hooke.

Robert Boyle was son of the Irish Earl of Cork. Wealthy and clever, he had settled in London at the birth of the Royal Society. Robert Hooke was similarly clever. Mechanically minded, Hooke worked as Boyle's contemporary and assistant for several years and as the curator of experiments of the Royal Society. Dolnick (2011) reported that, where Boyle was more temperate on the subject, Hooke was adamantly opposed to Scholasticism and its grip on Universities.

In Boyle's (1662) work—the second edition of his *New Experiments Physico-Mechanicall, Touching the Spring of the Air, and its Effects, (Made, for the most part, in a New Pneumatical Engine)*—the circumstances of 43 inductive and empirical experiments conducted by its author are offered in striking detail. As the title describes, although in archaic language, Boyle's experiments investigated the vacuum (spring of the air) through the use of an air-pump (pneumatical engine) of his and Hooke's design. A vacuum was not possible, according to Scholastic wisdom, and Boyle's account of it was not without critics. However, perhaps foreseeing its critical response, the detail of his descriptions embodies a technique that would eventually produce what we now understand as the mechanism of scientific authority: assent through trust.

Boyle (1662) offered, in the long passage quoted below, four mechanisms in a scheme intending to ensure the satisfaction of his reader with the veracity of his experiments, analysis, and conclusions.

> [T]he Experiments [herein] related, having been many of them try'd in the presence of Ingenious Men; and by that means having made some noise among the Virtuosi (insomuch that some of them have been sent into Foreign Countries, where they have had the luck not to be despis'd) I could not, without quite trying more then one Amanuensis, give out half as many Copies of them as were so earnestly desired, that I could not civilly refuse them.
>
> . . . Of my being somewhat prolix in many of my Experiments, I have these Reasons to render, That some of them being altogether new, seem'd to need the being circumstantially related, to keep the Reader from distrusting them: That divers Circumstances I did here and there set down for fear of forgetting them, when I may hereafter have occasion to make use of them in my other Writings: That in divers cases I thought it necessary to deliver things circumstantially, that the Person I addressed them to, might, without mistake, and with as little trouble as is possible, be able to repeat such unusual Experiments: and that after I consented to let my Observations be made publick, the most ordinary reason of my prolixity was, That foreseeing that such a trouble as I met with in making those tryals carefully, and the great expence of time that they necessarily require (not to mention the charges of making the Engine, and imploying a Man to manage it) will probably keep most Men from trying again these Experiments: I thought I might do the

generality of my Readers no unacceptable piece of service, by so punctually relating what I carefully observ'd, that they may look upon these Narratives as standing Records in our new Pneumaticks, and need not reiterate themselves an Experiment to have as distinct an Idea of it, as may suffice them to ground their Reflections and Speculations upon.

(pp. 3–5, *sic passim*)

To reiterate, Boyle is here designing an antecedent method of scientific practice that extended the inductive work of Bacon four decades earlier: (a) conduct your experiments in public, so that witnesses may attest to your actions and observations, and, following this, (b) a witness' reputation benefits your own; (c) publish your work widely and publicly for all those who would hold an interest in reading it; and (d) publish your work in details sufficient to render the reader a *virtual witness* (as the term was given by Shapin & Schaffer, 1985; Shapin, 1994) of your experiments and so that they may replicate your experiments if inclined to do so. Public scrutiny, peer review, replication, and scrupulous detail are the legacy we take from the science of Boyle. The results would constitute the universal authority by which ideas related to a particular phenomenon might become, as Boyle called them, *matters of fact*.

Robert Hooke's mechanical proclivity, acumen, and success made his work eminently valuable to the members of the Royal Society. So valuable was his technological production that his self-interest in the monetisation of his designs and inventions quickly rose to the forefront of the Society's discussions. The debate pitted the view that the scientific enterprise was a public good meant to be shared openly against the secrecy that ensures one's invention is protected against the tinkering of those unqualified to do so. Hooke was not alone in his want for secrecy—he was not the only engineer whose living was made through the sale of his designs—but his view did not prevail (Dolnick, 2011). For the Royal Society, science would be destined to generate matters of fact in the open, exposed to the tinkerings of the laity who might be so inclined.

BUILDING ON INDUCTION

As the seventeenth century became the eighteenth, then the nineteenth, and then the twentieth, few of the laity concerned themselves with scientific research. Few had the means, as Boyle had, to self-fund; fewer had the time. Natural philosophy was growing ever more specialised, and university training in the specialisations followed in close alignment—maintaining the gap between the educated, often elite, trained scientist and others in society (Meadows, 2004). In the eighteenth century, many advances were made: Among others, we see Linnæus' project in biology, resulting in the binomial classification scheme we still use today; the rise of chemistry through the testing of the theories of phlogiston and alchemy by Lavoisier and others; and geology from field work and debates surrounding Werner's neptunism and Moro's volcanism.

In 1847, a monumental review was made of Bacon's inductive scientific methods and the scientific specialisation and products that had emerged over the previous 200 years as a result. The author of the account was William Whewell, by all accounts a polymath and master at Trinity College, Cambridge (Meadows, 2004). In the preface to the second edition of *The Philosophy of the Inductive Sciences*, Whewell summarised his conclusions.

> We know that though Bacon's general maxims still guide and animate philosophical enquirers yet that his views, in their detail, have all turned out inapplicable: the technical parts of his method failed in his hands, and are forgotten among the cultivators of science.
>
> (p. v)

Whewell's take moved swiftly to an historical analysis of progress in, what by this time had earned the specialised status of, the physical sciences from which Whewell sought to understand the nature of what had in fact—if not Bacon's system—enabled their successes and achievements. Through his review, Whewell arrived at what he viewed as the common process or common principles that, in practice, functioned as the real modulator of successful science: hypothesis-generation followed by a type of return to deductive modes of reasoning.

Whewell's (1847) observation was that in the practice of knowledge generation, all methods are influenced by the subjectivity of the observer. This was a central piece of his revitalisation of Bacon's inductive method. Advocates of a more pure Baconian inductive method contemporary to Whewell—John Stuart Mill, for example (Forster, 2009)—argued, here simplistically put, that our mind is like a passive receptacle for the sensory exploration of the world; Whewell advocated the view that our knowledge of phenomena in the world is manipulated through the natural interpretive function of the mind. For Whewell, the scientist may encounter several examples of a particular phenomenon. As each encounter is accumulated into the observer's mind, the mind *colligates* (Whewell's word meaning the *process of thinking*) on these, and then superimposed over the phenomenon is the *colligation* (the mental conceptualisation formed by the observer). Colligations are, for Whewell, the real generator of new knowledge—influenced by observations, to be sure, but placed into a more generalisable system by the *mindful* and *thinking* observer (Snyder, 2009). Following the articulation of a colligation in an hypothesis, Whewell (1858) introduced three criteria by which the hypothesis may claim truth as a theory. First among these is *prediction*.

For a theory to merit a claim to truth, on Whewell's view, that theory must permit a scientist the ability to predict the presence or behaviour of a phenomenon in the future, as the case may be. An ideal example of this is found when one considers the great accomplishment demonstrated in Newton's theory of universal gravitation. In Newton's is found the striking ability to predict the motion of planets and other celestial objects. However, one might equally consider that, for over a thousand years previous, there had been a theory of celestial motion capable of predicting the behaviour of the known planets, the moon, and sun: the *doctrine of epicycles* (Barker, 2002). Before Copernicus, the predominant (and official Roman Catholic) model of the cosmos was based on the work of the Greek-Roman astronomer Claudius Ptolemy—the Earth was at the centre of everything, followed by the moon, then Mercury, Venus, the Sun, Mars, Jupiter, and Saturn, then came all else in the universe. Odd as it was, according to this model, each of the planets travelled on crystal spheres, occasionally reversing direction, then going back again on as they had been (that is, in fact, what we observe from our—unknown to the ancients—*moving* vantage point on Earth). Interestingly, the Ptolemaic system had been based on countless observations likely made by Babylonian astronomers inductively colligated in Ptolemy's mind. His hypothesis was published in the *Almagest* in the second century AD. Despite its ability to predict in very real and useful service to science, no modern account of astronomy perpetuates the Ptolemaic system; we must conclude, as Whewell (1858) did, that mere prediction from an hypothesis remains insufficient to demonstrate truth.

Second among Whewell's criteria for hypothesis testing is *consilience*. In some ways, consilience may be understood as an extension of the criterion of prediction; it is prediction beyond the phenomenon upon which the induction and colligation was originally made. Whewell suggested that consilience is found in those cases where newly observed phenomena do not require further colligations that alter an original hypothesis to explain and predict them, as well. Returning to the example drawn above in relation to Newton's universal gravitation, Whewell (1858) offered the example of the observation of the *procession of the equinoxes*[6] and its explanation through Newton's work—though Newton himself did not study this phenomenon in the creation of his original hypothesis. Nothing like the phenomenon of procession can be immediately explained by accounts of the Ptolemaic hypothesis, and on the horn of this criterion Ptolemy's account perishes.

Whewell's third criterion is *simplicity*. When a scientist whose hypothesis is challenged by prediction or consilience reacts by making that hypothesis more complicated, Whewell (1858) argued that the criterion of simplicity is abandoned and the hypothesis ought to be considered diminished in its service toward our view of truth. Once again, a helpful example is to compare Newton's work with that in the Ptolemaic system. Ptolemy's view assumed that the travels of planets about the Earth followed a path analogous to that which one would expect of a crystal sphere: perfectly circular about its circumference. If this were true, then observation of heavenly bodies through a telescope at any point in the year should render their size at a given magnification nearly identical to every other observation at any other time. But

Tycho Brahe's meticulous observations demonstrated that this was not the case, at least not for comets (Crombie, 1952). To reconcile, Keplar worked to modify Ptolemy's conception, but all attempts failed, on Whewell's account, to decrease complexity. In time, the simplicity of elliptical orbits provided in Keplar *cum* Newton's work strengthened its robustness as a viable theory (Huff, 2011).

While it is true that Whewell's conclusions suggested Bacon's inductive philosophy of science was problematic if taken as orthodoxy, he considered his work a refinement of the inductive tradition—and, further, that his manner of induction was demonstrable in how science was actually done by physical scientists, as well as by those who study social phenomena. There is some debate over whether or not in Whewell's work is found the roots of contemporary hypothetico-deductivism (the manner in which one can deduce from a hypothesis new knowledge)—important for a discussion of Evers and Lakomski's work on theory and science in educational administration a century and a half after the publication of Whewell's *Novum organon renovatum*. For some, it is clear that Whewell's work represented a contribution of value to inductivism (*cf.* Forster, 2009; Snyder, 2009); while for others the deduction performed in the assessment of the merits of a given hypothesis (where the [inductive] path one follows in pursuit of that hypothesis is of little consequence) represents a foray into the deductive process (*cf.* Sprenger, 2011). The relationship between inductive origins, the creation of hypotheses, and then the deduction of novel consequences to be tested in experimental or natural situations represents the culmination of scientific methods at the beginning of the twentieth century—and arguably much success, demonstrable through the advancement of human knowledge on many subjects, is attributable to the method(s) above discussed. The application of these methods (and the epistemological assumptions embedded within) in both the physical or natural sciences as well as the emerging social sciences is manifest as a key movement influential in educational administration into the 1950s. It is to this era that we now turn.

SOCIAL SCIENCE AND LOGICAL-POSITIVISM, LOGICAL-POSITIVISM AND THE THEORY MOVEMENT

In the mid-1800s, the influence of French philosopher Auguste Comte had become apparent. A contemporary of Whewell, Comte's *social positivism* is visible in the sociological and economic writings of Karl Marx and John Stuart Mill, among others. Comte's doctrine, from which the early methods of sociology were drawn, represented a perspective on social phenomena exposed through the methodology of science. As with inductive and hypothetico-deductive techniques emerging in the analysis of physical phenomena, Comte's sociology suggested that social phenomena might similarly be engaged and scrutinised. In essence, the tools and techniques of physical scientific analysis and mathematic logic are applicable to the social world (Pickering, 1993).

As an example of the translation of scientific methods into social phenomena, Marx, who was influenced generally by the grand historico-idealist theories of Hegel, offered an attempt to materialise the Hegelian grand progress of history, providing a scientific view of human historical progress through the material (real, physical, and empirically experienced) production of human beings. From the a priori relationship between a human and her material production, Marx suggested that a certain a posteriori consciousness emerged. This consciousness could be objectively analysed on account of its being dependent upon an individual's relationship with the means of production. Without offering too much in the way of Marxist theory, the larger point for our purposes is to articulate Marx and Engel's use of an objective scientific view of social phenomena, including the belief that history could be analysed scientifically.

Scientific and mathematical methods of analysis extended into values and morality through a school of thought known as Utilitarianism. Utilitarianism, which predated Whewell's and Marx's later writing, is a moral philosophical base upon which economics, governance, and other social systems may be founded. Jeremy Bentham devised a mathematical algorithmic *calculus* through which the amount of pleasure one ought to expect from a given action or behaviour can be calculated. Known as *felicific* or *utility calculus*, rightness or wrongness (and therefore the moral value) of an action was based on the pleasure or pain the action produced for the greatest number of people. Bentham's work was an attempt to devise a science of morality, the product of which would be happiness. As with any other science of the time, and consistent with our discussion above, Bentham argued that one ought to observe the physical and social world and base morality in reality, not in the unobservable otherworldliness of religious experience nor in the pre-defined *will of God*.

John Stuart Mill (1879), Whewell's contemporary, developed Bentham's utilitarianism. His was an influential account of, among other things, the intersection of education (through inductive means) as a mechanism for social improvement. Recalling Bentham, inductive observation was best achieved by educated observers who make it their practice of articulating individual and informed assessments that move oneself in the direction of greater happiness. Within this scheme, one ought to understand the physical and social world through observation, formulate hypotheses about outcomes given choices predicated on those observations, then deduce action to bring about the result most directed toward happiness and pleasure. Mill's (1846) descriptions of physical and social nature as interrelated causal networks provide a medium through which a scientific method can be followed in social analysis.

We may take from the above discussion a broad understanding that beginning in the 1800s, social science (a) offered a growing collection of fields of study with the potential for important contributions to social welfare and (b) was understood as sister to the physical sciences, employing successful scientific methods with little or no distinction. Problematic, however, for some, was the translation of scientific methods as a mechanism for discovering knowledge about objects of social experience, of growing interest to social scientists, that are unobservable or obscured from human empirical senses. In rational sciences, much weight had been placed on the role of mathematics as a means of demystifying, ordering, and testing observations caused by underlying or obscured phenomena—for some, the growth of work in the field of statistics, particularly during the latter half of the 1800s, appeared promising (*cf.* Gauss, 1801; Galton, 1869; Nightingale, 1858; Quetelet, 1842).

In the 1920s, a group of European scientists, philosophers, and mathematicians were drawn together in Vienna with the aim of aligning the purpose of philosophy as a tool useful for the pursuit of knowledge in the physical and social sciences. Otto Neurath, a political scientist and statistician and member of this group, was impressed with Albert Einstein's scientific advancements as well as with Alfred North Whitehead and Bertrand Russell's (1910) work in the decade previous on the defining of mathematics in logical proof. Neurath and his counterparts sought to find in logic the key to how one ought to proceed in science, and further, how to ensure the progressive organisation of society (Smith, 1987).

For the Vienna Circle, as the group would come to be called, the alignment of the social and physical sciences was proposed through a logic-based cleansing of theoretical questions asked and claims made. The founders of the Circle, including Neurath, were highly critical of the idealism of Hegelian philosophy, in particular, and any philosophy that put "vacuous" claims or questions analogous to those proposed by Hegel, in general. For members, any theoretical claim made in physical or social science that ought to be taken seriously ought to be meaningful; to be meaningful, a claim must be empirically testable in some concrete manner. Following this, one must be able to translate the language employed in the claim into symbolic logic, and then derive a result. Were the claim or question unintelligible under a system of logic, the claim or question should be abandoned as meaningless.

The school of thought embodied in the work of the Vienna Circle became known as both Logical-Positivism and Logical-Empiricism. At least in intent, this epistemological standpoint is not too dissimilar to the attempts made by Boyle in the 1600s to offer a mechanism for establishing scientific authority. The major difference, however, is in the arbiter of what ought to count as science—empirical reproducibility in the case of Boyle, the empirical rationalism of symbolic logic in the case of the Vienna Circle. Logical-Positivism had a profound effect on many fields of study. In the study of schools and educational administration, the Theory Movement holds direct lineage to the Vienna Circle in the post-World War II era through the work of Herbert Feigl. The insights of later Logical-Positivists/-Empiricists, including

Feigl and Carl Hempel, and kindred Analytic philosophers—along the line from Bertrand Russell, and including Charles Pierce, Willard Quine, and the Churchlands—continue to offer both support for, and foil against, the ideas promoted by contemporary thinkers in the philosophy of social science examining educational organisations.

THOUGHTS AND CONSIDERATIONS

Through the recitation of this chapter, we hope to provide the reader with a few important points related to the more contemporary circumstances of our field's debates. The first of these cautious observations is that no time is without differing opinion, and over 600 years we can see that the received view of any era is temporary. We are here reminded of a quote from Aristotle recalled by Boyle:

> . . . Of my wont to speak rather doubtfully, or hesitantly, then resolvedly, concerning matters wherein I apprehend some difficulty, . . . I shall now defend my practice but by the Observation of Aristotle, who somewhere notes, That to seem to know all things certainly, and to speak positively of them, is a trick of bold and young Fellows: whereas those that are indeed intelligent and considerate, are wont to imploy more wary and diffident Expressions.
>
> (Boyle, 1662, p. 5, *sic passim*)

Second, those who bring forward ideas for consideration, no matter how new or novel the ideas may be, are more often than not themselves unknowingly locked in a certain inescapability of the dominant view from which they emerged. Breaks from the past are difficult to accomplish, and to claim the ridiculousness of the received view is to claim, to greater or lesser degree, the same about oneself.

This brief exploration provides a backdrop for understanding the nature of debates that have occurred in educational administration over the past (at least) five decades. As students of educational administration ourselves, we remember our introduction to the work of Evers and Lakomski, and through their work, the writings of Greenfield, Hodgkinson, Bates, Foster, among others. At the time, the debates described in *Knowing Educational Administration* (Evers & Lakomski, 1991) did not perturb or disrupt our understanding of the field of study, although we sensed that it was intended to do just that. Without a clear understanding of the context in which Greenfield, for example, was writing, it is exceedingly difficult for students of educational administration to comprehend the revolutionary nature of the ideas proposed by our most distinguished scholars. Without such a perspective in which to locate the significance of these writers on educational administration, contemporary students of educational administration are left to "scratch their heads" and wonder what all the fuss is about. As a result, many students might be led to assume an eclectic stance or, perhaps, view the epistemological and methodological diversity as a smorgasbord from which one can pick and choose a selection that appeals at the moment. This, however, is an entirely unsatisfactory situation, for without understanding the context of theorists such as Greenfield, one is apt to take whatever feels comfortable in the contemporary context, rather than recognising the core of the purposes underlying the original critique of existing systems. It is our hope that this chapter, and the chapters that follow, will serve to situate the discourse on academic educational administration properly within the historical and theoretical contexts in which they arose.

NOTES

1. "Red sky at night; shepherds' delight,/Red sky in the morning; shepherds' warning," "April showers/bring May flowers," and "Ne'er cast a clout/'til May be out" are all English examples of informational rhymes originating at this time, employed by illiterate people to predict and ease their relationship with nature.
2. Particularly good examples can be found in the frescos and other artworks of Giotto di Bondone (*cf.* the Last Judgement, ca. 1305; the Ognissanti Madonna, ca. 1310; the Stefaneschi Triptych, ca. 1320); the polyptych of Ghent by the Dutch artist Jan van Eyck (1432); and on the tympana of St Foy Cathedral in Conques, St Lazare Cathedral in Autun, and Vézelay Abbey in Burgundy, all of which are in France.
3. Ptolemy's system differed slightly from that offered by Aristotle, and it was Ptolemy's that ultimately found its place as map of the medieval cosmos (Dear, 2009).
4. By this time, Gutenberg's press (invented in the 1450s) had easily reduced the cost of book printing by at least 340 times when compared with monastic handiwork. Burke (1986) reported this in terms of florins per page in Florence in 1483: For Ficino's translation of Plato's *Dialogues*, the scriptorium price was 1 per page, yet Ripola Press charged 3 florins per page setup and included a printed run of 1025 copies (p. 113).
5. On the whole, this was represented in the mutual gravitational attractions among all of the planets, which at some point ought to, thought Newton, throw the system out of alignment unless God became involved.
6. Also known as axial procession, this phenomenon occurs given the off-set orientation of the Earth's axis (which, when combined with the orbit of the Earth around the sun, causes the seasons) slowly rotating as a child's top does, and often causing a wobbling effect just before the top stops spinning. In the context of the Earth's axial procession, however, one complete "wobble" occurs roughly every 26 000 years.

REFERENCES

Allison, D. (1989). *Toward the fifth age: The continuing evolution of academic educational administration*. Paper presented at the Annual Meeting of the American Educational Research Association, San Francisco, CA.

Bacon, F. (1620/1901). *Novum organum* (J. Devey, Trans., Ed.). New York, NY: Collier.

Barker, P. (2002). Constructing Copernicus. *Perspectives on Science, 10*(2), 208–227.

Boyle, R. (1662). *New experiments physico-mechanicall, touching the spring of the air, and its effects (Made, for the most part, in a new pneumatical engine)* (2nd ed.). Oxford, UK: H Hall.

Burke, J. (1986). *The day the universe changed*. Boston, MA: Little Brown.

Butterfield, H. (1965). *The origins of modern science: 1300–1800*. New York, NY: Free Press.

Callahan, R. E., & Button, H. W. (1964). Historical change of the role of the man in the organization: 1865–1950. In D. E. Griffiths (Ed.), *Behavioral science and educational administration: The sixty-third yearbook of the National Society for the Study of Education* (Part II, pp. 73–92). Chicago: University of Chicago.

Crombie, A. (1952). *Augustine to Galileo: The history of science—AD 400–1650*. London: Falcon.

Culbertson, J. A. (1981). Antecedents of the theory movement. *Educational Administration Quarterly, 17*(1), 25–47.

Dear, P. (2009). *Revolutionizing the sciences: European knowledge and its ambitions, 1500–1700*. Princeton, NJ: Princeton University.

Dolnick, E. (2011). *The clockwork universe: Isaac Newton, the Royal Society, and the birth of the modern world*. New York: HarperCollins.

Ehrman, B. (2005). *Misquoting Jesus: The story behind who changed the* Bible *and why*. New York: HarperCollins.

Evers, C. W., & Lakomski, G. (1991). *Knowing educational administration: Contemporary methodological controversies in educational administration research*. Oxford, UK: Pergamon Press.

Evers, C. W., & Lakomski, G. (2000). *Doing educational administration*. Toronto: Pergamon.

Forster, M. (2009). The debate between Whewell and Mill on the nature of scientific induction. In D. Gabbay, S. Hartmann, & J. Woods (Eds.), *Handbook of the history of logic* (Vol. 10). Amsterdam: Elsevier.

Galton, F. (1869). *Hereditary genius*. London, UK: MacMillan.

Gauss, C. (1801). *Disquisitiones arithmeticae*. Leipzig, Germany: Fleischer.

Greenfield, T. B. (1974). *Theory in the study of organizations and administrative structures: A new perspective*. Paper presented at the Third International Intervisitation Programme on Educational Administration, Bristol, UK.

Grew, N. (1673). Some observations touching the nature of snow. *Philosophical Transactions, 8*, 5193–5196.

Henderson, F. (2007). Unpublished material from the memorandum book of Robert Hooke, Guildhall Library MS 1758. *Notes & Records: The Royal Society Journal of the History of Science, 61*, 129–175.

Huff, T. (2011). *Intellectual curiosity and the scientific revolution: A global perspective*. New York, NY: Cambridge University.

Kearney, H. (1971). *Science and change: 1500–1700*. New York: WUL.

Meadows, J. (2004). *The Victorian scientist: The growth of a profession*. London, UK: British Library Board.

Mill, J. (1846). *A system of logic, ratiocinative and inductive; Being a connected view of the principles of evidence and the methods of scientific investigation*. New York, NY: Harper & Brothers.

Mill, J. (1879). *Utilitarianism*. London, UK: Longmans, Green, and Co.

Nightingale, F. (1858). *Notes on matters affecting the health, efficiency, and hospital administration of the British Army*. London, UK: Harrison.

Oplatka, I. (2009). The field of educational administration: A historical overview of scholarly attempts to recognize epistemological identities, meanings and boundaries from the 1960s onwards. *Journal of Educational Administration, 47*(1), 8–35.

Oplatka, I. (2010). *The legacy of educational administration: Historical analysis of an academic field*. Frankfurt am Main, Germany: Peter Lang.

Pickering, M. (1993). *Auguste Comte: An intellectual biography*. Cambridge, UK: Cambridge University.

Quetelet, A. (1842). *Treatise on man*. Edinburgh, UK: Chambers.

Redi, F. (1666). Some observations of vipers. *Philosophical Transactions, 1*, 160–161.

Shapin, S. (1994). *A social history of truth: Civility and science in seventeenth-century England*. Chicago, IL: University of Chicago.

Shapin, S. (1996). *The scientific revolution*. Chicago, IL: University of Chicago.

Shapin, S., & Schaffer, S. (1985). *Leviathan and the air-pump: Hobbes, Boyle, and the experimental life*. Princeton, NJ: Princeton University.

Smith, B. (1987). Austrian origins of Logical Positivism. In B. Gower (Ed.), *Logical positivism in perspective* (pp. 35–68). London, UK: Croom Helm.

Snyder, L. (2009). William Whewell. In E. Zalta (Ed.), *The Stanford encyclopedia of philosophy*. Stanford, CA: Stanford University.

Sprenger, J. (2011). Hypothetico-deductive confirmation. *Philosophy Compass, 6*(7), 497–508.

Tartaglia, N. (1537). *Nuova scienza*. Venice, IT: Stefano Nicolini da Sabbio.

Whewell, W. (1847). *The philosophy of the inductive sciences, founded upon their history* (2nd ed.). London, UK: John W Parker.

Whewell, W. (1858). *Novum organon renovatum* (3rd ed.). London, UK: John W Parker.

Whitehead, A. N., & Russell, B. (1910). *Principia mathematica*. Cambridge, UK: Cambridge University.

Willower, D. J. (1979). Ideology and science in organization theory. *Educational Administration Quarterly, 15*(3), 20–42.

Wilson, D. (1882). Inaugural address. *Transactions of the Royal Society of Canada, sec. II*, 1–12.

Wray, J. (1669). Some observations concerning the odd turn of some shell-snailes, and the darting of spiders. *Philosophical Transactions, 4*, 1011–1016.

2 Toward the Fifth Age

The Continuing Evolution of Academic Educational Administration[1]

Derek J. Allison

From all sedition, conspiracy, and rebellion; from all false doctrine, heresy, and schism . . . Good Lord deliver us.

– *The Litany. Book of Common Prayer*

This chapter will trace the evolution of academic study in educational administration and discuss how each major stage in this evolution has led to increased sophistication and complexity within the academic realm, but at the same time has tended to further distance study from practice. In the final section, the chapter will discuss the recently proposed reforms and consider an alternative that would accommodate the current press for greater practical and experiential training in administrator preparation programmes without sacrificing the future promise of academic study.

ACADEMIC EDUCATIONAL ADMINISTRATION

As implied by the title, this chapter is primarily concerned with the development and future of what I will call *academic educational administration*. In this term, *academic* is meant to convey its generic meaning of being in and of the scholarly community of the university, with none of the pejorative or derogatory connotations of the word being intended or implied. Thus, *academic educational administration* might be operationally defined in terms of the characteristic activities undertaken, and the knowledge and culture consequently created and disseminated by, those who work in university departments of educational administration. The point of using this term is to make a clear distinction between the world of the practitioner and the world of the academic; between the concerns and interests of principals and superintendents, and those of scholars and students; between doing and studying educational administration.

Distinguishing between the action and academic worlds of educational administration is crucial to the thesis of this chapter, for I want to argue that each should properly be regarded as a separate realm with its own legitimate concerns and interests. This is not to imply or suggest that either can or should exist in isolation. The academic and the practical worlds naturally intermingle and overlap in many ways, and each must necessarily complement and inform the other. Indeed, from its beginnings to the present age, academic educational administration has always been concerned with the complementary practical world, as is entirely proper and appropriate for any applied field of academic inquiry. Even so, academics and practitioners typically view things of common interest in characteristically different ways. Those that must act within the real-time world of administration typically seek and value knowledge that will enable them to understand and deal sensibly with the immediately given: with their particular responsibilities and tasks; with the specific problems they encounter and decisions they must make; with ways of realising their professional hopes and plans; and, ultimately, with ways of retaining and enhancing control over the organisation and their future within it. While they may value such knowledge in their personal lives, the scholarly interests of those within the academic world characteristically encourage them to seek broader, more abstract and conceptually complex ways of understanding the realm of administrative action: ways that will be generalisable beyond specific situations, that connect actions and events in broader settings, that describe and explain things and processes in new and powerful ways, that offer novel ways of interpreting the practical world and provide illuminating insights into otherwise commonplace phenomena.

Viewed in this way, academic educational administration must be seen as having an implicit relevance to the world and work of school administrators, and it must also be credited with the potential power to influence, alter, and even transform the world of action through the creation and dissemination of new ideas, techniques, insights and conceptualisations. This, of course, is by no means a new notion. Indeed, a belief in the implicit relevance and power of academic approaches to the practical world undergirds the very idea of the university, and has provided the touchstone rationale for the establishment and development of educational administration as a subject of study within universities. Further, the adoption of major new approaches and emphases in the evolution of academic educational administration has consistently been prompted by desires to enhance the relevance of academic activity to the practical world. Yet the increased conceptual complexity and sophistication within the academic realm brought about by these developments has inevitably intensified the characteristically different ways in which academics and practitioners view the world, further complicating the innate difficulties of translating and relating academic knowledge to practical things. Ironically, then, the evolution of academic educational administration appears to have progressively distanced and isolated the work of university departments from the immediate concerns and interests of school administrators. This frustrating pattern of development has been exacerbated by the continued acceptance and pervasive influence of two deeply rooted assumptions. The first of these is that a science of school administration could be developed through academic work; the second, that school administrators can best be prepared for their roles by being trained in the emergent elements of this science through graduate degree programmes offered by university departments of educational administration. The prevalence of these assumptions, and the ironic consequences of successive attempts to realise and apply the implicit relevance and power of academic approaches to the practical world, can be illustrated by a brief historical review.

THE EVOLUTION OF ACADEMIC EDUCATIONAL ADMINISTRATION

University based approaches to the study and teaching of educational administration were first instituted in the United States a century or so ago, and for the most part the major developments in this academic domain have taken place within the context and culture of that country. Four broad but coherent stages in this evolution can be identified: inception, practical science, theoretical science, and the current stage of conceptual complexity.

Inception: 1880–1910

In Tyack and Hansot's (1982) apt terms, the foundations for public schooling in the United States were laid by middle-class, part-time educational evangelists, but the expansion and consolidation of the system that occurred during the first half of the twentieth century was managed by a new class of "administrative progressives." "Whereas the educational evangelists of the mid-nineteenth century aroused the citizenry against evils, the administrative progressives talked increasingly of problems to be solved by experts" (p. 106). There were indeed many practical and policy problems to be faced by the emergent class of professional school administrators, and a growing recognition among leading school and university administrators of the pressing need to codify and disseminate progressive ways of approaching and handling these problems stimulated the development of the first university courses in school management.

What Culbertson (1988) described as the "first course to train principals and superintendents" (p. 4) was established at the University of Michigan in 1881 by William Payne, who also published, in 1875, *Chapters on School Supervision*, which Culbertson hailed as the first book on educational administration (p. 3). Other courses in school management were established in the 1890s at Teachers College Columbia University (p. 8), the Universities of Colorado and Indiana, and apparently elsewhere (Newlon, 1934, pp. 85–86). These developments were sufficient to lead Newlon (1934) to declare that "by 1900, educational administration was definitely established as a field of professional training" (p. 85). Even so, at the turn of the century there were no departments or professors of educational administration, and the available literature was exceedingly thin. The next decade, brought significant advances.

The major developments were stimulated by and focused around Teachers College Columbia, which was destined to become the first temple of academic educational administration (Cremin, Shannon, & Townsend, 1954). A landmark event occurred in 1905, when the College awarded eight doctorates in education, the two most notable graduates being Ellwood Cubberley and George Strayer, both of whom had specialised in educational administration (Culbertson, 1988, p. 8; Campbell, Fleming, Newell, & Bennion, 1987, p. 4). Columbia was also home to Dutton and Snedden, who published *The Administration of Public Education in the United States* in 1908, which likely reflects some of the specialised work done by Cubberley and Strayer in their doctoral work. At least five other new textbooks on school management and administration were also published between 1900 and 1910 (Newlon, 1934, p. 271), and by the end of this period several other universities had begun to provide opportunities for doctoral study in the field.

The clearest indication that educational administration had become established as an academic subject was the first national meeting of professors to discuss the future development of the field, papers from which were published in *The Aims, Scope, and Methods of a University Course in Public School Administration* (Spaulding, Burris, & Elliot, 1910). The tone of the meeting was optimistic, even eager. Not only was educational administration being studied in graduate courses within the university, the conceptual and methodological ingredients for sound scientific work were believed to be at hand in, respectively, Frederick Taylor's ideas of organisational efficiency and Edward Thorndike's new techniques of statistical measurement. Moreover, the need for well-prepared professional school administrators to cope with the continuing problems of rapid growth and expansion, particularly in urban centres, appeared self-evident. Not all observers were convinced of the incipient maturity of the new field. Paul Hanus of Harvard, for one, declared that "a cynic, listening to the discussion at the meeting, might have said that most of us were not yet ready to study school administration, much less to give a university course in that subject" (cited in Culbertson, 1988, p. 10). This did not, of course, deter the faithful.

Practical Science: 1910–1950

Having established a firm, if slim, bridgehead in the universities, the pioneers of academic educational administration settled down to the serious work of building a corpus of specialist knowledge and applying their newly developed tools and techniques to the practical problems facing the schools and their administrators. Strayer, who remained at Columbia and published *Educational Administration* in collaboration with Thorndike in

1912, exercised a strong formative influence through his refinement and popularisation of school survey techniques, and his pioneering and still influential work in school finance. On the other side of the nation, Cubberley, the "Wizard of Stanford," exerted an indelible and powerful influence on the development of both academic and practical educational administration through his prolific writings, his broad historical grasp of American education, and his steadfast advocacy of expert, efficient, executive school leadership. His mammoth and monumental historical survey, *Public Education in the United States*, also helped form a national understanding of the roots and destiny of American schooling, some 80000 copies being sold between its publication in 1919 and the appearance of a revised edition in 1934 (Cremin, 1965, p. 5).

Yet while Strayer and Cubberley were without doubt the first high priests of academic educational administration, they were by no means alone in their simultaneous creation and advocacy of the gospel of professionalised, executive management. Other notable professors appointed during the first half of this era included Butterworth at Cornell, Hart and Morphet at Berkeley, Henzlik at Nebraska, Mort and Norton at Columbia, and Sears at Stanford (Campbell et al., 1987, p. 173).

Newlon's (1934) compilation of doctoral theses in educational administration submitted between 1910 and 1933 provides a useful picture of the extent of the academic community during this period, the 290 studies listed having been completed at 33 different universities. Newlon's list also dramatically illustrates the pre-eminent dominance of Teachers College at this time, with more than half (150) of the doctorates being earned at Columbia. It further reveals how thinly the academic community was spread in other parts of the country, 12 of the listed theses representing the only doctorate in educational administration completed at the university concerned during the period surveyed. Still, an average of a little more than one completed doctoral dissertation each month over 23 years represented a significant achievement for the new field. A considerably greater number of students, of course, studied for Master's degrees, enrolments in these programmes often being stimulated by the adoption of State certification requirements for school administrators in the middle and later years of this era. Many universities recruited instructors from amongst the ranks of locally experienced superintendents to teach in these programmes and staff the courses in school management that were increasingly being taught in their teacher training programmes. As a result, many of the professors that taught university courses in educational administration towards the end of this period possessed primarily professional, rather than academic, outlooks and interests.

In many ways, this development was an inevitable outcome of the period, for the great academics in the early decades of this age were intimately interested in promoting the professionalisation of school administration, and they were remarkably successful in doing so. They did not accomplish this alone, for they had powerful allies in the form of influential superintendents and the spirit of the times. In the first place, it is clear that the leading academics and superintendents shared a common vision of how schools should best be administered, but more importantly their respective efforts in promoting and implementing this vision were often intertwined and mutually supporting. Secondly, their vision of centralised, expert, executive, and, above all, efficient administration accurately reflected the then-popular principles of Taylorism and promised to bring the soaring costs and confusion created by rapid expansion of public school systems, especially in the cities, sharply to heel. The success of the administrative progressives in promoting their reform agenda is partly illustrated in Callahan's (1962) well known account of how the ideas and ideals of quantified efficiency were zealously applied, and also in the more recent works by Berman (1983), Tyack (1974), and Tyack and Hansot (1982).

Academic educational administration made three major contributions to this transformation of American schooling. First, the textbooks, particularly those penned by Dutton and Snedden (1908, 1916), Strayer and Thorndike (1913), Cubberley (1919, 1922, 1923, 1928), Engelhardt (1931), Moehlman (1940), and Reeder (1941), constantly reiterated the fundamental precepts and values of efficiency through expert executive administration, while typically supplying specific prescriptions as to how schools and school systems should be properly organised and administered. In many respects, they were virtual "bibles," which provided both direction and inspiration for established and aspiring administrators alike. But in addition to furnishing the expert knowledge that the new school managers needed in their work and fostering a growing sense of professional identity, the academics, particularly Cubberley, through his best-seller, also helped mould the way in which teachers, trustees, and other influential middle-class literati came to view the function and role of school administrators, a view which, of course, was founded on the expectation of professionalised expertise. Second, the academic community actively supported the diffusion and application of progressive administration by placing promising graduate students in key superintendencies and assisting in their subsequent advancement. The "Columbia barons"—particularly Strayer, Mort, and Engelhardt—established and managed particularly effective webs of influence, mentorship, and patronage, but professors at other universities also came to play important roles in the placement process as the network of academic educational administration developed during this era (Tyack & Hansot, 1982, pp. 140–142).

Third, and most importantly, the academic community created and disseminated a powerful form of practical science which had direct relevance to practising administrators and which was central to the transformation of American schools in the early and middle decades of this period. Strayer, Cubberley, and the other influential academics were naturally interested in making educational administration scientific, for then, as now, science was seen as a talisman of academic respectability. In that age administrative science was viewed as having a less complicated character, and for the most part those who sought to first make academic educational administration scientific concentrated primarily on the quantification, measurement, and comparison of variables that would yield facts about the functioning of schools and administrative systems, facts that could then be analysed to identify weaknesses or demonstrate accomplishments. The roots of this science were embedded in the pioneering work in statistical measurement techniques initiated by Thorndike in the first decade of this century and in Joseph Rice's earlier work on measuring student achievement. This developmental work led directly to standardised tests of student achievement, at least 300 of which had been developed by 1923 (Cubberley, 1934, p. 694), with more than 4000 mental tests of various kinds being available by 1939 (Cohen & Lazerson, 1977, p. 375). The significance of this to the administrative progressives preoccupied with Tayloresque notions of quantified efficiency was unambiguously explained by Cubberley (1934):

> The important underlying purpose in the creation of all such standards for measuring school work . . . is to give to supervisors and teachers means by which they may, quite definitely, measure the effectiveness of the work they do, and learn from the charted results where to shift the emphasis and how to improve the manufacturing process.
>
> (p. 698)

Moreover, the ability to accurately measure the outcomes of the "manufacturing process" was understood as providing a powerful means of enhancing executive control over administrative and instructional practices and policies, for as Cubberley (1934) further explained:

> For the superintendent, standardized tests have meant nothing less than the ultimate changing of school administration from guess work to scientific accuracy. The mere personal opinion of school board members and the lay public . . . have been in large part eliminated, and in their place has been substituted demonstrable proof as to the validity of a method or procedure or the effectiveness of the administration or the supervision of a school system.
>
> (p. 698)

Standardised measures of achievement, and the IQ tests that appeared at the same time, were not a creation of academic educational administration, nor, of course, were they used solely for administrative ends. Even so, the testing movement itself created conditions that encouraged the development and deployment of measuring devices that had explicit administrative purposes. The development and widespread use of teacher rating scales during this period, for instance, certainly owes something to the measurement movement, as does the wide use of various scales to measure and compare the adequacy of school buildings. But the exemplar of practical administrative science in this age was the school survey—described by Sears (1922), who authored the definitive handbook on this process in 1925, as "a technique for the scientific study of educational problems" (p. 281, as cited in Culbertson, 1988, p. 9). Early surveys, such as those undertaken at Boise, Idaho, in 1910 and Montclair, New Jersey, in 1911 (Cubberley, 1934, p. 695), concentrated on testing pupil achievement, but the technique developed into an omnibus process during which both student achievement and a host of other organisational and administrative variables were measured. Often these surveys were conducted by external consultants, many of whom were from the academic educational administration community, but some large school systems introduced "continuous surveys of production made from within by the superintendent of schools and his staff" (Cubberley, 1934, p. 696). In many cases, these internal surveys came to be conducted by specialist research units, which also conducted studies of other topics of specialist administrative interest such as "finance, accounting, attendance, budget preparation" and salary schedules (p. 696).

The school survey movement had a powerful and profound effect on American schools. Hundreds of surveys were conducted at system and state levels during this era, and it appears that the results and recommendations produced often led to operational changes (Campbell et al., 1987, p. 140). The use of this form of practical science declined during the Great Depression, and it was not revived, at least in the full-blooded form popularised by Sears, in the post-war years. A number of interesting developments did take place in academic educational administration as this age drew to a close, perhaps the most notable being the increasing interest in democratic forms of leadership reflected in Moehlman's (1940) text and other writings (Campbell et al., 1987, p. 141). But as this period drew to a close, academic educational administration seemed mainly content to maintain the course set by its founders and perhaps reflect on the great accomplishments in the earlier decades of the age. And in retrospect, they were great. In Newlon's (1934) words, academic educational administration had given "to government in this country the *only* administrative service staffed by executives who bring to their work extensive professional training and professional ideals" (p. 101).

Theoretical Science: 1950–1975

The post-war years brought with them new values, new ways of understanding and responding to social issues, and rapidly rising school enrolments, all of which placed educational administration, in both its action and academic realms, under strain. With financial support from the W.K. Kellogg Foundation, the Cooperative Program in Educational Administration was launched in 1950 with the main aim of adjusting to these changes through enhancing the quality of graduate preparation programmes. The success of this programme encouraged some thirty or so universities with larger departments of educational administration to support the creation of the University Council of Educational Administration (UCEA) in 1956. This organisation soon came to exert a dominant influence over the development of study and teaching in the field, even though the majority of North American professors of educational administration taught in non-UCEA affiliated universities. These developments in the institutional infrastructure of academic educational administration were driven by large increases in graduate enrolments, particularly in doctoral programmes, with some 1500 doctorates in educational administration being earned annually in the late 1970s (Ortiz & Marshall, 1988, Table 6.3).

By far the most important development was the dramatic change in the focus of academic work being done in the field as a consequence of the advent of the *Theory* or *New Movement*. Much has been written about how this paradigm shift came about, and the details need not concern us here. The main point to be made is that while the Theory Movement was initiated for sound academic reasons, it was understood as being ultimately dedicated to better serving practical ends.

In the transformed social and scientific climate of the post war years, the academic knowledge inherited from the previous age was deemed inadequate. Textbooks were considered to be far too prescriptive, too preoccupied with concrete minutiae and out-of-phase with the social and educational realities and values of the times. Getzels, for example, in personal correspondence quoted by Culbertson (1988), declared that the textbooks in educational administration that he examined in the early 1950s in an attempt to divine the conceptual foundations of the field "seemed more like training manuals than conceptual or research treatises" (p. 15). Similarly, the research being done was limited and weak. Most studies undertaken were largely based on the fact-gathering, school-survey–based traditions inherited from the practical science era; questionnaire driven methodologies were common, coherent conceptual foundation infrequent, and few, if any, of the advances in thinking that had taken place in the broader realms of social science were evident. These weaknesses were pointed out by new professors who took up appointments in departments of educational administration after receiving their academic training in other social science fields. With the able help of some recent graduates from doctoral programmes in educational administration, this new breed of academics set out to modernise the field.

In the article in which he first outlined the ingredients of what was to become the famous and massively influential "Getzels-Guba model," Getzels (1952) offered a paragraph that provides perhaps the clearest statement of the academic rationale behind the Theory Movement:

Systematic research requires the mediation of theory—theory that will give meaning and order to observations already made and will specify areas where observations still need to be made. It is here that we would place the root of the difficulty in educational administration: there is a dearth of theory-making.

(p. 235, as quoted by Culbertson, 1988, p. 15)

He was, of course, completely correct in both his diagnosis and his general prescription, for the understandings of the purposes and the processes of educational administration inherited from the practical science era needed an extensive conceptual reappraisal and overhaul. This did not really happen, for it was believed that an ample supply of conceptual material, theoretical perspectives, and appropriate research methods and techniques was readily at hand in the neighbouring social sciences. Advances in the broader domains of organisational and administrative theory appeared particularly appealing, and a sustained period of often indiscriminate pillaging of this literature began, supplemented with occasional forays into the fields of social psychology and political science. This resulted in considerable academic gains: new ways of understanding organisations and the administrative process proliferated; research became far more theoretically oriented and methodologically sophisticated; the field broadened and deepened as a more generic understanding of educational administration emerged and professors and students became interested in novel perspectives, problems, and possibilities; a new scholarly literature emerged and grew rapidly with the advent of specialised academic journals, while textbooks became far less prescriptive and shifted focus toward the presentation and analysis of conceptual models and research findings.

These academic developments were undeniably exciting, but most appeared to have no immediate relevance to the practical worlds of principals or superintendents. Many of those who earned graduate degrees in the transformed departments of educational administration found that the course material was interesting stuff, especially if there were professors around who could clearly explain the new ideas and concepts and if they could find the time to "do the readings" in their characteristically part-time programmes. Yet, the models, theories, and findings that were presented to these prospective or practicing principals and superintendents often appeared to them to lack any immediate relevance to the problems they would have to handle on Monday morning. This perception, of course, was substantially correct, for the conceptual knowledge that came to form the core of these programmes was never intended to provide specific answers to particular practical problems. On the contrary, it was initially created to provide the "meaning and order to observations" of the world referred to by Getzels above, and when presented in textbooks and seminar rooms was intended to offer generalisable ways of thinking about and gaining new understandings of generic aspects of educational administration. Ultimately, then, the usefulness of the new knowledge produced by the theory movement lay in the characteristic implicit relevance which any domain of academic inquiry has for the aspects of the world it addresses, rather than in any particular set of practical solutions that academic work may be able to offer to the ever-changing; always pressing; and locally complex issues, concerns, and problems in the realm of action.

Such an understanding of the implicit rather than direct relevance of modern academic knowledge of educational administration is now recognised in the literature, but at the beginning and throughout much of this period—and still today in some quarters of the field—the Theory Movement was expected to yield knowledge that would have direct practical relevance to the work of educational administrators. Many of the key assumptions that guided and constrained approaches to the study of educational administration during this period were grounded in Herbert Simon's (1945) *Administrative Behavior* (Culbertson, 1988, p. 14; Greenfield, 1986). As discussed in more detail by Greenfield (1986), Simon's approach rejected earlier understandings of administrative action—which were defined by March as consisting of any such knowledge that pre-dated 1950 (p. 58)—in favour of an objective, scientific analysis of administration as a technical process in organisations. For Simon, and for the founders of the Theory Movement, science was clothed in her then-modern robes as originally crafted by the logical-positivists of the Vienna Circle (Culbertson, 1983). Thus, educational administration was to be properly studied on the basis of objective observations informed by operationally defined concepts and directed and ordered by explanatory theories that would ideally take the form of "'hypothetico-deductive systems'. . . . 'from which can be derived by purely logico-mathematico [*sic*] procedures a larger set of empirical laws'" (Halpin, 1958, as cited in Culbertson, 1988, p. 17). As clearly implied by this celebrated definition of theory borrowed from Feigl and much venerated during the high years of the new movement, Simonesque science was expected to yield theoretical knowledge that would guide and inform administrative practice. In Greenfield's (1986) words:

> Such theory, it was held, would produce control over organizations in the same way that it permitted control over the physical world. The aim of the New [Theory] Movement in educational administration was to generate such theory about schools, to place it in the hands of administrators, and to train them in its use.
>
> (p. 65)

In this way, the theoretical science period in academic educational administration was originally understood as a way to produce knowledge that would be directly relevant to the action realm of administrative practice. Whereas the practical science of the previous age had been intended to yield facts that could provide the basis for action and support the legitimacy of professionalised expert executiveship prescribed in the Cubberlian doctrine, Theory Movement theoretical science was to furnish knowledge that would actually guide and inform action.

The high tide of this vaulting optimism crested early. Although papers from the second Chicago theory seminar were published under the revealing title of *Administrative Theory as a Guide to Action* (Campbell & Lipham, 1960), leaders of the movement were already recalibrating their original high expectations. While their faith in the power of positivistic science remained secure, the prospect of developing a general theory of administration was being increasingly seen as a remote, perhaps ultimately unreachable ideal, and attention was being directed toward selected aspects of organisational functioning and administrative behaviour. Nonetheless, the underlying rationale of generating practice-relevant knowledge through positivistic science and disseminating this knowledge to principals and superintendents via graduate programmes and other media remained the dominant motif during this period.

Conceptual Complexity: 1975–Present

Griffiths (1988a, p. 30) declared that after being in decline for perhaps a decade, the Theory Movement received its coup-de-grace from Greenfield's (1975) now-famous address to the 1974 *International Intervisitation Programme* (IIP) meeting in Bristol. While Greenfield certainly laid the original optimistic hopes for a theoretical science of educational administration to final rest, his first shots at the positivistic beasts that had come to graze in field of academic educational administration during the age of the Theory Movement scarcely wounded, let alone dispatched, them. Indeed, even a cursory glance through the pages of any recent [to the time of preparing this chapter] issue of *Educational Administration Quarterly* will show that the key notion of studying organizational functioning and administrator behaviour as objective, quantifiable, predictable, phenomena is still very much alive and even kicking. Yet a review of the contents of this flagship journal over time will also show the emergence of a variety of new emphases and approaches, a development which is even more marked in the broader literature. Thus, while Greenfield's initial attack on the epistemological foundations of theoretical science did not result in the overthrow of the construct and meta-paradigms characteristic of that previous period, it can certainly be taken as a landmark event that signifies the dawn of a fourth age in the evolution of academic educational administration.

This present age is characterised by, on one hand, the wide variety of the different orientations to the study of educational administration that are currently in use and, on the other, by the greater emphasis that many of the new approaches place on conceptually derived and informed understandings. While theory building remains an important activity, the narrow, positivistic ideal of theory epitomised by the grotesque Feigl definition has been succeeded by a much broader, more fluid, and contingent understanding that allows for diverse approaches to coexist and be pursued. Qualitative research methods have blossomed, while quantitative techniques have become more sophisticated and powerful. In this context, many of the new approaches that have emerged seek to understand administration through the power of discipline-based insights, ideas, and concepts. Thus, Bates (1983) and others have brought the power of Marxist critical theory to bear on the complexities of educational administration, while Hodgkinson (1978, 1983) has offered philosophical analyses of administration. In short, the single conception understandings of science that dominated each of the previous ages is being rapidly replaced with a much more flexible image of science as a dynamic, multifaceted, multi-level knowledge-generating and validating process.

Once again, the emergence of this new era of conceptual complexity was stimulated by a desire to increase the relevance of academic work to the realm of practice. The fundamental point of Greenfield's original denouncement of theoretical science was that Simonesque positivism was constitutionally incapable of yielding knowledge that could serve as a practical guide to administrative action, and thus whatever knowledge was generated through this approach would be inherently irrelevant to the realities faced by principals and superintendents in the action realm. Consequently, he and others consistently argued that academic educational administration should seek to develop more realistic and complete understandings of the indigenous complexities of the practical world by adopting approaches that are grounded in humanistic, rather than positivistic, assumptions. Such approaches would embody a more respectful and reflective attitude toward the experienced reality of administrators, with the main intent of simply helping them, and those who wish to join their ranks, to better understand the inherent complexities of their work. As expressed by Greenfield (1986),

> Scientists inspired by positivism approach administrators with the conviction that their theories and methods enable them to know administration in a way mere practitioners never could. The reverse assumption now seems a better point of departure: administrators know administration; scientists don't. The point of such inquiry would be to enable scientists to come to know what administrators know and to bring a fresh and questioning perspective to it.
>
> (p. 75)

In the context of the ideas developed in this chapter, this argument is an argument for capitalising unashamedly on the implicit relevance and power of academic approaches. Rather than attempting to dedicate and constrain academic work in educational administration to the production of either a practical or theoretical science of administration as in previous ages, this emergent stance would concentrate more directly on the study of administration. Rather than attempting to prescribe ideal practice, such study would seek to better understand and thus inform the realities of administrative action. Rather than assuming that academic work could and should concentrate on producing superior solutions to practical problems, a far greater emphasis would be placed on the ancient and always powerful academic practice of seeking to ask better questions. Rather than continuing the long established tradition of preparing administrators by attempting to train them in the dubious fruits of practical or theoretical science, the advent of such an orientation might also lead to graduate programmes based on the unique and time-honoured power of academic approaches to provide empowerment through education.

But these are only distantly glimpsed possibilities that might be realised if the evolution of academic educational administration continues into a possible fifth age. At the present time the conceptual complexity that currently characterises the field has been described alternatively by Greenfield (1986, p. 74) as "intellectual disarray," and by Griffiths (1979, 1988a, p. 40) as "intellectual turmoil," while Culbertson (1988, p. 18) has described the Theory Movement as currently being in "an embattled state." These internal perceptions of disarray and apparent confusion underestimate the inherent strength that resides in the growing diversity of the field, but they also communicate a sense of impotence to outside observers. From the perspective of practitioners and regulatory agencies, academic educational administration seems unable to deliver on its promises. Not only did the theoretical science era fail to create a workable science of school administration, the university programmes that were supposed to train a new generation of school administrators appear to be producing graduates who are ill-equipped to handle the practical realities of the world of action. As if this were not bad enough, rather than setting its own house in order, the academic community appears more interested in debating ever more esoteric points which seem even further removed from the pressing problems of the practical world. Which brings us back where this chapter began, and the dubious future for academic educational administration.

ALTERNATIVE SCENARIOS FOR THE FIFTH AGE

My main purpose in tracing the evolution of academic educational administration to this point was to try to show that: (a) academic educational administration has a longer and deeper history than is commonly acknowledged in the contemporary literature; (b) it has progressed though a number of essentially evolutionary stages, each one of which has enhanced the scope and sophistication of academic work; (c) each new stage was initiated in an attempt to make the academic field more directly relevant to the complementary practical world of action; (d) new stages developed so that prospective administrators might be better prepared; (e) despite continued attempts to increased the direct relevance of the academic realm to the practical, the main strength of the field has consistently resided in the implicit relevance of academic work and thinking; and (f) the potential power of academic work has been considerably enhanced with the advent of the conceptual complexity which currently characterises the field. Viewed in this broad context, it seems that the academic world of educational administration could well be on the verge of a new, more robust stage of development that could lead to the dawn of a fifth age of mature and sustained academic study.

Calls for education reform often generate pressures for change in the established form and content of administrator preparation programmes, changes intended to make them more directly relevant to the practical world of school management. The cumulative force of these pressures seems such that some kind of change along these lines appears inevitable, the consequences of which will force the development of a fifth stage in the development of academic educational administration in the United States, regardless of the evolutionary forces at work in the broader international field as a whole. Thus, a fifth age in academic educational administration appears likely. The crucial question is: What will be its character? Will it be the age of academic maturity promised in the continuing evolution of the field and outlined earlier, or will it be an age where a newly revived preoccupation with training subordinates academic gains to resurgent practical interests and values? Indeed, I fear that likely reforms threaten to sacrifice the last forty years of growth toward academic maturity on the altar of practical expediency.

Devolution Toward the Ideals of Past Ages

The University Council for Education Administration's *National Commission on Excellence in Educational Administration [NCEEA]* (1987) identified reforms that were primarily designed to increase the practical relevance of future administrator preparation programmes by adopting a more clinical and experientially based approach to training. University departments and their graduate programmes, it was proposed, would abandon liberal arts traditions and assumptions, including perhaps the PhD, in favour of a professional model of administrator training leading to a reconstituted and standardised EdD; programmes would be conducted in close cooperation with school systems, which would help determine content and provide opportunities for clinical experiences; the knowledge base would be restructured to directly address "problems of practice" (Griffiths, 1988a, p. 20), with research being focused on problems of "real significance" in schools (p. 23); finally, the university departments that are to offer and be ultimately responsible for the success of these new programmes would be overhauled to ensure that they were sufficiently well staffed and funded to effectively pursue their prime mission of training principals and superintendents.

The main dangers of these reforms reside in the way in which they seek to retain university level control over programmes of administrator preparation while simultaneously subordinating the legitimate interests and strengths of the academic realm to those of the practical world. This will inevitably result in a trivialisation of academic interests, which will tragically forfeit the immense gains promised by the growing scholarly maturity of academic educational administration. Indeed, the proposed changes appear to be largely based on and justified by a desire to regress the field toward the purposes, values and expectations exemplified in the earlier practical science era, with the knowledge presented being drawn mainly from that produced during the theoretical science age.

Ingredients for an Alternative Future

Is there a realistic alternative to these proposed reforms and the emasculation of academic educational administration that they will bring? In the context of the demand for enhanced relevance in administrator preparation programmes, the challenge is to find a model that will foster and take advantage of continued scholarly growth and sophistication in academic educational administration while at the same time providing appropriate opportunity for experiential learning in the realm of administrative action.

The "professional school" model of preparation advanced and employed by Griffiths (1988b), Greer (1989), and the NCEEA sought to bridge the boundaries between the academic and action realms of educational administration with a view to blending together the activities and interests of professors and practitioners in a common commitment to understanding and dealing with "problems of practice." In this Osterised model "responsibility for preparing educational administrators would be shared with the profession and the public schools" (Griffiths, 1988a, pp. 13–14). The university "should provide the intellectual dimension of preparation," Griffiths explained, "while the profession and the public schools" should cooperatively attend to "the clinical aspects of the program" and "bear major responsibility for supervision of field activities including the internship and the solution of practical problems in university classes" (p. 14).

The conception of "the profession" embedded in this division of responsibilities and promoted throughout Griffiths' (1988b) and Greer's (1989) papers deliberately attempts to separate professors of educational administration from their institutional base in the university and number them with practicing school administrators. This is a crucial element in the model of professional preparation promoted by some reformers, but it is by no means an accurate description of the current situation [at the time of writing], nor is it necessarily desirable or even logical. On the contrary, viewed in the light of the evolution of academic educational administration presented here it appears as an anachronistic conception that once again reflects the ideals of the second age in the development of the field, rather than the academic strength inherent in the current age of conceptual complexity. In this sense, the omnibus conception of "the profession" advanced by Griffiths must be seen as an inherently flawed notion that promotes muddled thinking about the proper and legitimate role of university departments of educational administration in modern times. A far more sensible and accurate approach would recognise and attempt to build on the very real and important institutional and phenomenological differences between the inhabitants of academic and action worlds of educational administration that have been stressed throughout this chapter. This preferable view would thus distinguish between the profession, composed of those who actually administer schools, and the academics who study educational administration.

This does not imply that there is no virtue in experiential approaches to the preparation of school administrators. To the contrary, it makes good sense to provide prospective school administrators with some kind of mediated exposure to, and involvement in, the realities of administrative work. Indeed, there is much to be said for this approach for surely the best way to learn about the working realities of administration is to be a principal, or superintendent, or work closely alongside one. But on what grounds and to what extent, should university departments of educational administration be involved in such activities? Given the apparently established irrelevance of their current programmes to the practical world then there must be doubt, the optimism of Griffiths and Greer notwithstanding, as to whether they can realistically claim the expertise necessary to be involved in the supervision of internships or other clinical experiences. Assuming that professors are or should be included within the profession of educational administration does not ensure or demonstrate that they can actually administer schools as well or better than those that do so on a day-to-day basis. Certainly the failure of the past age to produce a science of administration implies that while academics may well be able to bring insightful understandings to administrative problems and processes, they cannot necessarily lay claim to a special body of practical skill or expertise.

My point is that academic educational administration need not, and probably should not, be involved in all the formal elements of an ideal preparation programme for school administrators, nor should the academic community presume to exercise dominion over such programmes. Such a presumption represents another reversion to the ideals of the administrative progressives in the practical science age. And as Griffiths (1988a) said himself when explaining the rationale for the reform model: "Each should do what each does best" (p. 14). Academic educational administration should do what the evolution of the field has uniquely prepared it to do: It should provide a solid, stimulating, reflective, and mature intellectual treatment of the field. As such, university departments should rid themselves of the historically rooted grand delusion that they can or should train administrators in the specific techniques of their trade and accept that their modern mission is to educate prospective and practising administrators in the complexities of their work and responsibilities. To do this well, departments of educational administration must move closer to, rather than away from, the ideals of a liberal education traditionally embodied in the university arts and science faculties. This does not imply that they should attempt or desire to become part of these other university institutions. Academic educational administration has a rich, diverse and growing body of scholarly knowledge at its disposal and need not rely on, though it can certainly make use of, the knowledge contained in other academic fields and disciplines. The classical virtue of a liberal education is that it promises to liberate the thinking of beneficiaries by helping them see beyond the constraints and conventions imposed in the world of the immediately given. This should be the proper aim of graduate programmes in educational administration.

An Alternate Preparation Programme for the Fifth Age

What might a model of administrator preparation incorporating a liberal academic education look like? First and most fundamentally, such a model would recognise that an appropriate programme would be rooted in both the action and the academic realms. But rather than attempting to forcibly blend these together, as in the Osterised professional model, it would seek to preserve and capitalise on the differences between them. The professional school model tries to pretend that these differences are unimportant by promoting a spurious and anachronistic image of a community of practitioner-scholars. The dual model would acknowledge the force of a century of evolution in university-based approaches to the study of educational administration and attempt to build on the inherited strengths of that tradition. This would not mean that the academic and action worlds would operate as separate closed systems. As discussed in the introduction to this chapter, the two realms necessarily intermingle and complement each other, but they are still essentially different and distinct and the dual model would regard this distinctiveness as legitimate and inherently worthwhile.

The evolution of academic educational administration has produced a large and complex body of literature that offers many pathways to better understanding and gaining insight into the purposes, problems, and processes of practical educational administration. This literature contains many dead ends and many different, and some inherently contradictory, ways of understanding the world of practice, but when approached as a body of academic knowledge, these characteristics can be seen as strengths and not weaknesses. Ideally, degree programmes envisaged in the dual model advocated here would draw on and from all of these apparent and promised strengths in an open and free-ranging search for enhanced understanding. The fruits of the theoretical science era would not be ignored, but neither would inquiry be constrained by the bounds of that knowledge or the positivistic heritage it bears with it. Cubberley and Callahan, Griffiths and Greenfield, Halpin and Hodgkinson, the relics of the school survey movement, modern exploratory data analysis techniques, the insights of qualitative research; all these and other ways of seeking knowledge and insight into the nature of administration and the condition of administrators would be welcomed and available for use. But above all else, the courses and the degree programme itself would be designed to facilitate and further the study of educational administration through its extant and evolving academic literature and the application of the knowledge therein to the realm of administrative action. This emphasis would be communicated clearly and unambiguously to students and the professional community. Here, they would be told, we study, and do not teach, educational administration. Here, we offer insight and understanding, not training and technique. Here, we stand ready to learn from administrators, rather than tell them what is best.

Some of the specific emphases and content that would seem particularly appropriate in such programmes if academic educational administration were to move into its promised fifth age of academic maturity include:

1. Attempts to reflect on and learn from the rich history of academic and practical educational administration and relate such learnings to current and emergent situations. There is undoubtedly much work to be done in seeking a better understanding of the development of the field. Culbertson has helped to show us the way here, but we can also learn from educational historians and hopefully encourage them to work more closely with us.

2. Deeper and more sustained attention to the philosophical questions of administration and its inherently moral nature, with particular attention being given to the influence of values in administrative action. Hodgkinson has provided us with a good beginning in this area, but again there is a virtually limitless scope for inquiry, theory building, and seminar work.

3. Wider and broader attempts to understand schools as unique social phenomena. The literature of organisational theory will continue to have relevance here as it too evolves, but the perspectives of critical theory may provide particularly valuable material for classroom work. Specific attention could be paid here to exploring both the structure and effects of schools and the whole apparatus of state schooling. The construction of the curriculum and the sociology of knowledge should also be considered in this context.

4. Closer and more penetrating treatments of the nature and use of authority and power in organisational settings. Administrators are instruments and creators of authority, but there has been a tendency to cloak the difficult realities of this truth in abstractions and euphemisms. Both the personal and institutional exercise of authority provide much room for exploration, particularly with regard to policy formation, decision making and judgment, and the role of values and power in such activities.

5. Specific attention should also be given to the subjective reality of organisational life and action as experienced and constructed by both those who administer and those who are administered. Greenfield (1986), of course, has shown us the way forward here and he should

be heeded. In particular, his outline of a possible agenda for fifth age research provides additional topics for study which complement the few noted here.

CONCLUSION

In this chapter, I have tried to argue for the preservation and extension of the academic study of educational administration. I have tried to show that academic interest and work in the field has progressed through a number of relatively distinct stages to reach its present state of emergent maturity. At the present juncture, a popular press for excellence and effectiveness in the United States has generated proposals for the restructuring of departments of educational administration that threaten to impede or even destroy the prospect for mature and serious academic work in the field, at least in that country. An alternate model for the education and training of educational administrators was therefore presented as a means of sustaining the academic evolution of the field and capitalising on its implicit and promised strengths.

The arguments advanced in the development of the chapter are of course by no means new or novel. The inherent relevance of academic work to the everyday world has been recognised and demonstrated throughout our history, and many others have argued for its preservation in the face of zealous reformers seeking to diminish or overthrow its virtues in the name of practicality. Cubberley (1934) was one such defender and advocate of the value of academic work, and his frozen thoughts provide a fitting end to this chapter: "In education as in other lines of work, the old statement that the distinctive function of a university is not action, but thought, has been exemplified" (p. 690).

Let us keep it so.

NOTE

1. The original version of this essay was presented at a symposium on the future relevance of the academic study of educational administration in the preparation of administrators at the annual conference of the American Educational Research Association, San Francisco, March 1989.

REFERENCES

Bates, R. J. (1983). *Educational administration and the management of knowledge.* Victoria, Australia: Deakin University Press.

Berman, B. (1983). Business efficiency, American schooling, and the public school superintendency: A reconsideration of the Callahan thesis. *History of Education Quarterly,* 23(Fall), 297–321.

Callahan, R. E. (1962). *Education and the cult of efficiency.* Chicago: University of Chicago Press.

Campbell, R. F., Fleming, T., Newell, L. J., & Bennion, J. W. (1987). *A history of thought and practice in educational administration.* New York: Teachers College Press.

Campbell, R. F., & Lipham, J. M. (Eds.). (1960). *Administrative theory as a guide to action.* Chicago: University of Chicago.

Cohen, D. K., & Lazerson, M. (1977). Education and the corporate order. In J. Karabel & A. H. Halsey (Eds.), *Power and ideology in education,* (pp. 373–386). New York: Oxford University Press.

Cremin, L. A. (1965). *The wonderful world of Ellwood Patterson Cubberley.* New York: Teachers College, Columbia University.

Cremin, L. A., Shannon, D. A., & Townsend, M. E. (1954). *A history of Teachers College, Columbia University.* New York: Columbia University Press.

Cubberley, E. P. (1919). *Public education in the United States.* Boston, MA: Houghton Mifflin.

Cubberley, E. P. (1922). *Public school administration* (Rev. ed.). Boston, MA: Houghton Mifflin.

Cubberley, E. P. (1923). *The principal and his school: The organization, administration and supervision of instruction in an elementary school.* Boston, MA: Houghton Mifflin.

Cubberley, E. P. (1928). *Public school administration.* New York: Houghton Mifflin.

Cubberley, E. P. (1934). *Public education in the United States* (Revised and enlarged ed.). Boston: Houghton Mifflin.

Culbertson, J. A. (1983). Theory in educational administration: Echoes from critical thinkers. *Educational Researcher, 3*(10), 15–22.

Culbertson, J. A. (1988). A century's quest for a knowledge base. In N. J. Boyan (Ed.), *Handbook of research on educational administration* (pp. 3–26). New York: Longman.

Dutton, S. T., & Snedden D. (1908). *The administration of public education in the United States.* New York: Macmillan.

Dutton, S. T., & Snedden D. (1916). *The administration of public education in the United States* (Rev. ed.). New York: Macmillan.

Engelhardt, F. (1931). *Public school organization and administration.* Boston, MA: Ginn and Company.

Getzels, J. W. (1952). A psycho-sociological framework for the study of educational administration. *Harvard Educational Review, 22*(4), 235–246.

Greenfield, T. B. (1975). Theory about organization: A new perspective and its implications for schools. In M. Hughes (Ed.) *Administering education: International challenge* (pp. 71–99). London: Athlone Press.

Greenfield, T. B. (1986). The decline and fall of science in educational administration. *Interchange, 17*(2), 57–80.

Greer, J. T. (1989). UCEA Presidential address, 1988. An optimist's view. *UCEA Review, 30*(1), 5–7.

Griffiths, D. E. (1979). Intellectual turmoil in educational administration. *Educational Administration Quarterly, 13*(3), 43–65.

Griffiths, D. E. (1988a). Administrative theory. In N. J. Boyan (Ed.), *Handbook of research on educational administration* (pp. 27–51). New York: Longman.

Griffiths, D. E. (1988b). *Educational administration: Reform PDQ or RIP* (Occasional paper #8312). Tempe, AZ: UCEA.

Halpin, A. W. (1958). The development of theory in educational administration. In A. W. Halpin (Ed.), *Administrative theory in education* (pp. 1–19). Chicago: University of Chicago.

Hodgkinson, C. (1978). *Towards a philosophy of administration*. Oxford, UK: Basil Blackwell.

Hodgkinson, C. (1983). *The philosophy of leadership*. Oxford, UK: Basil Blackwell.

Moehlman, A. B. (1940). *School administration*. Boston, MA: Houghton Mifflin.

Newlon, J. H. (1934). *Educational administration as social policy* (Report of the Commission on the Social Studies, Part VIII). New York: Scribner.

Ortiz, F. I., & Marshall, C. (1988). Women in educational administration. In N. J. Boyan (Ed.), *Handbook of research on educational administration* (pp. 123–141). New York: Longman.

Reeder, W. G. (1941) *The fundamentals of public school administration*. New York: Macmillan.

Sears, J. B. (1922). Techniques of the public school survey. *Journal of Educational Research, 6*, 281–299.

Sears, J. B. (1925). *The school survey*. Boston, MA: Houghton Mifflin.

Simon, H. (1945). *Administrative behavior*. New York: Macmillan.

Spaulding, F. E., Burris, W. P., & Elliot, E. C. (1910). *The aims, scope and method of a university course in public school administration*. Indianapolis, IN: National Society for College Teachers of Education.

Strayer, G. D., & Thorndike, E. L. (1913). *Educational administration: Qualitative studies*. New York: Macmillan.

Tyack, D. B. (1974). *The one best system*. Cambridge, MA: Harvard University Press.

Tyack, D., & Hansot, E. (1982). *Managers of virtue: Public school leadership in America, 1820–1980*. New York: Basic Books.

University Council for Educational Administration. (1987). *Leaders for America's Schools. The Report of the National Commission on Excellence in Educational Administration*. National Commission on Excellence in Educational Administration. Tempe, AZ.

3   Thomas Greenfield and the Foundations of Educational Administration

Augusto Riveros

In this chapter, I explore the contribution of Canadian scholar of educational administration Thomas B. Greenfield. In the first part, I sketch the basic tenets of the Theory Movement and trace its origins to the principles of Logical Positivism proposed by the Vienna Circle. After setting the background, I introduce some key themes in Greenfield's work, showing how they articulate sound challenges to positivist conceptions of knowledge in educational organisations. Throughout this chapter, I highlight the links to authors and philosophies that influenced Greenfield's work to a certain extent.

THE BACKDROP: POSITIVISM AND THE STUDY OF EDUCATIONAL ADMINISTRATION

In an act of intellectual honesty, Thomas Greenfield stood before his colleagues in Bristol, England, in 1974 and challenged the very assumptions he used to uphold. His remarks soon initiated a turmoil (Griffiths, 1979) that impacted the study of educational administration for the years to come. He asked deep and perplexing questions about the role of subjectivity in the study of educational organisations, the meaning of actions, the role of values in the practice of educational administration, and the ontological status of organisations. Greenfield spoke to an intellectual tradition known as the *Theory Movement* that relied on ideas taken from the Vienna Circle and specifically from Logical Positivism. I will begin with a brief exposition of the Circle's ideas and their subsequent adoption by the Theory Movement. This initial discussion aims to contextualise Greenfield's critique to the positivist conception of educational administration.

The *Vienna Circle* was the name of a group of intellectuals that flourished in Europe in the 1920s and 1930s. They aimed to revamp empiricism by establishing the foundation of all human knowledge in logic and the physical sciences. Their reliance on logical reasoning and empirical experience originated the movement known as *Logical Positivism*. They claimed that scientific statements were meaningful only if they could be confirmed, tested, or verified by some scientific method. This criterion of verification was central to the Circle's opposition to any form of metaphysics and central to their hope to find a model that would unify the social sciences and the physical sciences. That is, logical positivists believed that human knowledge was a building-like structure in which the physical sciences and logic provided the support or foundations, and everything else was built upon them. Logical positivists believed that scientific theories were hypothetico-deductive systems, that is, systems that are structured upon law-like statements and are permanently tested by observation—thus the importance logical positivism gave to experimentation as a means to test scientific theories (Parrini, Salmon, & Salmon, 2003).

According to these philosophers there are only two types of meaningful statements: *a priori* and *a posteriori*. The former are logical truths that do not need to be verified by experience (e.g., principles of logic), the latter are statements that are true or false in virtue of the evidence gathered through experience. According to logical positivists, our knowledge of the world and our knowledge in general can only be represented through these two types of statements.

Logical positivists deemed scientific theory construction as a strictly rational enterprise based on logic and observation. Normative statements, or *ought* statements, of ethics had no place in theory building. Because a normative statement does not tell anything about facts and cannot be verified through observation, logical positivists believed that normative statements were meaningless and had no place in scientific theorisations. For example, Schlick (1979) argued that a scientifically oriented ethics is descriptive rather than normative, so instead of telling us what we *should* do to be morally right, a scientifically oriented ethics tells us what is good, right, and just, based on what we actually do to avoid pain and obtain pleasure. For instance, Schlick (1979) analysed egoist behaviour and altruist behaviour in terms of their role in our evolutionary history.

These ideas were taken up by some scholars of educational administration in the late 1950s and their adoption led to what we know as the Theory Movement. In 1957, during a career development seminar sponsored by the University Council for Educational Administration (UCEA) and the University of Chicago, a group of scholars produced a document in which they delineated the principles of the *New Movement* in educational administration (Halpin, 1958). This New Movement became known as the *Theory Movement*.

Halpin (1958), and Culbertson (1981, 1983), summarised the core ideas of the theory movement as follows:

1. Statements about what administrators and organisations ought to do cannot be encompassed in science or theory;
2. Scientific theories treat phenomena as they are;
3. Effective research has its origins in theory and is guided by theory;

4. Hypothetico-deductive systems are the best exemplars of theory;
5. The use of the social sciences is essential in theory development and training; and
6. Administration is best viewed as a generic concept applicable to all types of organisation.

I examine these ideas in more detail below.

On the Theory Movement

Statements about what administrators and organisations ought to do cannot be encompassed in science or theory. According to Culbertson (1981), "theory and research concentrate on the description, explanation, and prediction of administrative and organizational behaviour; generalizations prescribing courses of action or specifying what administrators or organizations should do are beyond the purview of researchers and the capacity of science" (p. 27). To Theory Movement advocates, any reference to values, ethics, and morality was meaningless because such references made use of unverifiable claims about *what should be* instead of claims about *what is*. This was, in part, the Theory Movement's reaction to the scholarship in educational administration of the time that offered prescriptions but lacked empirical support. The absence of a discussion on values and their silence about the moral purpose of educational administration was one of the principles that Greenfield, Hutchinson, Ribbins, and others condemned more forcefully in their critiques of the Theory Movement. Indeed, not talking about the moral purpose of administration is in fact a normative decision that has profound political and ethical implications regarding the purposes of educational administration and the role of people within educational organisations (Greenfield, 1991).

Scientific theories treat phenomena as they are. This idea has its origin in the conception of science as a purely descriptive endeavour. If educational administration were to be treated as a science then it had to conform to the protocols of natural science and develop a methodology appropriate to individuate and characterise its object of study.

Effective research has its origins in theory and is guided by theory. The scholars in the Theory Movement usually complained that educational research was permeated by a "naked empiricism" (Halpin, 1958, p. 1). According to these scholars, research without sound theoretical support is unable to generalise its findings. The alternative proposed by the Theory Movement was to derive hypotheses from the theory and to test such hypotheses through research. Another feature of the Theory Movement was the operationalisation of theoretical concepts. That is, making administration concepts measurable and understandable in terms of empirical observations.

Hypothetico-deductive systems are the best exemplars of theory. The Theory Movement endorsed Herbert Feigl's (1951) definition of theory, according to which a "'theory' is a set of assumptions from which can be derived by purely logico-mathematical procedures a larger set of empirical laws" (p. 182). Theory Movement proponents assumed that observation statements are ultimately derived from theoretical statements and the function of research was to verify and empirically test such observation statements, thus validating the theory in a process of continuous verification. Scholars in the Theory Movement believed that hypothetico-deductive systems were relevant to research in educational administration. In fact, their research was oriented to construct theories that could be tested by experimental methods.

The use of social sciences is essential in theory development and training. Authors within the Theory Movement thought that theory development in educational administration required methods from the behavioural and social sciences. They considered that the concepts of educational administration could be expressed as operational definitions offered by the behavioural sciences.

Administration is best viewed as a generic concept applicable to all types of organisation. Theory Movement advocates were interested in generalisations supported by the scientific method. The concept of administration was no exception. In their view (Halpin, 1958) administration was generalisable to other fields because they argued that there were no proprietary research methods to educational administration, and the resulting generalisations could be applied to any kind of organisation regardless of their nature.

REDEFINING THE NATURE OF EDUCATIONAL ORGANISATIONS

Several lines of thought can be drawn from Greenfield's work. Although these lines often intertwine and overlap, I will make an effort to make them visible. Greenfield (1980) was reluctant to frame his discussion of organisations within the classic metaphysical binaries. For example, when he said, "organizations are essentially arbitrary definitions of reality woven in symbols and expressed in language" (p. 44) he was intending to blur the classic philosophical distinction between ontology and epistemology. He noted that the nature of organisations could not be described as detached from our symbolic apparatus. Furthermore, in his work, Greenfield showed that any conception of organisational reality has deep ethical and political implications in relation to freedom, agency, and responsibility. His reviews of the positivist conceptions of educational administration revealed a picture in which individuals are seen as essentially separate from organisations, so, paradoxically, human will and values become irrelevant to the study of social institutions.

Greenfield's (1973) initial concerns were related to the nature of organisations. He asked, for instance, "What is an organization that it can have such a thing as a goal?" (p. 552). If organisations can have goals, then what is the role of individual agency and volition within the organisation? According to

Greenfield, an inquiry into the nature of organisations necessarily overlaps with questions about knowledge and truth in the organisational context. He not only interrogated the nature of organisations, he questioned the way people validate their knowledge and make sense of their actions in organised settings (Innes-Brown, 1993). In addition to these epistemological inquiries, Greenfield noted that organising is a symbolic act that carries political and ethical significance. He noted that meaning in organisations plays a pivotal role in defining our interpretation of organisational reality. In what follows, I focus on these overlapping themes in Greenfield's work, namely, (a) the *ontology of organisations*, (b) the *epistemology of organising*, (c) the *role of meanings in the interpretation or organisational realities*, and (d) the *ethical/ political significance of educational administration*.

In *Theory about Organization* (1975), Greenfield outlined two conflicting ways to understand organisational reality. On the one hand, there is the systems theory, which sees organisations as systems that can be studied as objects of nature. On the other hand, there is the conception of organisations as symbolic human creations. Greenfield saw the former as realist and objectivist, whereas he saw the latter as subject-centred, a "humane science" (Greenfield, 1991/1993). Systems theory portrays social science as a truth seeker that aims to find the universal laws that rule individuals and society, whereas a humane science portrays social sciences as sciences of meaning, in line with the Weberian project that seeks to study how people understand their experiences in the context of a culture.

In his critique of Simon's systems theory (Cyert & March, 1963; March & Simon, 1958; Simon, 1957, 1958, 1969; Vera & Simon, 1993), Greenfield rejected a type of ontological dualism that still pervades common parlance about organisations (e.g., Lunenburg & Ornstein, 2008; Senge, 2000). In his view, organisational literature "conveniently separates people and organizations . . . a mistaken belief in the reality of organizations has diverted our attention from human action and intention as the stuff from which organizations are made" (Greenfield, 1975, p. 1). A theory of administration that deals only with facts independent of human volition and intention assumes that organisations are entities in which the human dimension is just an accessory to the overarching goals of the organisation as a concrete reality. The questioned image is that of an organisation as a system that responds and adapts to the environment; the information gathered in the process of adapting to the environment is accumulated and systematised in the structure. In this arrangement, people in the organisation can come and go but the information and organisational structure stay (Fiol, 2002). According to this view, organisations provide an essential function to society, they provide structure to social relations, and they preserve information. Such separation between individuals and organisations relies on the assumption that organisations are necessary to individuals so they can obtain social benefits (Durkheim, 1957). A vision of organisations as systems that process information and adapt to the environment (Fiol, 2002), corresponds, in Greenfield's opinion, to the Theory

Movement's conception of administration as a science that deals with facts and is free of subjective influences.

Greenfield argued that what we call *organisation* is not a single abstraction with its own reality, but a variety of individual beliefs, values, and perceptions that often conflict with each other. He followed Weber's (1968) insights by indicating that organisational reality is socially constructed through the meanings shared among the different actors within the organisation. Weber's notion of *verstehen* was influential in the way Greenfield understood the construction of organisational reality (Harris, 2003). Weber (1968) indicated that observers of a culture engage in a systematic process of interpretive understanding (*verstehen*) in order to relate to that culture. The observers adopt an emphatic understanding of the social group trying to understand the culture's social reality from the perspective of the members of that culture. In reflecting about organisations as *talk, chance, and experience*, Greenfield (1979/1993) indicated,

> But what is an organization if it is not something separate from individuals? Organizations may be seen as pure process, as action where individuals change ideas into behaviour and possibilities into consequences. Our conceptions of organizations must be as complex as the reality we try to understand.
>
> (p. 55)

It is important to emphasise the intrinsic relationship Greenfield noted between the organisation and the individual (English, 2003). Positivist models of organisations create a relation of subordination in which people have to rely on a superior authority to find guidance (Greenfield, 1979/1993; Gronn, 1983, 2003). In a metaphysical sense, this separation cannot explain the origin of meaning in the organisational context. He conceived meaning as the symbolic framework used by the individual to make sense of his/her actions and to relate to the environment. H. L. Gray (1982) formulated this claim from a subjectivist perspective akin to Greenfield's position: "Organizational change occurs only as a consequence of changes in the individual self-concept. It is the individual's view of himself that changes, not the organization" (p. 38).

If the intertwining of individual meanings creates organisational reality, then the legitimation of the organisation as social institution depends on the participation of actors, as their meanings constitute the very substance of the organisation. Greenfield (1979/1993) noted how organisations are conventions; they comprise sets of rules and procedures so people can act towards a given goal. At this point, he noticed a crucial metaphysical problem for positivist conceptions of organisations: If it were the case that organisations have a separate existence from people, as external and independent realities, then we would have to explain the ontological status of the rules, procedures, symbols, and conventions in organisations (Evers & Lakomski, 1991). "It is the individual that lives and acts, not the organization. It is, therefore, the experience of individuals that we must seek to understand" (Greenfield, 1982, p. 4). Therefore, any talk about organisational change must take people's perceptions and experiences as its main focus (Ribbins, 2003).

Furthermore, Greenfield (1973) stressed that organisational transformation resides in the individual. "The transforming mechanism lies within individuals. It is found in individuals striving to change their demands or beliefs into definitions of reality that others must regard as valid and accept as limitations on their actions" (p. 560). This subjectivist perspective questions the ontological assumptions present in the positivist approaches to educational organisations. Specifically, Greenfield's subjectivism questions the very idea of organisational change as an effect of external forces (Greenfield, 1979/1993; Riveros, 2009). The change of focus proposed by Greenfield implies not only that organisational change does not belong to the realm of study of the natural sciences, but also implies that in order to transform organisations, individual perceptions must be subsequently transformed. In Greenfield's (1980) view, change is the transformation of a symbolic apparatus, a change in the content of meanings. Therefore, if organisational change were a transformation of meanings and meanings are subjective features of individuals, then organisational change does not happen independently of human action and experience:

> Organizations are the meanings we find in our lives, regardless of how those meanings came to be there. The self cannot escape organizations. Indeed, self *is* organization in a profound sense, though the self may behave and feel quite differently as it moves from organization to organization—from fragment to fragment of its personal world.
>
> (Greenfield, 1979/1993, p. 54)

The symbolic character of organisations inevitably ties them to human action and experience—organisations are the symbolic framework by which actors identify themselves as members or outsiders, that is, an action is *organisational* once it is understood against the symbolic backdrop of other organisational practices. In "Organization Theory as Ideology", Greenfield (1977) indicated that if we want to understand organisational reality we must go beyond a naturalist logic; in his view, "living in the world is synonymous with action. The individual can not escape doing; no more can the leader escape decisions or the agony that often goes with making them . . . [to] escape from action is impossible" (p. 106).

Greenfield's insights on truth, meaning, actions and organisational reality show us how he understood the evident connection between the ontological questions about the nature of educational organisations and the epistemological questions about knowledge in educational administration. In the next section, I discuss Greenfield's notion of meaning in connection to his conception of knowledge in educational administration, however, it is necessary to keep in mind that for him, organising is foremost a moral act that has profound implications for actors in schools.

GETTING TO KNOW EDUCATIONAL ORGANISATIONS

There are two important consequences of Greenfield's subjectivist notion of organisations. First, there is not a common organisation for all its members. Namely, there might be as many subjective versions of the organisation as individuals in it. Second, if there cannot be such a thing as an objective organisation, then there cannot be such a thing as an objective organisational goal.

In "Against Group Mind," Greenfield (1982) argued that each member has his/her own conception of the organisation, so organisational goals are a matter of subjective interpretation: "we live in separate realities. What is true for one person is not for another. In that sense, we live in different worlds. Each of us, Huxley says, is an island universe" (p. 5). Greenfield's relativism in this passage is supported by his subjectivism. We know by empirical evidence that people have different perceptions of the world, and the same applies to organisations:

> An anarchistic theory of organization may be summed up in two statements: first, a statement that rejects group mind and denies an overarching social reality thought to lie beyond human control and outside the will, intention and action of the individual; second, a statement that acknowledges the tumult and irrationality of thought itself.
>
> (p. 14)

It is clear that Greenfield was skeptical about notions akin to "shared meaning" or "group goals." In his view, agreement or coordination in organisations are the result of imposition and power, and not the product of group agency. This skepticism is present throughout his work: "In the production of organizations, we should be aware of what Giddens calls 'asymmetries' in meaning and morality and in the power of certain people to force their meanings and moralities upon others" (Greenfield, 1980, p. 46). The formulation of overarching organisational goals is absurd, on this view, because worldviews often collide and consensus is less likely to happen. However, how is it that there are organisations that clearly have the same goals for all their members? In Greenfield's opinion, we should not mistake consensus for powerful imposition:

> If we take the position based in common values, conflict occurs between the individual and the larger moral order. In this case, the administrator acts on behalf of the larger order against aberrant individuals who are to be coaxed and coerced into aligning themselves with it.
>
> (pp. 49–50)

Greenfield proposed that administrators should avoid coercion and instead adopt an open attitude towards dialogue and the acknowledgement of the differences in the organisation. He maintained that organisations are *moral orders*. Organisations prescribe and regulate people's behaviour, so the moral duty of the administrator is to be reflective—and respectful—of others in the organisation. The idea that organisations are moral orders has profound ontological, epistemological, and ethical implications, and Greenfield (1980, 1991/1993) stressed that these dimensions are essentially intertwined.

Greenfield's (1980) endorsement of the interpretive approach (*verstehen*) allowed him to distance himself from the naturalist presuppositions of positivism and, particularly, Systems Theory and the Theory Movement:

> The authentic administrator then becomes acutely aware of his decisions, choices, values and power—of the value choices *he* [*sic*] must make. Volition, interest, and intention enter the picture. Responsibility too. I can now no longer say that my finger moved, but that *I* moved my finger. It is not that my mind thinks and perceives the natural order of things, but that I think, conceive what is, and move to act upon it. Conflict, in other words, occurs between equals though their powers may be different.
>
> (p. 50)

In passages like this and elsewhere, Greenfield (1986, 1991) was responding to some of his critics (Griffiths, 1983; Hills, 1981) by stressing that it is not possible to study human beings in organisations by using the methods of the natural sciences. In his view, a naturalist approach makes "individuals disappear—and with them human agency, responsibility, and morality—and natural forces take over the conduct of human affairs" (Greenfield, 1986, p. 145). He stressed the epistemological primacy of experience: "any worthwhile explanations of social reality must not contradict that experience. It may reinterpret it but it must not contradict it" (Greenfield & Ribbins, 1993, p. 250). In his view, the study of educational administration is circumscribed to the individual's subjective experiences; namely, the subjective experience provides a glimpse into the structure and functioning of organisations (*cf.* Sackney & Mitchell, 2001, p. 8). However, in interpreting other people's actions in the organisational context, we could be easily lured by the old threat of solipsism:

> In the face of a multi-faceted, ambiguous "reality," one needs a conception, an idea of it, if one is to speak of organizations. The idea inevitably stands between us and what we think is reality; it links our experience and our sense of an outside world and others' behaviour in it. It is this mysterious void between behaviour and experience that the image must fill.
>
> (Greenfield, 1979/1993, p. 71)

In this remarkable fragment, Greenfield highlighted a very important issue for his epistemology of educational organisations, that is, the apparent gap, the "mysterious void," between my own experiences and other people's behaviour. How is it possible to interpret others' behaviour as "organisational behaviour" or "organisationally oriented behaviour" if I have no objective access to their own perceptions and knowledge? It is possible that their behaviour could be motivated by a completely different conception of the organisation. In other words, my interpretation of my own experience depends on my privileged access to my own experiential states, and in principle, according to this line of thought, I do not have such privileged access to anyone else's experiential states.

How is it possible to interpret the actions of other people in the organisation as organisationally oriented actions? Here, Greenfield seemed to suggest that one can interpret another's actions by analogy to one's own case (Ryan, 1988), creating a "conception"—an "idea that inevitably [. . .] links our experience and our sense of an outside world and other's behaviour in it" (Greenfield, 1979/1993, p. 71). He noted that we need symbols to understand our experience and other people's experience: "the only way we can gain access to another's experiences is in symbols of one kind or another, frequently linguistic symbols" (Greenfield & Ribbins, 1993, p. 250).

LEADER IN ACTION AND THE ORGANISATION AS MORAL ORDER

Conferring primacy to subjectivity in the study of educational organisations is not only an epistemological claim but also an ethical claim with profound implications for policy makers and administrators (Sergiovanni, 1992, 2000). To Greenfield (1991), organisations are first and foremost moral orders that legitimate a particular structure through symbols, meanings, and actions. It is worth noticing that Greenfield was not opposed to the idea of structure or hierarchy in organisations. He was interested in the *justification* of hierarchies as moral orders. He questioned models of organisation whose sole purpose is to impose and coerce. In his view, the legitimation of a hierarchical structure should rest on the recognition of different values and voices within the organisation; dialogue, conflict, and dissent become essential to the functioning of schools.

The notion of moral order contrasts with the idea of natural order, that is, the idea that the laws of nature determine the structure of reality. Greenfield (1986) considered that the idea of moral order allows us to understand how it is that conflict appears in organisations, and how dialogue becomes essential to the role of the administrator. The administrator must seek to legitimate the moral order not by imposition but by inviting and welcoming dissent and debate. Conflict is essential to organisations and the existent moral order is reflective of the way power is legitimated in, for example, schools. Greenfield's debt to Weber is evident here: "one cannot study the social order, therefore, without studying also the self, its values, conditions of creativity and power, and considerations of what ought to be" (p. 98).

In Greenfield's (1984) view, leadership emerges as the moral order is legitimated. He indicated that we should study the leaders in their context, their character and actions instead of elaborating abstract theories of leadership that do not reflect the complexities of the daily life of school leaders. It is the leaders and not the leadership that should attract the researchers' attention. Greenfield was not alone in his criticisms to positivism; another Canadian scholar, Christopher Hodgkinson (1978, 1983, 1991), proposed an alternative to positivism in educational administration by advancing the idea of administration as a moral art. According to Hodgkinson, the Theory Movement erred by stripping values from the study of educational administration. For Hodgkinson (1978), administration represents an act that is bounded by values and morality: "the intrusion of values into the decision making process is not merely inevitable, it is the very substance of decision" (p. 59). The administrator must decide between competing values, intentions, and purposes, and mere rational/logical analysis will not suffice. In Hodgkinson's view, education as a humane enterprise has a moral character and the administration of education must not detach from this primary concern.

In relation to the study of the nature of moral orders, there are two types of inquiry proposed by Greenfield. On the one hand, there is a description of the moral order and what happens within it; on the other hand, there is a normative or philosophical inquiry that asks the ethical questions about what is the best moral order. Greenfield (1984) acknowledged that this last question could not be conclusively resolved. In relation to the description of the moral order, he indicated that description "opens up the possibility that artistic and other non-rational modes of representation of reality might convey the meaning of social organizations as well as, or better than, the linear, concise, and highly quantified abstractions that now usually count as science" (p. 50). Harris (1996) has argued that Greenfield incorporated aesthetic thought into organisational theory in two ways: first, by surprising his audience challenging long-held assumptions in the field, making them see organisations from a new perspective—Harris called this the "aesthetic shock" (p. 490)—second, by proposing that knowledge in organisations is best expressed through symbolic means as it is originated in experience, meaning, and actions.

In relation to this point, Milley (2002) noticed a tension between Greenfield's moral and methodological enterprises. Milley argued that Greenfield's methodology is descriptive in the sense that it aims to articulate in a descriptive fashion the experiences of those within the organisation; however, Greenfield's portrayal of organisations as moral orders commits him also to a prescriptive approach that continuously seeks for the best of all possible moral orders. Although the best moral order may not be found, the argumentation process that accompanies this search is morally desirable as it makes us reflect about our current practices and situation. In other words, according to Milley, Greenfield seemed to suggest that from our description of the individual's experiences we could conclude what moral organisations ought to be. In Milley's opinion, Greenfield was guilty of deriving an *ought* from an *is,* namely, concluding a normative statement from a descriptive or factual statement. Milley considered that there is a problem in holding that "organizations are, and therefore ought to be, moral orders . . . [Greenfield] observed that certain people and their values hold sway, and argued that it ought to be this way" (p. 50). Personally, I find Milley's arguments unpersuasive. Greenfield's project was to advance the normative assumption that people are first and foremost moral beings and their moral nature is reflected in their social institutions. Furthermore, Greenfield (1979/1993, 1980, 1991/1993) was recurrent in rejecting the fact/value distinction. He consequently followed Weber, and was in tacit agreement, on this particular issue, with pragmatists and postmodern thinkers (English, 2003; Ryan, 2003):

> In interpreting the interwoven world of fact and value, the social scientist also bears—crucially so—the burden of determining what ought to be. Weber argued that the task for the social scientist could be framed within fact, at least within what we call historical fact, but he knew such inquiry inevitably stands on a value base. To determine what is in the social world, we must begin from a base that knows what ought to be in it.
>
> (Greenfield, 1979/1993, p. 72)

Greenfield was not claiming that he found a specific value or set of values in his descriptions of organisational life, neither did he claim that some specific moral order ought to be pursued. He argued that our observation is infused with values and therefore we cannot have neutral or objective perceptions of the social world. If observation is always value-laden (Kuhn, 1962) then the distinction between what *is* and what *ought to be* is meaningless, at least in the social sciences.

A FINAL NOTE ABOUT GREENFIELD'S LEGACY

Greenfield's work was revolutionary in the sense that it effectively disrupted the study of educational administration (Bates, 2003). He challenged the status quo by interrogating those assumptions that pervaded the study and practice of educational administration. In the current era of accountability and standardised testing, Greenfield's message is more relevant than ever (Macmillan, 2003). Indeed, the legacy of positivism, in the form of Systems Theory, remains pervasive in the contemporary academic landscape (Bush, Bell, & Middlewood, 2010; Lunenburg & Ornstein, 2008; Riveros,

Newton, & Burgess, 2012). Discourses centred on the *learning organisation* (Senge, 1990, 2000) maintain, perhaps unwittingly, the assumptions that organisations exist as entities that perform cognitive functions and, further, that people are instrumental to the achievement of overarching organisational goals. Greenfield's remarks on the ontological primacy of the individual's meanings, and his thoughts related to the importance of the subjective perspective as a means of understanding organisations, remain current and relevant. An approach to organisations focused on the subjective interpretation of social reality, as was offered by Greenfield, has the power to interrogate those current prevalent discourses that overlook issues of meaning, power, and politics in schools.

REFERENCES

Bates, R. (2003). The bird that sets itself on fire: Thom Greenfield and the renewal of educational administration. In R. Mcmillan (Ed.), *Questioning leadership: The Greenfield legacy* (pp. 117–143). London, ON: Althouse.

Bush, T., Bell, L., & Middlewood, D. (2010). *The principles of educational leadership & management*. Los Angeles: Sage.

Culbertson, J. A. (1981). Antecedents of the Theory Movement. *Educational Administration Quarterly,17*(1), 25–47.

Culbertson, J. A. (1983). Theory in educational administration: Echoes from critical thinkers. *Educational Researcher, 12*(10), 15–22.

Cyert, R. M., & March, J. G. (1963). *A behavioral theory of the firm*. Englewood Cliffs, NJ: Prentice-Hall.

Durkheim, E. (1957). *Professional ethics and civic morals*. London: Routledge & Paul.

English, F. W. (2003). *The postmodern challenge to the theory and practice of educational administration*. Springfield, IL: C.C. Thomas.

Evers, C., & Lakomski, G. (1991). *Knowing educational administration: Contemporary methodological controversies in educational administration research*. Oxford, UK: Pergamon.

Feigl, H. (1951). Principles and problems of theory construction in psychology. In W. Dennis (Ed.), *Current trends of psychological theory* (pp. 51–79). Pittsburgh, PA: University of Pittsburgh.

Fiol, C. M. (2002). Intraorganizational cognition and interpretation. In J. A. C. Baum (Ed.), *The Blackwell companion to organizations* (1st ed., pp. 120–137). Oxford, UK: Blackwell.

Gray, H. L. (1982). *The management of educational institutions: Theory, research and consultancy*. Barcombe, UK: Falmer.

Greenfield, T. B. (1973). Organizations as social inventions: Rethinking assumptions about change. *Journal of Applied Behavioral Science, 9*(5), 551–574.

Greenfield, T. B. (1975). Theory about organization: A new perspective and its implications for schools. In M. Huges (Ed.), *Administering education: International challenges* (pp. 71–90). London: Athlone.

Greenfield, T. B. (1977). Organization theory as ideology. *Curriculum Inquiry, 9*(2), 97–112.

Greenfield, T. B. (1980). The man who comes back through the door in the wall: Discovering truth, discovering self, discovering organizations. *Educational Administration Quarterly, 16*(3), 26–59.

Greenfield, T .B. (1982). Against group mind: An anarchistic theory of organization. *McGill Journal of Education, 17*(1), 3–11.

Greenfield, T. B. (1984). Leaders and schools: Wilfulness and non-natural order in organizations. In T. Sergiovanni, & J. Corbally, (Eds.), *New perspectives in administrative theory and practice* (pp. 44–68). Chicago: University of Illinois.

Greenfield, T. B. (1986). The decline and fall of science in educational administration. *Interchange, 17*(2), 57–80.

Greenfield, T. B. (1991). Re-forming and re-valuing educational administration: Whence and when cometh the phoenix? *Educational Management and Administration, 19*(4), 200–218.

Greenfield, T. B. (1979/1993). Organizations as talk, chance, action and experience. In T. Greenfield & P. Ribbins (Eds.), *Greenfield on Educational Administration* (pp. 53–74). London: Routledge. (Reprinted from: A. Heigl-Evers, & U. Streeck (Eds.), *Die Psychologie des 20. Jahrhunderts: Lewin und die Folgen, Band VII,* 1979, pp 547–558, Zurich: Kinder Verlag).

Greenfield, T. B. (1991/1993). Science and service: The making of the profession of educational administration. In T. Greenfield and P. Ribbins (Eds.), *Greenfield on Educational Administration,* (pp. 199–228). London: Routledge. (Reprinted from: *Thirty-fifth conference of the Department of Educational Administration,* September, 1991, Edmonton, AB: University of Alberta).

Greenfield, T. B., & Ribbins, P. (1993). Educational administration as a humane science: Conversations between Thomas Greenfield and Peter Ribbins. In T. B. Greenfield & P. Ribbins (Eds.), *Greenfield on educational administration: Towards a humane science* (pp. 229–271). London: Routledge.

Griffiths, D. E. (1979). Intellectual turmoil in educational administration. *Educational Administration Quarterly, 15*(3), 43–65.

Griffiths, D. E. (1983). Evolution in research and theory: A study of prominent researchers. *Educational Administration Quarterly, 19*(3), 201–221.

Gronn, P. (1983). *Rethinking educational administration: T B Greenfield and his critics.* Victoria, Australia: Deakin University.

Gronn, P. (2003). Thom. In R. Macmillan (Ed.), *Questioning leadership: The Greenfield legacy* (pp. 103–124). London, ON: Althouse.

Halpin, A. W. (1958). *Administrative theory in education.* London: Macmillan.

Harris, C. E. (1996). The aesthetic of Thomas B. Greenfield: An exploration of practices that leave no mark. *Educational Administration Quarterly, 32*(4), 487–511.

Harris, C. E. (2003). The naked participant: Balancing personal perspectives with the concept of 'Verstehen' in interpretive inquiry. In R. Mcmillan (Ed.), *Questioning leadership: The Greenfield legacy* (pp. 117–143). London, ON: Althouse.

Hills, J. (1981). A critique of Greenfield's "New Perspective". *Educational Administration Quarterly, 16*(1), 20–44.

Hodgkinson, C. (1978). *Towards a philosophy of administration.* Oxford, UK: Blackwell.

Hodgkinson, C. (1983). *The philosophy of leadership.* Oxford, UK: Blackwell.

Hodgkinson, C. (1991). *Educational administration: The moral art.* Albany, NY: SUNY

Innes-Brown, M. (1993). T.B. Greenfield and the interpretive alternative. *International Journal of Educational Management, 7*(2), 30–40.

Kuhn, T. S. (1962). *The structure of scientific revolutions.* Chicago: University of Chicago.

Lunenburg, F. C., & Ornstein, A. C. (2008). *Educational administration: Concepts and practices.* Belmont, CA: Wadsworth.

Macmillan, R. (Ed.). (2003). *Questioning leadership: The Greenfield legacy.* London, ON: Althouse.

March, J. G., & Simon, H. A. (1958). *Organizations.* New York: Wiley.

Milley, P. (2002). Imagining good organizations: Moral orders or moral communities? *Educational Administration Abstracts, 37*(4), 415–568.

Parrini, P., Salmon, W. C., & Salmon, M. H. (2003). *Logical empiricism: Historical and contemporary perspectives.* Pittsburg, PA: University of Pittsburgh.

Ribbins, P. (2003). Thomas Greenfield—A life and legacy: Lessons for educational administration. In R. Macmillan (Ed.), *Questioning leadership: The Greenfield legacy* (pp. 193–209). London, ON: Althouse.

Riveros, A. (2009). Thomas Greenfield and the quest for meaning in organizations: A postponed dialogue with Ludwig Wittgenstein. *Journal of Educational Administration and Foundations, 20*(2), 51–67.

Riveros, A., Newton, P., & Burgess, D. (2012), A situated account of teacher agency and learning: Critical reflections on Professional Learning Communities. *Canadian Journal of Education, 35*(1), 202–216.

Ryan, J. (1988). Science in educational administration: A comment on the Holmes-Greenfield dialogue. *Interchange, 19*(2), 68–75.

Ryan, J. (2003). Greenfield and the postmodern: Order, anarchy and inquiry in educational administration. In R. Macmillan (Ed.), *Questioning leadership: the Greenfield legacy.* (pp. 237–258). London, ON: Althouse.

Sackney, L. & Mitchell, C. (2001). Postmodern expressions of educational leadership. In. K. Leithwood & P. Hallinger (Eds.), *The second international handbook of educational leadership and administration* (pp. 881–914). Dordrecht, Netherlands: Kluwer.

Schlick, M. (1979). *Philosophical Papers, Vol. 2 (1925–1936).* Dordrecht, Netherlands: Reidel.

Senge, P. M. (1990). *The fifth discipline: The art and practice of the learning organization.* New York: Doubleday/Currency.

Senge, P. M. (2000). *Schools that learn: A fifth discipline fieldbook for educators, parents, and everyone who cares about education.* New York: Doubleday.

Sergiovanni, T. J. (1992) *Moral leadership: Getting to the heart of school improvement.* San Francisco: Jossey-Bass.

Sergiovanni, T. J. (2000) *The lifeworld of leadership: Creating culture, community, and personal meaning in our schools.* San Francisco: Jossey-Bass

Simon, H. A. (1957). *Models of man: Social and rational—Mathematical essays on rational human behavior in society setting.* New York: Wiley.

Simon, H. A. (1958). *Administrative behaviour.* New York: Macmillan.

Simon, H. A. (1969). *The sciences of the artificial.* Cambridge, MA: MIT Press.

Vera, A. H., & Simon, H. A. (1993). Situated action: A symbolic interpretation. *Cognitive Science, 17*(1), 7–48.

Weber, M. (1968). *Economy and society: An outline of interpretive sociology.* New York: Bedminster.

4 Critical Theory in Educational Administration
An Overview of the Field

Renate Kahlke

As has been demonstrated elsewhere in this text, the term *critical* can be applied to a wide range of theoretical frameworks. However, the term *Critical Theory* is most often used to designate a body of theory developed out of the works of Karl Marx and focused on understanding how culture works to obscure unequal and unjust power relations and distribution of wealth present in contemporary society. The role of Critical Theory in the context of educational administration is not yet well developed though Critical Theory offers much promise as an analytical and research tool for administrators and researchers interested in understanding how power is distributed and maintained in educational settings. Further, Critical Theory offers tools and techniques for responding to such inequities. This chapter begins by examining the origins and evolution of Critical Theory and its contemporary uses in the educational administration literature. It also provides some suggestions for future applications of Critical Theory in educational administration and research.

FIRST GENERATION CRITICAL THEORY: THE FRANKFURT SCHOOL

The term *Critical Theory* can be traced back to the Marxist thinkers of the Institute for Social Research in Frankfurt, Germany, known as the Frankfurt School. Herbert Marcuse and Max Horkheimer were particularly influential in the development of Critical Theory, publishing their foundational formulations of the field in 1937. However, even within the core group of Frankfurt School thinkers, the Critical Theory tradition is rife with tensions and is marked by a variety of disciplinary perspectives. Moreover, Critical Theory has significantly influenced the development of many later theorists and theoretical frameworks.

The fact that Critical Theory arose within the Frankfurt School in 1937 is no accident. Marxist thinkers at the time were caught in a particular historical moment marked by several major events that challenged orthodox Marxism. Marx had predicted that the revolt of the working class would cause the fall of capitalism and the rise of communism. However, in a time of historical tumult—including the fall of the Weimar Republic, the rise of Hitler's National Socialism (Kellner, 2001), and the rise of Stalinism (Kellner, 1989)—Marx's predictions appeared far from accurate. Many of the intellectuals of the Frankfurt School were forced to flee Germany to exile in America. Among these were Theodor Adorno, Herbert Marcuse, Max Horkheimer, Erich Fromm, and Friedrich Pollock (Crotty, 1998). There they sought an explanation for the rise of authoritarianism in both Germany and Russia, alongside the resilience of capitalism in Britain and America.

In working through this dilemma, the Frankfurt School's mission was to revise and build on Marx's thesis and to develop an updated "theory of contemporary society as a whole" (Kellner, 2001, p. 6). Because of the breadth of this mission—its attempt to explain many social and historical phenomena at the same time—the boundaries of Critical Theory are not always clear. However, there are some basic goals and parameters that define the field. As Bohman (2010) illustrated, Critical Theory must be

> explanatory, practical, and normative, all at the same time. That is, it must explain what is wrong with current social reality, identify the actors to change it, and provide both clear norms for criticism and achievable practical goals for social transformation.
>
> (p. 2)

From an explanatory perspective, Critical Theorists saw links between the material relations of society and the cultural structures that support them. Thus, they seek to analyse, understand, and explain the social-material relations within their historical moment. To do this, Critical Theory is grounded in an empirical analysis of the material practices and artefacts of late capitalism (Zuidervaart, 2011). Examples of major explanatory and analytic work in the field include Horkheimer's, Adorno's, and Marcuse's analyses of culture and the culture industry, best captured in *The Dialectic of Enlightenment* (Horkheimer & Adorno, 2002) and *The One Dimensional Man* (Marcuse, 1964). Adorno, Frenkel-Brunswik, Levinson, and Sanford (1950) also provided an account of authoritarianism in *The Authoritarian Personality*. In this explanatory work, Critical Theory seeks to bring together pure theory, which had been the domain of philosophy, with the empirical work of the social sciences. According to Horkheimer (1995), a robust theory of society can only emerge through a truly interdisciplinary perspective, which brings the theoretical and empirical together.

From a practical perspective, Critical Theory seeks to identify the actors and mechanisms through which society can be changed for the better. Pointing to the failure of Enlightenment approaches to reason and science—having produced social injustices of Late Capitalism, Stalinism, and Fascism—Critical Theorists of the first generation sought change through the actions of reasoning individuals who interrogate their society to expose its contradictions (Marcuse, 1968). Critical Theorists hold that these contradictions are inevitable when real social injustices are systematically obscured by the ideological illusion of freedom and choice inherent in Late Capitalism's commodity structure. Horkheimer (1995) and Marcuse (1968) argued that the work of Critical Theory is to provide the theoretical tools and empirical basis to support individuals in that interrogation. In *The Negative Dialectic*, Adorno proposed that this interrogation occurs through "'immanent critiques,' that is, through critique of the faulty inner logic of the works he examines—philosophical, literary, musical, or other. He seeks out their implied structure and sheds light on the contradictory elements" (Gerhardt, 2012, p. 2). Individuals can only be *free* when they are aware of how interrelated ideological and material structures limit how they are able to think and act in the world (Marcuse, 1968).

Finally, one of the most significant aspects of Critical Theory might be its unrelenting focus on the normative dimension—a conceptualisation of *what should be*. According to Kellner (2001), "critical theory is thus future oriented and has a utopian quality" (p. 15). There are many differences between the utopian visions of various Critical Theorists, particularly between the first and second generation Critical Theory, which will be further discussed in the context of Habermas' theory of communicative action. Moreover, Critical Theory has retained Marx' clear utopian vision to varying degrees. For many members of the Frankfurt School, and in the later work of Horkheimer and Adorno, in particular, the utopian vision is more implicit than explicit. In Finlayson's (2005) words, "Critical [T]heory's diagnosis of the social world is inherently a normative enterprise, since it involves judgments that the world ought not to be as it is, or about what is wrong with it" (p. 12). That is to say, Critical Theory occasionally shies away from an explicit vision of what the world *should* look like, but retains a negatively defined utopia, where critique of current society implies what the utopia *should not* look like, rather than what it *should* look like, as is the case in more orthodox Marxism.

While perhaps one of the most significant and intriguing aspects of Critical Theory, the normative dimension often comes under attack. Particularly when utopian visions are defined in the positive—what social relations *should* look like—they come under attack for their failure to *come true*, or their seeming impossibility from the perspective of the present circumstance. Marcuse (1968) dealt with this issue in *Philosophy and Critical Theory*. He argued that Critical Theory is not a stable thing, but rather must *evolve* with and from the material relations that exist within the present moment. Using this understanding of utopia, it is possible to imagine the normative dimension less as a fixed point that can *come true* or fail to do so; rather, the normative dimension is an actively negotiated sense of direction grounded in the material conditions of the moment. However, just as the positively defined utopia comes under attack, negatively defined utopian visions characteristic of Adorno's and Horkheimer's later work are also criticised for their failure to provide a utopian project, particularly by the Critical Theorists of the second generation.

SECOND GENERATION CRITICAL THEORY: HABERMAS

While first-generation Critical Theory sought to create an all-encompassing theory of society, second generation Critical Theory is marked by a move toward more practical approaches that

> are distinguished by the form of politics in which they can be embedded and the method of verification that this politics entails. But to claim that critical social science is best unified practically and politically rather than theoretically or epistemically is not to reduce it simply to demo-cratic politics. It becomes rather the mode of inquiry that participants may adopt in their social relations to others.
>
> (Bohman, 2010, p. 30)

Thus, Critical Theory becomes a constellation of ideas, rather than a sin-gle all-encompassing theory of society marked by certain commonalities in intent and approach—an attempt at a single all-encompassing theory.

Jürgen Habermas, the best-known theorist of the second generation of Critical Theory, initially advocated this approach. Though Habermas had a troubled relationship with the Frankfurt School (Wiggerhaus, 1986), his work reacted to and built on the work of the early Frankfurt School. Haber-mas took issue with the negative utopian vision and increasing pessimism of Adorno and Horkheimer, critiquing the theoretical foundations and weak normative dimension of their theory (Finlayson, 2005). He sought to build both the theoretical and practical basis on which a non-repressive society could be built. Unlike the first generation of Critical Theorists, Habermas' theory was grounded in the public sphere as the site where emancipation could come to fruition (Bohman, 2010). According to Bohman (2010), Habermas "brings democratic potentials back into view, since democracy makes sense only within specific forms of interaction and association, from the public forum to various political institutions" (p. 21).

Habermas' work can be divided into three major stages. First, he began an examination of knowledge and consciousness, as found in his early work *Knowledge and Human Interests* (Habermas, 1987a). In this work, he sought to differentiate instrumental knowledge, defined by an empha-sis on objectively *knowable* technical facts, and communicative knowledge, where knowledge is socially contested and constructed. In Habermas' view, this contested sphere of communication offers the space from which ideological critique can occur. Next, drawing on Marcuse's work, Haber-mas (1984, 1987b) developed his two-volume *Theory of Communicative Action*. Here, he sought to understand how conditions of domination are constituted through language. In situations of domination, speech is medi-ated by uninterrogated ideological structures that result in what he calls *distorted communication* (Habermas, 1984). He also sought to understand the characteristics of an *ideal speech situation*, which is a space where communication is free of relationships of domination and is instead guided by a rational consideration of perspectives (Habermas, 1984, 1987b).

From here, Habermas developed his theories of discourse and deliberative democracy in *The Philosophical Discourse of Modernity* and *Justification and Application*. For a productive and free public sphere to be possible, Habermas (1993) argued that individuals "must make a pragmatic presupposition to the effect that all affected can in principle freely participate as equals in a cooperative search for the truth in which the force of the better argument alone can influence the outcome" (pp. 49–50). Undistorted communication has its basis in the authenticity of participants' positions, the possibility of challenge, a universal ideal of justice in decision making, and freedom from ideological constraints (Kochan, 2002).

CRITICAL THEORY IN EDUCATION: CRITICAL PEDAGOGY

In the context of educational administration, theories of critical pedagogy, emanating from the work of Brazilian educator and theorist Paulo Freire, are of particular significance. Like earlier Critical Theory, this body of work is marked by an attention to explanatory, practical, and normative theoretical dimensions. Freire saw relations of social domination playing out in educational settings. What is unique about Freire's work is that, beyond explaining how relations of domination are enacted in these settings, he engaged in laying out the practical conditions required in order to transform educational settings from spaces where conditions of oppression and repression are reproduced, to spaces where those conditions can be challenged. He advocated for pedagogy in which the power differential between learners and teachers could be challenged, and where learners are invited to discuss and challenge the social conditions that they inhabit (Freire, 1996, 1998). He argued that such pedagogical spaces can and should invite *conconscietização*, translated as *critical consciousness* (Freire, 2008) or *conscietization* (Crotty, 1998)—referring to the learner's ability to critically analyse how ideology works, particularly through language, in order to see the real conditions of domination within which they live. From a normative perspective, Freire saw this process of critical pedagogy as paving the way for revolution. In fact, for Freire, critical thought and reflection cannot be separated from the world of action (Crotty, 1998); theory and practice are inextricably linked through the notion of *praxis*.

Drawing on Freire and Habermas, theorists of critical pedagogy in North America and Europe—such as Henry Giroux, Jack Mezirow, and Stephen Brookfield—began to further explore how learners can be invited to question the ideological structures in which they are embedded. Mezirow, in particular, draws on Habermas' emancipatory dimension of learning to understand how *transformative learning* takes place. For him, this type of learning is largely enacted through critical thinking, a process of individual and social interrogation of ideas through rational debate (Mezirow, 1991). Echoing Habermas, Mezirow (1990) contended that *"free, full participation in critical and reflective discourse* may be interpreted as a basic human right" (p. 11). Likewise, Brookfield (2010) contended that critical thinking is the process through which learners critique their own ideological assumptions and then test their ideas against the perspectives and views of others.

CRITICAL THEORY IN EDUCATIONAL ADMINISTRATION

The 1980s and 90s were a time of dissensus and branching out for the field of educational administration; theorists, researchers and administrators were beginning to question the dominant paradigm—positivism (Oplatka, 2009). Alongside other new administrative and research frameworks, in educational administration Critical Theory arose as an explicit reaction to the dominance of positivism in the field. Drawing on the work of Greenfield, these theorists argued that educational organisations are socially constructed; that is, what defines an *organisation* is culturally produced. Organisations do not exist outside of the social structures that created them. Thus, the positivist tradition of studying organisations as though they could be understood objectively and without attending to the social nature of their creation and maintenance makes little sense. The administration of educational organisations, according to Bates (2011), "cannot be viewed as a neutral, value-free, technical exercise and must be seen to be centrally concerned with ethics and the ways in which ethics inform social, cultural and political concerns" (p. 7).

Further, traditional educational administration literature had focused on ways to manipulate and control individuals within organisations as its subject matter. Rather than challenging the unequal basis on which society and the educational organisations within it are founded, positivist inquiry often explicitly seeks to perpetuate those relations. In Foster's (1986) words, "the orientation [of research questions in educational administration] to issues of motivation, leadership, climate, and communication often takes the form of a set of technical procedures designed to initiate the recalcitrant member into the organisational viewpoint" (p. 252). Critical Theory seeks to remedy this lack of attention to—and, indeed, support of—social relations of domination by focussing on the fact that "educational administration is a socially constructed system of behaviour which is the result of contestation between social groups of unequal power in terms of, for instance, class, race and gender" (Bates, 2011, p. 6).

Habermas in Educational Administration

A considerable amount of the Critical Theory perspectives in educational administration can be traced to the work of Habermas. Given that Critical Theorists in educational administration are explicitly reacting to the failure of positivism to address the social and communication-based nature of organ-isations, it makes sense that Habermas would be appealing. He explicitly sought to address issues of dominance through communication and offered a normative proposal regarding how social justice might be achieved through discourse ethics.

Analysis of Power in Speech Communities

The first task of Critical Theory in educational administration is to offer a way of analysing how unequal power relations are produced and repro-duced in organisations through language. In Foster's (1986) words,

> if the purpose of critical theory is to expose "coercion and unequal social relations" . . . as they occur in respect to social institutions, then it is prof-itable to consider the relationship between given speech communities and the distribution of knowledge and power in those communities.
>
> (p. 255)

Foster drew on Habermas' (1984, 1987b) *Theory of Communicative Action* when he proposed an analysis of the *systematically distorted communica-tion* resulting from the ideological and faulty premises that preserve unequal power relations.

To provide a slightly different look at the bases of systematically dis-torted communication, Bates (1996) suggested an analysis of the metaphors used in educational settings. He argued that these metaphors both produce and reveal the structure of dominance through communication in that set-ting. For example, when educational systems are viewed metaphorically as *machines*, students and teachers are stripped of their agency and reduced to *cogs*. Critical Theorists in educational administration advocate for these types of analyses both in research on educational administration (Bates, 1986, 1996; Foster, 1986) and in the practices of educational administra-tors themselves (Bates, 2005; Foster, 2005).

The Ideal of Distortion-Free Communication

From an analysis of distorted communications, researchers and adminis-trators can build an understanding of how to limit those distortions and facilitate conditions favourable to the *ideal speech situation*. In the con-text of educational administration, such a speech situation would be one in which all members of the organisation would have an equal voice in debates around a decision about to be made. This means that parents, students, teachers, and administrators can participate fully in decision making. Foster (2005) cautioned that this "attempt at democratization does not mean that every decision is open to full community participation; rather, adjustments have to be made for the type of decision and its importance to the commu-nity" (p. 59). Although Habermas suggested that the ideal speech situation might be fully realisable, "the ideal of distortion-free communication for the organizations becomes one toward which the critical administrator can work" (Foster, 1986, p. 256). That is, the concept of distortion-free communication offers a normative vision for educational administration.

Other Traditions of Critical Theory in Educational Administration

Although Habermas' theory dominates the discourse on Critical Theory in educational administration, it is not employed exclusively. Maddock (1995) traced the uses of other branches of Critical Theory in educational administration, such as the works of Horkheimer, Marcuse and Adorno. Additionally, the field of cultural studies is largely a product of the Frankfurt School's redirection of Marxist critique toward an examination of culture. Cultural Studies has often appeared in the literature on educational administration and offers insight into how culture, at both organisational and societal levels, works to reproduce relations of domination (Bates, 2006; Giroux, 2006). Significant work has also been done in applying the work of cultural theorist Pierre Bourdieu to the field of educational administration (e.g., Eacott, 2010; Kloot, 2009; Lingard & Christie, 2003; Lingard, Taylor, & Rawolle, 2005). Bourdieu's work focuses largely on the ways in which power is distributed in institutions. Critical Theory has a legacy in the field of critical race theory, which focuses particularly on the social inequalities perpetuated through the administration of educational institutions (e.g., Gillborn, 2005; Ladson-Billings & Tate, 1995; Parker & Villalpado, 2007).

CRITIQUES OF CRITICAL THEORY IN EDUCATIONAL ADMINISTRATION

In *Knowing Educational Administration* (1991), Evers and Lakomski included a critique of Critical Theory in educational administration, while proposing their "postpositivist" approach to the field. This sparked a vigorous debate between Evers and Lakomski and Bates, which appears in *Exploring Educational Administration*. (Bates, 1996; Evers & Lakomski, 1996a, 1996b, 1996c). Briefly, Evers and Lakomski (1996a, 1996b) hold three major critiques of Critical Theory in educational administration:

1. First, they explored Habermas' attack on the idea of *science* as a technology of social control, to say that if science is wrong (in that it is bent toward control, rather than toward the uncovering of truth), then Habermas must be arguing that all empirical work (on which he also relied) must be *wrong*.
2. They argued that Critical Theory is essentially subjectivist, and that *truth* for Critical Theory is entirely relative to the individual claiming it.

3. They argued that Habermas' call for the ideal speech situation is a transcendental argument that lacks adequate evidence. That is to say, they believed that Habermas argued that the ideal speech situation should, in some transcendental way, be fundamentally free, without adequate justification for that belief.

Bates (1996) replied convincingly to the first two arguments. To the first, he replied that Habermas' critique of science is sociological, not epistemological, and is based on a particular positivist construction and use of science within modernity, not an essential quality of science. To the second critique, he replied that it is simply wrong to characterise Habermas as subjectivist because

> Habermas explicitly rejects a purely subjectivist theory of meaning. His theory of communicative action ". . .relies on a cooperative process of interpretation in which participants relate simultaneously to something in the objective, the social and the subjective worlds even when they thematically stress only one of the three components in their utterances."
>
> (Bates, 1996, p. 192)

Habermas believed that subjectivity is an important aspect to human experience; however, the presence of subjectivity does not necessarily equate to pure subjectivism. Rather, reality can be objective, subjective, and social at the same time. Bates (1996) failed to reply to the third claim convincingly in *Exploring Educational Administration*. The claim that the "ideal speech situation" is a transcendental one that lacks adequate support goes unchallenged. However, Bates (1996) did argue that Evers and Lakomski focused too much on Habermas' early arguments, ignoring his later additions and amendments. This problem of unsupported transcendental claims may be resolved in Habermas' later work.

Finally, Maddock (1999) summarised two other critiques of Critical Theory in educational administration that should be considered. First, he paraphrased Ellsworth, who argued that Habermas' Critical Theory is too abstract to have contextual clarity in educational administration. As a result, in context, Critical Theory can be reduced to a jargon of empowerment, which is actually used to suppress dissent in the name of consensus. This is an issue that bears careful consideration when Critical Theory is employed in particular contexts, but does not constitute a critique of the theory in general. Like other theoretical frameworks, Critical Theory's language can be misappropriated and requires an authenticity and reflexivity when it is put into practice. Second, Maddock (1999) summarised the arguments of Love, who suggested that Habermas' general theory may not adequately attend to the diversity and complexity of the individuals and contexts in which decisions are made. Again, this is an issue that must be attended to in the individual, complex contexts in which discourse takes place. By developing conditions for the ideal speech situation, difference and diversity can be attended to without sacrificing the possibility of consensus; however, such difference can only be attended to in the specificity of each context, and may require additional theoretical frameworks, and an authenticity and reflexivity in practice.

CRITICAL THEORY IN PRACTICE

How might Critical Theory be useful in the work of the practicing educator, researcher, or administrator? When getting down to the nuts and bolts of research, teaching, or administrative practice, what can Critical Theory *really* look like? I offer a few suggestions on ways in which Critical Theory could offer practical help for critical practitioners.

Suggestion 1: Focusing on the Distribution of Power in Schools

Both in its origins and in its application to educational administration, Critical Theory is very explicit in its purpose: it seeks to unpack and remedy unequal and unjust distribution of power. Though not exclusively, this means focussing on the ways in which individuals' voices are constrained or omitted, particularly on the bases of their age, race, class, and gender. This can be an enormous challenge in educational institutions; however, taking Habermas' ideal speech situation seriously can focus efforts on a positive goal for the redistribution of power within the institutions themselves. Habermas' goal of domination-free communication provides inspiration and a general sense of what inclusivity in public institutions might look like.

Teachers and administrators might also look to the works of Freire (e.g., Freire, 1996, 1998; Shor & Freire, 1987) for help in theorising and building pedagogical spaces that allow for open inquiry. This means acting to preserve an open learning space where learners can safely discuss and contest distributions of power, including those between teachers, administrators, and learners.

As suggested by Bates (2005) and Foster (2005), administrators will also need to reconsider how they approach leadership. They may draw on some of the transformative leadership literature (Foster, 2005), provided that "transformative leadership" is not conceptualised as the manipulation of workers into "working harder" for some vague notion of efficiency. Rather, it must mean empowering colleagues to have a legitimate voice in educational decision making, and, when power is wielded unjustly, or when coercive arguments are employed, it may mean reasserting the openness of the discursive space. At their most fundamental level, all applications of Critical Theory rely on the reflexivity of practitioners, based in active self and institutional assessment that seeks to understand, reveal, and remedy unjust distributions of power.

Suggestion 2: Focusing on the Distribution of Power in Educational Research

As Maddock (1999) argued, democratic goals might also be incorporated into the methodology of the research, in addition to research topics. Given the arguments made above about the role of positivist research and theory in perpetuating relations of domination, critical researchers seek to avoid perpetuating relations of domination where the *ivory tower* of the University imposes its research interests on participants and research consumers, such as teachers and administrators. Maddock (1999) suggested action research as a potentially democratic approach to research, where participants are asked to configure their own research questions about their own settings, and to participate actively in the research process. Participants and *consumers* of research are thus actively engaged in the research process, unsettling the power imbalance between researchers, participants, and consumers.

Suggestion 3: Retaining the Normative Dimension of Critical Theory

As I have mentioned, Critical Theory often comes under fire with respect to its normative dimension. Many critiques look to the predictions of Critical Theory to *come true*, as though they are not theoretical positions taken by individuals in particular contexts and requiring action on the part of individuals within systems. Regardless of whether it is possible to identify the *right* normative predictions, the struggle over the utopian vision of Critical Theory is a crucial one. At the same time, neoliberal capitalism produces a cynicism over the possibility of social change. In Bohman's (2010) words,

> in this age of diminishing expectations, one important role that remains for the social scientifically informed, and normatively oriented democratic critic is to offer novel alternatives and creative possibilities in place of the defeatist claim that we are at the end of history. That would not only mean the end of inquiry, but also the end of democracy.
>
> (p. 65)

Normative theory offers hope, and the possibility of change: "this aspect of our work—active engagement in the politics of change implied by our critical theory—now requires more emphasis" (Collins, 2006, p. 121).

In fact, the struggle over the *rightness* of any utopian vision is exactly the struggle that must occur—the struggle itself is, perhaps, much more productive than an arrival at a static end decision on what our society *should* look like. As Habermas suggested, all social decisions should be open for debate. Critical educators, administrators, and researchers must continue to struggle over what educational systems should look like, and seriously engage with the idea of what democratic participation in institutions might mean. This struggle must, as Freire insisted, reunite theory and practice. As Elias and Merriam (1980) famously wrote: "theory without practice leads to an empty idealism, and action without philosophical reflection leads to mindless activism" (p. 4).

Such a grand struggle over meaning is also a struggle over the micro-interactions and communications occurring daily in institutions. It requires an unrelenting focus on remedying unequal power relations, the hard work of reflexivity, and certainly a struggle against the grain. In Foster's (1986) words,

> attention is focused on how members create moral universes which have as a characteristic unequal power relations. The role of the administrator becomes one of recognizing the existential quality of such relations and, mindful of their Promethean struggle, to simply do what they can.
>
> (p. 254)

REFERENCES

Adorno, T. W., Frenkel-Brunswik, E., Levinson, D. J., & Sanford, R. N. (1950). *The authoritarian personality*. New York, NY: Harper & Brothers.

Bates, R. J. (1986). Toward a critical practice of educational administration. In T. J. Sergiovanni & J. E. Corbally (Eds.), *Leadership and organizational culture: New perspectives on administrative theory and practice* (pp. 260–274). Chicago, IL: University of Illinois Press.

Bates, R. J. (1996). On knowing: Cultural and critical approaches to educational administration. In C. W. Evers & G Lakomski (Eds.), *Exploring educational administration: Coherentist applications and critical debates* (pp. 189–198). Bingley, UK: Emerald Group Publishing.

Bates, R. (2005). Leadership and the rationalization of society. In J. Smyth (Ed.), *Critical perspectives on educational leadership* [Taylor & Francis E-Reader version] (pp. 88–105). London, UK: RoutledgeFalmer.

Bates, R. (2006). Culture and leadership in educational administration: A historical study of what was and what might have been. *Journal of Educational Administration and History, 38*(2), 155–168.

Bates, R. (2011). And what rough beast, its hour come round at last, struggles . . . to be born? In R. Tinning & K. Simma (Eds.), *Educational, social justice and the legacy of Deakin University.* (pp. 1–13). Boston, MA: Sense Publishers.

Brookfield, S. (2010). Critical reflection as an adult learning process. In Lyons, N. (Ed.), *Handbook of reflection and reflective inquiry: Mapping a way of knowing for professional reflective inquiry* (pp. 215–236). New York, NY: Springer.

Bohman, J. (2010). Critical Theory. *The Stanford encyclopedia of philosophy.* Retrieved from http://plato.stanford.edu/entries/critical-theory/

Collins, M. (2006) The critical legacy: Adult education against the claims of capital. In T. J. Fenwick, T. Nesbit, & B. Spencer (Eds.), *Contexts of adult education: Canadian perspectives* (pp. 118–127). Toronto, ON: Thompson.

Crotty, M. (1998). *The foundations of social research.* Los Angeles, CA: Sage.

Eacott, S. (2010). Bourdieu's *strategies* and the challenge for educational administration. *International Journal of Leadership in Education, 13*(3), 265–281.

Elias, J. L., & Merriam, S. (1980). *Philosophical foundations of adult education.* Malabar, FL: Robert E. Krieger.

Evers, C. W., & Lakomski, G. (1991). *Knowing educational administration: Contemporary methodological controversies in educational administration research*. Oxford, UK: Pergamon Press.

Evers, C. W., & Lakomski, G. (1996a). Recent developments in educational administration. In C. W. Evers & G. Lakomski (Eds.), *Exploring educational administration: Coherentist applications and critical debates* (pp. 1–13). Bingley, UK: Emerald Group Publishing.

Evers, C. W., & Lakomski, G. (1996b). Educational administration as science: A postpositivist proposal. In C. W. Evers & G. Lakomski (Eds.), *Exploring educational administration: Coherentist applications and critical debates* (pp. 14–28). Bingley, UK: Emerald Group Publishing.

Evers, C. W., & Lakomski, G. (1996c). Response to commentaries. In C. W. Evers & G. Lakomski (Eds.), *Exploring educational administration: Coherentist applications and critical debates* (pp. 211–214). Bingley, UK: Emerald Group Publishing.

Finlayson, J. G. (2005). *Habermas: A very short introduction*. Oxford, UK: Oxford University Press.

Foster, W. P. (1986). Toward a critical theory of educational administration. In T. J. Sergiovanni & J. E. Corbally (Eds.), *Leadership and organizational culture: New perspectives on administrative theory and practice* (pp. 240–259). Chicago, IL: University of Illinois Press.

Foster, W. (2005). Toward a critical practice of leadership. In J. Smyth (Ed.), *Critical perspectives on educational leadership* [Taylor & Francis E-Reader version] (pp. 27–42). London: RoutledgeFalmer.

Freire, P. (1996). *Pedagogy of the oppressed*. Toronto, ON: Penguin.

Freire, P. (1998). *Pedagogy of freedom: Ethics, democracy, and civic courage*. Boulder, CO: Rowan and Littlefield Publishers.

Freire, P. (2008). *Education for critical consciousness*. New York, NY: Continuum.

Gerhardt, C. (2012). Adorno, Theodor W. *The Johns Hopkins guide to literary criticism*. Johns Hopkins University Press. Retrieved from http://litguide.press.jhu.edu/cgi-bin/view.cgi?eid=1

Gillborn, D. (2005). Education policy as an act of white supremacy: Whiteness, critical race theory and education reform. *Journal of Education Policy, 20*(4), 485–505. doi:10.1080/02680930500132346

Giroux, H. A. (2006). Cultural Studies, critical pedagogy, and the reponsibility of intellectuals. In C. G. Robbins (Ed.), *The Giroux reader*. (pp. 195–217). Boulder, CO: Paradigm Publishers.

Habermas, J. (1984). *The theory of communicative action* (Vol. 1: Reason and the rationalization of society; T. McCarthy, Trans.). Boston, MA: Beacon Press.

Habermas, J. (1987a). *Knowledge and human interests* (J. J. Shapiro, Trans.). Cambridge, MA: Polity Press.

Habermas, J. (1987b). *The theory of communicative action* (Vol. 2: Lifeworld and system: a critique of functionalist reason; T. McCarthy, Trans.). Boston, MA: Beacon Press.

Habermas, J. (1993). *Justification and application: Remarks on discourse ethics* (C. Cronin, Trans.). Cambridge, MA: MIT Press.

Horkheimer, M. (1995). *Critical Theory: Selected essays*. New York: Continuum.

Horkheimer, M., & Adorno, T. (2002). *The dialectic of enlightenment: Philosophical fragments* (G. S. Noerr, Ed.; E. Jephcott, Trans.). Stanford, CA: Stanford University Press.

Kellner, D. (1989). *Marxism and modernity*. Cambridge, UK: Polity Press.

Kellner, D. (2001). Introduction: Herbert Marcuse and the vicissitudes of critical theory. In D. Kellner (Ed.), *Towards a critical theory of society: Collected papers of Herbert Marcuse* (Vol. 2, pp. 1–34). New York, NY: Routledge.

Kloot, B. (2009). Exploring the value of Bourdieu's framework in the context of institutional change studies in higher education. *Studies in Higher Education, 34*(4), 469–481.

Kochan, F. K. (2002). Hope and possibility: Advancing and argument for a Habermasian perspective in educational administration. *Studies in Philosophy and Education, 21*(2), 137–155.

Ladson-Billings, G., & Tate, W. F. (1995). Toward a critical race theory of education. *Teachers College Record, 97*(1), 47–68.

Lingard, B., & Christie, P. (2003). Leading theory: Bourdieu and the field of educational leadership. An introduction and overview to this special issue. *International Journal of Leadership in Education, 6*(4), 317–333.

Lingard, T., Taylor, S., & Rawolle, S. (2005). Bourdieu and the study of educational policy: Introduction. *Journal of Education Policy, 20*(6), 663–669.

Maddock, T. H. (1993). Enlightenment and redemption: On the consequences of two different versions of Critical Theory in educational administration. *Educational Philosophy and Theory, 25*(2), 1–20.

Maddock, T. H. (1995). Science, critique and debate: The debate between critical theorists and the material pragmatists. *Educational Management, Administration & Leadership, 23*(1), 58–67. doi:10.1177/174114329502300107

Maddock, T. H. (1999). The nature and limits of Critical Theory in education. *Educational Philosophy and Theory, 31*(1), 43–62.

Marcuse, H. (1964). *The one dimensional man: Studies in the ideology of advanced industrial society.* Boston, MA: Beacon Press.

Marcuse, H. (1968). *Negations: Essays in Critical Theory* (J. J. Shapiro, Trans.). Boston, MA: Beacon Press.

Mezirow, J. (1990). How critical reflection triggers transformative learning. In A. B. Knox (Ed.), *Fostering critical reflection in adulthood* (pp. 1–20). San Francisco, CA: Jossey-Bass.

Mezirow, J. (1991). *Transformative dimension of adult learning.* San Francisco: Jossey-Bass.

Oplatka, I. (2009). The field of educational administration: A historical overview of scholarly attempts to recognize epistemological identities, meanings and boundaries from the 1960s onwards. *Journal of Educational Administration, 47*(1), 8–35. doi:10.1108/09578230910928061

Parker, L., & Villalpando, O. (2007). A race(cialized) perspective on education leadership: Critical race theory in educational administration. *Educational Administration Quarterly, 43*(5), 519–524. doi:10.1177/0013161X07307795

Shor, I., & Freire, P. (1987). *A pedagogy for liberation: Dialogues on transforming education.* South Hadley, MA: Bergin and Garvey Publisher.

Wiggerhaus, R. (1986). *The Frankfurt School: Its history, theories and political significance* (M. Robertson, Trans.). Oxford, UK: Polity Press.

Zuidervaart, L. (2011). Theodor W. Adorno. *The Stanford encyclopedia of philosophy.* Retrieved from http://plato.stanford.edu/entries/adorno/

5 Feminist Thought and/in Educational Administration
Conceptualising the Issues

Dawn Wallin

At the outset, I will suggest to you that if you are hoping to read about *the definitive answer* on feminist theory and/in educational administration in this chapter, you are bound to be disappointed. Feminist theorising has reshaped (rather than been additive to) the theories and practices of educational administration and is not singular in its conceptualisations or methodologies. In fact, feminism is more appropriately pluralised as *feminisms*, though there are some common *strands* of epistemological understandings that exist in its theorisations. For this chapter, I will limit my discussions to five avenues of feminist theorising that have conceptualised and problematised issues of/in educational administration: liberal feminism, radical feminism, socialist feminism, poststructural/postmodern feminism, and, most recently in Canada, postcolonial feminism.

A second point to make is that *feminisms are not only "for" women*. Nor are all feminists women, though there is some debate on whether men are acknowledged as feminists or pro-feminists (Lingard & Douglas, 1999). To make the topic even more complex, not all women would characterise themselves as feminist, though I believe it would be difficult to find a woman who does not advocate for equity to some degree, even if she does not engage in activism. The *f-word* is one that has been problematised in cultural media with negative connotations such that many women and men attempt to distance themselves from feminist theorising or activism without actually understanding much about it.

Equity concerns of feminists may (or may not) take up as a subject the equity concerns of all sexes, but regardless of the direct focus, the implications of feminist theorising are of concern for all. Feminist conceptualisations are generally concerned with how individual or social constructions of gender have differential implications for the sexes and lead to inequities in social roles and lived experiences. For example, contemporary feminist work recognises that the actions of women and men fall at any given moment and for different concerns along continua of masculinities and femininities, which are themselves difficult to define and highly contested (Blount, 2000; Lugg, 2003; Paechter, 2006; Reynolds, White, Brayman, & Moore, 2008). Therefore, rather than focus directly on biological sex differentiation (females and males, or males *versus* females, as the dichotomisation often infers), theorists consider how the social categories of masculinity and femininity shape how it is that women and men are *naturally* disposed and/or socialised to *perform* leadership, how differences between and among groups of women and men are experienced, how structures and assumptions enforce gendered expectations differentially, and the ways in which resistance and/or transformations occur (or are impeded).

The final point I wish to make is that *understandings of feminisms accrue from the individual theorists' positionality*: epistemologically, ontologically, and methodologically. Therefore, it becomes very important in any work using feminist theorising to first locate the individual feminist's social *location* so that those who read the work can *read into* the biases that may be shaping the understanding of feminism in any given text. For example, I am a Canadian, white, English-speaking, heterosexual, middle-class woman, which means I speak from a particular privileged social location. I am writing this chapter for a book about Educational Administration whose target audience is primarily those beginning their scholarly journey in systems organised along Western K–12 educational frameworks. I have to recognise that just being asked to write this chapter means that others have not. Though I would like to think that what I have accrued *along the way* of my career has been granted because of individual meritocracy, I also have to acknowledge that my social location has brought with it advantages that others may not have experienced (Wallin, 2008). This also means that I bring biases to my understandings of feminism as a consequence not only of my basic personality, but also because of my social location. Such an acknowledgement relates to the age-old *nature-nurture* debate related to sex/gender differences, but also pre-supposes that my understandings and experiences may not align with someone whose personal and social location differs from mine. It also means that, even with the best of intentions, I may inadvertently misrepresent someone else's work because of my own preconceptions. Hence the debates on feminist theorising, the critiques of differing feminist conceptualisations, and the reasons why a singular perspective of feminist theorising and/in educational administration is impossible. We don't all think the same, we don't all have the same experiences, and we don't always agree. *Vive la difference!*

Given this preamble, I will present some of the conceptual issues commonly debated by feminists whose work has some focus on educational administration. Though we could write forever on *what constitutes the nature of educational administration*, I will narrow my focus to the Western scholarly theorising and the postcolonial critique of Western scholarship in K–12 contexts. This subverts my ability to be comprehensive, but it also provides the locational context for this chapter, which may be helpful for those just beginning their understandings of what, for some of us, has been a career-long analytical focus. By extension, however, this narrowing of scope does not provide voice to feminists whose work falls outside of these parameters. Such limitations accrue in all texts, but it behoves the feminist to carefully locate her/his work such that those who read it know that she/he understands the limitations that exist. To that end, in this chapter I first provide a brief outline of the major conceptualisations of each of the five feminist theories mentioned, after which I comment upon some of the intractable tensions for feminist theorising in/and educational administration related to three *discourses of privilege* (Fitzgerald, 2003) commonly referenced in scholarship: profiles, patterns, and practice. I then add to these three discourses a fourth discourse, which includes agency, resistance, and transformation.

FEMINIST THEORISING

In this section, I provide a brief synopsis of the development of liberal, radical, social, poststructural/postmodern, and postcolonial feminist theories. It must be noted, however, that although I locate the development of this theorising in historical time periods, I believe there have been feminists all over the world from time immemorial whose voices may or may not have been privileged to be *written into* our documented (her)history, told primarily from the perspective of privileged men (Young, 1994). Given the limited pagination space for this chapter, there is little attempt to provide depth in these synopses or to outline the debates within each of these theories. Rather, it is hoped that the overview may interest readers to delve more voraciously into one or more of the theories outside of this text.

Liberal Feminism

Calas and Smircich (1996) wrote a comprehensive chapter in the *Handbook of Organization Studies* speaking to the premises of major feminist theories, of which liberal feminism was one of those perspectives. These authors cite Cockburn (1991), who suggested that liberal feminism "has its roots in the seventeenth and eighteenth centuries, when feudalistic, church dominated rule was giving way to capitalistic, civil society, and when aspirations for equality, liberty and fraternity were supplanting the monarchical order" (pp. 220–222). An individual rights perspective of the *just* society developed based upon two assumptions: mind/body dualism, whereby rationalism was separated from embodiment; and abstract individualism, whereby human action is conceived of in abstraction from social circumstances (Jaggar, 1983, cited in Calas & Smircich, 1996, p. 222). Given women's social location in the private realm and their exclusion from the public realm, liberal feminist theory developed as a means of conceptualising how it might be that women's access to the public realm could be achieved so that women had more control of their own economic and social destinies.

In one of my earlier papers, I suggested that "the premises of liberal feminism strive for a society in which all individuals have the opportunity to realize their potential" (Wallin, 1999, p. 4), which speaks to the theory's liberal emphasis on equal opportunity. To that end, the *Report of the Royal Commission on the Status of Women* (1970) advocated for changes in the social position of women through legal and political challenges and equalisation of economic opportunities for women, changes in family structure, and an increase in individual awareness of and action against sexism. Liberal feminists believe that the principles of liberty and justice should be applied to women and that society must work to remove laws and reform institutions that impinge upon equal rights. As a consequence, liberal feminism focuses primarily on systemic reform, but does not generally advocate for social or institutional upheaval or radical change. Liberal feminists fought for (and won) the rights to vote, to own property, to equal access to education, and to equal employment opportunity. Often described as *first wave feminists*, it was liberal feminists who paved the way for many of the equal opportunity rights found within our education system today. From a research perspective, liberal feminists are generally quite comfortable using positive scientific approaches (Calas & Smircich, 1996) because they do not champion the fundamental restructuring of social organisations and generally support liberal political assumptions that foster recognition of individual merit based on equal opportunity and access to current structures.

Radical Feminism

Although liberal feminists are acknowledged for the work they achieved in transforming systems to provide more access and opportunities for women, Elshtain (1982) critiqued liberal feminism on three grounds: (a) its claim that women can become like men if they set their minds to it, or the belief that nurture is the only difference between men and women, not dealing with potential real differences based on biology; (b) its potential to overestimate the number of women who want to abandon roles such as *wife* and *mother* for roles such as *citizen* and *worker*; and (c) its claim that all women would want to become *like men*, or aspire to masculinised values and/or roles. As well, there may be a tendency to over-emphasise the importance of individual freedom over that of the common good and community. There also exists a critique that in its attempt to be gender *neutral*, liberal feminism does not acknowledge the particular experiences and epistemologies of women.

In reaction to the first wave of liberal feminism, *second wave* feminists recognised that "sexual equality cannot be achieved through women's willpower alone. Also necessary are major alterations in the deepest social and psychological structures" (Tong, 1989, p. 38). Radical feminism developed in North America during the women's liberation movements of the late 1960s (Calas & Smircich, 1996). These feminists rejected mind/body dualism, and suggested that women's experiences were very much an extension of their embodied lives as women. Jaggar (1983) asserted that there is no distinction between the political and the personal; women's experiences must be examined in light of the systemic oppression of patriarchy where masculinised norms privilege the masculine (or male) over the feminine (or female).

In terms of education, those groups or ways of working that develop as a resistance to hierarchy, or that are based upon what we now call *grass roots* initiatives, are derived out of the radical feminist movement. Also, groups that focus deliberately on *girl power*, women's shelters or health centres, programmes for teenage mothers, or other ways of operating that create *safe spaces* for groups based on their particular needs and strengths have as their ideology of origin radical feminist thought. In terms of research methodology, case studies and consciousness-raising groups become key for the study of identity politics, power, and feminist organising (Calas & Smircich, 1996).

Social Feminism

As women's movements progressed, critiques of what it meant to be *the right kind of woman* or *the right kind of feminist* began to surface across disciplines as (primarily) women read the scholarship of feminism and did not necessarily see their experiences reflected in the discourses that were recognised as essentialising all women. In contrast, social feminists recognise that human nature is "created historically and culturally through dialectical interrelations among human biology, society and human labour" (Calas & Smircich, 1996, p. 220). Gender is understood, then, as socially constructed and impacted by intersections with sex, race, ideology, patriarchy, and capitalism.

It is in this frame that writers such as Dorothy Smith (1990, 2005), for example, developed her understandings of feminist standpoint theory. Essentially, standpoint theory suggests that women's experiences of oppression afford them *insider* access to social phenomena because of the disconnect between women's lived experiences and what is considered to be the objective knowledge of social practice. The gathering of these standpoints helps us to understand how categories of meaning come to reflect power relations, and to uncover the *relations of ruling* normally taken for granted. Methodologically, social feminists tend to utilise case studies, institutional ethnography, and ethnomethodology (Calas & Smircich, 1996); they focus on *micro* activities to collect the standpoints of particular women in particular historical and social locations in order to examine *macro* social processes.

Poststructural/Postmodern Feminism

Given growing recognition and resistance to essentialised understanding of power relationships and attention to how language itself structures our normative understandings and experiences with the world, Luke and Gore (1992) suggested that it is impossible for theorists to claim *recipes* of empowerment, emancipation, and liberation. In fact, to do so actually encourages the establishment of new hierarchies of power and control which themselves need to be critiqued. This understanding led me to consider the nature of postmodern feminism as it may affect policy development (Wallin, 2001).

Postmodern feminists champion diversity in perspectives and the necessity of deconstructing normative understandings in order to work towards a more equitable future. Then the process begins again, as it is assumed that there exists a constant need to critique, to deconstruct and to dismantle language/power relationships that begin to structure inequity in meaning-making and practice. For example, Rottmann (2006) drew from poststructural feminism to discuss how queer theory might contribute to the field of educational administration because of its "implicit challenge to normative structures and its embodiment of the physical and emotional elements of schooling that are so often hidden by a mask of mandated rationality" (p. 1). Poststructural/postmodern feminists typically utilise deconstruction methods of text and discourse analysis to illuminate power/language relationships and to search for the socially constructed gender norms embedded within language and organisational structures (Grogan, 2000).

Postcolonial Feminism

Though by no means a *new* feminist perspective, postcolonial feminism has recently gained much voice in Western scholarship, given the recognition in the Western world of the devastating affects of colonialism on Indigenous peoples. Postcolonial feminism opens a critique of primarily white, Western feminist ways of understanding the world that do not acknowledge or, alternately, homogenise, the experiences and knowledge of non-Western or Indigenous peoples (Fitzgerald, 2003; Grande, 2003).

Indigenous feminists advocate for the disruption of colonial norms within our social systems through the affirmation of Indigenous women's experiences and their intersections with race, class, nationhood, etc. (Cannella & Manuelito, 2008; LaRoche, 2007; St Denis, 2007). The focus of Indigenous feminism is not only on structural change, but also on pedagogies of action that are grounded in hope, local context, and new ways of being and understanding based on an Aboriginal or Indigenous worldview (Grande, 2008). In the subsequent sections, I demonstrate how various feminists have used these ways of theorising to transform understandings of educational administration, particularly with regard to career development.

FEMINISM AND/IN EDUCATIONAL ADMINISTRATION

I have organised the sections that follow in terms of what Fitzgerald (2003) suggested were "complementary and overlapping domains; profiles, patterns and practice" (p. 431) that she (additionally) critiqued as "discourses of privilege" organised around Western traditions that have produced "a particular kind of consensus" (p. 432). Her work legitimates a critique of Western scholarship, but her organisation also captures much of the work that has been done to date in Western countries on feminism and/in educational administration. It is, therefore, a useful way of framing this chapter while also recognising the need to move beyond these conceptualisations in future scholarship. I add to these domains a fourth domain, that of agency, resistance and transformation, as feminist academics speak not only to *what was* and *what is*, but *what may be*, and position women not only as passive victims at the whim of social systems, but also as agentic resistors of oppression and initiators of transformation.

Profiles

Fitzgerald (2003) characterised the domain of *profiles* as including "studies that provide demographic data and explore characteristics, attitudes, opinions and perceptions of selected issues. These data contribute to an understanding of the broader socio-political environment in which women as leaders operate as a numerical minority" (p. 432). Essentially, this domain of scholarship details the representation of women in leadership positions over time and attempts to disentangle why this might be so. Representation includes the proportion of administrators overall, as well as proportions delineated by different foci (e.g., elementary, middle, or secondary in-school administrators; etc.).

In the United States, Blount (2000), Lugg (2003), Mertz (2002), and Shakeshaft (1999) have written historical accounts of policy development and career representation of women and men in the United States subsequent to the mid-nineteenth century. They offer some rationales for changes over time that accrued due to economic, political, and socio-political concerns related to sex/gender assumptions underpinned by heteronormative and hypermasculinised understandings of leadership. Although these data provide a good historical perspective, they are now a decade old. Blount (2000) offered how in the United States, women account for 75% of school workers but for only 5% of school superintendents. Men account for 25% of all school workers, and "most teach in upper grades, coach, and/or assume administrative duties" (p. 97). Drudy (2008) examined UNESCO data and found that in the United States, women constituted 80% of primary teachers in 2008 and between 56% and 59% of lower and upper secondary teachers in 2003.

In Canada, Reynolds (2002) conducted interviews with 24 men and women administrators from the Toronto Board of Education from the 1940s to 1970s and analysed their reports to consider changing representation patterns and gender scripts for men and women over time based upon demographic, political, and legal shifts. Her work demonstrated that 75% of the teaching profession in the 1940s consisted of women, down from a proportion of 82% in 1921. In the Toronto Public school board, most

teachers were women, and male principals headed over 95% of all elementary schools, with 2 of the 18 secondary schools headed by females. She also
notes that by 1980, the data demonstrated that women constituted 15 of
105 elementary Toronto principals (14%) and 4 of 31 secondary principals
(13%) (Reynolds, 1995).

Young (1994) noted that although in the early 1990s, 60% of Canada's
elementary school teachers were women,

> in 1991/92, 25% of Canada's male teachers held school-based admin-
> istration appointments, a proportion unchanged from a decade ago.
> Although only 7% of our female teachers held comparable adminis-
> trative appointments in 1991/92, they did make up from one-quarter
> to one-third of the country's school-based administrators, more than
> double the proportion who were women a decade ago.
>
> (p. 356)

Drudy's (2008) statistics based on the UNESCO 2003 data indicated that
in Canada, women constituted 67% of lower and upper secondary teachers.

Current evidence suggests that women (and younger women, many with
children), are accessing leadership positions across the leadership spectrum
(Loder, 2005; Wallin, 2005a, 2010). However, there does exist some tension
for those who have advocated for their entry, because it is occurring amidst
growing concerns around the *feminisation of teaching* that creates its own
complex assumptions about gender scripts, professionalism, and schooling
(Drudy, Martin, Woods, & O'Flynn, 2005). For example, it has been noted
that when men leave professions or opt out of choosing them as a career
choice, the entire status of the profession may be minimised, which in fact
does not bode well for the women and men who may be leading within it.
This *tipping point* may be evidenced in growing negative public opinion of
public education being spun in the media and the research that demonstrates
that men are less often choosing education as a career.

In fact, those who write about the feminisation of teaching observe
that the phenomenon is much more complicated than it appears at first
glance, and that changes in the historical representation of women and men
in schooling has as much to do with shifting concepts about masculinity,
politics, and the economy than it does with feminisation *per se* (Blackmore,
2007; Coulter, 1998; Drudy, 2008).

Regardless of whether or not the feminisation of teaching is affecting
other levels of the education system, women remain underrepresented in the
superintendency (Brunner, 2004; Glass, Bjork, & Brunner, 2000; Grogan,
2000; Reynolds, 2002; Skrla, 2003; Wallin, 2005a, 2005b, 2010; Wallin &
Sackney, 2003). In 2010–2011, the percentage of women in the superintendency in Canadian public school systems ranged between 0% (Prince
Edward Island) to 60% in the Northwest Territories, with an average for
all provinces of 28% (Kachur-Reico & Wallin, in press). In my work on

the superintendency in Manitoba, I have noted that women generally hold anywhere from 3 to 7 superintendent positions of the 38 available in the public school system, even though they represent about half of the assistant superintendencies in the province (Wallin, 2010). Representation is further confounded when it is examined by context, because in 2006–2007, women constituted 14% of the population of rural superintendents (4 out of 28), and 22% of the population of urban superintendents (2 out of 7). Paradoxically, however, men constituted 65% of the rural assistant superintendent population (17 out of 26), but women constituted 65% of the urban assistant superintendent population (17 out of 26). Other research notes that women have obtained administrative positions in very small school divisions (Gupton & Slick, 1996; Wallin, 2005a, 2005b) and/or urban divisions with challenging work contexts, often in inner city placements (Lawson, 2008; Mertz, 2002; Murtadha-Watts, 2000). Added to this in the Canadian context is that "[p]olitical oppression of First Nations women has also resulted in their alienation from constitutional processes and from positions of leadership in White and Aboriginal male-dominated institutions" (Sankhulani, 2007, p. 22).

Researchers tend to agree that there exists a lack of reliable data on the statistics of representation (Fitzgerald, 2003; Reynolds, 2002; Shakeshaft, 1999; Tyack & Hansot, 1982; Young, 1994). Regardless of the complexities surrounding data and representation, we do know the following:

> Declaring that educators are making progress with regard to women's participation in leadership roles is a simplistic response to a complex issue. Women's participation rates vary over time and by context, and their participation rates are slow to change. Race, ethnicity, age, and sexual orientation can be factors that often interact with gender.
>
> (Reynolds et al., 2008, p. 39)

There is indeed a need to document the representation of women in educational administrative positions, but also a need to contextualise the spaces, contexts, and nature of such representation as it intersects with other categories of meaning and identity.

Patterns

The second discourse of *patterns* relates to "career aspirations, access to leadership opportunities, employment strategies, mentoring, professional barriers, retention and experiences of women leaders" (Fitzgerald, 2003, pp. 431–432). The American research indicates that women hold administrative licensure in greater numbers now than males (Brunner, Grogan, & Kim, 2005; Dana & Bourisaw, 2006). In Canada, it has been found that women often outnumber men in graduate programmes with a specialisation in educational administration (Bryant, 2004). Studies such as these beg the rhetoric around the ideas that women do not want to assume leadership positions or that they are not applying. Rather, the research indicates that women may not have the same access to mentoring or encouragement to apply for these positions (Young, 1994). For example, Wallin and Crippen (2008) concluded that "men have more mentors overall and more personal and professional mentors. Women are more apt to have more female mentors than men, though both males and females have more male mentors" (p. 22). In addition, women who access positions of leadership do not necessarily support each other (Skrla, Reyes, & Scheurich, 2000; Wallin & Crippen, 2007). Finally, while mentorship is usually viewed as a positive way of easing the entry into leadership positions, it also may become a way of socialising people into strict role definitions or presumed leadership styles or *gender scripts* to which women may feel pressured to conform (Blackmore, 2002; Reynolds, 2002; Wallin & Crippen, 2007).

In their award-winning article, Tallerico and Blount (2004) used occupational sex segregation theory and feminist scholarship to discuss the career patterns and work challenges of females in the superintendency over time. Tallerico and Blount (2004) attempt to illustrate the tensions between personal agency and sociocultural norms, but suggest that "labour queues operate fundamentally as gender queues, with males at the highest end of the hierarchical ordering and women at the lowest" (p. 635). In practice, this is reflected in Shakeshaft's (1999) work when she suggested that school boards tend to hire individuals who *look like themselves*. In fact, notions of *fit* are highly subjective and may be influenced by gendered assumptions about leadership (Grogan, 1996; Reynolds, 2002; Reynolds et al., 2008; Young, 1994).

Ridgeway (2001) outlined (a) the expectation of theory to problematise how it is that the social construction of gender ascribes differential status to men and women based upon their gender, race, ethnicity, or education, and (b) the generally associated perceptions of greater competence and worthiness in leadership to men rather than women. She suggested that "through their impact on goal-oriented interaction in the workplace and elsewhere, status beliefs affect many processes by which individuals are given access to rewards, evaluated, and directed toward or away from positions of power, wealth and authority" (p. 638). Gender status beliefs are salient in mixed-sex and gender-relevant contexts such as education, and they affect women differentially than men.

While many senior administrators indicated that they hired *the best person for the job*, and were adamant that they did not hire preferentially based on gender or ethnicity, they also contradicted themselves by speaking to the need for *gender balance* on leadership teams or by acknowledging targeted hiring for different contexts in order "to have at least one member of a school administrator leadership team reflect the social values, cultural understandings, and historical traditions of the local population" (Reynolds et al., 2008, p. 47). Additionally, when system needs are consistently placed above those of the individual, gender may become entangled in notions of individual merit, as "[v]iews about family as priority for women or about men needing to protect women, or women not as able to discipline students can affect decisions about their suitability as leaders" (pp. 42–43). There also exist tensions in the notions of "fit" when equity initiatives are employed to ensure that those hired for positions better reflect the diverse populations served by our school systems today, but without an attendant deconstruction of normative constructions around issues of gender, race, etc. Though the individuals hired may resist normative constructions, they may face challenging situations because of perceptions that they are not *a good fit* even though that may precisely be what the organisation needs.

Those women who achieve positions of leadership continue to face inequities, though often they are loyal to their employers and do not wish to indicate that their situations are inequitable or acknowledge that gender impacts upon their work (Reynolds, 2002; Wallace, 2004; Wallin, 2008; Young, 1994). Those who speak of inequities continue to reference lower wages; more challenging work conditions; disrespectful treatment from others; being *silenced* by comments, actions, and body language of board members, colleagues, and community members; isolation; lack of support from administrative colleagues; less prestige; being branded as *trouble-maker* for speaking critically; and highly challenging work contexts (Blackmore & Sachs, 2007; Blount, 1998; Brunner, 2000, 2004; Dana & Bourisaw, 2006; Grogan, 1996; Lawson, 2008; Reynolds, 2002; Shakeshaft, 1999; Skrla et al., 2000; Wallin & Crippen, 2007; Young, 1994). However, what is outlined clearly in these same studies is women's affirmation of their roles as leaders and the supports they build with their leadership teams and mentors, both female and male. Amidst the challenges they face, they also speak of being focused on their career development, of developing supportive networks, of focusing their energies on teaching and learning, of fostering the professional growth of others, of an awareness that they are role models for other women and champions of equity for others, and of being politically astute and using their positions to advocate for change (Reynolds, 2002; Wallin, 2010; Young, 1994).

Some researchers have argued that there are significant differences in the ways in which men and women lead that may affect perceptions of their effectiveness (Brunner, 2000; Gilligan, 1982; Marshall, Patterson, Rogers, & Steele, 1996; Pounder, 2000; Shakeshaft, 1989, 1999). The leadership styles of women are often characterised as nurturing, consultative, collaborative, and focused heavily on communication, professional development, teaching, and learning (Reynolds, 2002; Young, 1994). There is evidence to suggest that if women leaders maintain a more relational leadership style, they are perceived to be weak or not credible; however, women are sanctioned (by women as well as men) if they deviate from the "gender script" and act too assertively (Blackmore & Sachs, 2007; Brunner, 2000; Dana & Bourisaw, 2006; Wallin & Crippen, 2007; Young, 1994). Lugg (2003) added to this literature by suggesting that men also have had to live up to hypermasculin-ised understandings in order to be hired as leaders, and women who adopt a more masculinised approach may be barred from positions because they are suspected of being queer.

Others have argued that leadership style has little to do with gender and more to do with accommodations to socially constructed leadership norms (Astin & Leland, 1991; Eagly & Johannesen-Schmidt, 2001; Eagly, Karau, & Johnston, 1992; Reynolds, 2002; Reynolds et al., 2008). For example, Reynolds (2002) found that female administrators felt constrained by imperatives

> to always be warm and friendly, caring and nurturing. They saw this as an unfair gender stereotype that frequently diminished their contribu-tions in the organisation and hindered their ability to portray themselves as strong leaders who could handle confrontation and conflict.
>
> (p. 45)

In my work with superintendents, some women acknowledged the ten-sion between the gendered expectations (or their own desire) to be *lady-like* or *feminine* in their actions but also to be perceived as *strong* leaders who could accommodate the masculinised leadership norms of the superinten-dency (Wallin & Crippen, 2007).

Some researchers acknowledge that leadership styles of men and women have become more similar over time, and that styles that have been con-sidered more *feminine* (Brunner, 2000; Grogan, 1996, 2000; Wallin, 2010; Wallin & Crippen, 2007) are actually sought after in present day leadership circles (Leithwood & Jantzi, 2008; Leithwood & Levin, 2005; Robinson, Lloyd, & Rowe, 2008). In this way, both men and women are being freed from gender-biased views of what constitutes *appropriate* leadership styles for men and for women. However, leadership qualities that once may have given women *an edge* are becoming more commonplace in the self-reports of males (Wallin, 2010; Wallin & Crippen, 2007). This blending of styles can foster women's movement into leadership positions, yet at the same time potentially limit them if males who use these more feminine styles are still deemed by hiring committees to be more desirable as leaders (Wal-lin & Crippen, 2007). Interestingly, this phenomenon may be alluded to by Blackmore (2007), who wrote of how neoliberal reforms are strengthening a hypermasculinised *core* of control and management, but that "localized middle management in areas of curriculum, evaluation and quality became the new feminised organizational domain [. . .]. Devolution led to a remas-culinization of the center (executive management) and a feminisation of middle management" (p. 55).

In addition to their work contexts, women continue to have primary responsibility for managing their households (Loder, 2005). To that end, women administrators speak to the challenges of balancing home and career

(Lawson, 2008; Reynolds et al., 2008; Wallin, 2005b; Young, 1994) given time management issues and family-role conflicts, which can engender a heavy sense of guilt for not *performing* to their perceptions of expectations either at work or at home (Oplatka, 2002). In her work with four female principals in high-poverty community schools in Manitoba, Canada, Lawson (2008) considered the notion of boundary-spanning to examine the work-life balance of women principals. She supported the work of Noddings (2003) on the lack of family-friendly policies in work environments by suggesting that "[a]lthough progress has been made on a national level to warrant longer maternity leaves, school systems have not been forward thinking in their efforts to create flexible workplaces for working mothers" (p. 59). In my work with superintendents, I noted that although year-long maternity leaves are providing women (and younger women), with more time to manage their family lives when they have children, this may also lengthen the time some women take to access or move forward in administrative positions and potentially undermine perceptions of them as viable candidates (Wallin, 2010). I also noted that more superintendent contracts and collective bargaining agreements now include paternity leaves for men (though none of the men in my study had actually used the option). However, many of the men I spoke with looked back with regret for not spending as much time with their families as they believed they should have, and they acknowledged that it is becoming more common for male teachers and in-school administrators to access paternity leave clauses. Such commentary provides evidence to suggest that perhaps males in education do not have to accommodate to hypermasculinised norms of behaviour to the extent that has occurred in the past.

Over time, research has demonstrated that women in higher-level positions of administration were more often unmarried and/or childless (Reynolds, 2002; Young, 1994). However, this may be changing as research indicates that younger women, many with children, are accessing leadership positions (Loder, 2005; Wallin, 2005a, 2010). Of those women and men who are in relationships, having a supportive spouse is mentioned as the primary source of support, followed by family and friends. Overall, women speak to the various strategies they have implemented to help offset the demands, such as delegation or sharing of work at school and at home, hiring help at home, balancing the responsibilities for childcare or elder care, and ensuring they are taking time to maintain their personal wellness and relationships. In my own work, I have found women struggle with this aspect of their lives more so than men because they continue to hold the *double-shift* responsibility for home and career. Women whose partners have supported them have characterised that support as being emotional support or encouragement, whereas men are more apt to commend their partners for the roles their partners played in managing their home lives while they succeeded in their careers (Wallin, 2010).

As is evident in the preceding sections, though there is a certain level of agreement in the career experiences of women across time, there is no one pattern or experience that represents the experiences of all women, as there is no one pattern for all men. The dynamism of careers in educational administration plays out differently for different people in different contexts. By extension then, we are all part of the social constructions of our world, but we are also individual actors with agency within those social worlds. To think otherwise nullifies the complexity of the dynamics at play in the world of educational administration and sets up dichotomous and faulty understandings of individualistic meritocracy or social fatalism.

Practice

The final domain of practice is one that

> seeks to understand the nature of the various educational, managerial and political roles and draws attention to issues of power, visibility, collaboration, conflict and change management. In subliminal and subtle ways, this literature provides a relief map of women's ways of knowing and leading and furthermore charts ways in which women *inevitably* exercise leadership in schools.
>
> (Fitzgerald, 2003, p. 432)

This is perhaps the discourse in which the differences in feminist views become most apparent, and the areas in which much of the current work is now being developed because of the recognition of the need to move beyond dichotomous, essentialising notions of feminism and/in leadership that do not represent the multiple perspectives or complexity of issues at play in the collective experiences of educational leaders.

In her discussion of gender equity initiatives in Canadian education over time, Coulter (1996) examined the links between research, policy, teacher activism, and social change to suggest that "[a]t specific historical moments, events have conspired to make gender equity more or less possible" (p. 446). She went on to describe the 1970s as an era of vibrancy in the women's movement and teacher activism, but that the 1980s brought with it concerns about employment and the economy and therefore less public demand for action in schooling.

In her critique of the enactment of Canadian equity policy, Wallace (2007) used data collected from two studies conducted in Ontario, Alberta, and British Columbia to argue that both multiculturalism and gender equity policy work have not realised their potential due to the advent of neoliberal measures of accountability. Like Coulter (1996) and Wallace (2007), Australian scholar Blackmore (2006) critiqued the ways in which neoliberalism is shaping discourses of diversity in ways that premise them upon the maximisation of self-interest.

Reynolds et al. (2008) provided evidence for these contentions in their work on secondary principal rotation when they discussed how the privileging of system needs over that of the individual can lead to the promotion of some individuals over others based on gendered or racist assumptions. The authors wrote,

> we are not saying that the individuals we studied were deliberately blocking or advancing women, Aboriginals, or people from minority groups. We point out, however, that despite the good intentions and best efforts of those we studied, we observed and have described . . . how a complex set of organizational rules of control can operate to maintain, rather than alter, traditional patterns.
>
> (p. 48)

As another example, Rottmann (2006) cited many writers who work in the area of queer theory to provide three critiques of current conceptualisations of educational leadership: that the current North American socio-political context continues to marginalise sexually minoritised individuals; that sexuality remains largely absent in K–12 curriculum; and that the heterosexist organisation of educational administration goes largely uncritiqued because the lives and work of queer activists and theorists are separate from one another.

Lugg's (2003) writing supports that of Rottman (2006) as she cited a plethora of authors from the United States whose work demonstrates the prevalence of homophobia in schools found in gendered expectations for students and staff, in policy, in curricula, in inaccurate information provided to students regarding sexual orientation, in battles over Gay/Straight Alliances and in hypermasculine expectations faced by young men.

As a final example, writers such as Blackmore (1999), Fitzgerald (2003), Sankhulani (2007), Archuleta (2006), and LaRoche (2007) spoke to the challenges Indigenous women face as racially and colonially minoritised women in hierarchical systems led by white males, but numerically dominated by white women. These writers speak of the pressures of having to walk in multiple spaces simultaneously that are premised upon often conflictual and mutually exclusive understandings of the world, and of having to mediate the diversity within and among Indigenous peoples (AhNee-Benham, 2003).

In her critique of Western ideology and understandings of leadership, AhNee-Benham (2003) considered how the voices of Indigenous peoples have not defined how educational policy and practice have developed because research has been conducted by Western scholars whose perspectives differ from those of Indigenous peoples. Indigenous women's *ways of knowing and doing* educational leadership must be studied to avoid deficit understandings of their ability to provide leadership. She also suggests that "[d]espite the pressures to speak in current feminist and leadership language, native/indigenous scholars must take courage to define our own lexicon that best expresses our feminine traditions" (p. 224).

Given some of the concerns outlined in the preceding sections, it is little wonder that much of the earliest feminist work focused on the challenges for women who aspire to leadership positions. As previously indicated, women are not simply victims of social circumstance; they are also agents complicit within the systems in which they find themselves with various degrees of privilege given their personal histories and social location. However, because they are part of those systems, these women are able to act upon and within those systems to affect change. In the subsequent section, I examine notions of agency, resistance, and transformation offered by feminists working in the area of educational administration and leadership.

Agency, Resistance, and Transformation

Contrary to those who would suggest that feminists promote a negative *agenda* that centres on victimisation, fatalism, and hopelessness, feminists in fact *trouble the system* in order to jar people to consider how it is that inequity is structured and perpetuated within our systems and in our daily actions, with or without conscious thought. Feminist work is risky work; it is conceptualised to push our understandings and to have us reconceptualise and transform the system in ways that promote equity and that acknowledge the multiplicity of perspectives that inform educational leadership. Rather than being negative, these perspectives offer hope for all of us engaged as educational leaders and scholars who, by virtue of our engagement in the system, are complicit in the actions of that system (Wallin, 2008). We have to acknowledge our own privileges as leaders, try to deconstruct our own biases, and realise that we are all at different points in time victim and victimiser, agentic and passive, oppressor and oppressed.

So how is it that feminists have advocated for system transformation? It is impossible to provide a *list* of all the ways feminists have offered agentic responses to systemic inequities in this chapter. Suffice to say that many authors advocate for structural changes in equity policy, curricular and assessment practices, facilities supports, mobilising resources, or the restructuring of leadership positions to address the growing demands faced by educational leaders with attention to the differing gendered realities in our society (Blackmore, 2006; Lawson, 2008; Lugg, 2003; Rottmann, 2006). Others suggest that our understandings of normative masculinist assumptions underpinning leadership must change (Blackmore, 2006; Fitzgerald, 2003; Grogan, 2000; Lugg, 2003; Rottmann, 2006; Sankhulani, 2007) to reflect a social context more comfortable with contradiction, with the deconstruction of privilege and notions of power, centred on an appreciation of dissent and multiplicity of perspectives and ways of being, and a critique of how it is that we serve the needs of all children and those whose lives are affected by our education system.

In order to become more transformative, Blackmore (2006) suggested that conceptualisations of educational leadership must pay attention to principles of recognition, redistribution, participation, and agency. She offered practical examples of how each of these principles could be actualised in practice and theory. The first principle of *redistribution* necessitates that equity issues become prioritised in policy and resource agendas, with questions asked around who is privileged in the distribution of these and by extension, who is not. The principle of *exclusion* asks educators to consider how policies and practices exclude or include different groups within the system. The principle of *agency* asks educators to consider questions related to how decisions are made, who is involved in making those decisions, how communication occurs and the extent to which multiple perspectives and ways of understanding the world are acknowledged and affirmed. Finally, working towards recognition and representation means that educational leaders must consider the networks that exist, the extent to which they represent the educational community, how it is that misunderstandings or conflict develop or more inclusive ways of networking could occur, and how rewards are distributed, and to whom.

Wallace (2007) added to this the idea that these issues are "worked out at both the level of individual consciousness and systemic reform" but that "the growing discussion among academics and practitioners about the need to do both in theory and practice in educational administration and policy are encouraging" (p. 164).

To extend this thinking, Rottman (2006) suggested that we need to *queer* educational leadership: demystifying our understandings of leadership in theory and in practice, engaging in critical dialogue that disrupts categories of meaning making around sexuality and leadership, and providing supports for students and teachers to deconstruct and redress the homophobia and heterosexist assumptions embedded in our systems and ways of being with each other. Lugg (2003) advocated for a focus on intersectionality and multidimensionality that "stresses the various identities each individual can hold. Some of these identities can be shared across identity groupings, enabling seemingly diverse individuals to find common ground" (p. 123).

Indigenous scholars such as Archuleta (2006) stressed the hopeful nature of Indigenous feminism, with its focus on the next generation:

> Although not always recognized as political, Indigenous feminist rhetorical practices engage in a kind of political activism because they provide a commentary on Indigenous peoples' resurgence and recovery and because they instill in the younger generation pride, activism, and the power to resist injustice. Rather than view Indigenous women as victims, we should focus on their coming to voice and telling stories as a healing process. Rather than live in fear, Indigenous women speak out to promote resurgence and recovery.
>
> (p. 108)

Indigenous scholars acknowledge the multiplicity of perspectives within Indigenous communities. Fitzgerald (2003) added that leadership cannot be conceptualised superficially in dichotomous ways as being that of

Indigenous or non-Indigenous ways of being, but is instead about advocacy between Indigenous and non-Indigenous communities.

AhNee-Benham (2003) detailed a model for understanding leadership from an Indigenous feminist perspective that "advocates building strong educational communities that are family-centred, preserves and revitalizes native languages and cultures, and strengthens self-identity and sovereignty" (p. 241). Sankhulani (2007) wrote that educational systems must be designed to ensure that the "current situation of the First Nations people challenges political leaders, educators, and all society to decolonize former policies and practices in order to reclaim First Nations values" (p. 25) through the deconstruction/ reconstruction of cultural values, healing, and identity; acknowledgement of gender inequities; funding for women as breadwinners and not individuals; the recognition that education is lifelong and the necessity of supports to that end; and that elder and child care structures be in place.

CONCLUSION

Writing from "[a]n other perspective on the knowledge base in Canadian educational administration," in 1994, Young spoke of the lack of representation of feminist (and women's) voices in the development of the field of Educational Administration in Canada. In her paper, Young critiqued the *canon* of Canadian educational administration, which legitimated the voices of male scholars but in which women's voices were absent. Young (1994) suggested that "[t]he discourse underway and the research undertaken, like that in other social sciences of the time, consisted primarily of white middle-class men speaking to one another and assuming that their experiences and priorities could be generalized to all inhabitants of their world(s)" (p. 353). She spoke to the historical reliance on American literature by Canadian scholars working in educational administration and the recognition of the need in the 1950s and 1960s to contextualise the Canadian knowledge base. In effect, this recognition may have constituted the first attempt to *trouble* the notions of what *counts* in/as educational administration scholarship and a resistance to essentialising views of leadership based on nationalistic assumptions. Even at this early stage of feminist theorising in Canadian educational administration, Young (1994) acknowledged the danger of essentialising the voices and experiences of women as being overly simplistic and sentimentalising. During my own graduate studies as I was exploring feminist thought for the first time, I suggested,

> [t]here is a need to promote feminine ideology while at the same time remaining critical of emancipatory ideologies which define particular recipes for emancipation. Feminist ideology must be as critical of its own agenda for emancipation as it is critical of the current state of affairs in education.
>
> (Wallin, 1999, p. 7)

However, even in my own graduate and academic work, I resisted feminist theorising for many years, at least partially because my social location granted me privileges in ways that I was not yet ready to acknowledge or relinquish (Wallin, 2008).

As social herstory moves on, and as our theoretical perspectives become more nuanced, we begin to understand the need for continual critique and transformation of our understandings through feminist analysis. Today, feminists acknowledge the danger in doing feminist work in educational administration because of the risks it may engender as they move along in their academic or practitioner careers and/or because of the tendency to essentialise the experiences of women/men and/or to dichotomise the experiences and understandings of men and women. Neither position accurately reflects the real complexities found in the experiences of women and men in educational administration. As Lugg (2003) wrote, "[h]uman beings have multiple identities, and we live in highly complex and overlapping social systems" (p. 119). Though multiple perspectives of feminism still abound, and because individuals are at various ideological *points* in their understandings of feminism, there remains no *one way* of theorising the experiences of leaders in educational administration. I have offered in this chapter some *snippets* of the scholarship that has shaped much of our conceptualisations of feminism in/and educational administration. I also hope that I have given sufficient attention to the danger of essentialising or dichotomising understandings of leaders' experiences in leadership.

Much of the work by feminist scholars today recognises the need to consider feminist theory and educational administration in multi-dimensional, intersectional, and inter-disciplinary ways. There also is a need for women and men to claim feminist theorising as relevant and meaningful means of reconceptualising and transforming the theory and practice of educational administration. Finally, there is the need for all of us to contemplate how it is that each of us is shaped by, and shapes, the systems in which we are engaged as scholars and practitioners. In this way our agency is affirmed at the same time that our privileges and oppressions are unearthed and deconstructed. Ultimately, feminist theorising grants us the luxury of critiquing what has been and what is, in the desire to advocate for, and act upon, what may be a more equitable future for us all.

REFERENCES

AhNee-Benham, M. K. P. (2003). In our Mother's voice: A native woman's knowing of leadership. In M. Young & L. Skrla (Eds.), *Reconsidering feminist research in educational leadership* (pp. 223–245). Albany, NY: SUNY Press.

Archuleta, E. (2006). "I give you back." *Studies in American Indian Literatures*, 18(4), 88–114.

Astin, H. S., & Leland, C. (1991). *Women of influence, women of vision: A cross-generational study of leaders and social change*. San Francisco: Jossey-Bass.

Blackmore, J. (1999). *Troubling women: Feminism, leadership and educational change*. Buckingham, UK: Open University Press.

Blackmore, J. (2002). Leadership for socially just schooling: More substance and less style in high risk low trust times? *Journal of School Leadership, 12*(2), 198–219.

Blackmore, J. (2006). Deconstructing diversity discourses in the field of educational management and leadership. *Educational Management Administration and Leadership, 34*(2), 181–199.

Blackmore, J. (2007). Gender restructuring: Toxic, volatile and greedy organisations. In J. Blackmore, & J. Sachs (Eds.), *Performing and reforming leaders: Gender, educational restructuring and organizational change* (pp. 53–76). Albany, NY: SUNY Press.

Blackmore, J., & Sachs, J. (2007). *Performing and reforming leaders: Gender, educational restructuring, and organizational change*. Albany, NY: SUNY Press.

Blount, J. M. (1998). *Destined to rule the schools. Women and the superintendency. 1972–1995*. Albany, NY: SUNY Press.

Blount, J. M. (2000). Spinsters, bachelors and other gender transgressors in school employment, 1850–1990. *Review of Educational Research, 70*(1), 83–101.

Brunner, C. (2000). Unsettled moments in settled discourse: Women superintendents' Experiences of inequality. *Educational Administration Quarterly, 36*(1), 76–116.

Brunner, C. (2004). Women performing the superintendency: Problematizing the normative alignment of conceptions of power and constructions of gender. In J. Collard & C. Reynolds (Eds.), *Leadership, gender and culture in education: Male and female perspectives* (pp. 121–135). Cornwall, ON: MPG Books Ltd.

Brunner, C., Grogan, M., & Kim, Y. (2005) *Top women leaders and district size: A national study*. Paper presented at the American Educational Research Association, Montreal, Quebec, April 11–15.

Bryant, C. (2004). Women in the superintendency in Manitoba. *MASS Journal, 4*(1), 32–33.

Calas, M. B., & Smircich, L. (1996). From "the woman's" point of view: Feminist approaches to organization studies. In S. R. Clegg, C. Hardy, & W. R. Nord (Eds.), *Handbook of organization studies* (pp. 218–257). Thousand Oaks, CA: Sage.

Cannella, G., & Manuelito, K. (2008). Feminisms from unthought locations: Indigenous worldviews, marginalized feminisms, and revisioning an anticolonial social science. In N. Denzin, Y. Lincoln, & L. Smith (Eds.), *Handbook of critical and indigenous methodologies*, (pp. 45–60). Thousand Oaks, CA: Sage.

Cockburn, C. K. (1991). *In the way of women: Men's resistance to sex equality in organizations*. Basingstoke: Macmillan.

Coulter, R. (1996). Gender equity and schooling: Linking research and policy. *Canadian Journal of Education, 21*(4), 433–452.

Coulter, R. (1998). 'Us guys in suits are back': Women, educational work and the market economy in Canada. In A. Mackinnon, I. Elgqvist-Saltzman, & A. Prentice (Eds.), *Education into the 21st century: Dangerous terrain for women?* (pp. 107–117). Abingdon, Oxon: Routledge Falmer.

Dana, J. A., & Bourisaw, D. M. (2006). Overlooked leaders. *National School Board Association, 193*(6), 27–30.

Drudy, S. (2008). Gender balance/gender bias: The teaching profession and the impact of feminization. *Gender and Education, 20*(4), 309–323.

Drudy, S., Martin, M., Woods, M., & J. O'Flynn, J. (2005). *Men and the classroom: Gender imbalances in teaching*. London: RoutledgeFalmer.

Eagly, A. H., & Johannesen-Schmidt, M. C. (2001). The leadership styles of women and men. *Journal of Social Issues, 57*(4), 781–797.

Eagly, A. H, Karau, S. J., & Johnson, B. T. (1992). Gender and leadership style among school principals: A meta-analysis. *Educational Administration Quarterly, 28*(1), 76–102.

Elshtain, J.B. (1982). Feminism, family and community. *Dissent, 29*(1), 441–449.

Fitzgerald, T. (2003). Interrogating orthodox voices: Gender, ethnicity and educational leadership. *School Leadership and Management, 23*(4), 431–444.

Gilligan, C. (1982). *In a different voice*. Cambridge, MA: Harvard University Press.

Glass T. E., Bjork, L.G., & Brunner, C.C. (2000). *The study of the American superintendency: 2000*. Arlington, VA: American Association of School Administrators.

Grande, S. (2003). *Red pedagogy: Native American social and political thought*. Lanham, ML: Rowman & Littlefield Publishers.

Grande, S. (2008). Red pedagogy. In Denzin, L., Lincoln, Y., & Smith, L. (Eds.), *Handbook of critical and Indigenous methodologies* (pp. 233–254). Thousand Oaks, CA: Sage.

Grogan, M. (1996). *Voices of women aspiring to the superintendency*. Albany, NY: SUNY Press.

Grogan, M. (2000). Laying the groundwork for a reconception of the superintendency from feminist postmodern perspectives. *Educational Administration Quarterly, 36*(1), 117–142.

Gupton, S.L., & Slick, G.A. (1996). *Highly successful women administrators: The inside stories of how they got there*. (ERIC Document Reproduction Service No. ED 399 674).

Jaggar, A.M. (1983). *Feminist politics and human nature*. Totowa, NJ: Rowman and Allanheld.

Kachur-Reico, C., & Wallin, D. (in press). Tracing the career paths of female superintendents in Canada. *Journal of Educational Administration and Foundations*.

Laroche, E. (2007). Metis and feminist: Ethical reflections on feminism, human rights and decolonization. In J.A. Green (Ed.), *Making space for Indigenous feminism* (pp. 53–71). Halifax, NS: Fernwood.

Lawson, J. (2008). Women leaders in high-poverty community schools: Work-related stress and family impact. *Canadian Journal of Education, 31*(1), 55–77.

Leithwood, K., & Jantzi, D. (2008). Linking leadership to student learning: The contributions of leader efficacy. *Educational Administration Quarterly, 44*(4), 496–528.

Leithwood, K., & Levin, B. (2005). *Assessing school leader and leadership programme effects on pupil learning* (Research Report No. 662 prepared for the UK Department for Education and Skills). Toronto: OISE/UT. Retrieved from http://webarchive.nationalarchives.gov.uk/20130401151715/http://www.education.gov.uk/publications/eorderingdownload/rr662.pdf

Lingard, B., & Douglas, P. (1999). *Men engaging feminisms: Profeminism, backlashes and schooling*. Buckingham: Open University Press.

Loder, T. (2005). African American women principals' reflections on social change, community othermothering, and Chicago public school reform. *Urban Education, 40*(3), 298–320.

Lugg, C. (2003). Sissies, faggots, lezzies and dykes: Gender, sexual orientation and a new politics of education? *Educational Administration Quarterly, 39*(1), 95–134.

Luke, C., & Gore, J. (1992). Introduction. In C. Luke & J. Gore (Eds.), *Feminisms and critical pedagogy* (pp. 1–14). New York: Routledge.

Marshall, C., Patterson, J.A., Rogers, D.L., & Steele, J.R. (1996). Caring as career: An alternative perspective for educational administration. *Educational Administration Quarterly, 32*(2), 271–294.

Mertz, N.T. (2002). *Longitudinal study of women in school administration, 1972–2000*. (ERIC Document Reproduction Service No. ED 471 592).

Murtadha-Watts, K. (2000). Cleaning up and maintenance in the wake of an urban school administration tempest. *Urban Education, 35*(5), 603–615.

Noddings, N. (2003). *Happiness and education*. Cambridge, UK: Cambridge University Press.

Oplatka, I. (2002). Women principals and the concept of burnout: An alternative voice. *International Journal of Leadership in Education, 5*(3), 211–226.

Paechter, C. (2006, May). Masculine feminities/feminine masculinities: Power, identities and gender. *Gender and Education, 18*(3), 253–263.

Pounder, D. G. (2000). Book review. *Sacred dreams : Women and the superintendency, by Cryss Brunner. Educational Administration Quarterly, 36*(1), 143–148.

Report of the Royal Commission on the Status of Women. (1970). Report submitted to the Privy Council of Canada, September 28, 1970. Ottawa, ON: Canada. Retrieved from http://epe.lac-bac.gc.ca/100/200/301/pco-bcp/commissions-ef/bird1970-eng/bird1970-part1-eng.pdf

Reynolds, C. (1995). In the right place at the right time: Rules of control and woman's place in Ontario schools 1940–1980. *Canadian Journal of Education, 20*(2), 129–145.

Reynolds, C. (2002). Changing gender scripts and moral dilemmas for women and men in education, 1940–1970. In C. Reynolds (Ed.), *Women and school leadership* (pp. 29–48). Albany, NY: SUNY Press.

Reynolds, C., White, R., Brayman, C., & Moore, S. (2008). Women and secondary school principal rotation/succession: A study of the beliefs of decision makers in four provinces. *Canadian Journal of Education, 31*(1), 32–54.

Ridgeway, C. L. (2001). Gender, status and leadership. *Journal of Social Issues, 57*(4), 637–655.

Robinson, V., Lloyd, C., & Rowe, K. (2008). The impact of leadership on student outcomes: An analysis of the differential effects of leadership types. *Educational Administration Quarterly, 44*(5), 635–673.

Rottmann, C. (2006, Jan-Mar). Queering educational leadership from the inside out. *International Journal of Leadership in Education, 9*(1), 1–20.

Sankhulani, L. (2007). *Gender issues in Aboriginal learning.* University of Saskatchewan, Aboriginal Education Research Centre, Saskatoon, Saskatchewan and First Nations and Adult Higher Education Consortium, Calgary, Alberta. Retrieved from http://www.ccl-cca.ca/pdfs/AbLKC/SankhulaniGenderIssues20100827.pdf

Shakeshaft, C. (1989). *Women in educational administration.* Newbury Park, CA: Sage.

Shakeshaft, C. (1999). The struggle to create a more gender inclusive profession. In J. Murphy & K. L. Seashore-Louis (Eds.), *Handbook of research on educational administration* (2nd ed.; pp. 99–117). San Francisco: Jossey-Bass.

Skrla, L. (2003). Normalized femininity: Reconsidering research on women in the superintendency. In M. Young, & L. Skrla (Eds.), *Reconsidering feminist research in educational leadership* (pp. 247–263). Albany, NY: SUNY Press.

Skrla, L., Reyes, P., & Scheurich, J. J. (2000). Sexism, silence, and solution: Women superintendents speak up and out. *Educational Administration Quarterly, 30*(1), 44–75.

Smith, D. (1990). *Texts, facts, and femininity: Exploring the relations of ruling.* London: Routledge.

Smith, D. (2005). *Institutional ethnography: A sociology for people.* Walnut Creek, CA: Alta Mira Press.

St Denis, V. (2007). Feminism for everybody: Aboriginal women, feminism and diversity. In J. A. Green (Ed.), *Making space for Indigenous feminism* (pp. 33–52). Halifax, NS: Fernwood.

Tallerico, M., & Blount, J. (2004). Women in the superintendency: Insights from theory and history. *Educational Administration Quarterly, 40*(5), 633–662.

Tong, R. (1989). *Feminist thought: A comprehensive introduction.* Boulder, CO: Westview Press.

Tyack, D., & Hansot, E. (1982). *Managers of virtue: Public school leadership in America, 1820–1980*. New York: Basic Books.

Wallace, J. (2004). Learning to lead: Women administrators in twentieth century Ontario. *Oral History Forum/d'histoire orale, 24*, 87–106.

Wallace, J. (2007). Equity hierarchies and the work of female school administrators with/in the multicultural state. *The Journal of Educational Administration and Foundations, 18*(1 & 2), 147–170.

Wallin, D. (1999). *Liberal feminism and educational administration: Recruiting and supporting women in educational administration* (ERIC Document Reproduction Services No. ED 441 285).

Wallin, D. (2001). Postmodern feminism and educational policy development. *McGill Journal of Education, 36*(1), 27–43.

Wallin, D. (2005a). Shining lonely stars? Career patterns of rural female Texas administrators. *Journal of Women in Educational Leadership, 3*(3), 255–272.

Wallin, D. (2005b). Through the looking glass: A comparative analysis of the career patterns of rural female administrators in Saskatchewan and Texas. *Alberta Journal of Educational Research, 51*(2), 135–154.

Wallin, D. (2008). From "I'm not a feminist!" to CASWE President: Reflecting on space(s), time(ing), and his(her)-story. *Canadian Journal of Education, 31*(4), 795–810.

Wallin, D. (2010). *The career paths, supports and challenges of senior educational administrators in Manitoba: The effects of position, context and gender*. Research monograph written for the Manitoba Education Research Network, 80 pp.

Wallin, D., & Crippen, C. (2007). Superintendent leadership style: A gendered discourse analysis. *Journal of Women in Educational Leadership, 5*(1), 21–40

Wallin, D., & Crippen, C. (2008). Mentorship and gendered assumptions: Examining the discourse of Manitoba superintendents. *Journal of Educational Administration and Foundations, 19*(2), 56–76.

Wallin, D., & Sackney, L. (2003). Career patterns of rural female educational administrators. *The Rural Educator, 25*(1), 11–25.

Young, B. (1994). An other perspective on the knowledge base in Canadian educational administration. *Canadian Journal of Education, 19*(4), 351–367.

6   Postmodernism

Deborah Hicks

Postmodernism brings both challenges and opportunities to educational administration. It offers new ways of approaching traditional educational administration topics that allow researchers and practitioners to reassess concepts otherwise taken for granted, such as *organisation*. At the same time, this reassessment can cause uncertainty and confusion, thus challenging previously accepted notions and concepts. This chapter will present both the opportunities and challenges of postmodernism both broadly, as a theoretical stance, and specifically, as it applies to educational administration research and practice. To this end, this chapter will be divided into three sections. In the first section, I will provide an overview of postmodernism. In the second section, I will explore how researchers in educational administration have used postmodern thought in their work. Lastly, in the third section, I will look at where the postmodern-inspired educational administration researcher fits into the overall educational administration literature and suggest future directions for its use.

POSTMODERNISM

Offering an overview of postmodernism can be difficult. There is no one school of thought that can be characterised as *postmodern*. Instead it is best described as "a set of critical, strategic and rhetorical practices employing concepts such as difference, repetition, the trace, the simulacrum, and hyper-reality to destabilise other concepts such as presence, identity, historical progress, epistemic certainty, and the univocity of meaning" (Aylesworth, 2005, para. 1). The term *postmodernism* was first coined by Jean-François Lyotard in 1979 with the French publication of *The Postmodern Condition: A Report on Knowledge* (the first English publication came in 1984). Lyotard defined postmodernism as "incredulity toward metanarratives" (p. xxiv). Metanarratives are, he argued, the grand narratives that modern sciences use to legitimate their knowledge, or make their knowledges truthful at the expense of other knowledge. The metanarrative of science, for example, seeks to legitimise itself at the expense of traditional knowledge.

Certain kinds of knowledge, therefore, are seen to have a monopoly on truth. Lyotard's postmodernism, therefore, sought to destabilise this monopoly and question all kinds of legitimacy and truth: "Where, after the metanarratives, can legitimacy reside? . . . Postmodern knowledge is not simply a tool of the authorities; it refines our sensitivity to differences and reinforces our ability to tolerate the incommensurable" (1984, pp. xxiv–xxv).

Postmodernism, as its name implies, represents a response to *modernity*. Modernity, loosely defined, "is the dominant reality in the worldly affairs of Europe and North America and their vast imperial systems across the globe from the first age of exploration in the late fifteenth century through at least the two decades following World War II" (Lemert, 2005, pp. 26–27). Lemert described modernity as being the culture of the age between the late 15th century through to the 1960s and postmodernity as the culture of the decades following. We, therefore, live in a postmodern age. For some, this age is characterised by a *hyperreality* spread throughout the world not through imperialism, as was the mechanism for the spread of modernity, but through media, such as television and the Internet. Media, as the name implies, *mediates*, or makes indirect, our understanding of reality. It is not that reality does not exist; instead, reality is borrowed from and remade into "vastly more complex . . . forms than one ever experiences in the so-called real world" (p. 30). This mediated world has impacted everything from how we consume entertainment to how we understand other cultures.

Modernity was directly influenced by Enlightenment thinkers of the 18th century. The Enlightenment, alternatively known as the Age of Reason, replaced the more superstitious thinking of the medieval period with a desire to find human progress through the search for ultimate truths, rationalism, empiricism, and skepticism. The Enlightenment became *the* way of understanding the world. According to Lemert, in this understanding cultural differences become secondary to universal and essential qualities in human nature. This can be seen in contemporarily familiar phrases that emerged at the time—"all men are created equal," among others. Juxtaposed, postmodernism questions whether there can only be one way to understand the world and, as can be expected, there is no single postmodern approach.

Many different ways are available if we seek to characterise and discuss postmodern theoretical positions. For example, the contributions of select theorists could be examined, or various stances could be placed on a continuum measuring the presence or absence of postmodern and modern concern in each theorist's position (*cf.* Bloland, 2005). For use in this chapter, I find Lemert's (2005) understanding of postmodernism appealing to help unpack its theoretical landscape. Lemert divided postmodern thought into three broad categories: (a) radical postmodernism, (b) radical modernism, and (c) strategic postmodernism, each of which I describe in detail below. These categories represent approaches for answering what Lemert calls "the postmodern question" (p. 36): *How hyperreal is reality?*

Radical Postmodernism

Theorists in Lamert's (2005) radical postmodernism domain argue that modernity is dead and that everything is hyperreal. On this view, the postmodern world is a spectacle or a representation of itself. Social relations are formed around these representations and, as a result, rarely do we learn about our world through direct experience. Lemert used the example that most people receive their local information not by witnessing proximal events but by watching the news on television—thus reality is mediated through representations of reality. Even so-called live events, when watched on television, are mediated through the technology of the camera and television, and through the decisions made by the producers of the news programme.

One of Lyotard's main contributions to postmodernism was noted above: a scepticism of metanarratives. Lyotard identified how scientific knowledge can be understood as a kind of socially constructed discourse—it is through our social relations that we determine what is, and is not, true. In other words, a person becomes a scientist when they can create statements that other scientists recognise as true. Knowledge, therefore, is relational; as Lemert (2005) described it, "'$E = mc^2$' may be true scientifically, but it is also an article of cultural faith to those who believe the legends about Einstein and modern science, even to those who have no idea what it means" (p. 39). Through the social relations that support the truthfulness of scientific knowledge, scientific knowledge becomes its own metanarrative, and as a metanarrative it relies on the legitimacy given to it through cultural relations. That is to say, if a culture believes something to be true, then it becomes true. Ultimately, radical postmodernism questions the legitimacy of truth claims and, through the hyperreality of mediated events, even reality itself is open to question.

Radical Modernism

Radical modernists, such as the Frankfurt School's Jürgen Habermas, are not interested in questioning the legitimacy of truth claims in the same way as the radical postmodernists. Instead, radical modernists are interested in reinterpreting modernist texts, like Marx and Weber, and critically rediscovering the liberating potential of modernity (Lemert, 2005). Although other chapters in this volume will explore "radical modernist" thought in more detail, it is important to note here that radical modernists are committed to freeing and protecting the human spirit, but that they are critical of modernity's tendency to essentialise humanity and rid, or ignore, any difference—whether these differences be social, cultural, racial, or sexual.

Strategic Postmodernism

Lemert identified three qualities that strategic postmodernists share: (a) a commitment to reinterpret the modern classic social thinkers (Nietzsche, Husserl, and Freud, among others); (b) a conviction that language, or discourse, is fundamental to any science of the human; and (c) a rejection of any version of the ideal of a universal essence, totality, or center as a basis for social thought. An alternative descriptor for strategic postmodern thinkers might be *poststructuralists*. Lemert (2005) observed that strategic postmodern thought is often "lumped together" (p. 43) with the radical postmodernists, even though they share little in common. Jacques Derrida, Michel Foucault, and Jacques Lacan can all be considered strategic postmodernists.

The approach that strategic postmodernists take separates them from their radical postmodernist and radical modernist cousins. Their approach is arguably more modest than radical postmodernists—they do not attempt to articulate specifics of the new hyperreal world. In a manner similar to the radical modernists, they *reimagine* the modern world, employing an approach known as *deconstruction*.

Deconstruction is most often associated with the thinking and work of Jacques Derrida. Derrida described how deconstruction

> attacks not only the internal edifice, both semantic and formal, of philosophemes [i.e., a philosophical proposition], but also what one would be wrong to assign to it as its external housing, its extrinsic conditions of practice: the historical forms of its pedagogy, the social economic or political structures of this pedagogical institution.
>
> (Derrida, 1987, p. 19)

Simply put, this means that a text must be studied within its various contexts. Derrida argued that modernity assumes that discourse (or language) is an outward expression of an inward being, or that the words we use directly reflect our inner selves. Derrida wondered how it was that words acquired meaning. Modernity assumes that meaning appears to be an inherent quality of words—for example, the word *tree* appears to be intimately bound to both the object of a tree and to our idea of a tree (that is, a leafy, tall, green plant). Derrida, however, questioned whether meaning could ever be inherent in a word, arguing that meaning is constantly changing and context dependent. Words mean different things to different people, and particularly when they are being used under different circumstances. One example is the word *bit*. It can refer to equipment used in equestrian activities, or refer to a difficult task (*she took the bit in her mouth*), or a small role (*he took a bit part*), or to data transfer rates between computers, and so on. The meaning of *bit* is dependent on the context in which it appears (Gergen, 1994). Within these contexts, the word holds *traces* of other meanings. So, in the case of *bit part* the word holds the traces of the word *small*, which itself carries traces of other definitions or contexts. Language is, therefore, self-referential. So, as we encounter one word, like *bit*, we start to encounter many other words, like *small*. When we use language, we are not simply encountering the ideas that arise from other people's minds, but a host of other words (referred to as signifiers). Meaning, therefore, does not arise from the objects that words signify, but from other signifiers/words (Gergen, 1994).

Texts do not simply represent an archive of past knowledge; in the view of the strategic postmodernist, they take on meaning as they gain common usage (Davies & Harré, 1990). We are not conscious of this when we use language, but by doing so we are implicitly drawing upon the seemingly hidden references that exist in each word, while at the same time referring to alternatives that the word is not. For example, when we say *night* we are referring at the same time to what it is not: *day*. Derrida searched for these unspoken absences throughout his work. This analysis represents the essence of *deconstruction*. Strategic postmodernism, unlike radical postmodernism or radical modernism, does not seek to attack or transform the totalising aspects of modernism. Rather, it seeks to deconstruct modernism in an attempt to expose its inner workings.

Michel Foucault, particularly in his later works, approached the exposure of modernity's inner workings in a slightly different manner from that employed by Derrida. Foucault rewrote accepted histories to expose the workings of power embedded within. Where Derrida pointed out the referential quality of language, Foucault exposed the close relationship between language and social processes—which, for him, represented power relations. In Foucault's view, language allows us to construct knowledge. Knowledge, for Foucault, is neither objective nor timeless; knowledge is a prevailing worldview in a specific historical context. What might be understood as *mental illness* today, for example, was once considered demonic possession. Within their own contexts, both knowledges are *true*. For Foucault, knowledge is intimately bound to power. Because knowledge allows us to describe events and phenomena, it allows for certain versions of these events or phenomena to be accepted over other versions. The power to act within social processes is, following Foucault's reasoning, determined by prevailing knowledges. Power is used when the prevailing discourse is drawn upon to make our actions acceptable to our social context. Power, therefore, is a product of discourse.

Foucault's view of power is demonstrable in the ability to define others. "[P]ower produces; it produces reality; it produces domains of objects and rituals of truth. The individual and the knowledge that may be gained of him belong to this production" (Foucault, 1995, p. 194). He argued that modern society is a disciplinary society. Further, through *power/knowledge*—his preferred descriptor of how power is deployed by modernity—people are controlled. This control can simply be through the act of observation or through the more complex normalisation of behaviour where people come to control their own behaviours without overt punishment, through, for example, the use of national standards for education programmes. Foucault was moving beyond the maxim "knowledge is power" to the more subtle "in knowing we control and in controlling we know" (Gutting, 2003, para. 18).

The three approaches outlined above do not present what could be considered postmodernity in its entirety. Some may argue that important names have been ignored or, perhaps, that some of the theorists mentioned here are not, in fact, "postmodern." My intention is not to provide a complete picture of all postmodern thought. Rather, I here provide a starting place to understand the foundations of postmodern thought and to separate it from other approaches employed in the study of educational administration. There are clear differences between the three approaches outlined. Radical postmodernists argue that modernity is no longer a reality, that it has been replaced with a mediated hyperreality in which the differences between fact and fiction, real and unreal, are blurred. Radical modernists criticise modernity and its essentialist nature, but do not abandon it altogether. Rather, they seek to reinterpret it so that true human freedom can be achieved. Lastly, strategic postmodernists seek to unearth the inner workings of modernity to subvert accepted ideas around meaning, power, and knowledge.

THEMES IN POSTMODERN RESEARCH

An alternate approach to understanding postmodernism is to examine themes that researchers and thinkers who could be considered postmodern share. Alvesson (2002) identifies five themes of postmodern research: (a) the centrality of discourse, (b) fragmented identities, (c) the critique of the idea of representation, (d) the critique of metanarratives, and (e) the power/knowledge connection. Some of these themes were explored above; below I revisit them to clarify concepts and themes setting postmodern research apart from other research approaches.

Centrality of Discourse

Postmodernism is associated with the so-called *linguistic turn* in which philosophers paid ever-closer attention to the role language, and other systems of symbols, play in our experiences of the world. Vivien Burr explained why this focus on language is so important:

> The person you are, your experience, your identity, your "personality" are all the effects of language. This means that we can only represent our experiences to ourselves and to others by using the concepts embedded in our language, so that our thoughts, our feelings and how we represent our behaviour are all "prepackaged" by language.
>
> (Burr, 1995, p. 39)

Language is a social phenomenon. It does not merely arise for individuals out of the air. It occurs between people in conversations and in writing, and through other media. As Derrida pointed out, any meaning associated with language is temporary and contextual. This means that the "prepackaging" offered by language is "constantly sought after, contested, validated, maintained and so on" (Burr, 1995, p. 46). When language is used to present a particular version of events, or a particular version of a person or phenomenon, this is referred to as a *discourse*. Discourses are understood to be language structures or "a set of meanings, metaphors, representations, images, stories, statements and so on that in some way together produce a particular version of events" (p. 48). A discourse is, therefore, a "multidimensional social phenomenon" in which an individual's identity and social reality is constructed (van Dijk, 2009, p. 67).

Our understanding of objects, ideas, and indeed other people is informed by the discourses that surround them. As we encounter objects, ideas, and others, we encounter the discourses that construct and represent them. Each object, idea, and person is surrounded by multiple discourses; as a consequence, different people may construct each object, idea, and person in different ways. Discourses constrain and shape our actions, but do not predetermine them. They provide us with a sense of self, the ideas we think, and a narrative that we use to talk and think about ourselves. This narrative, however, is not self-generated. Instead, it is negotiated through our interactions with others in our lives and their discursive subject positions. However, not all discourses are equal. Some dominant discourses influence social arrangements and practices, which in turn support a status quo.

There are two ways to approach the study of discourse. One is to study it on the *micro* level of everyday interactions. The focus here is on the meaning and use of language. Language is a "sense-making apparatus" (Alvesson, 2002, p. 49) and a way to construct the world through interaction with others. Another way is to study discourse on a *macro* level or as a system of thought. Language here is still understood to be constructive, but it is also related to social and material structures (Burr, 2003). Foucault presented the clearest understanding of the *macro* notion of discourse. Discourse for Foucault is a system of thought that shapes the world through power/knowledge relations.

Fragmented Identities

Identity is traditionally understood to be a project of the self, meaning that a person is constantly becoming his or her *true* self through a process of self-fulfilment and improvement. Identity, through this lens, is the process of becoming this true, unchanging, and unified self. This understanding of identity is linked to Enlightenment thinking, where the self is a project of knowledge and experiences, and notions of the Romantic self, where identity is an expression of an innate self (Benwell & Stokoe, 2010; Potter & Wetherell, 1987). In essence, a modern conception of identity is as a binary concept: individual identity tied to a sense of self, or an internally based identity, and social identity tied to group membership, or an externally based identity. Postmodern analyses of identity have attempted to overcome this binary, to remove identity from either being an individually motivated search or a socially determined category. Broadly speaking, postmodernists have approached the self and identity as language-based social phenomena. Their focus is not on the self-as-entity, but on how the self is constructed and performed through socially based discursive practices. According to Potter and Wetherell (1987), "[t]here is not 'one' self waiting to be discovered or uncovered but a multitude of selves found in the different kinds of linguistic practices articulated now, in the past, historically and cross-culturally" (p. 102). In other words, depending on the context a person is in, she or he may be able to make sense of her- or himself in many different ways. The self, in this view, is historically and culturally bound and dependent on social practices. Identity is a *description* of the self within those boundaries and practices. The language used to describe identity exists on two discursive levels: (a) the micro, or situated, language use of everyday conversations and written communications and (b) the macro, "a set of meanings, metaphors, representations, images, stories, statements and so on that in some way together produce a particular version of events" (Burr, 1995, p. 48). Language provides the basis for discourses; it gives us categories for understanding our experiences and provides these experiences with meaning. A person's identity, therefore, is the product of language and not an inherent, unchanging, and knowable essence.

Critique of the Idea of Representation

Contrary to the modernist notion that words accurately represent the real life phenomena they are supposed to represent (i.e., when you think or say a word you immediately think of the phenomenon that word represents), postmodernists argue that the utterance of a word (a signifier) and the phenomenon the word is supposed to represent (a signified) are, in fact, never one-and-the-same. Alvesson (2002) used the example of *worker* to further illustrate this point. A worker is a social position that exists only through language and social relations. As Alvesson wrote:

> The questions "What is a worker really? . . . What makes one a worker?" are not answerable by looking at the something that can be described as a worker, but is a product of the linguistic and non-linguistic practices that make this something into an object.
>
> (p. 53)

These questions can only be answered by looking at the larger social and linguistic practices that shape what it means to be a worker in a particular context. What it means to be a worker today, for example, is very different from what it meant to be a worker during the eighteenth century. Therefore, to utter the word (signifier) *worker* today is to speak about a different phenomenon (signified) than if one said the same word in the eighteenth century.

Critique of Metanarratives

Alvesson (2002) outlined two approaches to the critique of metanarratives. First, metanarratives have always been a description used to support a particular (dominant) worldview. Since language does not directly represent a real external world, it is used to support these metanarratives. For example, a feminist might argue that historical narratives promote a masculine metanarrative given that the word is *history*. Second, for postmodernists, metanarratives of all forms are questionable, leaving only the truly local narratives that are "accounts focusing on a particular setting and with limited generalizability over space and time" (Alvesson, 2002, p. 55). Returning to the example of a feminist critique, gender relations would have to be studied within a particular social group and context. The findings of such a study would not be applicable to other groups and contexts.

Power/Knowledge Connection

Though the power/knowledge connection was discussed above, it is prudent to note that the fit of Foucauldian analysis to this postmodern *category* is not a comfortable one. Although power/knowledge is an influential idea within postmodernism, Foucault's focus on power is more explicit than most postmodernists' (Alvesson, 2002). Some postmodern theorists go so far as to question what is meant by power. Gergen (1994) wrote:

> To what does the concept of power refer? It is after all, multiply constructed . . . Further, these various concepts are used by different interest groups (Marxists, political conservatives, feminists) for often contrary purposes . . . [However] certain groups may find the concept of power invaluable at certain times—including [postmodernists].
>
> (p. 73)

Foucault's thought can be understood to be influential for postmodernists, even if he cannot be comfortably *classified* as one himself. But, perhaps a postmodernist researcher or theorist, when studying power, would question what kind of power she or he is studying. What is the context of this kind of power? And how is it being employed?

CRITIQUE OF POSTMODERNISM

There are at least three main criticisms of postmodernism. The first suggests that postmodernism has itself become a metanarrative, the second is that it tends toward relativism, and in a third it is argued that there is no political stance associated with postmodernism. The first criticism, that postmodernism has itself become a metanarrative, boils down to: "avoid master narratives other than those advocated by the [postmodernists]" (Alvesson, 2002, p. 39). Alvesson argued that this flaw in postmodernism is the result of the conflation of postmodernism as method for analysing phenomena, using the themes outlined above, and attempts to use postmodernism to develop a theory of the world in which we currently live (i.e., postmodernity). In this case, postmodernism is a signifier for two different phenomena: a critical position and a description of a society. These two phenomena may in fact be incommensurable and, as Alvesson wrote, "coherence may be an overvalued quality in social studies" (p. 39).

The charge of relativism comes from the postmodern stance that there is no single truth, that everything is contextual and referential. The concern for most postmodernists is that without a certain amount of relativism, you fall back into the trap of metanarratives—if there were one accepted truth then all other claims must be false. As Burr (1995) asked, "who has the right to make such judgements?" (p. 81). This does not necessarily mean that postmodernism accepts all truth claims as equal, as postmodernists would contend that all claims are equally open to deconstruction and examination.

In 1992, Baumann argued that "[t]he postmodern mind seems to condemn everything, propose nothing. Demolition is the only job the postmodern mind seems to be good at. Destruction is the only construction it recognizes" (p. ix). As a result, postmodernism is good at diagnosing social problems, but not good at providing solutions to those problems. Similarly put, Cole (2003) remarked, "[w]hat is *constructed* after the deconstruction?" (p. 491). Not surprisingly, postmodern theorists have mixed reactions to such charges. Some, like Derrida (1992), argued that deconstruction is itself an act of justice. Often, postmodern researchers appoint themselves as the representative of the people they study with the intention of providing their participants with a voice. Others view any attempt to provide other people or groups with a voice as an act of elitism and power. Alvesson (2002) argued that perhaps the only way forward for a politically informed postmodernist position would be to combine postmodernism with critical theory—and indeed it is not unusual to see the postmodern themes of the centrality of discourse and the critique of metanarratives in some critical theorists' research.

EDUCATIONAL ADMINISTRATION AND POSTMODERNISM

There are a variety of postmodern approaches in educational administration and some of them will be reviewed here. Greenfield contributed some of the first postmodern writings in educational administration. While this chapter will not explore Greenfield's thought in depth, it is important to note that his contribution to the postmodern approach in educational administration surfaced through attacks on the modernist assumptions of a *science* of educational administration. This is a foundational theme in postmodern educational administration theory and research.

Maxcy (1994) argued that, in the postmodern world, school leadership is seen as suspect because it has failed to improve such things as test scores and graduation rates. Further, the postmodern perspective suggests the discourse of school effectiveness has created competition amongst administrators and thus contributed to the breaking down of public perceptions about schools. The modernist approach to educational administration—valuing the practical application of modernist or positivist rules-based methods of administration focused on truth and universalism—has opened up educational administration programmes to criticism by further separating the theoretical, that is the work of educational administration researchers, from the practical, the work of school leaders. Maxcy stated that the reason for pursing a postmodernist answer to these problems with educational administration is:

> The structuralist/modernist mentality has taken for granted the virtues of a structured, nondemocratic school site, as well as stressing the value of control and bureaucratic manipulations of children, teachers, and parents. It has followed from the acceptance of this structuralist/ modernists metanarrative, with its assumptions regarding the nature of school culture and the superiority of a narrow band of so-called "scientific" methods of inquiry, that depictions of school administration have overemphasized the rational/technical and machine-like workings of the educational systems, as well as the derivative and powerless status of teachers, parents, and children within its boundaries.
>
> (p. 2)

There are a few different postmodern approaches presented in Maxcy's volume. Scheurich (1994), for example, articulated his version of a postmodern epistemology. Scheurich argued for what he called a social or postmodern relativism, meaning "the unabashed recognition that all epistemology, ontology, and the ways of thinking that yield such categories as epistemology and ontology are socially conditioned and historically relative or contextual" (p. 21). In essence, this means that there are social and historical constraints on what can be considered truth, and that it is the job of the postmodern critic to question and alter these constraints in an effort to uncover their truth-power, or power/knowledge, relationship. Scheurich was here attempting to address the critique of postmodernism as lacking a political project by bringing together what Lemert (2005) identified as radical modernism with strategic postmodernism.

Scheurich (1994) argued that social relativism means that all truth claims are constantly questioned—even one's own truth claims. Such questions include: Who does the truth claim benefit? Is expert knowledge required to gain access to the truth claim? Are experts privileged over others? What is the truth claim's social history? Under what social and historical conditions did the truth claim arise? Is one social group privileged over another? Does one social group advocate for it over others? Is one social group's interests represented by it over others?

Since a postmodern critique cannot privilege one position, or truth claim, over another, only political judgements about a truth claim can be made. Researchers, in this view, must be upfront with their political stances and select epistemologies that best express their views. To elucidate his stance, Scheurich (1994) compared his with how an administrator enacts a particular policy. The administrator, and the researcher, understands that how a policy is enacted will impact people and groups in different ways and that there is no single way to enact a policy. A postmodern approach to research, therefore, mimics the choices a school administrator must make in her or his job:

> An administrator . . . can choose to base her or his decisions on effectiveness, cost, equity, career needs, or on some combination of several possibilities. Each decision will have a certain politics (i.e., it will benefit some people or groups over others). . . . Each policy decision of the administrator . . . will express, explicitly or implicitly, the politics of that person and her or his social, historical positionality.
>
> (p. 38)

Scheurich used postmodernism as a tool for questioning essentialising or universalising truth claims of any sort. He argued that there can only ever be a political analysis of truth claims because no single interpretation can be considered better than another. Rather, all claims must be interrogated and political stances revealed.

Johnston (1994), also found in Maxcy's volume, presented an alternative politically informed understanding of postmodernism. Using Foucault's notion of power, Johnson argued that school administrators "create the social-political conditions under which others may raise their voice" (p. 128). This position rejects modernist notions of power as command, and replaces it with a version of Foucault's power/knowledge that emphasises care, concern, and connectedness with other people, relationships, and attachment, as well as an anti-bureaucratic discourse. Johnston claimed that a "postmodernist discourse is concern with 'right action'" (p. 129), meaning that schools must achieve their goals in a manner that respects people and community.

Scheurich and Johnston each offered a politically oriented postmodern stance, but they differ in significant ways. Johnston used postmodern ideas to deconstruct power relations in schools and provide *right actions* to remedy previous power imbalances. He thus used postmodern ideas to deconstruct current power relations to provide a new foundation of power relations where everyone has voice. He suggested that simply collecting and sharing stories about the school is enough to overcome discursive power imbalances. Scheurich took his critique further by calling for a constant questioning of all truth claims. As such, Scheurich might continue to question Johnston's *right actions* to discern which new position of power was being privileged. Foucault's own intention was to reveal the mechanics of power/knowledge in a particular social and historical context. Foucault challenged all truth claims because, on his view, all knowledge claims are dangerous and include elements of domination (Alvesson, 2002).

Johnston's postmodern stance used the ideas and tools of postmodernism to deconstruct some ideas but not others. Sackney and Mitchell (2002) described this as honouring the postmodern conditions. They used these postmodern conditions to promote a postmodern leadership theory and practice. Postmodern leadership is concerned with cultural processes and discourses that construct organisational meaning. Postmodern leaders "understand organizational and leadership narratives, . . . confront issues of power and empowerment, . . . emphasize action rather than contemplation, and . . . connect practice with theory" (p. 900). Leadership, in Sackney and Mitchell's view, is not associated with hierarchical organisational roles. Instead, all organisational members are seen as actors in the creation of school culture and the enactment of leadership. Qualities such as trust, flexibility, adaptability, and openness are encouraged. Critical reflection, dialogue and inquiry are necessary so that the political nature of schooling is always foregrounded. All organisational members are encouraged to discuss the previously undiscussed and allow people to disagree while still maintaining a space of trust. Sackney and Mitchell described an environment where organisational culture is continually constructed, deconstructed and reconstructed using the tools and ideas of postmodernism. Ultimately, "[postmodern] educational leadership is a democratic and empowering approach that honors localized thinking yet moves people beyond it to see multiple possibilities, multiple influences, and multiple perspectives" (p. 909).

Furman (1998) offered a similar use of postmodern conditions in her examination of the concept of community. Furman argued that postmodernism provides challenges to traditional metaphors of community and provides a foundation upon which to create new, postmodern, metaphors. A postmodern community is "a community of difference" (p. 312)—a place where such difference is accepted. This differs from other kinds of community that are based in sameness, such as a kinship community or a valuational community. By redefining community using postmodern ideas, Furman hoped to provide a new definition of community that schools in the postmodern age could use to build a "language of possibility for school community in postmodern times" (p. 324). In language similar to Sackney and Mitchell (2002), Furman advocated that schools become spaces where difference is accepted, where members feel that they belong, that they are safe and where trust is paramount. Co-operation and relationships are primary. Furman identified three challenges with a postmodern understanding of community: (a) decentring the norm of whiteness so that otherness is accepted; (b) promoting feelings of belonging, trust, and safety within a space of accepted difference; and (c) creating school structures that promote a sense of community. Furman accepted that the concepts of difference and belonging may never be truly resolved and that this means that a postmodern understanding of community may be somewhat unsatisfying because there is no single answer for administrators, teachers, and researchers to use to build this new postmodern community.

Finally, I explore English's (2003) postmodern approach to educational administration. Like Sackney and Mitchell (2002) and Furman (1998), English used the conditions of postmodernism to deconstruct and destabilise foundational concepts of educational administration. He deconstructed, for example, the ISLLC (Interstate School Leaders Licensure Consortium) standards, which he called the "epitome of the modernist agenda" (p. 125). According to English, ISLLC standards present an air of scientific neutrality and binary logic that implies the standards are applicable in all contexts. Instead, using postmodern ideas, English demonstrated how, at best, the ISLLC standards present a list of preferred habits, not *best* practices that are applicable in all situations—as, following postmodern ideas, nothing can be true in all contexts. English used a similar approach to deconstruct the discourses behind the popular management text *The 7 Habits of Highly Effective People* by Stephen R. Covey (1991) and expose its hidden use of Mormon theology. Herein English exposed how religion is disguised as science, giving the book a false modernist legitimacy even though it is not based on scientific evidence and therefore violates modernist rules about truth and legitimacy. He pointed to the need to question the origin and context of popular ideas, particularly if these ideas are to become part of the accepted knowledge base of our field. English looked to the writings of Paul Feyerabend and his notion of *epistemological anarchism* as grounding for his own postmodern stance. Feyerabend's definition of epistemological anarchism is:

> there is no view, however "absurd" or "immoral" he refuses to consider or to act upon, and no method he regards as indispensable. The only thing he opposes positively and absolutely are universal standards, universal laws, universal ideas . . . and the behavior they engender though he does not deny that it is often good policy to act as if such laws (such standards, such ideas) existed and as if he believed in them.
>
> (as cited in English, 2003, pp. 242–243)

Although the works of Feyerabend have not be examined here, we can easily see how Feyerabend's understanding of epistemological anarchism matches the perspective of postmodernism I outline in this chapter—a questioning of metanarratives and the deconstruction of universals.

All of the postmodern-inspired approaches to educational administration I outline above share one thing in common: they use postmodern ideas, tools, and conditions to challenge the status quo. Sometimes this challenge is explicitly political, as in the case of Scheurich (1994). Other times perhaps less so (for example, in English's work). Although English's can be at times highly political, he has not argued in favour of an explicitly political postmodern approach to educational administration. Instead, English's postmodern approach critiques and deconstructs the modernist foundations of educational administration, but does not attempt to use postmodernism as a source of *right action* as is found in Johnston (1994). Attempts to use postmodernism to guide political actions may seem at odds with the initial intentions of postmodernism. The postmodernist stance is inherently skeptical; however, it is easy to see why writers like Johnston and Sackney and Mitchell (2002) looked to postmodernism to provide some kind of answer, or at the very least some kind of alternative to the status quo. Furman's (1998) postmodern examination of community, however, demonstrated how uncomfortable and unsatisfying a postmodern *answer* might be.

POSSIBLE FUTURE DIRECTIONS FOR POSTMODERN EDUCATIONAL ADMINISTRATION

Generally, the application of postmodern approaches has been viewed with some skepticism (see, for example, the debate between Blake [1996, 1997] and Cole, Hill, & Rikowski [1997]). Constant questioning, destabilising of metanarratives, and deconstruction of core concepts and ideas means that future research and practice directions are shaky at best. Some researchers argue that future directions must be guided by "what educational practitioners *are willing to accept* as true, as desirable, as good" (Ramaekers, 2006, p. 256), meaning that research directions that pay attention to people and their relationship with the world and their individual context should be pursued. Others see postmodernism as providing a lens for students of educational administration to (re)view their world and work (Capper, 1998).

Many of the approaches I outline in the previous sections focus on postmodernism's central preoccupation with the power/knowledge connection and are highly influenced by the work of Foucault. Perhaps more attention could be paid to other postmodern themes of discourse, fragmented identities, the critique of representation, and the critique of metanarratives. Discourse analysis offers researchers a methodology for examining these themes by focusing on language and its use. Because discourse analysis is the analysis of language as a social practice, it aims to venture beneath the surface of the words we use to describe events or topics in an effort to understand how language is being used to construct the world in which we live (Potter & Wetherell, 1987). For Davies and Harré (1990), discourses are the institutionalised use of language. This institutionalisation can occur at many levels, from the individual to the cultural, and may develop around specific topics. Leadership, and its use within the *institution* of public school, for example, is its own discourse.

Discourse analysis allows researchers to study how language is used to create or build the world around us. Gee (2005) called this process *language-in-action*. By studying language-in-action, we can see how language makes certain events and ideas more significant than others, how language is used to get others to recognise the importance of certain activities, that certain identities are being enacted, that certain relationships between people exists, that certain perspectives are being taken, that some ideas and events are connected or relevant, and that some knowledge is privileged over other kinds of knowledge. Discourse analysis has been used to study issues of power and control in the ISLLC National Standards in Educational Administration (Anderson, 2001); the discord between the discourse of shared leadership in academe and the reality of shared leadership in practice (Hatcher, 2005); and the effect of the *glass ceiling* on the desirability of, and access to, leadership roles in schools (Moreau, Osgood, & Halsall, 2007). Again, these examples follow the power/knowledge theme; however, discourse analysis provides access to other postmodern themes by focusing on how language is used, the positionality of discourse users, the foundation and effects of text and speech, and the deconstruction of metanarratives by highlighting how discourses are used at the local level.

Postmodernism provides a direct challenge to traditional educational administration ideas and approaches. Some of these challenges may be unsettling. Postmodernism is, after all, better at interrogation and deconstruction than providing answers and reconstruction. But, it does allow accepted ideas to be subverted, making room for other voices and approaches. It demands that we interrogate the status quo and examine its inner workings. Some theorists argue that we live in a postmodern age, while others argue that we still live in the modern age but can use postmodern techniques and ideas to critique and reinterpret modernity. Regardless of the kind of world in which we currently live, postmodernism offers a new way of thinking about, talking about, and perhaps even acting in the world as we experience it.

REFERENCES

Alvesson, M. (2002). *Postmodernism and social research*. Philadelphia, PA: Open University Press.

Anderson, G. L. (2001). Disciplining leaders: A critical discourse analysis of the ISLLC national examination and performance standards in educational administration. *International Journal of Leadership in Education, 4*(3), 199–216.

Aylesworth, G. (2005). Postmodernism. In E. N. Zalta (Ed.), *The Stanford encyclopedia of philosophy* (Winter 2010 ed.). Retrieved from http://plato.stanford.edu/archives/win2010/entries/postmodernism/

Bauman, Z. (1992). *Intimations of postmodernity*. London: Routledge.

Benwell, B., & Stokoe, E. (2010). Analysing identity in interaction: Contrasting discourse, genealogical, narrative and conversation analysis. In M. Wetherell & C. T. Mohanty (Eds.), *The SAGE handbook of identities* (pp. 82–103). Los Angeles: Sage.

Blake, N. (1996). Between postmodernism and anti-modernism: The predicament of educational studies. *British Journal of Educational Studies, 44*(1), 42–65.

Blake, N. (1997). A postmodernism worth bothering about: A rejoinder to Cole, Hill and Rikowski. *British Journal of Educational Studies, 45*(3), 293–305.

Bloland, H. G. (2005). Whatever happened to postmodernism in higher education?: No requiem in the New Millennium. *The Journal of Higher Education, 76*(2), 121–150.

Burr, V. (1995). *An introduction to social constructionism.* New York: Routledge.

Burr, V. (2003). *Social constructionism* (2nd ed.). New York: Routledge.

Capper, C. A. (1998). Critically oriented and postmodern perspectives: Sorting out the differences and applications for practice. *Educational Administration Quarterly, 34*(3), 354–379. doi:10.1177/0013161X98034003005

Cole, M. (2003). Might it be in the practice that it fails to succeed? A Marxist critique of claims for postmodernism and poststructuralism as forces for social change and social justice. *British Journal of Sociology of Education, 24*(4), 487–500. doi:10.1080/0142569032000109396

Cole, M., Hill, D., & Rikowski, G. (1997). Between postmodernism and nowhere: The predicament of the postmodernist. *British Journal of Educational Studies, 45,* 187–200.

Covey, S. R. (1991). *The 7 habits of highly effective people.* New York: Simon and Schuster.

Davies, B., & Harré, R. (1990). Positioning: The discursive production of selves. *Journal for the Theory of Social Behaviour, 20*(1), 43–63.

Derrida, J. (1987). *The truth in painting* (G. Bennington & I. McLeod, Trans.). Chicago: University of Chicago Press.

Derrida, J. (1992). Force of law: The "mystical foundation of authority." In D. Cornell, M. Rosenfeld, & B. N. Cardozo (Eds.), *Deconstruction and the possibility of justice* (pp. 3–67). New York: Routledge.

English, F. W. (2003). *The postmodern challenge to the theory and practice of educational administration.* Springfield, IL: Charles C. Thomas Publisher.

Foucault, M. (1995). *Discipline & punish: The birth of the prison* (A. Sheridan, Trans.). New York: Vintage Books.

Furman, G. C. (1998). Postmoderism and community in schools: Unraveling the paradox. *Educational Administration Quarterly, 34*(3), 289–328. doi:10.1177/0013141X98034003003

Gee, J. P. (2005). *An introduction to discourse analysis: Theory and method* (2nd ed.). New York: Routledge.

Gergen, K. J. (1994). *Realities and relationships: Soundings in social construction.* Cambridge, MA: Harvard University Press.

Gutting, G. (2003). Foucault. In E. N. Zalta (Ed.), *The Stanford encyclopedia of philosophy* (Fall 2011 ed.). Retrieved from http://plato.stanford.edu/archives/fall2011/entries/foucault/

Hatcher, R. (2005). The distribution of leadership and power in schools. *British Journal of Sociology in Education, 26*(2), 253–267.

Johnston, B. J. (1994). Educational administration in the postmodern age. In S. J. Maxcy (Ed.), *Postmodern school leadership: Meeting the crisis in educational administration* (pp. 115–131). Westport, CT: Praeger.

Lemert, C. (2005). *Postmodernism is not what you think: Why globalization threatens modernity.* Boulder, CO: Paradigm Publishers.

Lyotard, J.-F. (1984). *The postmodern condition: A report on knowledge* (G. Bennington & B. Massumi, Trans.). Minneapolis, MN: University of Minnesota Press.

Maxcy, S. J. (Ed.). (1994). *Postmodern school leadership: Meeting the crisis in educational administration*. Westport, CT: Praeger.

Moreau, M.-P., Osgood, J., & Halsall, A. (2007). Making sense of the glass ceiling in schools: An exploration of women teachers' discourses. *Gender & Education, 19*(2), 237–253.

Potter, J., & Wetherell, M. (1987). *Discourse and social psychology: Beyond attitudes and behaviours*. London: Sage.

Ramaekers, S. (2006). No harm done: The implications for educational research of the rejection of truth. *Journal of the Philosophy of Education, 40*(2), 241–257.

Sackney, L., & Mitchell, C. (2002). Postmodern expression of educational leadership. In K. Leithwood & P. Hallinger (Eds.), *Second international handbook of educational leadership and administration* (pp. 881–913). Dordrecht, Netherlands: Klewer.

Scheurich, J. J. (1994). Social relativism: A postmodernist epistemology for educational administration. In S. J. Maxcy (Ed.), *Postmodern school leadership: Meeting the crisis in educational administration* (pp. 17–46). Westport, CT: Praeger.

van Dijk, T. A. (2009). Critical discourse studies: A sociocognitive approach. In R. Wodak & M. Meyer (Eds.), *Methods of critical discourse analysis* (pp. 62–86). Washington DC: Sage.

7 Naturalistic Coherentism

Madeline M. Press

Naturalistic coherentism is a post-positivist theoretical perspective on educational administration introduced by Colin Evers and Gabrielle Lakomski, and it has stimulated much discussion and critical examination by scholars. *Naturalistic coherentism* derived from a requirement for coherent evidence and a reliance on theories of natural science to inform knowledge development. In three books developed over ten years, Evers and Lakomski described a pragmatic and holistic approach to understanding in educational administration. They suggested a meta-paradigm with the potential to eliminate the dichotomies inherent in knowledge development and to unify all paradigms. Their dismissal of other ways of knowing in favour of a post-positivistic ontology created much discussion and controversy.

Through examination and amelioration of previous contributions to understanding in educational administration, Evers and Lakomski developed a naturalistic coherentism perspective of knowledge development. Evers and Lakomski (1996a) identified the following assumptions: The most coherent ontology is the natural world exists; the basic unit of social reality is individual interactions with the natural world; organizations are real patterns of human association, and they are relatively stable over time due to the stability of individual memories and collective records; and organizational pathologies occur as a result of dissonance between individuals, organizations, and society. These assumptions form the core of the naturalistic coherentism perspective.

Evers and Lakomski addressed the shortcomings inherent in logical empiricism by developing a more holistic definition of science and a pragmatic resolution to accepted dichotomies. They proposed the use of stable theories of natural science as the foundation for the development of coherent theories of educational administration and the application of coherence criteria as justification for theory choice and empirical adequacy. A theory of learning based on neural network models was proposed as the foundation for understanding practice in educational administration. However, the ambitious goal of bringing all knowledge development under one meta-paradigm met resistance from proponents of a variety of theoretical positions.

LOGICAL EMPIRICISM TO NATURALISTIC COHERENTISM

Arguably, over the lifetime of our field, the received view in educational administration has seen a significant shift in perspective. As other authors in this volume have explored, the original theoretical position of our field was characterised by the key assumptions inherent in logical empiricism/positivism that (a) observation is theory-neutral and (b) empirical evidence alone is sufficient to develop theory (Evers & Lakomski, 1996a)—the so called Theory Movement. However, beginning in the early 1970s, the nature of the relationship between theory and evidence was debated. Arguments were put forward that theory itself was the determinant of that relationship, and the justification for theory was specific to the paradigmatic approach in use (Evers & Lakomski, 2000)—the space created for theoretical diversity promoted by Greenfield.

As controversy over positivist understanding of knowledge development expanded, interpretive and post-modernist perspectives became more prominent. Evers and Lakomski (1993) believed the acceptance of alternative paradigms had resulted in numerous different epistemological positions with distinctive assumptions. Rather than making knowledge development easier, these paradigmatic approaches increased data screening and discounted the role of natural science (Evers & Lakomski, 2000). Post-modernist paradigms raised further concerns for Evers and Lakomski. In post-modernist paradigms, there was no distinction between fiction and non-fiction, failures were not filtered out, and random experiences were described (Evers & Lakomski, 2000). Evers and Lakomski (2000) proposed that human behaviour was not random; therefore, the contribution to science from post-modern paradigms was minimal.

The arguments against logical empiricism resulted in a rejection of science by researchers of educational administration. The logical empiricist understanding of science did not account for values, human subjectivity, and the social and political context inherent in the practice of educational administration (Evers & Lakomski, 1991). Thus, Evers and Lakomski proposed an alternative to the science of positivism by providing a post-positivist definition of science. They discussed the role of justification in the development of evidence, demanded empirical adequacy through super-empirical virtues, and insisted that understanding of knowledge cohere with how humans learn (Evers & Lakomski, 1991; Evers & Lakomski, 1996a; Evers & Lakomski, 2000). According to Lakomski (2005):

> Possibly the most important outcome has been that, unlike many contemporary theorists, we have opted for science and against many versions of subjectivism, interpretivism or critical theory approaches as the best way to explain the phenomena of our social and natural world.
>
> (p. 5)

A New Definition of Science

Science, as defined by logical empiricism, was too restrictive for the social practice of educational administration. As a result, the positivist approach to research and knowledge development was inappropriate for the practice of educational administration (Evers & Lakomski, 1996a). A rift between the science of logical empiricism and the practice of educational administration was inevitable. Evers and Lakomski's (2000) new definition of science acknowledged values, human subjectivity, complexity of practice, and particularity of practice situations. Therefore, rather than eliminating science from educational administration, naturalistic coherentism presented a more holistic definition of science.

Traditional science was found to be epistemologically inadequate because the subjective nature of social phenomena was not considered (Evers & Lakomski, 1991). The role of experience in practice was not addressed through the science of logical empiricism. Experience is ontologically different than the objective empirical reality defined by logical empiricism (Hodgkinson, 1993). According to Evers and Lakomski (1991), a naturalistic and coherent theory of science, based on neuro-scientific and cognitive theories, and encompassing human subjectivity and values, was the most coherent explanation. The naturalistic coherentism perspective was grounded in natural science. Therefore, this perspective cohered with scientific theories of how knowledge is acquired and represented (Evers & Lakomski, 2000).

Through the naturalistic coherentism perspective, knowledge is perceived as a dynamic web. At the center of the web, knowledge is more stable; therefore, theories from the physical sciences that are less likely to change reside there. The knowledge at the outside of the web, such as administrative theory, is less stable and is still being developed (Evers & Lakomski, 2000). Theories in natural science hold a foundational position for further theory development. The placement of natural sciences such as physics, chemistry, and neurobiology, close to mathematics and logic at the center of the web, inferred that these theories should be used to direct construction of theories further removed from the center (Allison, 2001), such as theories of educational administration. Evers and Lakomski (2000) maintained:

> The overall gain to be had from a focus on naturalism in research is an explanation of human thought and action which coheres with what is known about humans as biological beings who negotiate their complexly structured environments, mostly with success, often with great skill, and sometimes with finesse.
>
> (p. 162)

Naturalistic coherentism relies on a coherent theory of cognition based on theories of natural science. Evers and Lakomski addressed the limitations of logical empiricism and provided an expanded understanding of the role of science in educational administration. The most coherent theory of cognition was found in neuro-scientific and cognitive theories of learning. The requirement for empirical adequacy was met by the introduction of coherence criteria as a justification for theory (Barlosky, 1995). Through this process, Evers and Lakomski developed a post-positivist definition of science that addressed the dichotomies associated with inquiry in educational administration.

Resolving the Dichotomies

The dichotomies inherent in educational administration have become oppositional bases for different perspectives. Naturalistic coherentism reduced these dichotomies to inherent characteristics of scientific study (Evers & Lakomski, 2000). Evers and Lakomski addressed the controversies regarding facts and values, observation and theory, objectivity and subjectivity, and theory and practice. Rather than dichotomies, each of these diverse concepts is considered to be inseparable from the other.

Subjectivists maintained that facts and values fell into separate categories. Hodgkinson (1993) stated that there is a sharp distinction between facts and values that cannot be bridged by epistemology, and a naturalistic coherentist re-definition of these concepts falls short. Similarly, Maddock (1994) stated reducing values to an attribute of fact is unscientific because doing so omits the meaning of values. But, Evers and Lakomski (1996a) felt a distinction between facts and values was mistaken, and both facts and values were part of the total cognitive process. Thus, facts and values are intertwined. Educational administration is value-laden; therefore, facts derived from educational administration are value-laden (Evers & Lakomski, 1996a). As a result, there is no way to consider facts without also considering values, and values play an intrinsic role in establishing facts.

Logical empiricism maintained a distinction between theory and observation. This rigid distinction became indefensible because all observation is influenced by theory and open to interpretation (Allison, 2001). The observer is influenced by pre-conceived understandings. Observation is a construction rather than a discovery, and it is difficult to confirm or disprove theory by observation alone (Barlosky, 1995). Evers and Lakomski (2000) stated that observation can never be free of theory, and theory will alter the interpretation of the observer. As well, observation alone can be misleading. The same observations can confirm or refute more than one theory (Evers & Lakomski, 2000). Therefore, conclusions based on observations are subjective interpretations influenced by theory.

The practice of educational administration is subjective in nature. Subjective concepts, such as beliefs, values, ethics, and cultural influences, could potentially be used as evidence (Evers & Lakomski, 1993). However, subjective concepts that do not meet the coherency criteria may be overlooked.

Evers and Lakomski (1991) emphasized how theories about these concepts must cohere with scientific accounts of learning; therefore, some subjective concepts may be excluded. Rather than ruling out subjectivity, Evers and Lakomski (1996a) maintained the most coherent response would be the most objective response; so, objectivity becomes a matter of coherence. Even though subjectivists claimed meanings, intentions, actions, and experiences could only be understood subjectively, Evers and Lakomski (1991) contended objectivity is a matter of coherence and not hard data. Therefore, the most coherent response is the most objective.

Practical and theoretical knowledge are commonly perceived as distinct forms of knowledge. However, Evers and Lakomski (2000) advanced a common framework for both practical and theoretical knowledge. Evers and Walker (1983) believed there was no practical way to partition knowledge into distinct forms; therefore, a holistic epistemology was required. Theoretical structure in knowledge development is important. Good theories capture practical experience, resulting in accounts of learning that connect experience and theory (Evers & Lakomski, 1991); thus, linking situated and specific contexts to practice is necessary (Evers and Lakomski, 1996a). As a result, a common framework for practical and theoretical knowledge is essential for understanding in educational administration.

Through naturalistic coherentism, Evers and Lakomski (1993) attempted to resolve dichotomies inherent in educational administration by providing a pragmatic understanding of these divergent concepts. "One consequence of coherentism in general is a shift towards holism, with an attendant blurring of distinctions between observation and theory, fact and value, brute and non-brute data, foundational and derived knowledge" (p. 150). Although there are many dissenters, this holistic and pragmatic understanding of previously thought disparate concepts allows us to move forward in the development of knowledge in educational administration.

COHERENCY CRITERIA

An important criterion for the selection of theories in naturalistic coherentism is coherency. However, the act of choosing theory is subjective. Therefore, the choice of a coherent theory is a relative judgment in which one theory is found to be more coherent than another. Empirical evidence is not the only justification for theory. Super-empirical virtues such as consistency, comprehensiveness, simplicity, conservatism, fecundity, and explanatory unity are considered superior for choosing theory. The use of coherency criteria allow for epistemological diversity without the need for distinct paradigms (Evers & Lakomski, 1991). The super-empirical virtues would become a standard for all epistemologies. As such, coherency criteria could function as a unifying *touchstone* across divergent theoretical positions (Evers & Lakomski, 2000). These criteria are not limited to empirical claims. Coherent epistemology can be used to justify either subjective or scientific claims while still maintaining a scientific approach (Evers & Lakomski, 1996a). Therefore, application of coherency criteria could maintain empirical adequacy across divergent epistemologies.

The application of coherency criteria is useful in organising human experience and action, and it provides a holistic framework for knowledge development (Barlosky, 1995). But, these particular coherency criteria may not be the best criteria. Other virtues, such as complexity, situatedness, fluidity, and divergence, could be seen as more important (Barlosky, 1995). The criteria essential for understanding in one paradigm do not necessarily provide understanding within another paradigm. Hodgkinson (1993) argued proponents of feminism, Marxism, fascism, and radicalism all adhere to different standards. However, Evers and Lakomski (2000) insisted the naturalistic coherentism standard for theory justification is *the* touchstone because these coherency criteria are broadly used by other paradigms. Lakomski (2005) stated the use of super-empirical virtues imposes a tight discipline on theory choice because every rival claim is subject to the same examination, including the claims of naturalistic coherentism. However, universal agreement on coherency criteria may not be possible.

The way the coherency criteria are applied may also be a cause for concern. Even though Allison (2001) believed it was appropriate to use super-empirical virtues to guide inquiry, he believed these virtues could not be applied in a formal and context-free manner resulting in disagreement on how to apply them. Furthermore, there is little general agreement on coherency. Hodgkinson (1993) stated coherentism is one of many choices; Gronn and Ribbins (1993) suggested there is no clear definition of coherency or indication of where the super-empirical criteria come from. The use of coherency criteria in theory choice formed the basis of the naturalistic coherentism justification premise; however, there are many concerns about the definition and application of the super-empirical virtues in educational administration.

NEURAL NETWORKS AND COGNITION

All epistemologies contain assumptions related to how learning occurs. Evers and Lakomski (1996a) espoused a theory of cognition based on neural network models. They believed symbolic models of learning do not account for human learning, and only compressed experience into a representation expressed through language (Evers & Lakomski, 2000). Lakomski (2005) added that neural network models meet the coherency criteria and provide empirical evidence of learning within a dynamic environment; thus, they cohere with natural science theories of how the brain functions (Evers & Lakomski, 2000). Therefore, neural network models provided a more holistic understanding of learning than symbolic models.

The neural network theory of learning emphasized natural science and the role of the physical brain. Within the brain, knowledge is distributed across neurons rather than fixed in one spot, and patterns of neuronal activity form the internal representation of a specific thing. As learning occurs, a pattern of neuronal activation develops. Neurons are activated by sensory organs through stimulation from the environment; with repeated exposure to and feedback from the environment, the neural network is trained to respond to specific triggers (Evers & Lakomski, 1996a). Thus, a pattern develops and learning occurs. These patterns are under constant pressure from environmental feedback; therefore, the neural network continues to learn from experience and, as environmental factors trigger the neural network, previous learning is accessed (Evers & Lakomski, 2000). The neural network does not follow specific rules. Learning occurs because the network is susceptible to feedback and neuronal activation patterns can be changed over time (Lakomski, 2005). Therefore, knowledge within the brain is under constant pressure from the environment, either reinforcing or changing previously developed neuronal activation patterns.

Human subjectivity can be understood through neural network models. Behaviour is determined by the connections present in the neural network, not by the intention to act (Evers & Lakomski, 1991). A connection between the natural world and the social world exists. From a neural network perspective, will, choice, decisions, and passions are part of the cognitive process and reside in the neural network through a pattern of connections (Evers & Lakomski, 1993). Skills and expertise can be explained by neural network models. The practical skills and expertise gained through experience is a result of pattern processing within the neural network; these patterns have developed as a result of feedback that occurred during and after action (Evers & Lakomski, 2000). This process of learning accounts for all types of knowledge.

In the naturalistic coherentism perspective, the neural network is not confined to the human brain. Language is a collective process rather than an individual one; cognition is distributed in the world and not confined to the brain. The human brain and the environment are indivisible. Neural network models can influence theory development by viewing collective knowledge from the perspective of how the brain functions, and the neural network model can be extended into the social world, including the social world of the organization. Evers and Lakomski (2000) insisted individual learning and organizational learning were not separate entities, and organizational learning does not occur without individuals. The organization does not function as a brain. Accordingly, organizational learning occurs as a result of the distributed cognition, or learning, of the individuals within the organization. This network of individuals functions as the neural network for the organization; therefore, organizational knowledge is a result of this neural network.

According to Evers and Lakomski (2000), organizational knowledge is distributed through the patterns of activities of the individuals within the organization. Therefore, the neural network of the organization is susceptible to feedback from the environment as well. Artifacts, such as computers, languages, books, and tools, assist in pattern processing within the neural network. As individuals learn in response to environmental factors, the organizational network will continue to develop.

Neural network models cohere with stable natural science theories of how learning occurs in the human brain. From these models, Evers and Lakomski have developed theories of practice that cohere with their understanding of how neural network patterns develop. They have taken a physical understanding of how the human brain functions and applied it to abstract social concepts such as organizational learning and leadership. This dogmatic faith in the primacy of physical science to explain abstract conceptions of the social world may, nevertheless, be difficult for some philosophers in educational administration to accept.

CRITICISMS OF NATURALISTIC COHERENTISM

In naturalistic coherentism, Evers and Lakomski attempted to construct a universal theory of educational administration. Through the process of discussion, analysis and elimination of alternative beliefs, they proposed assumptions of naturalistic coherentism could answer any inquiry. However, this position met with resistance from proponents of alternate epistemologies. Willower (1996) suggested naturalistic coherentism gave little attention to paradigmatic differences and to the contribution these paradigms made to knowledge development. Cultural anthropology, phenomenology, hermeneutics, and interpretive social sciences all provide unique knowledge and contribute to the field. There may be something to gain from random experiences and alternative ways of knowing that proponents of naturalistic coherentism do not acknowledge.

A post-positivist definition of science is still science, and there were concerns about its role in educational administration. Barlosky (1995) felt naturalistic coherentism was another form of positivism because it proposed the same belief as logical empiricism that discrete paradigms held contradictory and incomparable forms of knowledge. Although acknowledging the importance of science to educational administration, Allison (2001) questioned the feasibility of a universal theory of educational administration. He believed naturalistic coherentism adopted all that was good about scientific inquiry but ignored the benefits of other approaches to inquiry. The superiority of science is assumed in naturalistic coherentism. Maddock (1994) stated that placing science over other ways of knowing does not acknowledge all thought is flawed and that philosophical debate should be encouraged. Hodgkinson (1993) suggested naturalistic coherentism placed scientific thought as the benchmark for knowledge development when science is often not coherent and does not offer enough for understanding in social science. He stated that reducing knowledge to physical processes of the brain ". . . rapidly becomes unscientific: it omits too much and it assumes too much . . . that we can explain what is meant by a *belief*; that all metaphysics will be reduced ultimately to physics; . . . [and] that science itself coheres" (Hodgkinson, 1993, p. 180).

Not only is there an ontological divide between the post-positivist perspective and other perspectives, but, according to Allison (2001), there is also an ontological divide between the natural world and the social world. Allison suggested no matter how much naturalistic coherentism is adapted or extended, it cannot interpret history in any meaningful way. Naturalistic coherentism does not acknowledge this divide. Even though administrative theory reflects social science, there is a strong coherence with natural science; the role of science is to describe the regularities inherent in social life (Evers & Lakomski, 1996a). Natural science satisfies the observation requirement because it identifies features of the world that result in what is observed (Evers & Lakomski, 2000). There are, however, those who take issue with this strong naturalistic approach. Allison stated that it would negatively influence the acceptance of science back into educational administration.

Alternative ways of knowing are discounted by naturalistic coherentism. Common or folk knowledge is regarded as inferior to natural science in its ability to explain and predict; neuroscience is used to explain inner states, such as beliefs and desires, reducing them to physical mechanisms (Allison, 2001). It may be difficult to overcome these ontological differences. Naturalistic coherentism focuses on individuals, either discrete or distributed systems, and other perspectives focus on a changing world of individuals within a historical, social, cultural, and linguistic reality (Allison, 2001). The pragmatism of naturalistic coherentism is claimed to be superior to other philosophical theories. However, some argue that the notion of one overarching theory that can explain everything is unrealistic in a contradictory world driven by opposing forces, ideas, needs, and convictions (*cf.* Maddock, 1994). Naturalistic coherentism is only one belief in a world of many.

The concept of coherency does not generate a universal understanding. Coherency is a vague concept, and coherency criteria do not always do the job expected of them (Maddock, 1994). The coherency criteria may not be generally accepted virtues. Maddock (1994) stated there is no indication of how to combine the super-empirical virtues and why these virtues are superior to other virtues. The use of the term *coherency* positions naturalistic coherentism as a superior paradigm. To differ with the concept of coherency suggests adoption of incoherency in place of knowledge (Barlosky, 1995). Yet, administrative practice may not be coherent. Hodgkinson (1993) asserted administration is a combination of incoherence, contingency, and change. Therefore, coherency criteria do not necessarily provide enlightenment for truth-seekers in educational administration.

Evers and Lakomski sought to provide a coherent structure for examining issues in educational administration. Naturalistic coherentism is a holistic and pragmatic perspective that acknowledges subjective and scientific evidence as long as the coherency criteria are met. The choice of natural science theory as the foundation for development of educational administration theory was based on the belief that epistemology must cohere with natural science and with theories of human learning. Evers and Lakomski proposed naturalistic coherentism as a grand, unifying meta-paradigm for educational administration. However, this proposed position has met with considerable opposition from those advocating alternative theoretical perspectives.

REFERENCES

Allison, D. J. (2001). Riding the E and L roller-coaster: How I came to fear naturalistic coherentism. *Journal of Educational Administration, 39*(6), 539–553.

Barlosky, M. (1995). Knowledge, certainty, and openness in educational administration. *Curriculum Inquiry, 23*(4), 441–455.

Evers, C. W., & Lakomski, G. (2000). *Doing educational administration: A theory of administrative practice.* Oxford, UK: Pergamon.

Evers, C. W., & Lakomski, G. (1991). *Knowing educational administration: Contemporary methodological controversies in educational administration research.* Oxford, UK: Pergamon.

Evers, C. W., & Lakomski, G. (1993). Justifying educational administration. *Educational Management Administration & Leadership, 21*(3), 140–152.

Evers, C. W., & Lakomski, G. (1996a). *Exploring educational administration: Coherentist applications and critical debates.* New York: Pergamon.

Evers, C. W., & Lakomski, G. (1996b). Science in educational administration: A post-positivist conception. *Educational Administration Quarterly, 32*(3), 379–402. doi:10.1177/0013161X96032003005

Evers, C. W., & Walker, J. C. (1983). Knowledge, partitioned sets and extensionality: A refutation of the forms of knowledge thesis. *Journal of Philosophy of Education, 17*(2), 155–170. doi:10.1111/j.1467-9752.1983.tb00027.x

Gronn, P., & Ribbins, P. (1993). The salvation of educational administration: Better science or alternatives to science? *Educational Management Administration, 21*(3), 161–169. doi:10.1177/174114329302100303

Hodgkinson, C. (1993). The epistemological axiology of Evers and Lakomski: Some un-Quineian quibbling. *Education Management Administration & Leadership, 21,* 177–184.

Lakomski, G. (2005). *Managing without leadership: Towards a theory of organizational functioning.* Oxford: Pergamon/Elsevier.

Maddock, T. H. (1994). Three dogmas of materialist pragmatism: A critique of a recent attempt to provide a science of educational administration. *Journal of Educational Administration, 32*(4), 5–27.

Willower, D. J. (1996). Explaining and improving educational administration. In C. W. Evers & G. Lakomski, *Exploring educational administration* (pp. 165–175). New York: Pergamon.

Part II

Diverse Perspectives

8 Critical Realism

Robin Mueller

Critical realism is a methodological orientation that is relatively unknown in the fields of education and educational administration. When, as a developing educational scholar, I spent many months looking for a research methodology that best resonated with my sensibilities, it was due only to a happy accident that I was introduced to the critical realist's perspective. I experienced an immediate affinity with the tenets of critical realism, and I consequently found the absence of critical realist discourse in educational administration somewhat puzzling. The perspective has, admittedly, been criticized by some; however, such critical debate is common among adherents to a number of paradigms that continue to be robustly represented in administrative scholarship. I believe that the majority of critique with respect to critical realism is due to a misreading of the methodology as an intensely and, perhaps solely, theoretical perspective. Counter to this misunderstanding, my colleagues and I have found in critical realism a research orientation that inspires curiosity, theoretical rigour, *and* significant practical utility.

Before proceeding, I will offer some clarity about what I mean by *methodology*, a term that is used variously within social science research. I use the word not to imply specific modes or traditions of data collection, but more broadly as an ontological philosophy of inquiry. This interpretation follows Olsen and Morgan's (2005) definition of methodology as

> a combination of techniques, the practices we conform to when we apply them, and our interpretation of what we are doing when we do so. Methodologies often have embedded in them assumptions about the nature of reality and underlying or implicit axioms about human behaviour.
>
> (p. 257)

Philosophers began articulating a methodology of *critical realism* in the 1970s (Bhaskar, 1975). While a variety of authors have adopted a critical realist theoretical position over the past decades, the approach is relatively new and consequently *developing*. Critical realism, as Danermark and colleagues (2002) most succinctly put it, "is not a homogenous movement in social science" (p. 1); sources regarding the methodology are admittedly variable and critical realism is not easily reduced to a few core principles. Further, the link between theory and method in critical realism is often perceived as something of a mystery, and writing is sparse with respect to application of critical realist principles in research. However, when viewed holistically, use of critical realism presents many opportunities for the development of valuable inquiry in the social sciences broadly, and within the domain of educational administration particularly. In this chapter, I outline the theory of critical realism and demonstrate how the critical realist's alternative view of reality and inquiry is significant to research in educational administration.

ORIGINS OF CRITICAL REALISM

Critical realist discourse was initiated partly in response to the dominance of *logical positivism* in both natural and social sciences. Hume (1711–1776) and Comte (1798–1857), widely considered the *inventors* of positivism, theorized and wrote during a historical period when researchers were preoccupied with the task of establishing an empirical foundation for science, partly in response to the then-prevalent religious influences on inquiry (Manicas, 2006). The philosophers of the Vienna Circle adopted Comte's ideas in the early 1920s, and while there were a great many more nuances inherent in the development and establishment of positivism, it is enough for my purposes to note that by the mid-1900s logical positivism had become a dominant methodology in most natural and social science traditions (Manicas, 2006). The legacy of positivism remains influential in current inquiry, and although many scientists have rejected positivist epistemology, much research is still conducted based on embedded positivist assumptions and by utilising positivist language and conceptualisations (Manicas, 2006).

Positivism is heavily grounded in principles of formal logic and frequently expressed in the language of mathematics. Deductive and inductive reasoning are used to describe the relationship between specific conditions, events, and scientific laws. This is exemplified in the deductive argument "if a, then b,"—which has also been called the *covering law model* (Manicas, 2006). Laws are construed as broad explanations of regular patterns, and are generally substantiated, or *proven*, through empirical observations; for example, "if water is heated to one hundred degrees Celsius, it boils." Hume also extended law-like relations to enable an understanding of causality; he suggested that "if a, then b" *is equivalent to* "a is the cause of b" (Manicas, 2006). Hume, in an effort to defy spiritual influences on research, argued that there is nothing further to be known about causal relationships. The covering law model and its associated conception of causality came to be primarily associated with natural sciences, but positivist language use and research design is readily reflected in the social sciences, as well (Manicas, 2006). Widespread acceptance of the positivist model of causality has tended to suppress strategic efforts to more deeply understand what produces phenomena in both natural and social science traditions.

Rejection of Logical Positivism

Despite the necessary role of deduction and induction in science, critical realists suggest that reliance on empirical investigation and the covering law model is ill-founded and misleading (Danermark, Ekström, Jakobsen, & Karlsson, 2002; Manicas, 2006; Searle, 1995). A critical realist view offers an alternative option for perceiving causality and for further comprehending the notions of predictability, understanding, and explanation. According to the positivist covering law model, "*explanation and prediction are symmetrical. If you are in a position to explain some event b, then b could have been predicted—and conversely*" (Manicas, 2006, p. 11, emphasis in original). Prediction, as a consequence, has become a widely acknowledged hallmark of quality scientific inquiry. However, this equation is only reasonable when it is applied to laws that are typically expressed by way of the covering law model, and with respect to phenomena that are typically tested in closed, experimental kinds of conditions. The range of events and phenomena that are not explainable or predictable based on the covering law model are vast: from the destruction wrought during an earthquake, to acts of mob violence, to poverty in developing nations. In short, the complexity inherent in the expression of real-life phenomena defies explanation *and* prediction based on the covering law model. Adherence to the model and the associated conception of causality are consequently inadequate, and the positivist-inspired emphasis on prediction is also largely unreasonable.

The most important aspect of a critical realist's rejection of positivism emerges in a reconceptualization of *explanation* and *understanding* (see a visual comparison of positivist and critical realist conceptions of explanation and understanding in Figure 8.1). In the positivist tradition, explanation is associated with identification of empirical patterns; laws express regularities, the measurement of regularities inform laws, and theories broadly articulate systems of laws. Explanation is *descriptive* in nature. So, the consistent observation that water boils at one hundred degrees Celsius provides an accurate picture of the phenomenon, but does little (or nothing) to promote understanding about *why* this happens. Positivist understanding frequently does not move past explanation, and many positivist scientists have indicated a belief that understanding is not actually necessary in science (Manicas, 2006). However, this kind of science provides only a limited view of reality, as the empirical patterns tell us very little about what constitutes phenomena, what causes events, and the variety of conditions that make the expression of activity possible. A realist notion of explanation and understanding then pertains first to the acknowledgement of a *deep reality*

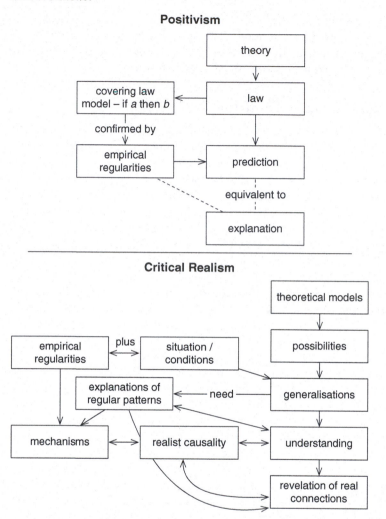

Figure 8.1 Comparative mapping of prediction, explanation, and understanding in positivism and critical realism.

that is comprised of the distinct mechanisms that cause real phenomena. The empirically observable patterns that we take note of in the world provide a starting point, and become the materials that inform research questions (Manicas, 2006). In the process of directing inquiry, generalizations observed do not *equal* explanation, but *require* explanation, and by way of explanation we achieve better understanding of the way real phenomena actually work. Explanation is consequently *facilitative* in nature. Various explanations (or possibilities) are expressed by way of theoretically informed models, which are selective representations of reality.

CRITICAL REALISM: HISTORICAL CONTEXT

Early critical realists explicitly pushed against "the shadow cast by the great scientific thought of the past" (Bhaskar, 1975, p. 7) in an effort to provide an alternative to positivist approaches to inquiry. More recently, critical realism has been characterized as a functional middle ground between positivist and constructivist or relativistic paradigms (Egbo, 2005), likely because adherence to critical realist methodology allows a *both-and* approach to inquiry that runs contrary to the normative binaries evident in many other methodological positions. Responses to established methodologies—positivism, for example—typically occur in a pendulum-like swing toward other extremes (Danermark et al., 2002), and because critical realism does not mark such an extreme it can be construed as occupying an intermediate position between paradigms. Critical realism is often erroneously situated as a kind of compromise between philosophical orientations that, when roughly placed along a continuum, reflect what have historically been viewed as opposite and incommensurable paradigms. However, none of these views adequately reflect the ontological underpinnings of critical realism, and I will demonstrate that while a critical realist approach includes insights that are also present in research orientations located on either end of the paradigmatic continuum, it is not in fact a middle ground but a "distinct alternative" (Danermark et al., 2002, p. 2). Such a demonstration is best begun by outlining the tenet of realism that most informs a critical realist's perspective.

REALISM

The term *realism* has been used in philosophy for hundreds of years, but has also assumed a wide variety of meanings (Searle, 1995). Theorists in recent decades have referred to classical realism, pragmatic realism, deep realism, methodological realism, subtle realism, modal realism, ethical realism, and intentional realism, among others. This proliferation of realist approaches leaves many scholars wondering what it is—exactly—that sets a critical realist methodological perspective apart. The answer is not easily located within realist discourses, so I will begin with a description of the facet of realism that is most typically considered to represent realist perspectives. I will then distinguish critical realism as a related but distinct methodological perspective.

Foundational to realism is an ontological belief that what is real in the world exists independently of observers (Gutek, 2009; Hammersley, 1992; Kivinen & Piiroinen, 2004). Physical and social realities, then, express themselves, persist, and function regardless of our perceptions of them; the real world does not depend on whether or not we see it, or what we think about it. This subscription to a person-independent reality is tempered by the varying degrees of belief in contextual influence and social construction that are evident in realist philosophies, which represent a number of ways of understanding human *perception* of reality. Nevertheless, realists essentially believe that a real world exists independently of language, human thought, and belief (Searle, 1995).

DISTINGUISHING FEATURES OF CRITICAL REALISM

The realist's person-independent reality is frequently criticized, particularly within the realm of social science, and it can be difficult to imagine how a realist view might work when inquiring into social phenomena. Critical realist philosophers, in response to confusion about realist applications, have invested in a painstaking effort to thoroughly align critical realism with social science research. Such alignment is illustrated in the following aspects of critical realism that distinguish the methodology from other types of realism: (a) an alternative conception of objectivity; (b) an acknowledgement that social realities are constructed, but that they are also independently real and consequently knowable; and (c) a belief in a layered reality with *deep structures* that include largely unobservable causal or generative mechanisms.

Critical Realist Objectivity

The critical realist's ontological position is routinely questioned with respect to the idea that social phenomena have a person-independent reality. When thinking about natural objects such as trees or mountains, and even man-made objects like tables and computers, it is generally reasonable for someone to acknowledge the possibility that those objects exist even when they are beyond our immediate view. However, such acknowledgement becomes more problematic in consideration of social phenomena. How can things like values, motivation, marriages, money, power, conflict, and pain exist outside of human interaction? While a thorough response to this question is beyond the scope of this chapter, it will suffice for now to suggest that such social phenomena can be simultaneously socially constructed *and* objectively real.

Searle (1995) offered one of the most comprehensive explanations of the reasons why we can consider social phenomena as independently real, and much of it has to do with a critical realist's conception of *objectivity*. Realist objectivity here departs from conventional use of the word, and therefore does not refer to the objectification of social phenomena, nor to a belief that it is possible to observe any kind of absolute truth (Searle, 1995). Objectivity also departs from traditional positivist and post-positivist reference to impartiality or emotional detachment (Kirk & Miller, 1986). In these previous (and still prevalent) uses of the word, objectivity reflects an epistemic judgement of worth (Searle, 1995), or an *opinion* about the characteristic nature of something. Alternatively, critical realists refer to objectivity in an ontological sense, where the word simply implies *existence*. Social phenomena, while they may be constructed, *must be constructed of something*; something real exists *a priori* of the construction, and is also expressed in real material practices (Danermark et al., 2002; Searle, 1995). Therefore, even a socially constructed reality requires "an ontologically objective reality out of which it is constructed" (Searle, 1995, p. 191). Examples can be noted at individual and social levels. Love between two people, for example, is a socially constructed phenomenon, but it is *constructed out of* the proximity, activities, and interactions between those people. Love is further expressed in other material practices—holding hands, living together, having a family, and so on—that are more readily identifiable as ontologically real or existing despite what others think of them. The precursors and mechanisms inherent in love are objectively real. They exist regardless of our experience or observation of them, and they are expressed in a way that is potentially knowable by others. Consequently it is possible for researchers to achieve an incrementally more precise understanding of such a phenomenon.

Understanding Through Causal Mechanisms and Stratified Reality

Further to the critical realist's understanding of objectivity, the directives of common sense and a long history of scientific inquiry suggest there is a *deep structure* to both physical and social phenomena; this deep structure is constituted by a layered or stratified reality. The image of a layered reality "allows an immediate distinction to be drawn between surface [expression of] phenomena and what may... lie beneath that surface. The impetus is to go deeper—to identify causal mechanisms which lie beneath the surface of what we observe or experience" (McGrath, 2006, p. 219). Critical realists most commonly refer to three distinct strata or layers of reality: (a) *the empirical*, or aspects of reality that are largely observable and that may be directly or indirectly experienced; (b) *the actual*, or features of reality, events, or activities that actually occur but may not be detected; and (c) *the real*, or mechanisms and/or deep structures that can and do generate phenomena (see Figure 8.2 below; Bhaskar, 1975; McEvoy & Richards, 2006; Wuisman, 2005). It is important to emphasize that critical realists, while concerned with layers of reality, do not suggest that the empirical, actual, and real are mutually exclusive categories. They are overlapping, mutually influential, iterative domains that pertain to the reality of any given phenomenon (Wuisman, 2005). Understanding is predicated by discovery and description of deeper strata (Bhaskar, 1975), where the ultimate goal is to understand the strata of reality where generative mechanisms are found.

The layering of reality is a foundational point of departure and hallmark for critical realists, and assumptions regarding stratification often drive critical realist oriented research agendas (Bhaskar, 1975, 1998; Danermark et al.,

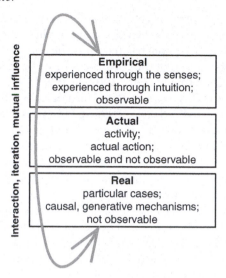

Figure 8.2   Levels or strata of critical realist reality.

2002; McEvoy & Richards, 2006; Wuisman, 2005). Despite the prevalence of deductive inquiry and a historically steadfast refusal to acknowledge causality, natural science research has uncovered stratified realities for centuries, and examples of incremental discovery of strata abound. Human beings, for example, are construed as biological wholes; however, incremental inquiry revealed that humans are made up of internal systems (endocrine, digestive, neurological, etc.), and that these systems in turn are comprised of tissues and cells. Given the critical realist assumption that social phenomena are independently real, it is reasonable to assume that cumulative discovery and description from stratum to stratum also yields greater understanding in the social sciences (Bhaskar, 1975).

Causal mechanisms. Causal mechanisms are features of any given phenomenon that are responsible for producing an outcome, or expression of, that phenomenon (Danermark et al., 2002). Mechanisms are consequently imbued with *power*: the power to make something happen, produce a result, generate a particular circumstance, enable an activity, or determine an outcome. The things that make a mechanism powerful, however, are not necessarily or automatically realized. Generative mechanisms operate only when they are catalyzed by particular kinds of triggers, influenced in turn by the particular context or circumstance. It is also important to note that causal mechanisms do not work in isolation. Many mechanisms may influence, compound, or contradict one another (Danermark et al., 2002). Figure 8.3 illustrates the relationship between conditions, triggers, mechanisms, and outcomes, and indicates the levels of reality that correspond to each. A trigger arises from a particular context to catalyze a mechanism. Active mechanisms interact with one another to generate activities that

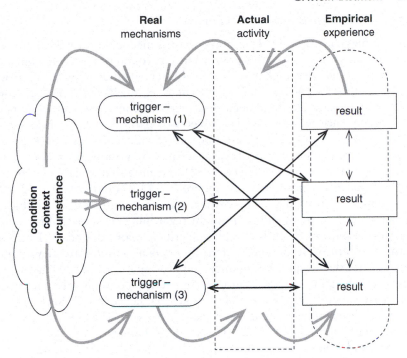

Figure 8.3 The relationship between conditions, triggers, mechanisms, activity, and experience in critical realist reality.

influence results; the results together comprise the empirical, observable expression or experience of a phenomenon. Note that any one mechanism can influence a number of results, and that results, activity, and mechanisms are recursive, meaning that they influence or *feed* one another. Further, results are holistically and empirically experienced, meaning that they are not perceived in a compartmentalized manner.

These facets of causal mechanisms may be best understood through use of an illustrative example. This example is still the subject of debate, and as such it is not intended to be scientifically exact; in any case, it does demonstrate the nature of causality by way of a commonly perceived physical phenomenon. Electricity may be viewed as a causal mechanism in terms of its function within meteorological systems—electricity in weather systems is commonly cited as the *cause* of lightning (Betz, Schumann, & Laoche, 2009). In order to exert causal influence, electricity must be *triggered* by collisions between liquid and ice particles. Further still, the appropriate *conditions* must be in place, conditions that might be characterized by particular ambient temperatures, up and down drafts of air, the rate at which drops of water/flakes of snow are falling, the amount of dust in the clouds, and so on. The triggered mechanism results in the unseen *activity* of an electric field, and results in the observable *empirical experience* of a lightning bolt.

Causal Mechanisms in Social Science

The examples I have provided pertaining to stratified reality and the nature of causal mechanisms have, to this point, centred around physical phenomena. It is important now to emphasize that the objects of study in natural science differ from those in social science (Danermark et al., 2002; Manicas, 2006; Searle, 1995). Natural phenomena exist without consciousness, awareness of, or dependence on humans. The objects of natural science, then, while socially perceived and defined, are naturally produced (Danermark et al., 2002). In contrast, the objects of social science are both dependent on people *and* perceived by people (Sayer, 1992), meaning that social phenomena are "both socially defined and *socially produced*" (Danermark et al., 2002, p. 31, emphasis in original). This critical difference with respect to objects of study requires a slight shift in thought regarding causal mechanisms and their correspondence to levels of reality in critical realist discourse. The people that are ultimately the focus of study in social inquiry are changeable and adaptive; they respond to inquiry and are capable of producing, maintaining, or changing social structures. People are consequently conceived of as possessing *agency*, or the ability to act (Manicas, 2006). Such agency requires a different view of the connection between levels of reality, the expression of social phenomena, and causal mechanisms.

Agents and structures. Stratified reality in the social world is complex and peopled: it is comprised of individuals, or *agents*, whose activity is informed by resources, constraints, and causal mechanisms. Giddens (1984) labelled the levels of social reality as (a) systems, (b) structures, and (c) structuration (see Figure 8.4 for an illustration of these labels as they pertain to levels of critical realist reality). The critical realist's meanings of these labels depart from conventional interpretation, so it is important to be clear with respect to what systems, structures, and structuration are taken to mean.

Systems are the observable aspects of society, meaning that in systems we can see relationships, actions, and regular practices (Manicas, 2006). Systems are groups of such activity that are interconnected and perceived as loosely bounded. While the activity in systems is not integrated, it is often thought of as being so. Practical examples of the activity observable by way of social systems include parenting, working, supervising, and lawmaking (Manicas, 2006). Examples of social systems are myriad, and might include families, schools, governments, countries, and even people in and of themselves; it is important here to remember that systems are not mutually exclusive, and that they overlap, interact with, and influence one another. *Structures* are abstract properties that inform, enable, constrain, facilitate and/or limit activity and expression of social phenomena. Structures correspond to the *activity* level of critical realist reality. The activity actualized by structures is that of *bridging*. Although structures are abstract in the sense that they cannot be seen, they can be thought of as bridges (or links) between the observable expression of an activity and its mechanisms. A metaphorical illustration may help clarify this point. A literal, physical bridge provides

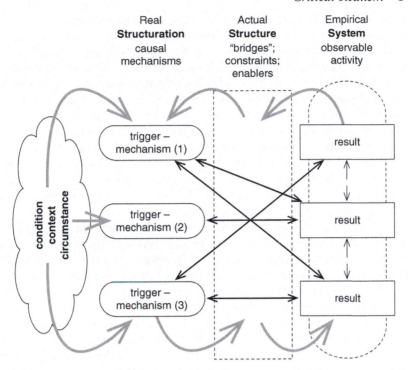

Figure 8.4   Systems, structures, and structuration in critical realist social reality.

options: a person may cross the bridge, perch on it, go around it, or ignore it all together; because the bridge is available does not mean a person must cross it, and a bridge may be crossed from either direction. In this sense, *structures are options* that create meaning in systems (Manicas, 2006), and while they do not determine activity, they do enable, facilitate, limit, or constrain it. *Structuration* refers to the causal mechanisms of social reality. Here mechanisms are viewed in much the same way as described previously: They are features of any given phenomenon that are responsible for producing an outcome, or expression of, that phenomenon. In the social world, however, mechanisms take very different form than in the natural world; social mechanisms are located within people, and can include reasons, motives, dispositions, powers, and capacities (Manicas, 2006).

Contingency in Open Systems

The complex interaction between systems, structures, and structuration is further influenced by contingency in the social world. Here an integrated consideration is necessary. The nature of a causal mechanism has already been noted: It is "that which can cause something in the world to happen" (Danermark et al., 2002, p. 55). There is an internal, necessary connection between objects or phenomena and their mechanisms, as mechanisms make a phenomenon uniquely what it is. However, mechanisms are not always active, and the relationship between mechanisms and outcomes is not obligatory; here enters the notion of *contingency*. The result of mechanistic activity is not a matter of design. The context—conditions, circumstances, and environment—plays a significant role in influencing whether or not a mechanism will operate and what the resulting effect will look like (Danermark et al., 2002). Contingency is illustrated by way of several examples in Table 8.1 below. The changeable nature of contingency renders predictability impossible, in both natural and social science inquiry. However, upon closer inspection we begin to see that, given an understanding of causal mechanisms we can "speculate about the potential consequences of social phenomena given certain conditions" (Newton, Burgess, & Burns, 2010, p. 580).

A predominant claim generated by natural science inquiry is that of predictability. Assessment of regularities and consistencies, generally formulated based on observation of the aspects of phenomena that are empirically notable, enables scientists to predict how and when natural phenomena will occur. However, since the inquiry that generates regularities in activity is generally conducted within *closed systems*, such predictability is often not possible in the real world. A closed system is one characterized by constancy. Conditions that enable isolation of causal mechanisms and eliminate the possibility of change or variation are necessary in order to create a closed system. Such manipulation of conditions is generally called an *experiment*, and is traditionally used in natural science inquiry. Experimentation is

Table 8.1   Simple illustrative examples of contingency at work.

Object	Mechanism	Trigger	Mediated By (circumstance)	Potential Result(s)
person	immune system	virus	amount of sleep, nutrition, stress, immunization	death, major illness, minor illness, no illness
camera	flash	trigger button pressed	lens cap on or off, distance from subject, movement of subject, light levels	no photo, poor photo, good photo
stove	stovetop element	switch turned on	level of heat, type of pan, attention of cook, type of food in pan	stove fire, burned food, cooked food, undercooked food

possible in the natural sciences partly because of the nature of the objects under study; these are objects that exist independently and regardless of human interaction or activity (Danermark et al., 2002). In other words, natural phenomena are not affected by inquiry—they do not respond to social manipulation and continue to exist in their real state regardless of our knowledge of them. The cellular activity in muscle tissue, for example, does not discern observation and continues to behave as it naturally does despite its being observed. It is possible, then, to situate most natural phenomena within the experimental conditions of closed systems, which in turn allows for the kind of observation necessary to generate predictions.

While it is possible to create experimental conditions within which to observe many natural phenomena, it is not possible to do so with social phenomena (Danermark et al., 2002). The reason for this is that "studying people is not the same as studying 'things'" (Manicas, 2006, p. 43). First, people exhibit consciousness (Danermark et al., 2002; Manicas, 2006), which means, as we have already noted, that they are changeable, adaptive, developmental, and responsive. When people are studied, they know they are being studied; this alone precludes the manipulation of people within closed experimental systems, and informs ethical guidelines that prohibit us from doing so. Second, people are independently real, but we interact and are necessarily perceived and represented in a social manner (Manicas, 2006). Humans are not moveable from their social context. What this ultimately means is that we cannot negate the influence of contingency because all social research takes place within changeable open social systems. Consideration of contingency is, then, one of the factors that drives the necessity for hermeneutic interpretation in social science inquiry.

Hermeneutics

Understanding of natural phenomena within natural sciences involves a *single hermeneutic*, meaning that natural science investigations require just a single, unidirectional cycle of interpretation. Interpretation of natural phenomena is one-sided (Danermark et al., 2002), so the phenomena will continue to exist as they are regardless of a researcher's inquiry. Natural phenomena, including physical man-made objects like chairs and desks, do not display consciousness and are unresponsive to our interpretations; the earth would be round even if we thought it flat, and cells would exist in bodies even if we thought them comprised solely of water. The objects of natural science then, while certainly influenced and modified by human behaviour, "exist and work independently of what meaning and significance we assign to them" (Danermark et al., 2002, p. 34), and they consequently remain unaltered by the kinds of knowledge we create about them through the interpretation of inquiry.

In contrast to the natural world, investigation of social phenomena requires a *double hermeneutic*. Interpretation in the social sciences is multi-sided and reflexive (Ellingson, 2009), and the researcher's job is to interpret interpretations. This notion is driven by the situated-ness of social under-standing, where the researcher's perceptions and the perceptions of those being studied are inseparable and mutually influential (Danermark et al., 2002). Further, meaning is assigned to social phenomena at multiple levels, so there should be a reflexive interplay in consideration of interpretations that are meaningful subjectively to individuals who experience a phenom-enon, conceptually to groups of people who express the phenomenon, and theoretically to scholars or "communicators" (Giddens, 1984, p. 285) who engage in descriptive activity with respect to the phenomenon.

In the context of a critical realist's ontological holism, the most significant epistemological considerations are then tied to the process of hermeneutics. The process of iterative interpretation begins with the identification of a phenomenon of interest and the generation of questions about that phenom-enon (Danermark et al., 2002). The idea of a double hermeneutic is meant to provide awareness that knowledge produced is not representative of the *truth* regarding any phenomenon, but is representative of the phenomenon's reality from one perspective. Use of a double hermeneutic in social science research and practice means that there is a persistently critical dimension to social inquiry and knowledge production (Danermark et al., 2002).

METHOD: A CRITICAL REALIST'S PERSPECTIVE

The ontological unity presented here precludes any need for a prescribed *method* of critical realism. A critical realist makes only an ontological claim: that phenomena exist independently. There are no inherent epistemologi-cal prescriptions. Consequently, those who make claims that particular research methods are better suited to critical realist inquiry than others are mistaken because inquiry as part of this methodology is driven solely by the phenomenon of interest. The typical and traditional binaries between quan-titative and qualitative forms of inquiry are irrelevant, as it is the researcher's imperative to determine which strategies will best yield increasingly accurate representations of the phenomenon at hand.

It is this point at which accusations of relativism are usually made with respect to those aiming to criticize a critical realist's methodology. The asser-tion, however, that inquiry be driven by the phenomenon at hand does not mean *anything goes*. A critical realist's research agenda is ideally crafted around use of multiple methods of data collection, engagement in multiple forms of reasoning, and application of a double hermeneutic of interpre-tation; what emerges from inquiry are numerous representations of the phenomenon that, when compared and integrated with one another, reveal patterns, consistencies, and differences that push researchers incrementally closer to understanding the reality of the phenomenon. There is nothing relativistic about this; in fact, such comprehensive research agendas are demonstrably rigorous and yield an authenticity of understanding that is unparalleled. However, some effort must be maintained to ensure the critical capacity of critical realist inquiry, and to ensure clarity and transparency with respect to research methods.

Discussion of critical realist methods is typically perceived as somewhat mysterious. This is because there are no ready prescriptions to offer with respect to methods of data collection and analysis, a situation that is infuriating to some. It is most important for a critical realist researcher to maintain a level of openness to utilising whichever methods and strategies are most appropriate for the purpose of generating increased understanding of the phenomenon she is interested in. I must emphasize again that this is not a relativistic process, but one driven by careful consideration of the ways in which a variety of methods might generate knowledge regarding the reality of any given phenomenon. This means that one must be equally amenable to statistical analysis of empirical information as they are to conducting and analysing narrative interviews. It is crucial to remember that all data collected reflects *representations* of reality (Newton et al., 2010), and as a consequence both reflective analysis and comparative analysis of trends across methods of inquiry are extremely important (Manicas, 2006). Such a range of possibility is especially useful in the domain of educational administration, where quantitative and qualitative attempts to understand educational realities have traditionally occurred in diametric opposition to one another.

CRITICAL REALISM IN EDUCATIONAL ADMINISTRATION

Scholars have struggled over the past century to theorize and articulate paradigms of inquiry that are suitable for the objects of social research. Burrell and Morgan (1979) attempted to map existing paradigms in sociological and organizational theory, in what they considered a comprehensive view of all the available possibilities. They indicated that there are four distinct paradigms of inquiry, and that these are readily mapped according to their placement along two descriptive axes: the horizontal axis describes the nature of social science along a subjective/objective continuum, and the vertical axis describes the nature of society along a regulated/change-oriented continuum (Ortenbläd, 2002). The paradigms arising from Burrell and Morgan's (1979) framework are: (a) the *functionalist* paradigm, characterized by objectivity and regulation; (b) the *interpretive* paradigm, indicated by subjectivity and regulation; (c) the *radical structuralist* paradigm, which is objective and change-oriented; and (d) the *radical humanist* paradigm, demonstrated by alignment to subjectivity and continuous change. Furthermore, Burrell and Morgan (1979) suggested that an individual's positioning within any particular paradigm of inquiry is absolute, indicating, for example, that one cannot conduct research simultaneously from both functionalist and interpretivist orientations. Burrell and Morgan's (1979) extremely influential effort has been useful to those involved in the study of educational administration for two reasons: It allows scholars to track the persistent and evolving influence of logical positivism in our field, and it presents an opportunity for framing and illustrating critical realism as a distinct and unifying paradigm suitable for administrative research.

Even a brief comparative analysis reveals that the majority of theoretical positions advanced throughout the short history of educational administration fall within Burrell and Morgan's (1979) *functionalist* domain, which is characterized by objectivity and order. For example, educational administration has been considered as a practical science (Allison, 1989), as part of the theory movement (Culbertson, 1981), and as a practice occurring within the natural science confines of deductive reasoning (Oplatka, 2009). Upon closer inspection, it is most clear how Burrell and Morgan's (1979) functionalist domain exhibits the characteristics of logical positivism and consequently illustrates the profound influence positivism has exerted within research agendas in educational administration.

Scholars such as Greenfield (1986), Willower (1979), Sackney and Mitchell (2002) and others have done much to introduce phenomenological, constructivist, and postmodern approaches to administrative inquiry. These approaches have positively affected the research emerging from educational administration, and they have pressed scholars to reconsider what constitutes meaningful inquiry and discourse. However, these emerging paradigms also represent theoretical positioning that is diametrically opposed to the tenets of positivism, and the ensuing debate has resulted in fracture, entrenchment, and perceived disarray within educational administration (Oplatka, 2009). The current methodological debate is construed as highly problematic by some, but it also illustrates how a critical realist's research orientation could best utilized in educational administration.

Critical realism does not fit within Burrell and Morgan's (1979) framework. Their framework of paradigms pre-supposes particular kinds of epistemologies and prescriptions about how knowledge is best created. Critical realism, in contrast, is founded on ontological holism and consequently requires no commitment to any particular epistemological stance. This holism is perhaps best illustrated through comparison of the *ontological beginnings* of the paradigms that have been most frequently discussed here. Positivists take the empirically observable aspects of social reality as their ontological baseline. Constructivists, in diametric opposition to positivism, take the construction of social reality as their ontological starting point. Critical realism, in a distinct point of difference, takes independent reality and the layering of social reality as its ontological beginning (Wuisman, 2005). There are, then, no claims about the *most useful* methods or traditions of inquiry, and research instead becomes focused on identifying a phenomenon of interest, finding the most suitable methods for inquiry, and engaging in critical consideration and hermeneutic interpretation. Critical realism "involves a switch from epistemology to ontology, and within ontology a switch from events to mechanisms" (Danermark et al., 2002, p. 5). Such a switch marks a profoundly different way of viewing the world and the research that follows.

Critical realism is not, then, a *middle ground*, but represents an altogether different ontological commitment. As such, critical realism generates hope for a reconciliation of epistemological perspectives and methods within educational administration. It is safe within the realm of critical realism to acknowledge that multiple conceptual frameworks, methods, and modes of interpretation may be utilized to investigate any particular social phenomenon. At the outset those differences may appear problematic, but in context of a critical realist's methodology they are not incommensurable as often thought elsewhere. Use of a critical realist's orientation in administrative inquiry allows researchers, while *doing their own thing*, to engage in productive dialogue and to identify and utilize patterns noted across multiple methods of data collection and analysis.

A side note must be made here in mention of the various ways critical realism is interpreted within discourses of educational administration. Many scholars appear to take the traditional social science affiliation toward dualistic binaries to heart, utilising those binaries to characterize critical realism as something much different than what has been outlined here. In my experience, the language of critical realism, for example, has often been construed as indicating alignment between critical realist and positivist paradigms, when positivism is in fact the orientation that realists most often take issue with. Alternatively, critical realism has also been interpreted as a research paradigm most concerned with phenomenological consideration and subsequent emancipatory action (Egbo, 2005), an interpretation that swings to the opposite end of the positivist-postmodern continuum. It is crucial to reiterate, then, that critical realist methodology makes room for an account of and reflection on both empirical evidence and real-life experience, and acknowledges that both make a distinct and valuable contribution to educational research. However, it must also be emphasized that the philosophical goal of critical realism is not regulation *or* transformation. *Critical realism merely offers a way of talking about what is, and for structuring ways at getting at that reality with the methodological strategies that are most appropriate given the context and phenomenon at hand.* While critical realists do not make any claim to value-neutrality, there is no implicit moral imperative inherent in the critical realist's orientation.

The focus on ontological unity and an intense theoretical underpinning also lends a distinct practical utility to critical realism in educational administration. While this may seem counterintuitive at first, consider what the results of critical realist inquiry and analysis look like. If a research agenda were conducted in alignment with the principles of critical realism, with methods chosen in a deliberate manner to most effectively elicit information and understanding about a given phenomenon, the results would be surprisingly simple. The researcher is left with a descriptive *picture* of observable realities, a representative model of the mechanisms that make a phenomenon unique, and some particular notions about the ways in which context influences the operation of mechanisms. This all translates in colloquial terms to *real-world understanding*, enabling utility for both theorists and practitioners alike.

The field of educational administration has long been characterized by what has been dubbed a theory/practice gap—an inability or reluctance to apply theory in practice (Begley, 1996; Newton et al., 2010). Clearly such disconnect is problematic because of the applied nature of administration; this is a field most concerned with the social planning and facilitation inherent in educational practice. The critical realist's research agenda contributes to both an understanding of, and reduction in, the theory/practice gap. The rigorous theoretical underpinning of critical realism allows for the opportunity to *engage theory* (Newton et al., 2010), and practical relevance is ensured because we are aware of how to best apply the knowledge of mechanisms given certain conditions. A critical realist's methodology, then, is ideally suited to the demands of inquiry in educational administration.

CONCLUSION

Critical realism is a methodological orientation that is well suited to make a significant contribution to the field of educational administration. A critical realist's methodology is distinguished by the following characteristics: an understanding that physical and social realities exist independently of human perception; a re-defined conception of objectivity and a corresponding acknowledgement that social realities are constructed, but that they are also independently real and consequently knowable; and a belief in a layered reality with *deep structures* that include largely unobservable causal mechanisms. Greater understanding and explanation of phenomena is driven by meaningful inquiry into observable aspects of phenomena and their underlying causal properties, tempered by an acknowledgment of context and conditions. Consequently, there is no prescribed method within critical realism, and research is driven by a selection of methodological approaches that best suit the phenomenon under study. Critical realism is indeed theoretically oriented, but it also yields simple results that are easily applied in a pragmatic manner within administrative practice, making this methodology ideally suited to informing inquiry in educational administration.

REFERENCES

Allison, D. (1989). *Toward the fifth age: The continuing evolution of academic educational administration*. Paper presented at the Annual Meeting of the American Educational Research Association, San Francisco, CA. Retrieved from http://eric.ed.gov/PDFS/ED306662.pdf

Begley, P. T. (1996). Cognitive perspectives on values in administration: A quest for coherence and relevance. *Educational Administration Quarterly, 32*(3), 403–426. doi:10.1177/0013161X96032003006

Betz, H. D., Schumann, U., & Laroche, P. (Eds). (2009). *Lightning: Principles, instruments and applications.* Springer. Retrieved from http://www.springerlink.com/content/p76564/#section=142503&page=4&locus=26

Bhaskar, R. (1975). *A realist theory of science.* Leeds, UK: Leeds Books.

Bhaskar, R. (1998). *The possibility of naturalism* (3rd ed). London: Routledge.

Burrell, G., & Morgan, G. (1979). *Sociological paradigms and organisational analysis.* London: Heinemann.

Culbertson, J.A. (1981). Antecedents of the theory movement. *Educational Administration Quarterly, 17*(1), 25–47. doi:10.1177/0013161X8101700103

Danermark, B., Ekström, M., Jakobsen, L., & Karlsson, J. (2002). *Explaining society: Critical realism in the social sciences.* London: Routledge.

Egbo, B. (2005). Emergent paradigm: Critical realism and transformative research in educational administration. *McGill Journal of Education, 40*(2), 267–284. Retrieved from http://mje.mcgill.ca/article/viewFile/568/457 .

Ellingson, L. L. (2009). *Engaging crystallization in qualitative research.* Thousand Oaks, CA: Sage.

Giddens, A. (1984). *The constitution of society.* Berkeley, CA: University of California Press.

Greenfield, T. B. (1986). The decline and fall of science in educational administration. *Interchange, 17*(2), 57–80. doi:10.1007/BF01807469

Gutek, G. L. (2009). Realism and education. In G. L. Gutek (Ed.), *New perspectives on philosophy and education* (pp. 40–72). Upper Saddle River, NJ: Pearson Education.

Hammersley, M. (1992). *What's wrong with ethnography?* London: Routledge.

Kirk, J., & Miller, M. L. (1986). *Reliability and validity in qualitative research.* Newbury Park, CA: Sage.

Kivinen, O., & Piiroinen, T. (2004). The relevance of ontological commitments in social sciences: Realist and pragmatist viewpoints. *Journal for the Theory of Social Behaviour, 34*(3), 231–248. doi:10.1111/j.0021–8308.2004.00246.x

Manicas, P. (2006). *A realist philosophy of social science.* Cambridge, UK: Cambridge University Press.

McEvoy, P., & Richards, D. (2006). A critical realist rationale for using a combination of quantitative and qualitative methods. *Journal of Research in Nursing, 11*(1), 66–78. doi:10.1177/1744987106060192

McGrath, A. E. (2006). *A scientific theology: Reality.* London: T&T Clark.

Newton, P., Burgess, D., & Burns, D. P. (2010). Models in educational administration: Revisiting Willower's 'theoretically oriented' critique. *Educational Management, Administration and Leadership, 38*(5), 578–590. doi:10.1177/1741143210373740

Olsen, W., & Morgan, J. (2005). A critical epistemology of analytical statistics: Addressing the sceptical realist. *Journal for the Theory of Social Behaviour, 35*(3), 255–284. doi:10.1111/j.1468–5914.2005.00279.x

Oplatka, I. (2009). The field of educational administration: A historical overview of scholarly attempts to recognize epistemological identities, meanings and boundaries from the 1960s onwards. *Journal of Educational Administration, 47*(1), 8–35. doi:10.1108/09578230910928061

Örtenblad, A. (2002). Organizational learning: A radical perspective. *International Journal of Management Reviews, 4*(1), 87–100. doi: 10.1111/1468-2370.00078

Sackney, L., & Mitchell, C. (2002). Postmodern expressions of educational leadership. In K. Leithwood, & P. Hallinger (Eds.), *Second international handbook of educational leadership and administration* (pp. 881–913). London: Kluwer Academic.

Sayer, A. (1992). *Method in social science: A realist approach* (2nd ed.). London: Routledge.

Searle, J. R. (1995). *The construction of social reality*. New York: Free Press.

Willower, D. J. (1979). Ideology and science in organization theory. *Educational Administration Quarterly, 15*(3), 20–42. doi:10.1177/0013131X7901500304

Wuisman, J. J. J. M. (2005). The logic of scientific discovery in critical realist social scientific research. *Journal of Critical Realism, 4*(2), 366–394. Retrieved from http://www.marjee.org/pdfs/Wuisman_2005.pdf

9 Cognition and Administrative Practices in Education

Augusto Riveros

Naturalistic perspectives on educational administration have turned to the cognitive sciences in order to understand some organisational practices and processes such as decision making, leadership, and professional development, among others. In this chapter, I explore further the contributions of classic and contemporary perspectives on distributed and situated cognition to the study of educational administration. The cognitive sciences have revolutionised the study human thought and action; however, the contribution of the cognitive sciences to the epistemology of educational administration is still relatively unexplored. Herein, I summarise the recent scholarship that explores the connections between the cognitive sciences and educational administration. This exploration suggests new avenues for research and offers new insights regarding the nature and object of educational administration. I begin by illustrating how the researchers in organisational theory introduced models of cognitive processing in order to explain administrative practices in organisational settings. The theories derived from these studies (e.g., Senge, 2000) have exercised wide influence in the scholarship on the administration of educational organisations (Evers & Lakomski, 2000; Fullan, 2007; Lakomski, 2005). These theories have portrayed schools as systems that process information, and they offer a group-level analysis of school functioning.

ORGANISATIONS AS INFORMATION PROCESSING SYSTEMS

Spender (1998) noted that organisational theorists have been interested in cognition from the very beginning of organisational studies when they noticed that cognitive processes like decision making, understanding, and interpretation had an impact in the functioning of organisations. However, the early theorists from the 1920s to the 1950s lacked the theoretical tools to explore cognition in depth.

Herbert Simon's (1957, 1958, 1969, 1989; Vera & Simon, 1993) work on group rationality and group cognition (Haugeland, 1993) inspired a number of studies on cognition in organisations during the 1960s, 1970s, and 1980s (Feuer, 2006). These studies aimed to explain decision making, adaptation, and change in organisations and provided an entry point for researchers interested in administrative practices in education. Simon (1957) aimed to explain organisational functioning using the language of information processing theories. The operating assumption was the *computational theory of mind* (Horst, 2009), consisting in the claim that mental states involve symbolic representations (Baum & Rowley, 2002). In this model, organisations are seen as information processing systems that manipulate symbolically encoded information through computational procedures (Fiol, 2002). Two key assumptions supported this model. First, the idea that individuals represent the environment through internal mental models that characterise stimuli from the environment in a certain way, and second, the assumption that decision making in organisations is a rational process—organisations are in the business of searching, selecting, and processing information in order to make the best possible decisions based on the limited alternatives or choices available (Cyert & March, 1963; March & Simon, 1958). The system's computations are embedded routines that store and enact information. According to this view, the main task for any given organisation is to efficiently achieve its goals by searching and processing relevant information. For these authors, efficiency is important because resources are usually limited and procedures consume resources; thus, the less processing, the fewer resources consumed. Aguilar (1967), Galbraith (1973), and Milliken (1990), among others (Daft & Weick, 1984; Levinthal & March, 1993; Sitkin, 2001), have suggested that organisations develop different strategies to *scan* the environment for information. March used the notion of *organisational intelligence* (March, 2001) to indicate that organisations make decisions in conditions of uncertainty. Lant (2002) indicated that the problems of uncertainty and ambiguity are a matter of *interpretation*, because preferences, desires, and concepts are not necessarily defined homogenously within the organisation, which opens the door for individuals to have different understandings of their organisational reality.

The Group Mind Hypothesis

There is an obvious sense in which cognition is present in organisations: Organisations are inhabited by individuals who have cognitive properties of their own; if individuals are present in organisations, then cognition is present in organisations. However, some authors in the field of organisational theory like Greeno and Moore (1993), Hutchins (1990), Lant and Shapira (2001), Lakomski (2005), March (2001), Walsh (1995), and Weick (1979) had a more radical understanding of the nature of cognitive properties in organisations. They argued that cognitive properties in organisations are instantiated in virtue of the group dynamics of organisations

(Ocasio, 2001). These authors endorsed the idea that organisations instantiate *group minds*.

There are two different ways to understand the group mind hypothesis (Wilson, 2004). One is through a *literalist* reading that suggests that groups have minds in the same way individuals have minds. For instance, ant colonies (Wheeler, 1911, 1923, 1928) and human social groups (Le Bon, 1895/1968) have been studied as single entities that literally have cognitive properties of their own; however, the cognitive properties instantiated by these groups may not be as complex as those instantiated by individuals. Most studies in the field of group cognition focus on specific mental properties, like memory (Wegner, 1986) or decision making (Hutchins, 1990, 1991, 1995).

Another way to understand the group mind hypothesis is to see group minds as examples of the *cognitive metaphor*—namely, individual cognitive traits can be used to explain groups' behaviour, allowing researchers to treat groups *as if* they had a psychology of their own. In this case, the group mind hypothesis is used as a methodological tool to understand the behaviour of groups. Weick and Roberts (1993) used the concept of "collective mind" to argue that some organisational performances can be properly analysed as the product of "heedful interactions" (p. 357). They indicated that "collective mind" does not mean "within-group similarity of attitudes, understanding, or language, nor can it be understood without close attention to communication processes among group members" (p. 358). Similarly, Wegner (1986) and Wegner, Erber, and Raymond (1991) proposed the notion of *transactive memory* to explain how information is distributed among the individuals and is retrieved through the use of language. People in groups enact an integrated and interdependent system that helps them remember information.

The notion of *neural network* has been extrapolated to organisations in order to understand group decision making and information processing. In short, a connectionist network is a computational model that consists of several interconnected units. Information is represented as distributed in the connection patterns within the network, as opposed to residing in individual units. These patterns are created by inhibitory or excitatory stimuli differentiated by their strength (Rumelhart & McClelland, 1986). Sanderlands and Stablein (1987) argued that organisations could be characterised as neural networks, because organisations encode information through interrelated activities in a similar way to how neural networks encode information thorough the interaction of their units.

Along a similar vein, Hutchins (1990, 1991, 1995) has investigated how groups act in a coordinated fashion. Hutchins explained cognition as a distributed property in human groups; however, according to Weick and Roberts (1993), connectionist models constitute a "shaky basis on which to erect a theory of organisational mind" (p. 359). These models are mostly designed to represent the operation of the nervous system, but it is not evident how a connectionist network can account for the complexity of human interactions within organisations.

Cognitive perspectives on organisational functioning are not exempt from criticism. According to Fiol (2002) and Jones (1995) there remains great controversy regarding the appropriate account of cognition in organisations.

> Do influential individuals bring their own schema to the group causing it to become a frame of reference for the group? Do shared schemata emerge that characterize a group mind? Should researchers examine each individual's cognitive responses and treat them as nodes in a network?
>
> (Fiol, 2002, p. 130)

Along the same lines, Spender (1998) argued that the connection between cognitive studies and organisational theory is not evident by itself because the inquiry about *how the mind works* is different from the inquiry about how *organisations work*. In his opinion, cognition is perhaps one among several dimensions to look at when studying organisations—cognitive analyses of organisations must clarify in what sense organisations are *cognitive entities* so researchers can extrapolate individual cognitive schemes to organisations. Spender argued that computational models in general and Simon's model in particular assume that there is only one type of knowledge to be acquired and mapped, namely propositional knowledge. According to Spender, Simon's model remains silent about *procedural knowledge*, also known as *know-how*, or, in Polanyi's (1967) terminology, *tacit knowledge*.

More recently, List and Pettit (2011) argued, "we must think of group agents as relatively autonomous entities—agents in their own right, as it is often said, groups with minds of their own" (pp. 77–78). In their view, there are three features of agency that groups must satisfy: first, an agent has "representational states that depict how things are in the environment" (p. 19). Second, an agent has "motivational states that specify how it requires things to be in the environment" (p. 19), and third, and agent has "the capacity to process its representational and motivational states, leading to intervene suitably in the environment whenever that environment fails to match a motivating specification" (p. 19). In order to support their argument, they adopted a version of the principle of methodological individualism, that is, the idea that social phenomena can only be explained as a result of the action of individual agents (Weber, 1968): "Our theory maintains this realist view of group agents without compromising the individualist claim that no psychologically mysterious forces should be invoked in giving an account of the social world" (List & Pettit, 2011, p. 6). They argued that "the attitudes and actions of a group agent supervene on the contributions of its members" (p. 66) so groups must be treated as agents that offer explanations of social phenomena.

EXPLORING THE COGNITIVE DIMENSIONS OF EDUCATIONAL ADMINISTRATION

Schools differ from other type of organisations given their goals, their practices, their actors, and the kind of interactions between these actors. It is worth noting that the literature that explores administrative practices in education from a cognitive perspective is not extensive. Cognitive studies in the field of education have mostly focused on student learning and instruction, and, beyond a few notable exceptions, researchers have not explored in depth the cognitive dimensions of educational administration.

Weick (1976) argued that educational organisations are *loosely coupled systems*, that is, systems in which the different components loosely interact with each other without compromising the system's identity. This makes the system's operation difficult to predict: "loose coupling also carries connotations of impermanence, dissolvability, and tacitness all of which are potentially crucial properties of the 'glue' that holds organisations together" (p. 3). Alternatively, a tight coupling implies rigidity and high dependence between groups and low capacity for adaptation. In a tightly coupled system, errors propagate easily because the links between groups are too rigid and highly interdependent. In a loosely coupled organisation, groups working independently have the autonomy to deal with systemic irregularities and unexpected situations. Weick did not endorse Simon's idea of organisations as symbol-processing systems. Instead, he used the notion of *enactment* (Varela, Thompson & Rosch, 1991; Weick, 1979) to argue that an organised system plays an active role in creating its own environment. "According to the enactive approach in cognitive science, cognition is grounded on the sense-making activity of autonomous agents—beings that actively generate and sustain themselves, and thereby enact or bring forth their own domains of meaning and value" (Thompson & Stapleton, 2009, p. 1).

To translate the idea of loose coupling into the context of educational organisations, Weick (1976) argued:

> to the extent that two systems either have few variables in common or share weak variables, they are independent of each other. Applied to the educational situation, if the principal-vice-principal-superintendent is regarded as one system and the teacher-classroom-pupil-parent-curriculum as another system, then by Glassman's [1973] argument if we did not find many variables in the teacher's world to be shared in the world of a principal and/or if the variables held in common were unimportant relative to the other variables, then the principal can be regarded as loosely coupled with the teacher.
>
> (p. 3)

Weick indicated that a loosely coupled organisation is better suited to scan and gather information from the environment and has the capacity to innovate because the high levels of specialisation in the system's components produce deeper knowledge about the environment; promoting flexibility and capacity to adapt. Schools vary depending on the population, projects, programmes, and curriculum; however, we still label such structurally dissimilar institutions as *schools*. In Weick's words: "How can such loose assemblages retain sufficient similarity and permanence across time that they can be recognized, labelled, and dealt with? (p. 2). According to Weick, loosely coupled organisations are defined by their *practices* rather than by their formal *structures*.

In a related line of argumentation, Rogoff (2003) argued that people's participation in sociocultural scenarios that are performed, preserved, and transformed through successive generations, bring about the development of new and more elaborate forms of cognition. So as people transform their cognitive structures through the use of cultural artefacts, they simultaneously transform the cultural artefacts that transform their cognitive structures. Rogoff argued that individualistic analyses of human cognitive processes mistakenly focus on the internal processes, assuming that a description of internal causal events suffices for psychological explanation. In her view, human activity is constituted by a number of interrelated aspects, the personal, interpersonal, and cultural-institutional. No aspect can be analysed independently. In these models, learning is a situated process, influenced by the cultural artefacts, the inter-subjective relations, and the sociocultural/ institutional contexts in which the agents are situated. The introduction of the institutional context as one of the determinants of human learning is important for educational administration because it opens the door for the study of administrative practices as contexts for action, decision making, and professional learning.

Lave and Wenger (1991) offered a theory of learning as an activity situated in institutional contexts. They provided a theoretical framework to conceptualise learning as a situated process in the context of *communities of practice*. Lave and Wenger's model substantiates the claim that there is a cognitive dimension to administrative practices in schools. In their study, they used the notion of *legitimate peripheral participation* to explain how participation in communities of practice is essential to the institutionalisation and dissemination of professional knowledge (Wenger, McDermott, & Snyder, 2002). Coburn and Stein (2006) argued that practitioners develop their own learning dynamics in their communities, which, in turn, has an impact in the way policies are enacted in the classroom.

The cognitive sciences have the potential to generate new conceptualisations of leadership, decision making, professional development, policy implementation, and other areas of interest for educational administrators. Evers and Lakomski (1991, 1996, 2000) have advanced a systematic account of an epistemology of educational administration that positions cognition as pivotal in the analysis of educational organisations. In the following section,

I will review Evers and Lakomski's contribution to the epistemology of educational administration

REPRESENTING KNOWLEDGE IN EDUCATIONAL ADMINISTRATION: THE NATURALISTIC COHERENTISM OF EVERS AND LAKOMSKI

Evers and Lakomski (1991, 1996, 2000) discussed the representation of knowledge in educational administration as an attempt to develop an epistemology of educational administration. Their starting point was the coherentist theories of epistemic justification. Coherentism, as a theory of epistemic justification, contains a critique of foundationalist epistemologies. In a foundationalist epistemology, the entire structure of knowledge is ultimately justified by *non-inferential beliefs* or *infallible foundational beliefs*. A classic example of foundationalism is the empiricist claim that all knowledge rests in perception (Russell, 2010). Indeed, if X is the justification of Amy's belief in Y, then Amy must believe in X and she must be justified in believing X, in virtue of some other belief, say, Z, which must be also believed by Amy in order for Amy to justify her belief in X. According to foundationalism, the regress of justifications will end at the point where the subject justifies the whole inferential chain by reference to a non-inferential belief or a set of non-inferential beliefs. Empiricists, like Russell, were not the only ones who held foundationalist views; rationalists, such as Descartes, also maintained that the inferential chain of justifications must end at some point, such as a set of indubitable beliefs that sustain the whole structure of knowledge (*cf.* Rorty, 1979).

Kvanvig (2007) indicated that coherentists have offered two main critiques to foundationalism; first, according to them, it is not clear when the justification chain ends. In other words, the question "why do you believe this?" can always be asked. Second, coherentists question the idea that a limited number of foundational beliefs can support the vast diversity of human knowledge, such as our knowledge about the past, our beliefs about the future, our beliefs about unobservables, and abstract knowledge. Evers and Lakomski (2000) also characterised their coherentism as a reaction against the logical positivism that influenced early conceptualisations of educational administration. Those conceptualisations responded to the following principles:

1. A theory is a hypothetico-deductive structure;
2. Theories are justified by meeting certain conditions of empirical testability;
3. All the theoretical terms of a theory must be able to be given operational definitions; and

4. Scientific theories of educational administration exclude substantive ethical claims. (Culbertson, 1981, 1983; Evers & Lakomski, 2000; Halpin, 1958)

In contrast to positivism, Evers and Lakomski (2000) argued that a coherentist approach to the study of knowledge in educational administration would respond to the following principles:

1. Theories are part of a "continuous web of belief" included in the global theory we develop from childhood. "Statements at the perimeter, perhaps singular observation reports, are those which should be most readily revised in the light of experience" (p. 7). At the centre of the structure they locate "logic, mathematics and branches of physics, [that] function as major organizing features of the web and are least revisable unless doing so makes for substantial gains in simplicity, or some overall gain in the coherence of the global theory" (p. 7);
2. Theories are justified by the overall coherence of the whole web of belief;
3. Theoretical terms obtain their meaning by the conceptual relations they have in a particular conceptual scheme in a theory and not by their capacity to measure the world in a particular way; and
4. Observation is value laden and values also make part of the web of belief.

To Evers and Lakomski, values are subject to "coherent adjustment in the light of experience, [they] take it as uncontroversial that values are embedded throughout educational administration theory" (p. 7). Evers and Lakomski called their approach *naturalistic coherentism*—that is, their model aims to naturalise coherentist epistemology. Particularly, they aimed to provide a conceptualisation of knowledge in educational administration that coheres with our knowledge of the natural sciences. To achieve this goal they indicated that a model of the material mind would give us insights about the way administrators make decisions in schools. They chose the *connectionist model of the mind* (Rumelhart & McClelland, 1986) to show how the knowledge of administrative practices could be naturalised, that is, expressed in the language of the natural sciences.

Briefly, connectionism explains cognition by reference to computational neural networks. These computational models are simplified representations of the brain in which the units or nodes in the network are portrayed as analogous to neurons. The units in the network connect following a certain pattern; they react to the incoming connections forwarding activation inputs to other units. The connections between units have different weights that can be measured numerically; the weight determines the strength of connections between units. Connectionist networks process information in a way different from a classic computer, because they do not require strings of symbols, rules, or representations to function. In a connectionist network, the information is stored in a non-symbolic way, as it is *distributed* between the network's units (Baxt, 1990; Rumelhart & McClelland, 1986).

According to Evers and Lakomski (2000) neural networks can be used for "data extraction and analysis" (p. 157). Namely, they can be useful for "discovering patterns" (p. 157) through compression algorithms that "summarize the regularities the network has extracted from the data comprising its experience" (p. 157). In other words, connectionist models would allow us to identify regularities in the knowledge of practices—these regularities, once codified, inform future practices and provide us with analytical tools to understand school functioning.

Evers and Lakomski (2000) identified six implications of computational neural networks for understanding the decision making process in educational administrators. First, neural networks may give us some insights into how humans represent their practical knowledge in a non-symbolic distributed fashion. Second, we learn our practical knowledge when we interact with our peers and the environment and we receive feedback from them. Third, connectionist models let us see reasoning processes as pattern processing rather than following a set of rule-like sentences. They exemplify this principle as follows:

> When a school principal makes a decision, say, to admit a child with a particular disability into that school, instead of seeing the result as a deduction from a set of unarticulated premises, it is more plausible to see the input information as triggering a prototype of a successfully integrated child, a prototype that has been built up by experience.
> (Evers & Lakomski, 2000, p. 18)

Fourth, if neural networks can process simultaneous inputs, then they would be better suited to represent human cognitive processing and would provide us a better understanding of the influence of different inputs in the decision-making process. Fifth, Evers and Lakomski said that it is useful to see "linguistic/symbolic formulations of knowledge as ways of *compressing* experience into a representation" (p. 18). However, they indicate that an algorithm that compresses a practice like teaching or leading is of little use if contextual factors dominate. In their view, fine-grained distributed representation of practices like leadership, decision making, or teaching would be useful if they take into account the contexts in which these practices are held (Lakomski, 2005). They suggested that connectionist networks would facilitate the creation of simulations for training purposes. In their view, connectionist models can be used to introduce contextual variables into the compressed representations so professional training based on connectionist models could be more useful and realistic. And sixth, connectionist models would represent thought in an accurate fashion because they model thinking as a "dynamic process that occurs in real time" (p. 18).

Evers and Lakomski (2000) suggested that the traditional view of cognition as symbol processing is insufficient to explain the complexity of administrative practices in institutional contexts. In their view, connectionism can be used to explore cognition as "*distributed* between other knowers and their material contexts" (p. 37). Other authors have identified similarities between connectionist networks and systems of distributed cognition (Mason, Conrey, & Smith, 2007; Van Overwalle & Heylighen, 2006; Smith, 2009). It must be noted, however, that their argument for this methodological jump from the individual to the collective is not clearly revealed. They indicated that Hutchins (1991, 1995) and Clark (1997) endorsed connectionist principles. However, it must be noted that Hutchins (1991) explicitly expressed some caution on this regard.

> Because the processing in connectionist networks is distributed across units in a network, and the processing in a system of socially distributed cognition is distributed across a number of people, there is a strong temptation to adopt a superficial mapping between the two domains, in which units in a network are seen as corresponding to individual people and the connections among units are seen to correspond to the communication links among people. In this way a single network would be taken as a community of people . . . this most obvious mapping is a quite likely a dead end.
>
> (p. 293)

In Hutchins' view, the real value of connectionism for the study of socially distributed cognition would be in the use of a more elaborated analogy in which individuals are represented as networks, and groups of individuals where cognition is socially distributed are represented as *communities of networks*.

What are the implications of this theorisation for our knowledge of educational administration? Evers and Lakomski argued that representing the knowledge of practice is paramount to understanding the nature of school administration because encoding practices into concrete representations: (a) improves our knowledge of decision making in schools; (b) improves our knowledge of leadership processes in education; (c) provides us with useful insights about the functioning of educational organisations; and (d) provides systematic knowledge of practices in educational administration that would have a positive impact in training programmes for teachers and educational administrators.

Evers and Lakomski's model is one of the most recent and systematic attempts to explain practices in schools by reference to cognitive theories. However it is worth noting that connectionist models such as the one endorsed by Evers and Lakomski aim to simulate the brain's neural connections, without taking into consideration the role of the environment in cognitive processing. In the next section, I will introduce some conceptualisations that take the social context into consideration when talking about administrative practices in education.

TWO EXAMPLES: PROFESSIONAL LEARNING AND POLICY ENACTMENT

Professional Learning and Situated Cognition

Two areas that are interrogated consistently by researchers in education are teacher learning and professional development. Putnam and Borko (2000) indicated that most of the scholarship on learning from a situated perspective has focused on students' learning but scarce attention has been paid to teachers' learning. They noted that an individualistic view of learning has dominated the field (Bredo, 2009). This individualistic view portrays "knowing as the manipulation of symbols inside the mind of the individual, and learning as the acquisition of knowledge and skills thought to be useful in a wide variety of settings" (Putnam & Borko, 2000, p. 4). They followed suggestions from Lave and Wenger (1991) and Greeno, Collins, and Resnick (1996) regarding the role of *activity* in the learning process. These authors indicated that activity is always externally oriented because it takes place in physical and social contexts (Clancey, 1997). They also pointed out that activity is an integral part of learning. According to Putnam and Borko (2000), teacher education programmes should foster *authentic* environments—that is, a context of teaching-related activity in which teachers can exercise problem-solving skills. They characterised these environments as *discourse communities* (Resnick, 1991) comprising people that share common interests and similar cultural codes: a professional language, similar values, or similar social-cultural background. According to these authors, mastering the community's discourse and participating in changes to the discourse are ways of learning. Similarly, Lave and Wegner (1991), for example, characterised learning as a participatory process in which individuals gradually gain access to communities of practice. In this regard, Greeno et al. (1996) elaborated on the situated perspective on thinking and learning, arguing that

> success in cognitive functions such as reasoning, remembering, and perceiving is understood as an achievement of a system, with contributions of the individuals who participate, along with tools and artefacts. This means that thinking is situated in a particular context of intentions, social partners, and tools.
>
> (p. 20)

Similarly, Carter (1990) and Carter and Doyle (1989) suggested that teachers' knowledge is *event-structured* or *episodic*—that is, teachers' knowledge is "developed in context, stored together with characteristic features of the classrooms and activities, organized around tasks that teachers accomplish in classroom settings, and accessed for use in similar situations" (Putnam & Borko, 2000, p. 13). Putnam and Borko (2000) gave importance to the socio-cultural environment of teaching; they proposed a situated account of cognition that portrayed teachers' learning as an activity that takes place in the interaction between the teachers and their surroundings.

The Enactment of Instructional Policy

James Spillane (2004) studied how policymakers and teachers made sense of science and math teaching standards in Michigan during the 1990s. He noted that the stakeholders developed their own understanding of the policy message based on unsuitable interpretational schemata. Teachers and local policymakers understood math and science policy

> as familiar ones, without sufficient attention to aspects that diverged from the familiar . . . [They missed] deeper, more conceptual core elements . . . the result was modest change in existing local understanding and thereby in the ideas about science education promoted by school-district policies.
>
> (p. 89)

Spillane concluded that the cause of the insufficient transformation in the educational practices was the unsuitable interpretational schemata used by teachers and policymakers.

In another study, Hill (2001, 2006) found that the enactment of mathematics and language arts standards in California resulted in practices that did not correspond to the policy objectives, even though no resistance or opposition was reported at the classroom/district level. She pointed out that classroom practices remained unaltered after policy introduction. Studies of this sort suggest that the gap between the policy as designed and the policy in practice is created, in some cases, by the interpretational schemata that the stakeholders use when they try to understand the new curriculum (Cobb, McClain, Lamberg, & Dean, 2003; Coburn, 2001). All these cases have one element in common: They assume that individuals interpret policy and act accordingly. For example, according to Yanow (2000), it is usually assumed that the policy message is unambiguously understood by the policy-relevant public or policy communities (Pal, 2006). However, in Yanow's view, this is not always the case: The policy message could be reinterpreted by means of the interpretive filters the community uses to make sense of new policy. In the same vein, Cuban (1998), Spillane (2004), and Hill (2006) concluded that the interpretation of policy messages at the classroom-/school-/district-level might be different from the interpretation of the policy messages at the ministry or governmental level, and this makes it possible that the policy outcome might be different from what policy designers intended.

Researchers that make use of the notion of *interpretation* have turned to cognitive models aiming to identify how individuals interpret messages (Spillane, 2004). Most of the work in this field has been centred on how individual cognition makes for individual differences and similarities, extrapolating the results to groups by generalisation. Such generalisations provide the grounds for using terms like *distributed leadership* (Spillane, Reiser, & Gomez, 2006), *shared meanings* (Fullan, 2007), or *interpretive communities* (Yanow, 2000). For example, Spillane et al. (2006) indicated:

> we argue that cognition is an essential lens for understanding education policy implementation, especially the implementation of policies that demand significant shifts in teachers' practice, but that investigations of the role of cognition in policy implementation to date, including some of our own investigations, have failed to grapple with cognition as a distributed practice.
>
> (p. 48)

In the reported cases of the Michigan (Spillane, 2004) and California (Hill, 2001, 2006) standards, the researchers seemed to assume that the stakeholders *share* an interpretational scheme, because the stakeholders seemed to share a similar understanding of the policy; however, the *nature* of the similarity between interpretive schemata yet remains to be explained. One explanation could be provided by Thomas Greenfield's (1993) suggestion, according to which the consensus can be explained as a matter of persuasion or forceful imposition, but neither Spillane (2004) nor Hill (2001, 2006) reported political or power controversies within the studied communities. Another option is to use the notion of communities of practice (Lave & Wenger, 1991). This idea might be helpful for understanding this phenomenon because teachers can be seen as participants in structured practices that enable them to perform their jobs in certain ways. However, both Spillane and Hill seem to assume that teachers somehow *acquire* an internal cognitive interpretational scheme, which is opposed to Lave and Wenger's theory "as they locate learning not in the acquisition of structure, but in the increased access of learners to participating roles in expert performances" (Hanks, 1991, p. 17).

EXPLORING THE COGNITIVE DIMENSION OF EDUCATIONAL ADMINISTRATION

Throughout this chapter, I have reviewed classic and contemporary contributions to the cognitive study of administrative practices in education. The scholarship on cognition in educational administration is scarce, but as I have shown, research in some areas, such as decision making, leadership, policy implementation, knowledge diffusion, and professional learning, yields promising results.

The cognitive sciences have generated a revolution in the way we understand the human mind; however, this revolution has yet to be seen in the study of educational administration. The studies that I have reviewed in this chapter provide an entry point to explore theories and concepts that, albeit useful, are rarely used in the research and scholarship on educational organisations. Exploring the cognitive dimension of administrative practices in education would give us new insights about the epistemology of educational administration. There are unanswered questions about the nature and the object of educational administration that could be explored through the theoretical frameworks provided by the cognitive sciences. Perhaps organisations are nothing but assemblages of human intention and meaning, as Thomas Greenfield (Greenfield & Ribbins, 1993) argued. An inquiry into the cognitive aspects of school administration could give us useful insights into the way school stakeholders understand educational institutions.

A study of the cognitive dimension of the practices of educational administrators would give us new way to understand the nature of knowledge of educational administration. Practitioners have a wealth of practical knowledge about their profession, and a cognitive approach would help researchers to characterise and systematise such knowledge. Authors in the field of philosophy of mind (Robbins & Aydede, 2009) have identified substantive connections among the cognitive sciences, phenomenology, and hermeneutics (Rowlands, 2010). Potentially, the study of educational administration would gain by exploring the connections among cognition as a cultural phenomenon, embodiment (Dall'Alba, 2009; O'Loughlin, 1995), and interpretation (Gadamer, 1975). This promising area of inquiry would allow us to investigate how our understanding of social reality informs our actions and, simultaneously, how our actions constitute the very nature of social reality (Giddens, 1984).

REFERENCES

Aguilar, F. J. (1967). *Scanning the business environment*. New York: Macmillan.

Baum, J. A. C., & Rowley, T. J. (2002). Companion to organisations: An introduction. In Baum, J. A. C. (Ed.), *The Blackwell companion to organisations* (pp. 1–34). Oxford, UK: Blackwell.

Baxt, W. G. (1990). Use of an artificial neural network for data analysis in clinical decision-making: the diagnosis of acute coronary occlusion. *Neural Computation, 2*(4), 480–489.

Borko, H. (2004). Professional development and teacher learning: Mapping the terrain. *Educational Researcher, 33*(8), 3–15.

Bredo, E. (2009). Is educational policy making rational—and what would that mean anyway? *Educational Theory, 59*(5), 533–547.

Carter, K. (1990). Teachers' knowledge and learning to teach. In W. R. Houston, M. Haberman, & J. Silkula (Eds.), *Handbook of research on teacher education* (pp. 291–310). New York: Macmillan.

Carter, K., & Doyle, W. (1989). Classroom research as a resource for the graduate preparation of teachers. In A. Woolfolk (Ed.), *Research perspectives on the graduate preparation of teachers* (pp. 51–68). Englewood Cliffs, NJ: Prentice Hall.

Clancey, W. J. (1997). *Situated cognition.* Cambridge, UK: Cambridge University Press.

Clark, A. (1997). *Being there: Putting brain, body and world together again.* Cambridge, MA: MIT.

Cobb, P., McClain, K., Lamberg, T. S., & Dean, C. (2003). Situating teachers' instructional practices in the institutional setting of the school and district. *Educational Researcher, 32*(6), 13–24.

Coburn, C. E. (2001). Collective sensemaking about reading: How teachers mediate reading policy in their professional communities. *Educational Evaluation and Policy Analysis, 23*(2), 145–170.

Coburn, C. & Stein, M. (2006). Communities of practice theory and the role of teachers professional community in policy implementation. In M. Honig (Ed.), *New directions in education policy implementation: Confronting complexity* (pp. 65–82). Albany, NY: SUNY Press.

Cuban, L. (1998). How schools change reforms: Redefining reform success and failure. *Teachers College Record, 99*(3), 453–477.

Culbertson, J. A. (1981). Antecedents of the Theory Movement. *Educational Administration Quarterly, 17*(1), 25–47.

Culbertson, J. A. (1983). Theory in educational administration: Echoes from critical thinkers. *Educational Researcher, 12*(10), 15–22.

Cyert, R. M., & March, J. G. (1963). *A behavioral theory of the firm.* Englewood Cliffs, NJ: Prentice-Hall.

Daft, R. L., & Weick, K. E. (1984). Toward a model of organisations as interpretation systems. *The Academy of Management Review, 9*(2), 284–295.

Dall'Alba, G. (2009). *Learning to be professionals.* Berlin: Springer.

Evers, C. W., & Lakomski, G. (1991). *Knowing educational administration: Contemporary methodological controversies in educational administration research.* Oxford, UK: Pergamon.

Evers, C. W., & Lakomski, G. (1996). *Exploring educational administration: Coherentist applications and critical debates.* New York: Pergamon.

Evers, C. W., & Lakomski, G. (2000). *Doing educational administration: A theory of administrative practice.* Amsterdam: Pergamon.

Feuer, M. J. (2006). *Moderating the debate: Rationality and the promise of American education.* Cambridge, MA: Harvard Education Press.

Fiol, C. M. (2002). Intraorganisational cognition and interpretation. In J. A. C. Baum (Ed.), *The Blackwell companion to organisations* (1st ed., pp. 120–137). Oxford, UK: Blackwell.

Fullan, M. (2007). *The new meaning of educational change.* New York: Teachers College Press.

Gadamer, H. G. (1975). *Truth and method.* New York: Continuum.

Galbraith, J. R. (1973). *Designing complex organisations* (Addison-Wesley series on organisation development). Reading, MA: Addison-Wesley.

Glassman, R. B. (1973). Persistence and loose coupling in living systems. *Behavioral Science, 18*(2), 83–98.

Giddens, A. (1984). *The constitution of society: Outline of the theory of structuration.* Cambridge, MA: Polity Press.

Greenfield, T. B. (1993). Organisations as talk, chance action and experience. In T. Greenfield & P. Ribbins (Eds.), *Greenfield on educational administration* (pp. 51–71). London: Routledge.

Greeno, J. G., Collins, A. M., & Resnick, L. B. (1996). Cognition and learning. In D. Berliner & R. Calfee (Eds.), *Handbook of educational psychology* (pp. 15–46). New York: Macmillan.

Greeno, J. G., & Moore, J. L. (1993). Situativity and symbols: Response to Vera and Simon. *Cognitive Science, 17*(1), 49–59.

Halpin, A. W. (1958). *Administrative theory in education.* London: Macmillan.

Hanks, E. (1991). Foreword. In J. Lave & E. Wenger (Eds.), *Situated learning: Legitimate peripheral participation* (pp. 13–24). Cambridge, UK: Cambridge University Press.

Haugeland, J. (1993). *Artificial intelligence: The very idea.* Cambridge, MA: MIT Press.

Hill, H. (2006). Language matters: How characteristics of language complicate policy implementation. In M. Honig (Ed.), *New directions in education policy implementation: Confronting complexity* (pp. 65–82). Albany, NY: SUNY Press.

Hill, H. C. (2001). Policy is not enough: Language and the interpretation of state standards. *American Educational Research Journal, 38*(2), 289–318.

Horst, S. (2009). The computational theory of mind. In N. Zalta (Ed.), *The Stanford encyclopedia of philosophy.* Retrieved from http://plato.stanford.edu/entries/computational-mind/#EmbEmbCog

Hutchins, E. (1990). The technology of team navigation. In J. Galegher, R. E. Kraut, & C. Egido (Eds.), *Intellectual Teamwork* (pp. 191–220). Hillsdale, NJ: Erlbaum.

Hutchins, E. (1991). The social organisation of distributed cognition. In L. B. Resnick, L. M. Levine, & S. D. Teasley (Eds.), *Perspectives on socially shared cognition* (pp. 283–307). Washington, DC: American Psychological Association.

Hutchins, E. (1995). *Cognition in the wild.* Cambridge, MA: MIT Press.

Jones, M. (1995). Organisational learning: Collective mind or cognitivist metaphor? *Accounting, Management & Information Technologies, 1*(5), 61–77

Kvanvig, J. (2007). Coherentist theories of epistemic justification. In. E. Zalta (Ed.), *Stanford encyclopedia of philosophy.* Retrieved from http://plato.stanford.edu/entries/justep-coherence/

Lakomski, G. (2005). *Managing without leadership: Towards a theory of organisational functioning.* Amsterdam: Elsevier.

Lant, T. K. (2002). Organisational cognition and interpretation. In J. A. C. Baum (Ed.), *The Blackwell companion to organisations* (pp. 344–362). Malden, MA: Blackwell.

Lant, T. K., & Shapira, Z. (2001). *Organisational cognition: Computation and interpretation.* LEA's organisation and management series. Mahwah, NJ: Erlbaum.

Lave, J., & Wenger, E. (1991). *Situated learning: Legitimate peripheral participation.* Learning in doing. Cambridge, UK: Cambridge University Press.

Le Bon, G. (1895/1968). *The crowd: A study of the popular mind.* Dunwoody, GA: Norman, S. Berg.

Levinthal, D., & March, J. (1993). The myopia of learning. *Strategic Management Journal, 14*, 95–112.

List, C., & Pettit, P. (2011). *Group agency: The possibility, design, and status of corporate agents.* Oxford: Oxford University Press.

March, J. G. (2001). The pursuit of intelligence in organisations. In T. K. Lant & Z. Shapira (Eds.), *Organisational cognition: Computation and interpretation* (pp. 61–72). Mahwah, NJ: Erlbaum.

March, J. G., & Simon, H. A. (1958). *Organisations.* New York: Wiley.

Mason, W. A., Conrey, F. R., & Smith, E. R. (2007). Situating social influence processes: Dynamic, multidirectional flows of influence within social networks. *Personality and Social Psychology Review, 11*(3), 279–300.

Milliken, F. J. (1990). Perceiving and interpreting environmental change: An examination of college administrators' interpretation of changing demographics. *Academy of Management Journal, 33*(1), 42–63.

Ocasio, W. (2001). How do organisations think? In T. K. Lant & Z. Shapira (Eds.), *Organisational cognition: Computation and interpretation* (pp. 39–60). Mahwah, NJ: Erlbaum.

O'Loughlin, M. (1995). Intelligent bodies and ecological subjectivities: Merleau-Ponty's corrective to postmodernism's subjects in education. *Philosophy of Education Society Yearbook*. Urbana-Champaign, IL: Philosophy of Education Society.

Pal, L. (2006). *Beyond policy analysis: Public issue management in turbulent times*. Scarborough, ON: Thomson/Nelson.

Polanyi, M. (1967). *The tacit dimension*. New York: Anchor Press.

Putnam, R. T., & Borko, H. (2000). What do new views of knowledge and thinking have to say about research on teacher learning? *Educational Researcher, 29*(1), 4–15.

Resnick, L. B. (1991). Shared cognition: Thinking as social practice. In L. B. Resnick, J. M. Levine, & S. D. Teasley (Eds.), *Perspectives on socially shared cognition* (pp. 1–20). Washington, DC: American Psychological Association.

Robbins, P., & Aydede, M. (2009). *The Cambridge handbook of situated cognition*. New York: Cambridge University Press.

Rorty, R. (1979). *Philosophy and the mirror of nature*. Princeton, NJ: Princeton University Press.

Rogoff, B. (2003). *The cultural nature of human development*. Oxford, UK: Oxford University Press.

Rowlands, M. (2010). *The new science of the mind: From extended mind to embodied phenomenology*. Cambridge, MA: MIT Press.

Rumelhart, D. E., & McClelland, J. L. (1986). *Parallel distributed processing: Explorations in the microstructure of cognition*. Cambridge, MA: MIT Press.

Russell, B. (2010). *The problems of philosophy*. New York: Cosimo Books.

Sandelands, L. E., & Stablein, R. E. (1987). The concept of organisation mind. In S. Bacharach & N. DiTomaso (Eds.), *Research in the Sociology of Organisations* (Vol. 5; pp. 135–161), London: JAI Press.

Senge, P. M. (2000). *Schools that learn: A fifth discipline field book for educators, parents, and everyone who cares about education*. New York: Doubleday.

Simon, H. A. (1957). *Models of man: Social and rational; mathematical essays on rational human behavior in society setting*. New York: Wiley.

Simon, H. A. (1958). *Administrative behaviour*. New York: Macmillan.

Simon, H. A. (1969). *The sciences of the artificial*. Cambridge, MA: MIT Press.

Simon, H. A. (1989). *Models of thought*. New Haven: Yale University Press.

Sitkin, S. (2001). The theoretical bases of organisational cognition. In T. Lant & Z. Shapira (Eds.), *Organisational cognition: Computation and interpretation* (pp. 73–99). Mahwah, NJ: Erlbaum.

Smith, E. (2009). Distributed connectionist models in social psychology. *Social and Personality Psychology Compass, 3*(1), 64–76.

Spender, J. C. (1998). Dynamics of individual and organisational knowledge. In C. Eden & J. C. Spender (Eds.), *Managerial and organisational cognition: Theory methods and research* (pp. 13–29). London: Sage.

Spillane, J. P. (2004). *Standards deviation: How schools misunderstand education policy/James P. Spillane*. Cambridge, MA: Harvard University Press.

Spillane, J., Reiser, B., & Gomez, L. (2006). Policy implementation and cognition: The role of human, social, & distributed cognition in framing policy implementation. In M. Honig (Ed.), *New directions in educational policy implementation: Confronting complexity* (pp. 47–64). New York: SUNY Press.

Thompson, E., & Stapleton, M. (2009). Making sense of sense-making: Reflection on enactive and extended mind. *Topoi, 28*(1), 23–30.

Van Overwalle, F., & Heylighen, F. (2006). Talking nets: A multiagent connectionist approach to communication and trust between individuals. *Psychological Review, 113*(3), 606–627.

Varela, F. J., Thompson, E., & Rosch, E. (1991). *The embodied mind: Cognitive science and human experience*. Cambridge, MA: MIT Press.

Vera, A. H., & Simon, H. A. (1993). Situated action: A symbolic interpretation. *Cognitive Science, 17*(1), 7–48.

Walsh, J. P. (1995). Managerial and organisational cognition: Notes from a trip down memory lane. *Organisation Science, 6*(3), 280–321.

Weber, M. (1968). *Economy and society: An outline of interpretive sociology*. New York: Bedminster Press.

Wegner, D. M. (1986). Transactive memory: A contemporary analysis of the group mind. In B. Mullen & G. R. Goethals (Eds.), *Theories of group behavior* (pp. 185–205). New York: Springer-Verlag.

Wegner, D. M., Erber, R., & Raymond, P. (1991). Transactive memory in close relationships. *Journal of Personality and Social Psychology, 61*(6), 923–929.

Weick, K. E. (1976). Educational organisations as loosely coupled systems. *Administrative Science Quarterly, 21*(1), 1–19.

Weick, K. E. (1979). *The social psychology of organising*. New York: Random House.

Weick, K. E. (2001). *Making sense of the organisation*. Oxford, UK: Blackwell.

Weick, K. E., & Roberts, K. H. (1993). Collective mind in organisations: Heedful interrelating on flight decks. *Administrative Science Quarterly, 38*(3), 357–381.

Wenger, E., McDermott, R., & Snyder, W. M. (2002). *Cultivating communities of practice: A guide to managing knowledge*. Boston, MA: Harvard Business School.

Wheeler, W. M. (1911). The ant-colony as an organism. In W. M. Wheeler (Ed.), *Essays in philosophical biology* (pp. 3–27). Cambridge, MA: Harvard University Press.

Wheeler, W. M. (1923). *Social life among the insects*. New York: Harcourt Brace.

Wheeler, W. M. (1928). *The social insects*. New York: Harcourt Brace.

Wilson, R. (2004). *Boundaries of the mind*. Cambridge, UK: Cambridge University Press.

Yanow, D. (2000). *Conducting interpretive policy analysis*. Thousand Oaks, CA: Sage.

10 Sociological Approaches to Educational Administration and Leadership

Scott Eacott

In this chapter, I examine the question of whether social theory—and, in particular, sociological approaches—can be mobilised to understand the leadership, management, and administration of educational institutions. This may seem an odd question to pose, given that orthodoxy in both scholarly and lay communities establishes and sustains both educating and leading as social activities, yet social theory remains marginalised in educational leadership, management, and administration despite a well-established sociology of education and a sociological tradition of organisational studies. Sociology is, however, a large and intellectually diverse scholarly discipline. Given the brevity of a chapter, I pay particular attention to critical social theory, especially that rooted in French social thought, to describe its history, outline current usage, and provide *a* (not *the*) means of mobilising a sociological approach for the scholarship of educational administration and leadership.

WHAT DO I MEAN BY SOCIOLOGY?

Sociology, at its simplest, is the study of human social behaviour and its origins, development, organisation, and institutions. Understandably, given its focus, sociological thinking predates the establishment of sociology as an academic discipline in universities. The analysis of the social world was central to early Western philosophy, and the generation and classification of data about society and social groups was pivotal in the establishment and advancement of public administration.

While it is difficult to pinpoint the moment of origin for sociology as an academic discipline, three scholars considered to be the founding architects of contemporary sociology are Émile Durkheim, Karl Marx, and Max Weber. Durkheim held a strong belief in a *science* of the social world—comparable to the natural sciences—and it is this stream of sociology that was influential during the early phases of the *Theory Movement* in educational administration. Marxist analysis of the social world, and the centrality of power, remains prominent—even if not always identified—in the critical stream of scholarship. Weber, who incidentally was writing at around the same time as Frederick Winslow Taylor—arguably the father of contemporary management sciences—wrote a highly influential, but significantly misunderstood, account of the role of the economy, administration, and society,[1] and initiated discussion of charismatic leadership. The work of Pierre Bourdieu, which is experiencing popularity in contemporary educational leadership, management, and administration discourses, draws from and extends the work of Durkheim, Marx, and Weber.

In addition to its multiple traditions, sociology also operates at two distinct—although deeply connected—levels: sociology *of* and sociology *for*. In other words, there is sociology of a field of practice, and the sociology of and for knowledge production. The former, a sociology *of*, is concerned with describing events in the social world, and the latter, a sociology *for*, is concerned with the epistemological and ontological preliminaries of knowledge production. This is not to suggest the simplistic and unproductive binary of theory and practice or theoretical and applied. Rather, it is to recognise the different levels of the research object and its implications for scholarship. An approach that merges both of these levels in the research process is articulated in a text by Pierre Bourdieu, Jean-Claude Chamboredon, and Jean-Claude Passeron (1968/1991) entitled *The Craft of Sociology: Epistemological Preliminaries*. Attention to the epistemological preliminaries of research is particularly important in the context of educational leadership, management, and administration, given the "embedded and embodied" nature of the researcher (Eacott, 2014).

This embedded and embodied context is important for a sociology of knowledge production in educational administration. The central issue is that educational administrators are, as are all social agents, *spontaneous sociologists* (Bourdieu & Wacquant, 1992, p. 66). This is particularly so in the professions, such as education. In the case of educational administration, most, if not all, academics are former administrators at school and/or systemic levels (a quick scan of recruitment advertisements will attest to the privileging of this). Further to that, many hold administrative positions in the academy, further blurring the boundary between the native (naïve) perception of the spontaneous sociologist and the research objects constructed through the *scientific* method of the researcher. Following Bourdieu, this does two (considerably overlapping) things, first, the manner in which the social world is perceived is the result of the internalisation of the objective structures of the social world in the cognitive schemata through which they apprehend the social world. Alternatively, the social world exists in the body as much as the body exists in the social world. Second, there exists a belief in administration and, most importantly, the stakes of the task at hand. That is, administration functions only in so far as it produces a belief in the value of its product (e.g., policy, security, order) and means of production (e.g., governance). What I have brought to attention here is the importance of engaging with the epistemological (and ontological) preliminaries that shape, and in turn are shaped by, scholarship in educational administration.

The potential of sociology and a sociological approach to educational leadership, management, and administration has long been acknowledged. In 1965, Burton R. Clark noted:

> . . . sociology should be able to make a major contribution to the study of administration within formal structures. It is also notably a discipline whose sensitivity to emergent phenomena and informal patterns should aid greatly in extending the study of educational administration to the many influences on policy and practice that are located outside of formal structures.
>
> (p. 69)

Weber's (1922/1978) work on bureaucracy highlights the potential of sociology for the study of administration, as does the work of Talcott Parsons (see 1956a, 1956b) and many others. Bourdieu and Passeron (1970/1990) also showed the potential of sociology for bringing to the level of analysis the many structural means in which education serves to (re)produce the existing social order. A key, and ongoing, challenge is the reciprocity between sociology and educational administration. As Beryl Tipton (1977) identified over 35 years ago:

> It follows from this argument that educational administration needs sociology (or the social sciences). But does sociology need educational administration? Sociology, after all, already has a well-developed sociology of education and sociology of organisations, and constitutes the backbone of social administration.
>
> (p. 47)

Sociology, including the sociology of education, has continued on with little reference to leadership, management, and administration. This also includes the recent trend towards education policy sociology. A cursory scan of the table of contents of flagship journals such as *Sociology of Education*; *British Journal of Sociology of Education*; and sociology-informed journals such as *Discourse: Studies in the Cultural Politics of Education*, *Critical Studies in Education*, and *Journal of Education Policy* supports such a claim. This highlights a fundamental challenge for any interplay between sociology and educational administration.

Moving beyond the sociology of knowledge production in educational administration for a moment, there are two ways of using sociology for education administration. The first is to use sociological writings or great thinkers and apply or map these onto events. This is arguably the most common usage of sociology, yet in doing so, the research object remains intact, just described using new or different language. The second approach is to mobilise the intellectual resources of sociology to understand the research object(s) in new ways. These new ways may unsettle some, or many, of the existing ways of thinking. Both approaches hold potential but it is in moving beyond novelty of applying or mapping onto educational administration that the second provides for innovative and possibly discipline-defining contributions.

Gaston Bachelard (1934/1984) argued that a key distinction between the social and natural sciences is that in the social, research traditions are most important, whereas in the natural, it is the pursuit of perfect theory. When making any claim to be using sociology, it is imperative to locate your argument within a particular research tradition of sociology. This may be through adherence to a particular great thinker or to a research methodology. Whatever it is, it should be clear for the reader.

In short, sociology is many things but is fundamentally concerned with human activity. In an increasingly globalised world, where the boundaries between policy, administration, and social behaviour are blurred, sociology offers important intellectual resources for understanding the different ways in which the socio-political and temporal nature of the social world influences the leadership, management, and administration of educational institutions.

SOCIOLOGY AND EDUCATIONAL ADMINISTRATION

The role of sociology within the study of educational leadership, management, and administration is one of many ebbs and flows. Initially, in the pursuit of validity within the academy, educational administration established boundaries around itself as a discipline. In doing so, any disciplinary knowledge from beyond the boundaries of educational administration was excluded. Then, during the early phases of the *Theory Movement*, sociology played a role, but this was a particular brand of sociology—one based on logical empiricism. The contemporary discipline of educational administration and leadership is seeing a re-emergence of sociological approaches, but unlike the earlier stream, these contributions have a grounding in critical social theory, and the most prominent thinker mobilised has been Pierre Bourdieu.

To the Exclusion of All Others

Richard Bates (2010) argued that the history of educational administration and leadership as a field of knowledge production and practice is evidence of what John Dewey (1902) observed as "the habit of regarding the mechanics of school organisation and administration as something comparatively external and indifferent to educational ideals" (pp. 22–23). In particular, Bates cites the establishment of departments of educational administration in US universities in the 1900s as a key point for the field. Notably, it was the recruitment of early professors who had little disciplinary training in education that highlighted the problem. An important appointment was that of Ellwood Cubberley at Stanford. With a background in geology and physical science, he had little background in the study of education, with the exception of having served as a superintendent in San Diego for two years (Tyack & Hansot, 1982). During this period, he came to the conclusion that school boards should be apolitical. This was consistent with the Municipal Reform Movement, which, in drawing from industry management research, sought to develop large school systems and administrative structures (e.g., much like what Weber described in his work on bureaucracy). This is why the take-up of Taylor's (1911) scientific management was so successful in the US, as described by Raymond E. Callahan (1962) in his classic *Education and the Cult of Efficiency*. The construction of these disciplinary boundaries, legitimising the educational administration professor as *the* teacher of the profession, enabled the de-legitimation of those who might stake a claim to offering something of use for educational administrators (English, 2002). As a result, the critical stream of sociology became *othered* in the scholarship of educational administration.

A Re-Injection

In the US, the WK Kellogg-supported Cooperative Program in Educational Administration (CPEA) centres were important mechanisms for encouraging sociologists, psychologists, and others to conduct scholarship on educational administration during the mid-1900s. As a result, psychology and sociology were influential during the importation of *science* in the lead-up to the *Theory Movement* (Bates, 2010). The sociological influences in the *Theory Movement* were built upon an appropriation of Talcott Parson's systems theory through Jacob Getzel's (1952) *A Psycho-Sociological Framework for the Study of Education Administration*. From a sociological perspective, this approach reflects a very particular form of scholarship, one built upon logical empiricism as *the* way to do science. In mainstream discourses, this approach was popular. The use of survey techniques and the construction/classification of social groups for analysis provided the basis of substantive applied research. From a knowledge production standpoint, however, there remain issues around the artificial partitioning, or epistemic categories, of such research and the relationship between the researcher and the researched.

When Thomas Greenfield launched his attack on the apparent objectivity of the *Theory Movement*[2] he received far greater support from Commonwealth-based scholars than he did from US-based ones. There had long been a general agreement across the Commonwealth academy that the social sciences were a useful source of theory and methodology for educational administration (*see* Baron & Taylor, 1969). Unlike in the US, where early professors and then the *Theory Movement* sought to establish an apolitical account of educational administration, across the Commonwealth there was a stronger recognition or conceptualisation of educating as a political activity. In England, for example, schooling had a long history of class warfare, and scholarship could not easily overlook this socio-cultural context. At scale, and contingent on temporality, the effects of colonialism/imperialism still linger across the Commonwealth, and socio-political accounts of educational administration are far more evident in both practice and scholarship. The closest equivalent in the US is the attention to matters of race, particularly through the University Council for Educational Administration (UCEA) and general education societies such as the American Educational Research Association (AERA). However, this takes less of an explicit sociological approach, drawing from a range of social sciences.

The Rise of the Phoenix

It has long been recognised that contemporary educational administrators are faced with increasingly complex problems (Biesta & Mirón, 2002; Maxcy, 1993). As a result, the last 30 years has seen a diversity of scholarship in educational leadership, management, and administration. Within the opening-up of the field—the extent to which remains in question (*see* Wilkinson & Eacott, 2013)—Helen Gunter (2010) identified an emerging trend of using sociological approaches in educational leadership, management, and administration. In many ways, this is not surprising, given the global spread of the managerialist project, the neo-imperialism underway through education interventions (including school leadership preparation and development) in developing countries, policy borrowing, and the comparative turn in educational administration and policy. This opening-up was captured by Helen Gunter and Tanya Fitzgerald (2008), when they argued that

> the demand for evidence is stifling understandings and explanations of practice, and at the same time the self-reverence of a person's story of their victory in turning round a failing school does little to explain who determines whether a school is failing and for what purposes.
>
> (p. 7)

Sociological approaches have the potential to open up scholarship and ask large-scale or theoretical questions that are then explored through their empirical manifestation. As Clark (1965) noted:

> there are no boundaries around a sociology of educational administration, but rather open terrain and rambling roads that connect to the interests of researchers in a number of other specialities in sociology, and the interests of psychologists, anthropologists, economists and political scientists.
>
> (p. 51)

Currency within sociology, and in broader public discourse, is easiest maintained when the subject of research is of heightened or sustained public interest. In the case of education, there is almost always sustained public and scholarly interest. After all, as Bates (1980) noted, "the processes through which learning is organized in society are of central importance in both the production of knowledge, the maintenance of culture, and the reproduction of social structure" (p. 1).

It is arguably for this range of reasons that the work of the French sociologist Pierre Bourdieu has found increasing traction in education, and, in particular, in educational administration and leadership. Although he never wrote on educational administration per se,[3] and earlier claims that his work is minimally used in educational administration despite his theoretical attention to the relationship between individual agency and structural determinism (Lingard & Christie, 2003), the use of Bourdieusian social theory in educational administration and leadership has increased substantially since his death in 2002. His theoretical resources have been used to interrogate aspects of educational administration, such as school reform (Gunter, 2012), leadership preparation and development (Eacott, 2011), leadership standards (English, 2012), strategy (Eacott, 2010), autonomy (Thomson, 2010), questioning *leadership* as a concept (Eacott, 2013a), educational leadership at large (Thomson, 2014), its application for undertaking case studies in educational leadership (Eacott, 2013b), or even the intellectual field of educational administration (Gunter, 2002). A cursory scan of the geographic location of the key people working in this space does continue the trend of Commonwealth-based (Gunter and Thomson in England, myself in Australia) as opposed to US-based scholars (the exception being English). That being said, with the global spread of ideas courtesy of conferences, but more importantly electronic access to journals, the increased usage of Bourdieusian social theory is a trend, albeit a small one, in the discipline.

A *Relational* Approach

If this chapter is to have an audience beyond itself, then it is vital that I can demonstrate further how a sociologically informed mode of scholarship plays out in educational administration and leadership. To do so, I am going to outline a *relational* approach to the study of educational leadership, management, and administration that I am advancing here and elsewhere (Eacott, 2014)[4] that explicitly fuses multiple sociological analytical frames. The intellectual heritage of this *relational* approach is eclectic, drawing heavily on French social theory, such as the critical sociology of Pierre Bourdieu and the pragmatic sociology of Luc Boltanski,[5] but also critical management studies, political science, organisational studies, and given my own disciplinary location, recognised educational administration thinkers such as Richard Bates, Colin Evers and Gabriele Lakomski, Thomas Greenfield, and contemporaries such as Helen Gunter, Pat Thomson, and Fenwick English. Centrally, in bringing critical pluralism to scholarship,

I engage with what I see as the key theoretical problem of the legitimation of the social world and its empirical manifestation in the administration of educational institutions. Through this theoretical and empirical focus, the *relational* research programme investigates how the production of knowledge about the legitimacy, effectiveness, efficiency, and morality of administration connects with the practices of administration. In doing so, this *relational* approach blends a focus on knowledge production with a sociology of the field of practice. Questions are raised regarding the extent to which *new* forms of administration—leadership, participatory, distributed, authentic, and so on—are generative or thwarting of new knowledge and ways of being. Such a move is not surprising, given that for the most part scholars, at least those who take such matters seriously, are looking for an alternate ontology as the Newtonian/Cartesian universe inhabited by self-interested, atomistic individuals—that which fits nicely with managerialist accounts of administration—does not logically fit prescriptions for collaborative practice nor the image of educational institutions as a nebulas unit. A *relational* focus enables scholarship to move beyond internal tensions and external pressures by opening up institutions and engaging with the dynamic relations that they hold with other social institutions and those that constantly redefine their very existence. As a means of highlighting the key features of my argument, below I list five identifying features of the *relational* approach:

- The centrality of *administration* in the social world creates an ontological complicity that makes it difficult to epistemologically break from our spontaneous understanding of the social world;
- Rigorous social *scientific* scholarship would therefore call into question the very foundations on which the contemporarily popular discourses of *leadership*, *management*, and *administration* are constructed;
- The contemporary social condition cannot be separated from the ongoing, and inexhaustible, recasting of administrative labour;
- Studying administration *relationally* enables the overcoming of the contemporary, and arguably enduring, tensions of individualism/collectivism and structure/agency; and
- In doing so, there is a productive—rather than merely critical—space to theorise administration.

The primary point of departure I make with mainstream educational leadership, management, and administration scholarship is my attention to matters of epistemology and ontology, or knowledge production. However, rather than locate this work in a more philosophy of science space, I explicitly bring this into discussion with contemporary discourses of educational leadership, management, and administration. This move enables the argument to speak across intellectual (e.g., education, political science, philosophy, economics, management, organisational studies) and socio-geographic boundaries through the provision of a theoretical argument that is not confined to any one empirical problem or socio-geographic location. Adopting this analytical strategy enables an interdisciplinary approach to scholarship while also fusing multiple lenses for the specific intent of opening new lines of inquiry and renewal in a field of knowledge production—educational leadership, management, and administration—under question for its scholarly value within the academy.

The type of analysis made possible by this *relational* approach offers a means of crafting theoretically charged narratives illuminating the situated nature of administration. Struggles for legitimacy are at the very core of institutions (Barley, 2008). Social institutions, particularly modern institutions such as education, are the configuration of individual actors in a particular socio-geographic space. As such, groups are an epistemic construction as much, if not more so, than an empirical reality. While individual actors exist in the empirical, it is the epistemic classification of groups on the basis of a particular attribute (that could include physical locality) that gives rise to institutions. In addition, administrative analysis is frequently based on an underlying generative assumption that this collection of individuals operates as a coherent whole. However, I, as with many others, argue that such configurations of individuals in a particular time and space are dynamic contested terrains. The binding attributes of institutions, as social groupings, are performative in the sense that they only exist in practice and cannot be solely reduced to particular structural arrangements of the empirical. The binds that hold a group of individual actors together in the form of a social institution are therefore problematic, active, and, by virtue of these qualities, fragile.

The work of institutional actors is the ongoing construction of the social world through the embedding and embodying of it with meaning centred on what is legitimate. Therefore, change in institutions can only take place through shifts in the logics whereby legitimacy is assessed, or, in other words, the standards whereby alternatives are deemed to be appropriate. For the purpose of this chapter—outlining the potential uses of sociological approaches to scholarship—this *relational* approach provides an analytical lens for interrogating the moment-to-moment social relations that define the political activity of educating. Specifically, it opens up analysis that breaks down the unproductive binaries that have existed in the scholarship of educational administration and leadership centred on individualism/collectivism and structure/agency. Furthermore, it brings to the fore the role of description in the scholarly narrative. Following Michael Savage (2009), I mobilise *description* not as the enduring rhetorical criticism that constructs description as a lowly, if not the lowest, form of scholarly work, but rather the rich or *thick* (to think with Clifford Geertz [1973] following Gilbert Ryle [1971]) description of the scholarly narrative.

Although this may at first appear to be a vague account of the *relational* approach to scholarship in educational administration and leadership, it is in adhering to the five identifying features that the research takes shape. Rather than an a priori definition of the research object prior to the study (e.g., an operational definition of what is *leadership*) the research object is deconstructed and the re-constructed (arguably partially) as a result of initial analysis. In the context of a thesis or dissertation, this initial phase may replace the traditional literature review. In doing so, careful attention is paid to ensuring that the construction of the research object is not merely the reproduction of ordinary language, but a systematic scholarly act. This research object is then considered in relation to the various key influences that seek to redefine its existence. This is where empirical work may or may not be mobilised for greater insight. In crafting the scholarly narrative, the goal is a theoretical informed description of what is taking place in the empirical. It is not about trying to understand why someone is doing something or creating linear flowcharts, but relating actions to other actions. Establishing causality is not the purpose; rather, the purpose is the description of the unfolding political work of social groups and institutions in a particular time and space. Importantly, it is about producing scholarship that suspends judgement (as this frequently is based on an original normative orientation) and sees value in description.

CONCLUSION

In this chapter, I have argued that in social theory we find unexpected and surprising resources to think through leadership, management, and administration. As Jill Blackmore (2004) stated, to understand how educational leadership, management, and administration are "perceived, understood and enacted, one has to have a sense of the broader social, economic and political relations shaping educational work" (p. 267). Within the confines of a chapter, I have sought to provide a brief history of the role of sociology in educational administration and leadership, focusing on its initial role through to contemporary trends including the Commonwealth bias in the usage of sociological approaches. In addition, I provide articulation, albeit brief, of a *relational* approach to educational administration and leadership scholarship that is built upon a sociological tradition. If you seek to undertake a sociological approach to your study, you will need to go well beyond this single chapter. As with any approach, there is a need to read and read widely. Most importantly, sociology is an intellectually diverse discipline—if working in the space, it is important to name the tradition in which you are working. There is substantial potential in sociological approaches for advancing our understanding of the ways in which educational institutions go about their work, and because of the dynamic and contradictory nature of the social world, this is an ongoing and inexhaustible intellectual project.

NOTES

1. As a case in point, Tony Bush (2014), among others, described Weber as the developer of "the bureaucratic model of leadership". This is not accurate. In *Economy and Society* (1922/1978), Weber, as a sociologist, described the bureaucracy and in doing so provided a set of conceptual tools for thinking through the administration of the social world. This is very different from the highly applied provision of a conceptual framing to be used to improve practice—as is often the case in educational administration discourses. An often-overlooked aspect of Weber's work is his initiation of a dialogue around charismatic leadership.

2. While Greenfield's attack is often credited to his 1974 paper at the International Intervisitation Programme at Bristol, others consider it to have actually begun at the 1973 Annual Meeting of the American Educational Research Association in New Orleans (see Bates, 1980). This supports the argument that it is impossible to demarcate an exact point of origin for thought.

3. A somewhat overlooked thread in Bourdieusian scholarship is his work around "prophets". Building from his study of Martin Heidegger, Bourdieu argued that a prophet is a person who expresses already existing, albeit intuitive, presumptions or values within a social field. The status of the prophet, much like that of a leader, comes from acting upon latent social needs. The strength of the prophet rests on the dialectic relationship between authorised, authorising language and the group which authorises it and acts on its authority (Bourdieu, 1972/1977, p. 171).

4. In addition to the 2014 book, I have in-press papers at *European Studies in Educational Management*, *Educational Philosophy and Theory*, *Leadership & Policy in Schools* (with Judith Norris), and *Critical Studies in Education* (with Kimbalee Hodges), and a number of doctoral supervisions.

5. Boltanski was a former collaborator with Bourdieu, but since breaking away has developed a pragmatic sociology based around situated moral judgement and logics of worth (see also the work of David Stark). In *The New Spirit of Capitalism* (1990/2005, which pays homage to Weber's classic: *The Spirit of Capitalism*), Boltanski and Eve Chiapello use management literatures to build their argument, and this work is being increasingly taken up in organisational studies, but has yet to gain traction in educational administration and leadership.

REFERENCES

Bachelard, G. (1934/1984). *The new scientific spirit* (P. A. Heelan, Trans.). Boston: Beacon Press. (Originally published as *Le nouvel esprit scientifique*. Paris: Presses Universitaires de France).

Barley, S. R. (2008). Coalface institutionalism. In R. Greenwood, C. Oliver, R. Sahlin, & R. Suddaby (Eds.), *The SAGE handbook of organizational institutionalism* (pp. 491–518). Thousand Oaks, CA: SAGE.

Baron, G., & Taylor, W. (Eds.). (1969). *Educational administration and the social sciences*. London: Athlone.

Bates, R. J. (1980). Educational administration, the sociology of science, and the management of knowledge. *Educational Administration Quarterly, 16*(2), 1–20.

Bates, R. J. (2010). History of educational leadership and management. In P. Peterson, E. Baker, & B. McGraw (Eds.), *International encyclopedia of education* (3rd ed.; pp. 724–730). Oxford: Elsevier.

Biesta, G. J. J., & Miron, L. F. (2002). The new discourses on educational leadership: an introduction. *Studies in Philosophy and Education, 21*(2), 101–107.

Blackmore, J. (2004). Restructuring educational leadership in changing contexts: A local.global accout of restructuring in Australia. *Journal of Educational Change, 5*(3), 267–288.

Boltanski, L., & Chiapello, E. (1990/2005). *The new spirit of capitalism* (G. Elliott, Trans.). London: Verso. (Originally published as *Le nouvel esprit du capitalisme*. Paris: Editions Gallimard).

Bourdieu, P. (1972/1977). *Outline of a theory of practice* (R. Nice, Trans.). Cambridge: Cambridge University Press. (Originally published as *Esquisse d'une théorie de la pratique, précédé de trois études d'ethnologie kabyle*. Switzerland: Libraire Droz S.A.).

Bourdieu, P., Chamboredon, J.-C., & Passeron, J.-C. (1968/1991). *The craft of sociology: Epistemological preliminaries* (R. Nice, Trans.). Berlin, Germany: Walter de Gruyter. (Originally published as *Le métier de sociologue: préalables épistémologiques*. Paris: Mouton).

Bourdieu, P., & Passeron, J.-C. (1970/1990). *Reproduction in education, society and culture* (R. Nice, Trans.). London: SAGE. (Originally published as *La reproduction*. Paris: Les Éditions de Minuit).

Bourdieu, P., & Wacquant, L. (1992). *An invitation to reflexive sociology*. Cambridge: Blackwell Publishers. (Originally published as *Résponses: pour une anthropologie réflexive*. Paris: Seuil).

Bush, T. (2014). Emotional leadership: A viable alternative to the bureaucratic model? *Educational Management Administration & Leadership, 42*(2), 163–164.

Callahan, R. E. (1962). *Education and the cult of efficiency*. Chicago, IL: University of Chicago Press.

Clark, B. R. (1965). The sociology of educational administration. In W. W. Charters, B. R. Clark, J. A. Culbertson, D. E. Griffiths, W. Z. Hirsch, D. Lee, & N. A. Masters (Eds.), *Perspectives on educational administration and the behavioral sciences* (pp. 51–69). Eugene, OR: The Center for the Advanced Study of Educational Administration.

Dewey, J. (1902). *The education situation*. Chicago, IL: Chicago University Press.

Eacott, S. (2010). Bourdieu's *strategies* and the challenge for educational leadership. *International Journal of Leadership in Education, 13*(3), 265–281.

Eacott, S. (2011). Preparing 'educational' leaders in managerialist times: An Australian story. *Journal of Educational Administration and History, 43*(1), 43–59.

Eacott, S. (2013a). 'Leadership' and the social: Time, space and the epistemic. *International Journal of Educational Management, 27*(1), 91–101.

Eacott, S. (2013b). Towards a theory of school leadership practice: A Bourdieusian perspective. *Journal of Educational Administration and History, 45*(2), 174–188.

Eacott, S. (2014). *Relational administration: A theory and methodology for educational administration*. Rotterdam, The Netherlands: Sense Publishers.

English, F. W. (2002). The point of scientificity, the fall of the epistemological dominos, and the end of the field of educational administration. *Studies in Philosophy and Education, 21*(2), 109–136.

English, F. W. (2012). Bourdieu's misrecognition: Why educational leadership standards will not reform schools or leadership. *Journal of Educational Administration and History, 44*(2), 155–170.

Geertz, C. (1973). *The interpretation of cultures*. London: Hutchinson.

Getzels, J. W. (1952). A psycho-sociological framework for the study of educational administration. *Harvard Educational Review, 22*(3), 235–246.

Gunter, H. (2002). Purposes and positions in the field of education management: Putting Bourdieu to work. *Educational Management & Administration, 30*(1), 7–26.

Gunter, H. (2010). A sociological approach to educational leadership. *British Journal of Sociology of Education, 31*(4), 519–527.

Gunter, H. (2012). *Leadership and the reform of education.* Bristol, UK: Policy Press.

Gunter, H., & Fitzgerald, T. (2008). Educational administration and history part 1: Debating the agenda. *Journal of Educational Administration and History, 40*(1), 5–21.

Lingard, B., & Christie, P. (2003). Leading theory: Bourdieu and the field of educational leadership: an introduction and overview of this special issue. *International Journal of Leadership in Education, 6*(4), 317–333.

Maxcy, S. J. (1993). *Postmodern school leadership: Meeting the crisis in educational administration.* Westport, CT: Praeger.

Parsons, T. (1956a). Suggestions for a sociological approach to the theory of organizations-I. *Administrative Science Quarterly, 1*(1), 63–66.

Parsons, T. (1956b). Suggestions for a sociological approach to the theory of organizations-II. *Administrative Science Quarterly, 1*(2), 225–239.

Ryle, G. (1971). *Collected papers.* London: Hutchinson.

Savage, M. (2009). Contemporary sociology and the challenge of descriptive assemblage. *European Journal of Social Theory, 12*(1), 155–174.

Taylor, F. W. (1911). *The principles of scientific management.* New York: W.W. Norton.

Thomson, P. (2010). Headteacher autonomy: A sketch of a Bourdieuan field analysis of position and practice. *Critical Studies in Education, 51*(1), 5–20.

Thomson, P. (2014). *Bourdieu and educational leadership.* London: Routledge.

Tipton, B. (1977). The tense relationship of sociology and educational administration, *5*(2), 46–57.

Tyack, D., & Hansot, E. (1982). *Managers of virtue: Public school leadership in America, 1820–1980.* New York, NY: Basic Books.

Weber, M. (1922/1978). *Economy and society: An outline of interpretive sociology* (G. Roth & C. Wittich, Trans.). Berkeley, CA: University of California Press. (Originally published as *Wirtschaft und gessellschaft: grundriss der verstehenden soziologie,* Tübingen, Germany: J. C. B. Mohr/Paul Siebeck).

Wilkinson, J., & Eacott, S. (2013). Outsiders within?: Deconstructing the educational administration scholar. *International Journal of Leadership in Education, 16*(2), 191–204.

11 Cultural Perspectives on Schooling

Pamela Timanson and José da Costa

There has been pervasive curiosity about *culture* in many fields of research; education proves no exception. Researchers studying educational administration have been, and continue to be, profoundly interested in culture, particularly as it relates to school reform and school improvement initiatives. Here, we offer an historical overview of both organisational and educational administration research focused on educational organisations and school culture. Following an examination of the historical context for culture research, we explore how culture has come to be defined in organisations and in schools. Culture, given these definitions, provides the backdrop for examining other dimensions of organisational research applicable to schools. We conclude the chapter with a discussion of contemporary perspectives and uses of culture studies in educational administration and leadership.

HISTORICAL OVERVIEW

Research into organisational culture began in the 1930s. These preliminary investigations relied primarily on quantitative research methods to explore shared attitudes of employees, organisational learning, and the behaviours and perceptions of organisational members (Park & Schulte, 2004). Until the 1970s, organisational culture research remained relatively inactive. As societal changes led researchers and practitioners to place greater value on cultural diversity in the workplace and on overcoming stagnation in organisations, managers began to examine conceptions of culture in promoting organisational change. Martin and Frost (1996) noted that many North American organisations had, in the early 1970s, blindly adopted Japanese management styles (for example, those rooted in the post-WWII management ideas taught in Japan by Deming) without paying heed to cultural differences among countries. Arguably, in the absence of critical cultural considerations or investigations into the effects of cultural difference on organisational participation, North American organisations were unable to overcome the challenges of stagnation.

In the late 1970s and early 1980s, research into organisational culture experienced a renaissance as researchers recognised the intensification of managerial interest toward organisational culture. Simultaneously, researchers focused on organisational culture began to rely more on qualitative methods and less on quantitative ones as the basis for theorising (Martin & Frost, 1996).

There were two main perspectives arising from the early 1980s research: The *integration perspective* and the *differentiation perspective*. The *integration perspective* relied primarily on qualitative research methods. Researchers drawing on integration believed cultural leaders in organisations could bring about *strong* cultures if focused on *values* (Martin & Frost, 1996). Cultural transformation occurred when organisations broke down old patterns, replacing them with new ones, and, in this process, permitted conflict to occur as the new culture formed around the values of the organisation's leader (Martin & Frost, 1996).

The *differentiation* perspective also drew heavily on qualitative research methods, but highlighted *ethnography* in organisational studies. Within the differentiation perspective, there were two dominant organisational culture conceptual frameworks: (a) a critical theory approach and (b) a pluralistic approach (Martin & Frost, 1996). Researchers drawing on *differentiation* focused their attention on employees, not on those in leadership positions, examining their views of organisational culture. Cultural researchers used a material approach to their research, largely because it was more general and holistic. This allowed them to examine inconsistencies in organisational culture in greater depth. Research demonstrated how subcultures provided insight into the broader cultural context and exposed differences in organisations' subcultures with increased clarity and coherence. As Martin and Frost noted, "from a differentiation viewpoint, an organisational culture is not unitary; it is a *nexus* where environmental influences intersect, creating a nested, overlapping set of subcultures within a permeable organisational boundary" (p. 604).

With the increase in qualitative research into organisational culture studies in the 1980s, a methodological debate ensued. Qualitative researchers focused on interpreting experiences of non-managerial employees and differentiating subcultures. They accused quantitative researchers of lacking research detail, ignoring the importance of context, and focusing exclusively on managerial preferences. Quantitative research was further critiqued for providing contradicting empirical findings, focusing solely on high-ranking managers or loyal employees in their samples, and excluding any aspects of the culture producing ambiguous interpretations (Martin & Frost, 1996).

Contemporaneous to the critiques of qualitative research, researchers drawing primarily on quantitative approaches purposely focused their attention on the managerial level—developing scales and models to measure culture within organisations. These researchers were interested in investigating links among culture and variables in organisations (e.g., financial performance, school effectiveness). Quantitative researchers accused qualitative researchers of failing to provide consistent or convincing support for either of their integration and differentiation perspectives. They similarly critiqued qualitative researchers for using non-random samples of low-level employees; missing was a holistic view of organisations' shared values at all levels (Martin & Frost, 1996).

This debate was not solely a debate between quantitative and qualitative researchers. Interestingly, several disagreements ensued among researchers working exclusively within the qualitative methods perspective. One such disagreement centred on questions related to the appropriate duration for ethnographic studies. *True ethnographers* criticised the "smash and grab" ethnographic studies completed on short timelines; they believed that studies of this nature should take several months, or even years, to complete (Martin & Frost, 1996). This debate stirred some researchers to attempt mixed-methods and hybrid approaches. Quantitative and qualitative methods were blended together in attempts to address the shortcomings identified by each group of researchers. However, because of vast epistemological differences between the two general approaches, many researchers saw mixed-methods research as highly problematic. The methodological debate ultimately led to chaos within the organisational culture research community, causing managers to lose trust in the viability of the notion of culture to bring about change within organisations (Martin & Frost, 1996). In the early 1990s, chaos and lack of trust opened the door for a third cultural perspective to emerge: *fragmentation*.

Researchers aligned with the fragmentation perspective believed culture is chaotic and ambiguous within organisations; consequently, obtaining clarity is impossible since a singular and unified view of an organisation's culture is simply an illusion created by managers seeking organisational harmony (Martin, 2004; Martin & Frost, 1996). "Lack of consistency, lack of consensus, and ambiguity are the hallmarks of a fragmentation view of culture" (Martin & Frost, 1996, p. 609). Researchers drawing on the fragmentation perspective focused on the contexts of organisations to create cultural portraits illustrating ambiguity and inconsistency within the cultures of organisations being studied.

As a result of the three conflicting organisational culture perspectives, an attempt was made to create a theoretical approach that synthesised all three. The argument for this synthesis was "any culture at any point in time [would] have some aspects congruent with all three perspectives" (Martin & Frost, 1996, p. 610). The use of a synthesis approach allowed researchers to delve deeper into their understandings of culture in organisations. However, Martin and Frost argued that synthesis has limitations, particularly as the theory relates to knowledge creation and the evaluation of studies. It does not account for studies that straddle the boundaries between perspectives, it omits unclassifiable research, and the uniqueness of individual contributions is lost.

The most significant contemporary discourse to enter the organisational cultural research has been *postmodernism*. Although the three earlier perspectives are still prevalent, postmodern discourse draws attention to disorder, offers many contradictory interpretations, and views culture as arbitrary (Martin & Frost, 1996). The main goal of postmodern cultural researchers is to "challenge the foundations of modern cultural scholarship" by disrupting the hierarchical order of dominance in seeking truth (p. 612). Martin and Frost contended the main critiques of postmodern cultural research is that "it is esoteric, reactionary, apolitical, too relativistic, or nihilistic" (p. 612). Despite these critiques, Martin and Frost maintain postmodernism in organisational culture research affords opportunities for cultural texts to be more self-reflexive and for multiple voices to be represented and deconstructed.

CULTURE RESEARCH IN EDUCATIONAL ADMINISTRATION

The presence of cultural research in the educational administration literature first appeared in 1932 when Waller identified school cultures as manifest in their complex networks of relationships, shared beliefs, and moral code (Maslowski, 2006). Cultural research in educational administration circles remained relatively dormant until the 1970s, when researchers again began to look to culture as a possible means for bringing about change in schools. However, it was in the 1980s that educational culture research truly accelerated, and culture was considered an important determinant of how schools function (Firestone & Seashore-Louis, 1999; Maslowski, 2006). This acceleration coincided with the re-emergence of organisational culture research, as described above. Educational culture appealed to researchers and administrators because of its apparent ability to bring meaning to schools. Furthermore, there was optimism embodied in its potential to assist leaders to influence the cultures of their schools and to affect student achievement (Firestone & Seashore-Louis, 1999).

Educational culture research in the 1980s, primarily qualitative and interpretive, focused on a small number of schools in which perceptions of staff members were analysed in terms of shared values and beliefs (Dumay, 2009; Firestone & Seashore-Louis, 1999; Maslowski, 2006). However, in the 1990s, moves toward larger-scale quantitative studies incorporating surveys, questionnaires, and models appeared (Maslowski, 2006). Nevertheless, the majority of cultural studies remain narrowly focused on linking school culture to school effectiveness and improvement, and linking administrator roles to the cultivation of culture (Firestone & Seashore-Louis, 1999; Maslowski, 2006). Although most contemporary educational cultural research has focused on identifying cultural traits of schools, there remains some research focused on other dimensions (e.g., homogeneity, strength) of culture in schools (Dumay, 2009; Luria, 2008; Zohar & Tenne-Gazit, 2008).

Most cultural research, past and present, fails to sufficiently account for organisational conflict: focusing exclusively on the micro-cultures of the school under study rather than examining the interplay between the school and the organisational subcultures or the school and other micro-cultures (Firestone & Seashore-Louis, 1999).

DEFINITIONS OF CULTURE

Organisational culture has been defined in many different ways. Smircich (1983) defined culture as systems of meanings shared to greater or lesser extent within the group. Later Reichers and Schneider (1990) argued that culture offers an understanding of shared group conceptions and of culture's deficits, goals, and practices. The concept of *sharing* continued in Hoy and Miskel's (2008) definition in which they stated that organisational culture is a system of shared orientations that gives a distinctive identity to the organisation. However, these definitions bring question to and highlight differences of opinion as to what is shared. Schein offered one of the most enduring definitions in 1985. His remains the most persuasive definition used in organisational studies, largely because of its focus on the different levels of culture existing within organisations.

Schein (2010), drawing on his 1985 definition, described culture as a dynamic phenomenon that is "constantly reenacted and created by our interactions with others and shaped by our own behavior" (p. 3). For Schein, organisational culture is a pattern of shared basic assumptions, values, and beliefs that are continually taught to new employees ensuring they can perform optimally and relate to the nuances of organisational life. In social contexts, there exists a reciprocal structure in which the individual influences the culture of the organisation and the culture of the organisation influences the individual. This reciprocal relationship of individual and group culture extends around the employee, both in the physical and abstract space of the organisation (Schein, 2010).

Schein (2010) conceptualised three levels of culture: artifacts, espoused beliefs and values, and basic underlying assumptions. *Artifacts* are those objects in the physical space of an organisation. Artifacts are visible to outside observers; "both easy to observe and very difficult to decipher" (p. 24). Deciphering of artifacts is difficult because researchers are not able to understand their meaning until explored with an insider to the organisation. Artifacts can include: (a) technology and products used by the organisation; (b) language used by employees; (c) physical space designed and furnishings; (d) artistic creations of the organisation; (e) dress-code style embodied by employees, formality of interactions with each other, and display of emotions; (f) the narratives or myths told about the organisation; (g) published organisational mission or values statement; and (h) the observable rituals and ceremonies.

Espoused beliefs and values arise and are sustained by a dialogical process in which employees decide, through critical discourse, the knowledge that will be shared (Schein, 2010) and the standards of desirability (Maslowski, 2006). Espoused beliefs and values can appear through an empirical process when one employee believes a practical course of action is appropriate to solve a particular problem, the group carries out the course of action, and members of the group transform this into shared belief. Espoused beliefs and values can also be confirmed through social validation—social experiences are represented much like ideologies, or they can be rationalisations for desired organisational behaviours; these may not be reflected in the observed organisational behaviour (Schein, 2010).

The third level of culture entails *basic underlying assumptions*. When espoused beliefs and values are repeatedly demonstrated to be successful, they transform to become a basic assumption, shared and mutually reinforced by members of the organisation (Schein, 2010). Mutually shared organisational assumptions guide the behaviour of the employees and "tell group members how to perceive, think about, and feel about things . . . what to pay attention to, what things mean, how to react emotionally to what is going on, and what actions to take in various kinds of situations" (pp. 28–29). They are very much a part of the employees' identities and sense of self-esteem. Basic underlying assumptions offer a center to organisational life—"the nature of reality and truth, the nature of human nature, the nature of human activity and the nature of human relationships" (Maslowski, 2006, p. 8). As a result, basic underlying assumptions are very difficult to change; employees neither debate nor confront these (Schein, 2010).

Similarly, Maslowski (2006) contended that there are three aspects of culture—content, homogeneity, and strength. *Content* is "the meaning of basic assumptions, norms, and values as well as cultural artifacts shared" by organisational members (pp. 8–9). These members decide on the priority of assumptions, values, and beliefs (Dumay, 2009). *Homogeneity* is the degree to which members of an organisation share basic assumptions, norms, values, and artifacts. Homogeneity is variable between and within organisations. A high degree of homogeneity exists if nearly all members share and uphold basic assumptions, norms, values, and artifacts (Maslowski, 2006). *Strength* is the extent to which member behaviour "is actually influenced or determined by the assumptions, values, norms and artifacts" (Maslowski, 2006, p. 9). The normative pressure placed upon members to act and behave in certain ways, an interaction between cultural values and homogeneity, is understood as strength (Dumay, 2009). A strong school culture places pressure on teachers to behave in certain ways. This is due to the influence of the majority who strongly prescribe those normative behaviours that are acceptable.

Detert, Schroeder, and Mauriel (2000) completed a qualitative content analysis on culture literature; they describe eight dimensions embodied in the organisational culture phenomenon. The *basis of truth and rationality* in the organisation emanates from various ideas about truth and reality held by individuals. These are based on personal experience or scientific study. The *nature of time and time horizon* focuses on how organisations use long-term planning and goal setting or how time is defined and measured as well as its importance to the organisation (Detert et al., 2000). Examples from school settings include: instructional minutes, the timetable, and the measurement of student achievement.

Motivation "encompasses ideas about whether people are motivated from within or by external forces, whether people are inherently good or bad, whether people should be rewarded or punished, and whether effort or output can be changed by manipulating others' motivation" (Detert et al., 2000, p. 855). *Stability versus change/innovation/personal growth* classifies organisations as risk-taking or risk-aversive. Risk-taking organisations are open to change and innovation. Risk-aversive organisations prefer stability, consistency, routine, are not open to change, and are satisfied with the status quo (Detert et al., 2000). Educational organisations are often mandated toward continuous improvement yet, paradoxically, they are "almost impervious to change" (Firestone & Seashore-Louis, 1999, p. 297), looking and operating much as they did in the past.

Orientation to work, task, and coworkers describes how employees envision work. Some employees within organisations view work as a means to an end; they work solely to perform a *job* for which they are paid. Other employees view work as being both a place to complete their job and to socialise with their coworkers (Detert et al., 2000). This notion holds true for schools; teachers and leaders fall into similar categories (Firestone & Seashore-Louis, 1999).

Isolation versus collaboration/cooperation describes the extent to which leaders believe whether individual or team performance is the best method to achieve desired results. If the belief is that teams of employees work better than individuals, then work is organised such that it is group-oriented; structures are enacted to encourage employees to collaborate (Detert et al., 2000). Historically, schools have operated very much as *one-room schoolhouses*; teachers work in their own classrooms and in isolation from colleagues. Over the past decade, there have been a variety of initiatives to have schools function as professional learning communities in which teachers are provided opportunities to collaborate (*cf.* Alberta Education, 2011a).

With respect to *control, coordination, and responsibility,* organisations valuing centralised decision making are considered to be *concentrated,* while organisations valuing collaborative decision making enact shared approaches (Detert et al., 2000). Concentrated organisations are structured with few employees at higher levels making decisions and policies guiding and regulating others' behaviours. Shared organisations, by comparison, do not have as many rules and formal procedures; guiding policies tend to be created to inform decisions made by members of the organisation.

The final dimension consists of *orientation and focus—internal and/or external*. Organisations can either be controlled internally, externally, or a combination of both. Organisations are internally controlled if focused on their employees and processes; they are externally controlled if focused on customers, the environment, or competitors (Detert et al., 2000). Educational organisations experience a combination of both internal and external control. Teachers are seen as internal experts trusted to make pedagogical decisions addressing the learning needs of students (Alberta Education, 2011b) while, simultaneously, schools and school jurisdictions are externally controlled through input from stakeholders (e.g., parents, industry, government, universities). Furthermore, school improvement efforts are often judged comparatively through externally identified measures, allowing comparisons to other schools on provincial, national, and international levels (Alberta Education, 1999).

School Culture

It can be argued that schools have their own particular cultures, as they have their own "system of basic assumptions, norms and values, as well as the cultural artifacts, which are shared by school members and influence their functioning at school" (Maslowski, 2006, p. 9). Both the visible physical structures of the school and the invisible ways of being and acting influence how members of the school behave. These comprise the norms and character of any school (Díaz-Maggioli, 2004). Physical structures can profoundly influence schools' cultures. For example, some schools are physically structured to emphasise teacher isolation—the act of teaching is individual and private, thus emphasising barriers to conversations among professionals and the sharing of professional knowledge. Other schools may be highly open in structure and collegial in nature; leaders encourage collaborative learning while teachers actively seek out the collegial support of peers in a non-contrived fashion (Firestone & Seashore-Louis, 1999).

Schools can have cultures based on their clearly defined populations (e.g., adult employees, students) and their distinct political structures. There is frequently a complicated network of social relationships within a school, enabling school members to each experience a sense of belonging (Bullock, 2011). Schools also hold a commitment to, and responsibility for, student learning. This emerges as a shared sense of purpose and values, shared norms for continuous learning and improvement, and in collaborative and collegial relationships (Díaz-Maggioli, 2004).

Schools as Microcultures

Microcultures are microsystems within organisations that are dynamic and varied in comparison to overall organisational culture (Schein, 2010). They "provide special opportunities to study culture formation and evolution" because they are a small part of the larger organisation and reflect their own culture and that of the larger organisation (p. 3). Schools are microcultures commonly influenced by organisational cultures and subcultures. The larger organisational cultures, which directly influence the microcultures of schools, include: cultures of school systems and governmental organisations and the subcultures of occupational groups within organisations (Schein, 2010). The macro-level concerns of organisational culture and subcultures are inherently linked with the internal concerns of the microculture. These macro-level concerns are particularly evident as the microculture tries to balance macro-level policies and practices against pedagogical practices of the microculture. As a result, individual schools are able to change based on, for example, an influential administrator; however, there are aspects of this microculture that also reflect the larger organisational cultures' and subcultures' aversion to change (Firestone & Seashore-Louis, 1999).

Firestone and Seashore-Louis (1999) asserted that macro-level policies and practices are designed to keep schools either homogeneous or heterogeneous. For example, *homogeneous policies* demonstrable in accountability frameworks (*cf*. Alberta Education, 1999) include characteristics such as: (a) common curriculum from kindergarten through to grade twelve, (b) common resources (e.g., textbooks) that are used for instruction, (c) governmental achievement and diploma examinations, (d) accountability measures for determining funding for schools (e.g., jurisdiction plans, reports), and (e) the number of instructional minutes and the types of courses that must be offered. On the other hand, heterogeneity is present in jurisdictions where school choice is a key element. Heterogeneity is further enhanced through decentralised decision making and site-based management in which specific local needs can be addressed.

Minimally, there are two microsystems existing within the microculture of a school—the *adult* and the *student* microsystems (Firestone & Seashore-Louis, 1999). Three themes have been identified with respect to these microsystems. First, there is inherent conflict between the adults in the school and the students because of roles adults play in setting rules and standards for academic performance and student behaviour. This hierarchy innately sets a structure of adult-dominance over students. Second, teachers and administrators determine pedagogical practices. Traditional pedagogical practices typically allow for very little input from students, whereas, for example, constructivist practices are student-centred and collaborative. Third, the nature of interactions amongst teachers is either isolated or collaborative. Teachers are either isolated from each other physically—primarily working alone in classrooms—or they collaborate often with each other, during time specific for collaboration, or in shared workspaces. Interaction among teachers can also occur across department or grade groupings. Departmental and grade groupings vary in their adherence to the school culture based on how much time they spend together, the discipline-base of the department (e.g., science, math, English), and interpersonal relationships (Firestone & Seashore-Louis, 1999).

In the student microsystem, students often identify difference and categorise peers in terms of intellect and physical stature. The categorisation continues into junior high school, where different cliques form. This age grouping is often a time for rebellion against the adult microsystem; students pursue independent social lives, resist adult control, and rebel against societal expectations (Firestone & Seashore-Louis, 1999). In high school, cliques become increasingly distinct and, occasionally, rebellion also becomes a prominent feature. The dynamics of adult and student microsystems and the interplay of the organisation and subcultures "compete with administrative efforts to shape the culture in a school" (p. 311).

Cultural change appears in schools as a result of socialisation and the introduction of new individuals into the microculture (Firestone & Seashore-Louis, 1999). "School culture is responsible for the way members of a school regard themselves, their relationships with one another, and the institution and its goals" (Díaz-Maggioli, 2004, p. 10). Most new teachers entering schools are educated within the same, or a similar, system. They tend to replicate the culture of a predominately white, middle-class education system, where knowledge is transmitted from the professional teacher to the student (Firestone & Seashore-Louis, 1999).

Cultural Research in Schools

A majority of cultural research remains focused on linking school culture to school effectiveness and improvement. Additionally, this research focuses on investigating administrator influences on school culture and student achievement (Firestone & Seashore-Louis, 1999; Maslowski, 2006). This form of research has been pervasive in educational administration for twenty-five years and continues, although contested in the study of educational culture (Kythreotis, Pashiardis, & Kyriakides, 2010). At best, the research evidence examining how leadership effects school culture, and ultimately student achievement, has been mixed. Some studies demonstrate that school leadership focused on culture reform does effect student achievement, while others argue the effects are too difficult to measure (Kythreotis et al., 2010). For example, transformational, symbolic, and distributed leadership models have been found to change school culture and improve schools (Firestone & Seashore-Louis, 1999). In recent studies, Dumay (2009) and Kythreotis et al. (2010) found similar results in their investigation of the effects of leadership and culture on student achievement. However, most of the effects on student achievement were small, having only a modest impact. School culture seemed to produce only small changes in student achievement (Dumay, 2009), and direct leadership effects on student achievement appear to be rare (Kythreotis et al., 2010).

Another trend in educational administration culture research examines building learning communities within schools and school jurisdictions to bring about organisational change and school reform. These efforts place the emphasis on developing teacher capacity in terms of pedagogical strategies and commitment to and support of district goals for student achievement (Johnson & Chrispeels, 2010). Learning communities have been found to be rich spaces for teacher learning and growth (Hodkinson & Hodkinson, 2005; Levine, 2010; Sirna, Tinning, & Rossi, 2010). However, there is a tendency in schools for this collegial interaction to be contrived (Firestone & Seashore-Louis, 1999) and for teachers to view the learning community as an administrative directive, as opposed to a teacher-led learning opportunity (Johnson & Chrispeels, 2010).

CONCLUDING COMMENTS

As educational administration culture research has continued to investigate the themes of the past quarter century, with a limited number of empirical studies reported, Firestone and Seashore-Louis (1999) have argued that it is time for cultural research in education to extend to other areas. They have suggested that these areas could include the investigation of linguistic and behavioural codes that provide the basis for interactions among members within organisations. Furthermore, organisational culture research needs to make use of: (a) more eclectic methodologies to study culture in education, (b) international comparative analyses, (c) macro and micro investigations of culture, and (d) examinations of student culture beyond existing studies limited to the culture of adults in organisations.

REFERENCES

Alberta Education. (1999). *Framework for the Alberta initiative for school improvement.* Retrieved from http://education.alberta.ca/apps/publications/PublicationItem.asp?ID=173

Alberta Education. (2011a). *Alberta's commission on learning.* Retrieved from http://education.alberta.ca/department/ipr/archive/commission/report/reality/school/devlcomm.aspx

Alberta Education. (2011b). *Teaching quality standard applicable to the provision of basic education in Alberta.* Retrieved from http://education.alberta.ca/department/policy/standards/teachqual.aspx

Bullock, S. M. (2011). *Inside teacher education: Challenging prior views of teaching and learning.* Rotterdam, Netherlands: Sense Publishers.

Detert, J. R., Schroeder, R. G., & Mauriel, J. J. (2000). *A framework for linking culture and improvement initiatives in organisations.* Academy of Management Review, *25*(4), 850–863.

Díaz-Maggioli, G. (2004). *Teacher-centered professional development.* Alexandria, VA: ASCD.

Dumay, X. (2009). Origins and consequences of schools' organisational culture for student achievement. *Educational Administration Quarterly, 45*(4), 523–555. doi:10.1177/0013161X09335873

Firestone, W. A., & Seashore-Louis, K. (1999). Schools as cultures. In J. Murphy & K. Seashore-Louis (Eds.), *Handbook of research on educational administration* (pp. 297–332). San Francisco: Jossey-Bass.

Hodkinson, H., & Hodkinson, P. (2005). Improving schoolteachers' workplace learning. *Research Papers in Education, 20*(2), 109–131.

Hoy, W. K., & Miskel, C. G. (2008). *Educational administration: Theory, research, and practice* (8th ed.). New York: McGraw-Hill.

Johnson, P. E., & Chrispeels, J. H. (2010). Linking the central office and its schools for reform. *Educational Administration Quarterly, 46*(5), 738–755. doi:10.1177/0013161X10377346

Kythreotis, A., Pashiardis, P., & Kyriakides, L. (2010). The influence of school leadership styles and culture on students' achievement in Cyprus primary schools. *Journal of Educational Administration, 48*(2), 218–240. doi:10.1108/09578231011027860

Levine, T. H. (2010). Tools for the study and design of collaborative teacher learning: The affordances of different conceptions of teacher community and activity theory. *Teacher Education Quarterly, 37*(1), 109–130.

Luria, G. (2008). Climate strength: How leaders form consensus. *Leadership Quarterly, 19*(1), 42–53.

Martin, J. (2004). *Organisational culture* (Stanford Graduate School of Business research paper no 1847). Stanford, CA: Stanford University.

Martin, J., & Frost, P. (1996). The organisational culture war games: A struggle for intellectual dominance. In S. R. Glegg, C. Handy, & W. R. Nord (Eds.), *Handbook of organisation studies* (pp. 599–621). Thousand Oaks, CA: Sage.

Maslowski, R. (2006). A review of inventories for diagnosing school culture. *Journal of Educational Administration, 44*(1), 6–35. doi:10.1108/09578230610642638

Park, H., Ribière, V., & Schulte Jr., W. D. (2004). Critical attributes of organisational culture that promote knowledge management technology implementation success. *Journal of Knowledge Management, 8*(3), 106–117.

Reichers, A. E., & Schneider, B. (1990). Climate and culture: An evolution of constructs. In B. Schneider (Ed.), *Organisational climate and culture*. San Francisco: Jossey-Bass.

Schein, E. (2010). *Organisational culture and leadership* (4th ed.). San Francisco: John Wiley and Sons.

Sirna, K., Tinning, R., & Rossi, T. (2010). Social processes of health and physical education teachers' identity formation: Reproducing and changing culture. *British Journal of Sociology of Education, 31*(1), 71–84.

Smircich, L. (1983). Concepts of culture and organizational analysis. *Administrative Science Quarterly, 28*, 339–358.

Zohar, D., & Tenne-Gazit, O. (2008). Transformational leadership and group interactions as climate antecedents: A social network analysis. *Journal of Applied Psychology, 93*(4), 744–757.

12 Daoist Perspectives on Educational Leadership

Trâm Trương Anh Nguyễn

The best soldier is not soldierly;
The best fighter is not ferocious;
The best conqueror does not take part in the war;
The best employer of men keeps himself below them.

—Te, Taoism [99a] (as cited in Watts, 1975, p. 108)

In the sixth century BCE, a so-called *guidebook for rulers* appeared in the Chinese states of the Zhōu dynasty. Titled *Dào Dé Jīng* (translated as, *Book of the Way and its Powers*), the work has historically been attributed to the philosopher Lǎozi[1] (literally, *Master Lǎu*) and exists as the most important of scriptures in the oriental religious philosophy of Daoism. Underlying Daoist thought is the search for harmony in the universe. Practitioners believe this is achievable through a system of rules and practices that focus the individual upon *the way* (or the *Dào*) of natural being in the cosmos, health, longevity, and action through inaction. Over the 2600 years that have followed, the Daoist movement has spread widely, and this ancient philosophy is deeply ingrained in the psyche of many contemporary Asian cultures.

In this chapter, I propose a conceptual framework for the practice of democratic leadership in education by drawing on Daoist perspectives. To do this, I first explore Daoist ontology—particularly in terms of its perspectives on individuals in relation to themselves and others. Second, I demonstrate the intersection between Daoism and democratic leadership. Lastly, I propose a conceptual framework for the practice of democratic leadership in education from a Daoist worldview, employing four tenets: (a) a view of the *individual as microcosm* and of the *organisation as macrocosm*; (b) an acknowledgement of *interrelationships* among the leader, the individual, the organisation, and the environment; (c) the identification of a *space of freedom* for exercising intersubjectivity and democracy; and (d) the necessity for building an organisational *culture grounded in mutual trust*. The central thread underlying all four tenets can be summarised in the notion of *harmonious interconnectedness* with two procedural concepts: *intersubjectivity* and *democracy*.

A DAOIST ONTOLOGY

> The way begets one;
> one begets two;
> two begets three;
> three begets the myriad creatures.
>
> (Lao Tzu, c. 600BCE/1963, Chapter XLII)[2]

Daoists believe that the Dào creates all creatures; and practitioners seek to know what the Dào is. The Dào is the central concept running throughout the classical Chinese work of Lăozi. In the *Dào Dé Jīng*, the concept of the Dào is understood as *the Way*:

> The way that can be spoken of is not the constant way.
> The name that can be named is not the constant name.
>
> (Lao Tzu, c. 600BCE/2001, Chapter I)

And hence "[t]he way is forever nameless" (Lao Tzu, c. 600BCE/1963, Chapter XXXII). Indeed, "[t]here is no name that is applicable to the *tao* because language is totally inadequate for such a purpose" (Lau, 1963, p. 16). In other words, the Dào cannot be named because of its greatness. It is the creator of all beings, and in this sense, the Dào is "responsible for the creation as well as the support of the universe" (Lau, 1963, p. 16). More than that, it is also an endless living source of the universe, neither born nor dead:

> The Tao is like a well
> Used but never used up.
> It is like the eternal void:
> Filled with infinite possibilities.
> It is hidden but always present.
> I don't know who gave birth to it.
> It is older than God.
>
> (Lao Tzu, c. 600BCE/1999, Chapter IV)

As the Dào creates "myriad creatures" or the "ten thousand beings," it thus creates human beings. Noticeably, in creation, "the human being occupies no special position, except that of the most complex conglomerate, incorporating all the differentiated energies of the universe" (Schipper, 1982/1993, p. 34). That is, contemporaneously, human beings are part of the universe and contain all the energies of the universe; humans and the universe are interrelated. Man is a microcosm for the cosmos; "all things correspond to each other, . . . microcosm reflects macrocosm, and vice versa." (Ebrey, Schipper, Steinhardt, & Hung, 2000, p. 14). This stands as the central cosmological principle of Daoist thought, and is interpreted to mean that if each *individual* is a microcosm, then *the world* is also a macrocosm—thus these two entities are mutually inclusive and operate as a functional unity. On the view of Daoists, the macrocosm functions as everlasting source of life and the microcosm possesses all features of the macrocosm. The microcosm functions as not only a *living cell* of the macrocosm but also a *diminished version* of the universe. Given this position, when humans fail to recognise themselves as a microcosm, they demean and separate themselves from the macrocosm. They become *dead* (figuratively and spiritually speaking) and, at the same time, unwittingly deny their own great potential. Daoists do not consider it hyperbole to associate such a state of disconnectedness with death. For the Daoist, disconnection is contrary to the inherent nature of humanity.

As microcosm, Daoists emphasise how each individual has his or her own uniqueness and great potential because each microcosm—sharing the same source—is no different from the macrocosm:

> The Tao is great.
> The universe is great.
> Earth is great.
> Man is great.
> These are the four great powers.
> (Lao Tzu, c. 600BCE/1999, Chapter XXV)

On this principle, a person can grow fully only when he or she recognises and makes the best use of his or her inner potential and, at the same time, establishes connections with the outside world. For Daoists, this suggests the individual, turned inward, makes a link with his or her internal world while simultaneously, turned outward, establishes relationships with his or her external world. Such interconnectedness is characteristic of human maturity.

For the uninitiated, a question may arise: Given our creation by the Dào and the contention that we are, from genesis, connected to the universe, does it remain necessary to establish *connections with the macrocosm*? The Daoist would explain how our creation represents merely an *initial* connection in an ongoing process. During a lifetime, the individual should, on the Daoist view, wittingly and continuously maintain and develop the relationship for the sake of *long-lasting* existence and *healthy* growth. Lǎozi argued that "[w]hoever is planted in the Tao/will not be rooted up. / Whoever embraces the Tao/will not slip away" (Lao Tzu, c. 600BCE/1999, Chapter LIV). From this, the uninitiated may pose another question: How can people know whether their microcosm has been successfully united with the macrocosm in the requisite manner? Daoists find an answer as implicitly expressed in the notion of *harmony* as expressed in the *Dào Dé Jīng*: "[t]o know harmony is called the constant;/to know the constant is called discernment" (Lao Tzu, c. 600BCE/1963, Chapter LV) Here, harmony is one's harmony with the Dào, "[i]n harmony with the Tao,/the sky is clear and spacious,/the earth is solid and full,/all creatures flourish together,/ content with the way they are,/endlessly repeating themselves,/endlessly renewed" (Lao Tzu, c. 600BCE/1999, Chapter XXXIX).

The primary sign of the unity between microcosm and macrocosm arises when the individual finds herself able to live *in peaceful harmony* with her internal and external world. Key is the fact that the Daoist notion of *harmony* does not imply an existence *without conflicts*. Rather, harmony denotes the ability to maintain peaceful harmony in the face of conflicts by realising the shared source of all existence:

Each separate being in the universe returns to the common source.
Returning to the source is serenity.
If you don't realize the source,
you stumble in confusion and sorrow.
When you realize where you come from,
you naturally become tolerant
(Lao Tzu, c. 600BCE/1999, Chapter XVI)

Furthermore, "[s]he who is centred in the Tao/can go everywhere she wishes, without danger./She perceives the universal harmony,/even amid great and pain,/because she has found peace in her heart" (Lao Tzu, c. 600BCE/1999, Chapter XXXV). To this end, Daoism not only acknowledges conflicts but also offers a possible means to deal with conflicts through *harmony*. Procedurally, for Daoism, harmony is synonymous with the state of *moderation*, *flexibility*, and of keeping all *in balance*. Moderation is synonymous with avoiding extremist positions; "any over-determined behavior produces its opposite" (Heider, 1985, p. 3). Moderation is also essential for good Daoist leadership. "[f]or governing a country well/there is nothing better than moderation" (Lao Tzu, c. 600BCE/1999, Chapter LIX).

In Daoist thought, the mention of moderation cannot be divorced from balance. "[b]e aware of when things are out of balance./Stay centred within the Tao" (Lao Tzu, c. 600BCE/1999, Chapter LIII). Put simply, it is critical for a leader, indeed all people, to remain moderate and keep balance. "Fill your bowl to the brim," wrote Lǎozi, "and it will spill./Keep sharpening your knife/and it will blunt" (Lao Tzu, c. 600BCE/1999, Chapter IX). Hence, a sage should know how to avoid letting one extreme or one opposing force repeatedly dominate the other—for then it may become the *opposite* in accord with the principle of *yīn-yáng*.

For Daoists, "[a]ll behavior consists of opposites or polarities. If I do anything more and more, over and over, its polarity will appear" (Heider, 1985, p. 3). These polarities are expressed in the unified principle of *yīn* (shadow) and *yáng* (light). The *yīn-yáng* represents the Daoist belief that nothing is without an interconnected opposite. However, when out of balance, "any excess, whether of *yin* or *yang*, is considered dangerous" (Oldstone-Moore, 2003, p. 78).

In addition to moderation and balance, flexibility is no less encouraged. "He who is in harmony with the Tao/is like a newborn child./Its bones are soft, its muscles are weak,/but its grip is powerful" (Lao Tzu, c. 600BCE/1999, Chapter LV). Put another way, to the Daoist, flexibility implies life or victory while rigidity signifies death or defeat. "At birth, a person is flexible and flowing. At death, a person becomes rigid and blocked" (Heider, 1985, p. 151).

From the above discussed essential elements, one can conclude that in a Daoist ontology emphasis is placed upon individual *human value*, the necessary *interconnectedness* between an individual's internal world and his or her external world, and that *expected harmony* is found in the practice of moderation, balance, and flexibility in all belief, action, and behaviour. In this, the Daoist infers that one only *exists* when one is connected with oneself and with others; one only *grows* healthily and persistently when one maintains *harmonious interconnectedness* with oneself (internally) and with others (externally). In the section that follows, the core of Daoist thought is offered as a lens through which leadership may be examined.

DAOISM AND DEMOCRATIC LEADERSHIP

I herein develop a framework for the practice of democratic leadership based on Daoist cosmology. In the work of Lǎozi can be found a view on leadership that I believe shares much with the occidental conception of *democratic leadership*. According to Lǎozi, ideal Daoist leaders maintain a low profile, leading mostly by example and allowing followers to take ownership:

> The best of all rulers is but a shadowy presence to his subjects.
> Next comes the ruler they love and praise;
> Next comes one they fear;
> Next comes one with whom they take liberties.
> (Lao Tzu, c. 600BCE/1963, Chapter XVII)

This point resonates with much in the Western view of democratic leadership, but particularly in terms of the belief that leaders ought not be controlling. As Cunningham and Cordeiro (2003) defined, democratic leaders are those who "delegate authority and responsibility and permit subordinates to function within defined limits. . . . Organization members develop an understanding of themselves and prepare for and accept ownership of their work" (p. 183). Fiore (2004) similarly defined democratic leadership as an approach in which "[l]eaders encouraged the group to be involved in the decision-making process. They informed subordinates about all conditions affecting their work, and they encouraged subordinates to express their feelings and ideas openly" (p. 15). Thus, a democratic leadership style is one that decentralises power and delegates authority and responsibility to subordinates by permitting them to engage in the policy-making or decision-making processes through open dialogue. Consequently, members of a democratically led organisation maintain a sense of owner-ship in their work. Equally, the Daoist would hold that "[t]he wise leader stays centered and grounded and uses the least force required to act effec-tively" (Heider, 1985, p. 57). Daoists thus advocate a minimal—or the least controlling—leadership approach, requiring little use of institutional or personal force (in all of their manifestations). "When force is used, conflict and argument follow. The group field degenerates. The climate is hostile, neither open nor nourishing" (p. 59), and leaders "think that their con-stant interventions are a measure of ability, when in fact such interventions are crude and inappropriate" (p. 57). Alternatively stated, the controlling leadership approach, for Daoists, provokes negative responses from mem-bers and is consequently counterproductive. "Governing a large country [or organisation]/is like frying a small fish./You spoil it with too much poking" (Lao Tzu, c. 600BCE/1999, Chapter LX).

A CONCEPTUAL FRAMEWORK FOR THE DAOIST PRACTICE OF DEMOCRATIC LEADERSHIP

Upon a foundation of Daoist cosmology—recalling its strong emphasis on the *equal* interrelations between and among microcosms and macrocosm—I posit that the *harmonious interconnectedness* between and among individu-als and the larger world exists only when there is *intersubjectivity* among them on the foundation of *democratic* principles. This is my primary thesis. The notion of harmonious interconnectedness (with two procedural concepts of intersubjectivity and democracy) is central to my proposed framework. It will be conceptualised as follows: (a) a view of the individual as microcosm and organisation macrocosm; (b) acknowledging the interrelationships among leaders, individuals, organisations, and environments—a minimal-ist leadership approach; (c) assuring an individual space of freedom—an agent for intersubjectivity and democracy; and (d) building an organisa-tional culture grounded in mutual trust—another agent for intersubjectivity and democracy.

A View of the Individual as Microcosm and the Organisation as Macrocosm

To begin, I define an organisation as a macrocosm consisting of a complex system of microcosms that (a) adhere together through the gravity of a power created not only by cultural, political, philosophical, social, and economic influences but also by emotional constraints, and that (b) operates on a certain principle toward desired goals. Accordingly, I mean that individuals are the primary agents and creators of organisation, while simultaneously an organisation is comprised of individuals. In a similar manner, Greenfield (1979) assumed that "organizations are nothing other than people doing and acting for whatever reasons seem adequate or desirable to them" (p. 107). In this respect, although Greenfield's beliefs about organisation and individuals are shared in that framework that I propose, I would argue for a more optimistic view of the connections between and among members and their organisation. Specifically, unlike Greenfield's emphasis on separate individuals' subjectivity, the framework assumes the role of intersubjectivity as mechanism of connection.

Greenfield's (1979) account of an organisation is as a collection of different separate individuals. Like Daoist leaders, Greenfield (1979) addressed the individual's uniqueness in an organisation and, in turn, how an organisation is constituted of different individuals; however, his was shy of the conclusion that individuals are interconnected in the manner discussed above:

> We live in separate realities. But we live with each other. . . . We need to move from the conviction that there is only one social reality to a recognition of the possibility that many exist. How we are to understand and appreciate these alternate perspectives as theorists and as human beings is not altogether clear.
>
> (p. 109)

It seems that the failure to enunciate how individuals who operate as differentiated subjective entities can be interlinked resulted from Greenfield's doubt about the possibility of mutual understanding, which is primarily conditioned by emotional understanding. Indeed, the inability to understand interconnected human existence is more explicitly expressed when Greenfield cited words from one of Pirandello's (1954) six characters to support his assumption:

> Each one of us has a whole world of things inside him. . . . And each of us has his own particular world. How can we understand each other if into the words which I speak I put the sense and the value of things as I understand them myself. . . . While at the same time whoever is listening to them inevitably assumes them to have the sense and value that they have for him. . . . The sense and value that they have in the world that he has within him? We think we understand one another. . . . But we never really do understand!
>
> (as cited in Greenfield, 1979, pp. 98–99)

As was held by Greenfield, individuals hardly understand one another because

> [t]he self that lives by one set of values, by one ideology, within one social organization, is not the self that lives by other values, within

other ideas, or other organizations, though the same consciousness may connect the two realities. Even more so, then, do different people live within different realities.

(p. 99)

Accordingly, the only factor possibly linking people together, on Greenfield's account, is *consciousness* moulded by rules or by a violent imposing force driven by a coercive ideological vision. The connection among individuals (to create organisation) is so weak, *emotionally* at least again on Greenfield's account, and rests on account of its *compulsory*, rather than *voluntary*, nature. "And the social system now appears, not as an objective reality, but as an ideological social order accepted by individuals or forced upon them" (p. 101). In advancing my Daoist alternative, below, I briefly digress to explain why Greenfield's consciousness-based link is fragile.

Friedrich Nietzsche held that "consciousness is the latest development in the organic world, of which humans are part, and as such is the most unfinished and weakest part of the self. Much stronger are the human instincts" (Burkitt, 2008, p. 13). From this argument, I question the solidity of Greenfield's consciousness-based link—particularly in the absence of emotional understanding—among individuals in an organisation that springs from mere consciousness.

A Daoist perspective presumes that each individual exists as a microcosm laden with personal uniqueness and potential. However, this presumption does not entail that a microcosm can be separated from other microcosms and from the macrocosm. Although it is true that "each one of us has a whole world of things inside him. . . . And each of us has his own particular world," there are still common things held among individuals. It is *not* necessarily true that "we never really do understand" one another. In contrast to Greenfield's assumptions, in Daoist thought, the distinction between the self and others is artificial: all come from the same source, the Dào. Barriers among people that create the different realities articulated in Greenfield's work are merely *constructed* by the human mind. To fully appreciate this statement, however, one must understand how the Daoist defines construction as the imposition of judgment. Thus, in Daoist terms, to understand others is a function of one's willingness to *deconstruct* (that is, to abandon judgment and see the world as it is) the reality infused by one's own values and experiences. Only at this point is one's heart open to connect and merge with others' realities.

In Daoist cosmology, any belief in the self as discrete substance is illusion; *intersubjectivity* accounts for interrelatedness between and among individuals. Revisiting Greenfield's (1979) position, perhaps it is not unfair to say that his implicit assumption, the self as separate, leads to his belief that "[w]e think we understand one another. . . . But we never really do understand" because for him each person has his or her own world that others cannot penetrate. Conversely, for Daoists "[t]hat which has no substance/enters where there is no space" (Lao Tzu, c. 600BCE/1999, Chapter XLIII). Put differently, the self has no substance because it is merely contingent flux created by the nameless, formless, and infinite Dào. Yet, paradoxically, thanks to this attribute it can enter where there is no space. With this thought, Daoists disrupt the barrier between self and others, and strongly believe that we *can* gain reciprocal understanding, empathy, and compassion even though there *seems* to be a gap between and among people—as long as we abandon the illusion that the self is real and discrete. "When we don't see the self as self,/what do we have to fear?" (Lao Tzu, c. 600BCE/1999, Chapter XIII). Metaphorically, the Dào is assumed by followers to be the central thread that weaves the intangible web of individuals, organisation, society, and the world.

Ultimately, viewing individual as microcosm and organisation as macrocosm allows me, like Greenfield, to value the importance of individuals embodying their own uniqueness within the organisation. However, unlike Greenfield, Daoists would argue that individuals *can* be interconnected, and hence mutual understanding can be gained through their intersubjectivity, despite subjective differences.

Acknowledging the interrelationships among leader, individual, organisation, and environment—a minimalist leadership approach. The interconnectedness among microcosms *and* between microcosms and macrocosm in Daoist philosophy allows me to argue for a leadership style that encourages *harmonious interrelationships* among leader, individual, organisation, and environment. It is important to recall that the notion of *harmonious* here does not mean *without conflicts*, but rather keeping peaceful harmony in the face of conflicts.

Recall how Lǎozi described the best leaders: "When the Master [best leader] governs, the people/are hardly aware that he exists" (Lao Tzu, c. 600BCE/1999, Chapter XVII). Alternatively, he said,

> the Taoist sages advocate a minimalist approach to leadership because government reflects a distrust of the working of the Tao and human nature. . . . When left alone, followers obey natural laws and society as a whole benefits. Therefore, she/he who governs best governs least.
>
> (Johnson, 2000, p. 85)

On this principle, and at the center of my proposed model, a leader's power is made *invisible* and *minimal* such that *all* individuals within the organisation feel theirs is an *equal* contribution. As such, they engage participation in organisational decision making, rather than fear the power from above.

Assuring an individual space of freedom—an agent for intersubjectivity and democracy. Daoists view the individual-microcosm as embodying great potential. To germinate this potential, I argue for *individual spaces of freedom* in organisations. In this section, I provide a definition of individual spaces, and articulate attributes that facilitate emotional and intellectual intelligence. These two kinds of intelligence, I argue, facilitate the creation of intersubjectivity and further enhance democracy in an organisation. Finally, I offer a conceptual framework for building such individual spaces.

An individual space of freedom is a space that allows each person to be herself or himself. I call it a space of freedom because I assume in this space people liberate themselves from external impositions. One such imposition emerges from ideologies with instrumentalised dominating discourses.

Ideologies and discourses free humans from immediate oppression, but also create new and sophisticated prisons that confine. In such prisons, "humans 'see' what their language, culture, and context permit them to see" (English, 2008, p. 55). Wittingly or not, most people live a life others have defined. Consequently, when the mind is confined, the heart cannot find peace. That is why Lǎozi advised, "Empty your mind of all thoughts./Let your heart be at peace" (Lao Tzu, c. 600BCE/1999, Chapter XVI). This advice does not mean, for Daoism, that the mind should be completely emptied of thoughts or the acts of thinking. Rather, *thoughts* in the Daoist tradition can be understood as social values and even biases internalised by individuals. With these values and biases individuals are shaped, and also with them individuals shape the world—or, at least, the ways individuals see the world. Such a shaped mind, for Daoists, is like a *carved block*: unnatural and antithetical to the Dào.

Unsurprisingly, Lǎozi valued the *uncarved block*, which he described as "blank, childlike, untutored, dark, [and] nameless. . . . To reach it is to 'know oneself', to 'return to the root from which we grew,' [and] to 'push far enough towards the Void'" (Welch, 1965, p. 46). For Lǎozi, the "uncarved block" is "connected with intuition as opposed to discursive reasoning" (p. 47). Hence, a space of freedom facilitates an individual's return to him- or herself. There they may regain their liberty from external impositions, be true to themselves, connect with themselves. Further, there they may recognise those connections with the external worlds they may need to (re)establish to satisfy their interests and make themselves and others grow intellectually and emotionally.

Due to external and causal constraints, I do not expect people will experience *absolute* freedom, no matter how free the space provided. Dewey (1987, p. 220) similarly cautioned against the overly idealist view of absolute freedom when he recognised that organisational freedom "is not the right of each individual to do as he pleases but [it is] freedom of mind and [it is] whatever degree of freedom of action and experience . . . necessary to produce freedom of intelligence" (as cited in Olssen, Codd, & O'Neill, 2004, p. 270). It is this individual space of freedom, or what Goens (2005) called "the inner context"—that defines "who we are and who we want to be and affects our relationship to and in the outside world" (p. 17). Space helps us grow emotionally because "in our inner world, . . . true learning and growth come when we take experiences and emotions to heart–feel them, embrace them, and sense them" (p. 20).

My notion of individual space of freedom may overlap that of Goens (2005) in the sense that space may affect its owner's behaviour and his or her relationships with the external world. However, the inner space does not necessarily define who we are and who we want to be. The important point is that in this space one can come to understand the nature of one's *self*. Inner space brings inner freedom to deconstruct our social self. It permits letting go of social and cultural impositions held over us, and we come nearer to our inner self to know its nature. To some extent, inner freedom as I have articulated it may overlap with Maslow's (1970) concept of *inner freedom*:

> It is an inner freedom that they have. So long as they are independent of the approval and disapproval of other people, and seek rather self-approval, so long may they be considered to be psychologically autonomous, in other words, relatively independent of the culture.
>
> (p. 279)

It is worth noting that *letting go* does not here mean resisting or separating from one's bias. Letting go is to manifest an impartial and calm mind that does not attempt to hold fast objects of consciousness. It is the realisation that all is impermanent and contingent. Thus, inner space is not a space in which we construct our *self*; rather, we deconstruct our self in search of liberty (not only *from*, but also *to*). For these reasons, the Daoist democratic leader will recognise and help members of the organisation to build their individual space of freedom.

An individual space of freedom helps develop *emotional intelligence* (to borrow the term from Scharmer [2009], who expressed a similar idea) inasmuch as it helps open one's heart, and consequently facilitates intersubjectivity. In Scharmer's (2009) words, the open heart "relates to our ability to access our emotional intelligence, or EQ; that is, our capacity to empathize with others, to tune into different contexts, and to put ourselves into someone else's shoes" (p. 41). In this respect, the individual space is an intersubjective *agent* (so to speak) that both links microcosms together and links microcosms to the macrocosm, by enhancing understanding and empathy between and among people. Although, in this space, people try to liberate themselves from external constraints and gain some independence from the outside world, the space does not give rise to selfishness and isolation. The space facilitates the linking of one to others, after linking to oneself, in the way that promotes mutual understanding and empathy. On this, Lǎozi explained, "our inner nature is an extension of the nature of the universe" (Welch, 1965, p. 45). Indeed, returning to themselves, *truly* knowing themselves, and understanding their origins helps individuals turn to others in the spirit of tolerance and compassion. Lǎozi taught that "when you realize where you come from,/you naturally become tolerant,/. . . kind-hearted as a grandmother" (Lao Tzu, c. 600BCE/1999, Chapter XVI).

No doubt, in different traditions, there are different ways to articulate the above discussed connection between knowing one's *self* and compassion. It is generally believed that when we know ourselves, we will, more or less, gain empathy for others. Indeed, Sinagatullin (2006) held that "understanding and learning more about yourself . . . will greatly promote your understanding of other people who are, by nature, very much like you" (p. 173). For the Buddhist, there is no permanent substance to one's selfhood. To know one's self *truly* is to realise that a permanent self does *not* exist, and "the realization of the absence of such a permanent self leads to selfless loving kindness and compassion for others" (Mitchell, 2002, p. 37). Thanks to our self-awareness, the heart is open and emotional intelligence is developed.

In summary, no matter how the relation between self-knowledge and compassion is explained, inner space—as an intersubjective agent—facilitates self-knowledge and helps link one to one's self, to others, and to the world, through understanding and empathy, built in the virtue of an open heart.

Individual space helps promote *intellectual intelligence* (once again borrowing Scharmer's [2009] term to express the link between *open mind* and *intellectual intelligence*) and self-empowerment. It is foundational to a Daoist vision of democracy in an organisation. With respect to the relationship between mind and intellectual intelligence, Scharmer (2009) held that "The first instrument, or capacity, the *open mind*, is based on our ability to access our intellectual, or IQ, type of intelligence. This allows us to see with fresh eyes, to deal with the objective figures and facts around us" (p. 41).

Revisiting Daoist cosmology, all sentient living beings are *equal* because they all come from the same source, the Dào. In this respect, I explore how the individual space will dispose people toward equality in a Daoist manner in virtue of *mind*, or intellectual intelligence, and through its desired mode of thinking. To do this, I will make a comparison between modes of thinking—as a means of self-empowerment and hence a move towards equality—from Western and Daoist perspectives.

In the Western paradigm, equality is hardly achieved without a *free* mind that makes room for critical thinking. As mentioned above, although people cannot have absolute freedom, they should be at least assured a space to return to themselves and, according to Socrates, to make "their own selves fully their own" (Nussbaum, 1997, p. 21). Along a similar vein, Dewey (1987, p. 220) argued "it is not the right of each individual to do as he pleases but freedom of mind and of whatever degree of freedom of action and experience is necessary to produce freedom of intelligence" (as cited in Olssen, Codd, & O'Neill, 2004, p. 270). In fact, Western perspectives contend that freedom of mind facilitates critical, deliberative, and creative thinking. Each of critical, deliberative, and creative thinking form self-empowerment. With self-empowerment, the Western perspective suggests, individuals can achieve greater equality with their fellow humans.

This is vital for democracy because "lacking their own independent visions of what to do or what to be, most individuals become what others now, or before them, have created for them" (Greenfield, 1979, p. 107); and hence, domination and oppression ensue. As Greenfield (1980) demonstrated in his theory of organisation, "there is no group mind that thinks for the rest of us and will have its way. It is we who must have our way or who acquiesce" (p. 40).

At a macro social level, talking about the relationship between critical thinking and democratic citizenship, Philips (1997) held that:

> Good thinking is a prerequisite for good citizenship because it helps the citizen form more intelligent judgments on issues and to the democratic solution of social problems. There can be no liberty for a society that lacks the critical skills to distinguish lies from the truth.
>
> (p. 264)

Daoists would *not* challenge this belief. Here, readers may wonder if there is any contradiction where I earlier noted how Daoists advocate the idea of freeing the mind from thoughts or the acts of thinking while not opposing critical thinking (at least as defined in Western perspectives). There is *no contradiction* intended. Daoists advise people to free their mind from thoughts so that their heart can be opened. This does *not* mean that they ought to keep a completely *void* mind or a mind in the absence of thoughts. Rather, there ought to be absence of judgment and bias in their mind so that the mind perceives the world as it is. To this end, the empty mind does not block critical, deliberative, creative, or any other manner of thinking generally advocated by Westerners. Hence, in this sense, Daoist thought is not antithetical to a Western conception of thinking. However, Daoists persist further by advocating contemplation, an altogether more abstract level of thinking. Contemplation is not necessarily different from thinking in the ordinary sense, but it denotes a higher level of thinking: thinking to *unthink*. In this way, a Daoist mode of thinking consists of not only thinking critically but also thinking *desconstructively* about what one is taught by tradition. For Lăozi, *unthinking* thinking represents the highest and most ideal level at which the mind is completely free from its own bias to see things as they are: "Stop thinking, and end your problems./What difference between yes and no?/What difference between success and failure?/Must you value what others value,/avoid what others avoid?/How ridiculous!" (Lao Tzu, c. 600BCE/1999, Chapter XX).

Unthinking thinking lets the mind reside in the Dào, the oneness, and non-duality by avoiding attachment to ideas. "The Master keeps her mind/always at one with the Tao;/that is what gives her radiance./The Tao is ungraspable./How can her mind be at one with it?/Because she doesn't cling to ideas" (Lao Tzu, c. 600BCE/1999, Chapter XXI). It is through non-attachment that practitioners see the world without bias; hence, they treat all livings equally and impartially.

In the individual space of freedom, people are taught not only how to think in the ordinary sense but also at the higher level of unthinking. The individual space of freedom allows the individual to reach the highest level of thinking, contemplation, and enter a realm of thought beyond the duality of thinking and non-thinking to see the world as it is. For Daoists, this is the highest stage of intellectual development because in the individual space of freedom the mind is completely open, dispensing with its accumulated biases. As Scharmer (2009) succinctly put the matter: "the mind works like a parachute: it only functions when it is open" (p. 41). The individual space of freedom is instrumental in intellectual intelligence; it is of paramount importance to the facilitation of democracy—not only in organisation but also in the larger environment. In the next section, I propose a way to build an individual space of freedom.

Building Individual Spaces of Freedom

Generally speaking, building individual spaces of freedom requires effort by leaders and followers.

On the part of leaders. Leaders ought not impose their own ideologies on their followers. Daoists believe that to secure an individual space of freedom, democratic leaders should help all members of the organisation build their own space so that they can think with their own minds, speak with their own voices, and act on their own will. Indeed, in Lǎozi's opinion, "The Master has no mind of her own./She works with the mind of people" (Lao Tzu, c. 600BCE/1999, Chapter XLIX). This is understood by Daoists to reflect the notion that leaders ought not use their own will to bend others' toward a set of established controlling virtues. Equally, interpreting *Dào Dé Jīng*, Heider (1985) shared a similar view. "The wise leader does not impose a personal agenda or value system on the group" (p. 97), and hence leaders will "learn how fruitful the blocked group or individual suddenly becomes when you give up trying to do just the right thing" (p. 95). To achieve this, leaders should first be open to, and tolerant towards, a diversity of points of view. In the Daoist tradition, "[b]eing open and attentive is more effective than being judgmental," and in this case "[p]erhaps the leader seems naïve and childlike in this uncritical openness to whatever emerges. But openness is simply more potent than any system of judgments ever devised" (p. 97).

Leaders should create opportunities for their followers to innovate and discover. Leaders should neither push nor intervene unnecessarily in a group's work. Daoist leaders acknowledge that "[t]oo much force will backfire. Constant interventions and instigations will not make a good group" (Heider, 1985, p. 57). Similarly, in the Western paradigm, leadership demonstrating excessive force and control is often synonymous with authoritarian leadership. As put by Fiore (2004):

[a]lthough authoritarian leadership [has] led to an initial increase in productivity, this style [tends] to yield either aggressive or apathetic

behavior from subordinates. This [has been] thought to be the result of frustration subordinates felt [as a consequence of] the authoritarian leadership style.

(p. 16)

Equally, in Daoist philosophy, force provokes hostility and even an aggressive response. "When force is used, conflict and argument follow. . . . The climate is hostile" (Heider, 1985, p. 59), and there will be "a deeper resistance and possibly even resentment" because paradoxically "while they [subordinates] may do what you tell them to do at the time, they will cringe inwardly, grow confused, and plot revenge" (p. 61).

At a higher level, leaders should pay attention to the concept of unity. This proposition adheres to the principle of Dào (Heider, 1985). To do this, leaders should bridge the gaps among members of the organisation by providing opportunities for connection with one another in the form of teamwork and collaboration. As noted earlier, connectedness nurtures the individual spaces of freedom. In the literature on educational organisations, Glickman, Gordon, and Ross-Gordon (2009) have called this connectedness "a cause beyond themselves." These authors explained:

Teachers do not view their work as simply what they carry out within their own four walls. In successful schools, teachers see themselves as part of the larger enterprise of complementing and working with each other to educate students. For successful schools, education is a collective rather than an individual enterprise.

(p. 35)

For Daoists there are relationships among microcosms and between microcosms and macrocosm because they share the same essence, the Dào. Indeed, for Daoists what there was in the beginning "refers macrocosmically to the universe, microcosmically to oneself" (Welch, 1965, p. 47). Translated into the field of educational administration, this principle would ensure equal co-operation between and among teachers or members of the institution, which in turn is pivotal to a successful organisation.

On the part of followers. It is critical that followers perceive themselves as microcosms with great potential. In Lǎozi's assumption, the universe is great and *man* is also great. Individuals ought to recognise that they need to grow and be treated as full and capable members of their organisation. Although Daoists would understand that no man is perfect, subordinates in organisations are not to see themselves as defective or *perpetually* reliant on a flawless leadership cadre. With such *persistent* passiveness, people in organisations will find themselves being controlled under the guise of *assistance* or *dependence*.

To set themselves free from domination, individual members of the organisation must build a space of freedom for themselves. This is often no easy task, for, as a matter of familiarity, *prisoners* may at times feel safer in the prison—the devil they know. To tackle this, emancipation begins with the de-construction of the *prisons of dominating ideologies*. Members of the organisation need to arrive at an awareness of their diverse identities— not only as human-*beings* and-*doings*, but also human-*thinkings*; not only through *critical thinking* but also through *unthinking thinking*. The "Tao does not preach sermons or dictate behavior. . . . Instead of asking for advice, learn to become more conscious of what is actually happening. Then you will be able to see for yourself how things happen. You can make your own decisions about what to do" (Heider, 1985, p. 145).

Building an Organisational Culture Grounded in Mutual Trust—Another Agent for Intersubjectivity and Democracy

To obtain harmonious interrelationships between and among individuals in an organisation, the Daoist emphasises a prerequisite healthy milieu, feeding on a supportive and constructive culture built on trust. On my Daoist understanding, trust fulfils the role of agent for intersubjectivity and democracy. In this section, I present the relationships among trust, intersubjectivity, and democracy; I then offer a Daoist means of building trust.

The relationships among trust, intersubjectivity, and democracy. Building an organisational culture grounded upon mutual trust is vital for the practice of Daoist democratic leadership. Lǎozi said that, "If you don't trust the people, you make them untrustworthy" (Johnson, 2000, p. 86). It is worth noting that the notion of trust developed in this section is the trust expected among *all* members in an organisation who are emotionally attached thought what I shall call *universal trust*. It was held by Levin (2008) that "the first requirement to build commitment and engagement is mutual respect and trust among all the partners in a school system" (p. 121). No doubt, this kind of trust is different from the trust that was described by Clegg (2007) in his analysis of *family-based trust of Chinese organizations*: "family can be trusted, outsiders cannot" (p. 594). More accurately stated from the Daoist tradition, the relationships among trust, intersubjectivity, and democracy can be articulated as I present in the paragraphs that follow.

First, trust draws people together so that they can live, work, and grow in peace with each other. This brings about a shift from subjectivity to intersubjectivity, the capacity that connects people and where different elements of subjectivity converge. This, in turn, paves the way for democracy—at least to the extent that people may become increasingly open to expressing their own ideas and gaining certain satisfaction in interpersonal relationships and work. Although each individual has his or her own inner world, thanks to mutual trust, people are presented with viable opportunities to understand and see themselves in one another. Undoubtedly, trust draws people closer together with both their *head* and their *heart*. Indeed, Starratt (2004) emphasised the importance of trust in building a coherent democratic community:

> This is building democracy from the ground up, from the recent pain, fears, and nightmares; learning to trust that the social fabric can be healed, learning to trust that the community will hold together for yet another day. This is a democracy of the human heart sharing the burdens of others, working together to rebuild shattered lives, constructing in the educating process, as Goddard suggests, bridges to a liveable future.
>
> (p. 725)

On the contrary, in the absence of trust, people will live in constant fear and suspicion. This limits their freedom of speech and action, and, undeniably, a lack of freedom is the enemy of democracy. Such culture is harmful. It creates a climate of fear and suspicion that hinders people from daring to think and act; it impedes both personal and organisational development.

How to build trust. Leaders must be impartial. As articulated, this proposition stems from the Daoist belief that all sentient beings are equal, and leaders should free their own mind from bias. In Daoist cosmology, "Neither is one person or one people better than the rest of humanity . . . Why play favorites?" (Heider, 1985, p. 9). Being unbiased, leaders will be able to create a coherent culture where factions and conflicts are minimised, peace is maximised and trust is built. Similarly, Glickman, Gordon, and Ross-Gordon (2009) acknowledged the relationship among justice, interconnectedness (or intersubjectivity), peace, and trust. "Consistent efforts on behalf of compassion, wholeness, connectedness, inclusion, justice, peace, and freedom can lead to trusting relationships among members of the school community" (p. 342). Noticeably, applied to educational domains and wholly consistent with the Daoist spirit, impartiality should also be translated into teaching learners how to *unlearn* and *unthink*.

Leaders' words should match their actions. Lǎozi even preferred actions over words, "The Master doesn't talk, [she] acts" (Johnson, 2000, p. 86). Likewise, as English (2008) put it, leaders "must not only 'talk the talk.' They must also 'walk the walk.' The key to credibility is congruence in action" (p. 94).

Leaders should create a climate that is open to sincere conversations among all participants. Recalling the interconnectedness between and among microcosms and macrocosm posited in Daoism, it is necessary for leaders to connect all employees together during their process of building trust. In this respect, Daoist leaders create a friendly climate that allows *all* participants to engage in and share their stories. As a matter of fact, when people can speak and be heard, they will trust one another. In education, to facilitate this, leaders should willingly talk to teachers, sincerely and intimately, and simultaneously listen to share their experiences and feelings. As Levin (2008) put it, "two-way communication is vital [. . .] to the motivational work of building trust" (p. 193). In addition, open and sincere conversations can connect people together because they then feel understood and appreciated, and hence they need to be linked to others to grow. From a Daoist perspective, this is a good way for microcosms to be interconnected and, at the same time, to be connected to the macrocosm *harmoniously*.

> Through reflection on individual lives and shared dialogue, teachers and administrators can begin to construct new organizational realities that allow all members to grow and work more productively together. In such an atmosphere of support for individual growth and a sense of community, the earlier stories of pain and hurt might not occur.
>
> (Lambert et al., 2002, p. 121)

This view implies that open and shared dialogues facilitate trust. In turn, this enhances healthy intersubjectivity and democracy in schools.

CONCLUDING COMMENTS

Using a Daoist cosmology as a fundamental theory, I proposed a framework for the practice of democratic leadership in education. Noticeably, *harmonious interconnectedness* is the key point underpinning my work. Underlying this notion are two procedural concepts, *intersubjectivity* and *democracy*; each help build harmonious interconnectedness. However, it is important to note that the notion of *harmony*, as conceptualised herein, does not mean *without conflicts*. On the contrary, it allows conflicts to happen in a limited fashion. Daoists view conflict as synonymous with development; to deal with conflicts, a leader should employ ways to keep opposing forces in balance and avoiding extremes. In this chapter, I argued for an intersubjective capacity that helps connect individuals together while simultaneously linking them to their organisation and, ultimately, to the environment. In addition, in the framework, I developed a model of democratic leadership characterised by a minimalist leadership approach. This structure, with its proposed minimalist leadership and diminished use of coercive power, allows all members of the organisation to maintain a strong sense of ownership, rather than followership, of their enterprise while simultaneously linking their interests to others, to the benefits of their organisation, and to the surrounding environment.

I also conceptualised the notion of individual space of freedom, which a Daoist would see as instrumental for the development of emotional and intellectual intelligence. These, it was argued, respectively facilitate intersubjectivity by virtue of an open heart, and democracy by means of an open mind characteristic of the mode of unthinking thinking. Finally, in this chapter, I offered a way to build trust in a Daoist fashion. To be sure, this proposed conceptual framework for the Daoist practice of democratic leadership in education is in its initial formation. Nevertheless, I have offered what I believe to be an emergent view of organisational leadership through the lens of Daoist traditions for the Western scholar of educational administration.

NOTES

1. There exist several alternative methods for transliteration of Chinese into Latin characters. At times, this leads to alternative spellings (where, for example, Lǎozi can also be transliterated as Lao Tzu, Lao Tse, Lao Tu, Lao-Tsu, Lao-tze, Laosi, and Laocius; where *Dào Dé Jīng* may commonly appear as *Tào Té Chīng*; and where *Dào* may equally commonly appear as *Tào*)—but in all cases, the spellings rely on pronunciation rules that are frequently inconsistent with common English usage. In the text of this volume, we employ the more contemporary and standard Pinyin system; citations remain true to their original method.
2. Quotations of passages from ancient texts are referenced by their *historical* methods.

REFERENCES

Burkitt, I. (2008). *Social selves: Theories of self and society*. London: Sage.

Clegg, S. R. (2007). Modernist and post-modernist organization. In D. S. Pugh (Ed.), *Organization theory: Selected classic readings* (pp. 577–615). London: Penguin Books.

Cunningham, W. G., & Cordeiro, P. A. (2003). *Educational leadership: A problem-based approach*. Upper Saddle River, NJ: Pearson.

Dewey, J. (1987). Democracy and educational adminstration. In J. A. Boydson (Ed.), *John Dewey: The later works, 1925–1953*. Carbondale and Edwardsville, IL: Southern Illinois University Press.

Ebrey, P., Schipper, K., Steinhardt, N. S., & Hung, W. (2000). *Taosim and the arts of China*. Chicago: The Art Institute of Chicago.

English, F. W. (2008). *The art of educational leadership: Balancing performance and accountability*. Thousand Oaks, CA: Sage.

Fiore, D. J. (2004). *Introduction to educational administration: Standards, theories and practice*. New York: Eye on education.

Glickman, C., Gordon, S., & Ross-Gordon, J. (2009). *The basic guide to supervision and instructional leadership*. Boston, MA: Allyn & Bacon Inc.

Goens, G. A. (2005). *Soft leadership for hard times*. Lanham, MD: Rowman & Littlefield.

Greenfield, T. B. (1979). Organization theory as ideology. *Curriculum Inquiry*, 9(2), 97–112.

Greenfield, T. B. (1980). The man who comes back through the door in the wall: Discovering truth, discovering self, discovering organizations. *Educational Administration Quarterly*, 16(3), 26–59.

Heider, J. (1985). *The Tao of leadership: Lao Tzu's Tao Te Ching adapted for a new age*. Atlanta, GA: Humanics Limited.

Johnson, C. (2000). Taoist leadership ethics. *Journal of Leadership and Organizational Studies*, 7(1), 82–91.

Lambert, L., Walker, D., Zimmerman, D. P., Cooper, J. E, Lambert, M. D., Gardner, M. E., & Szabo, M. (2002). *Constructivist leader*. New York: Teachers College Press.

Lao Tzu. (c. 600BCE/1963). *Tao Te Ching*. (D. C. Lau, Trans.). Toronto, ON: Penguin.

Lao Tzu. (c. 600BCE/1999). *Tao Te Ching*. (S. Mitchell, Trans.). London: Frances Lincoln.

Lao Tzu. (c. 600BCE/2001). *Tao Te Ching*. (D. C. Lau, Trans.). Hong Kong: Chinese University.

Lau, D.C. (1963). X. In *Tao Te Ching* (D. C. Lau, Trans.) (p. 66). Toronto, ON: Penguin.

Levin, B. (2008). *How to change 5000 schools: A practical and positive approach for leading change at every level*. Cambridge, MA: Harvard Education Press.

Maslow, A. H. (1970). *Motivation and personality*. New York: Harper & Row.

Mitchell, D. W. (2002). *Buddhism: Introducing the Buddhist experience*. New York & Oxford: Oxford University Press.

Nussbaum, M. C. (1997). *Cultivating humanity: A classical defense of reform in liberal education*. Cambridge, MA: Harvard University Press.

Oldstone-Moore, J. (2003). *Understanding Taoism*. London: Duncan Baird Publishers.

Olssen, M., Codd, J., & O'Neill, A. M. (2004). *Education policy: Globalization, citizenship & democracy*. London: Sage.

Philips, T. (1997). Professional education and the formation of democratic relationships between 'experts' and 'ordinary' citizens. In D. Bridges (Ed.), *Education, autonomy and democratic citizenship: Philosophy in a changing world* (pp. 237–247). London: Routledge.

Pirandello, L. (1954). *Six characters in search of an author*. Translated by Frederick May. London: Heinemann.

Scharmer, C. O. (2009). *Theory U: Learning from the future as it emerges*. San Francisco: Berrett-Koehler Publishers.

Schipper, S. (1982/1993). *The Taoist body* (K. C. Duval, Trans.). Berkeley, CA: University of California Press.

Sinagatullin, I. M. (2006). *The impact of globalization on education*. New York: Nova Science Publishers.

Starratt, J. S. (2004). Leadership of the contested terrain of education for democracy. *Journal of Educational Administration*, 42(6), 724–731.

Watts, A. (1975). *Tao: The watercourse way*. New York: Pantheon Books.

Welch, H. (1965). *Taoism*. Boston, MA: Beacon Press.

13 Rethinking Conceptions of First Nations Educational Leadership and Ethics

Gerald Fallon and Jerald Paquette

There is no single, comprehensive definition that encompasses all divergent views about educational leadership. A seemingly endless variety of definitions have been developed referring to varying themes of educational leadership traits, behaviours, role relationships, interaction and learning patterns (facilitation of collaborative relationships and team work), change, organisational structures, or sense making (see Bush & Barker, 2003; Cranston, 2002; Danielson, 2007; Fullan, 2006; Lam 2002; Ryan, 1998). Educational leadership is a concept that is contingent upon the sociocultural and educational context in which it is enacted and exercised (Gonzales-Parra & Simon, 2011; House, 2004). Capturing the essence of educational leadership in a First Nations educational setting has been an elusive goal sought by scholars in Canada (see Blakesly, 2008; Jules, 1999; Ottman, 2005). Nonetheless, leadership in a First Nations educational setting has not been systematically examined in Canada, particularly given the absence of (an) appropriate First Nations cultural len(se)s through which to examine educational leadership in terms of implicit beliefs, convictions, and assumptions concerning attributes, behaviors, and practices that inhibit or contribute to outstanding educational leadership in First Nations contexts. "This limits the opportunity for contextually and culturally relevant leadership development which takes into account the aspirations of First Nations communities" (Blakesly, 2008, p. 441), especially in terms of a culturally relevant and effective educational system for their children.

The values, beliefs, and assumptions held by members of societies or communities regarding (a) concepts of knowledge, (b) concepts of relationships among individuals, (c) the nature of their community ties and ecosystems, (d) ways things should be done, and (e) overreaching purposes of living in society each influence the nature of leadership actions and practices of individuals, groups, or institutions within those communities, and the degree to which such actions and practices are viewed as legitimate, acceptable, and effective (House & Javidan, 2004). Constructing a culturally relevant conception of educational leadership within a First Nations setting has been "hindered by the predominant hegemony of Euro-centric paradigms of educational leadership" (Blakesly, 2008, p. 445) that resulted in having indigenous ways of knowing the world devalued, marginalised, or ridiculed in the marketplace of ideas (Turner, 2006). As a result, assumptions, attitudes, and activities have been imposed on current First Nations education entities that include material acquisition, expansion, privatization of common goods, competition, and an obsession with technology and sciences. In overemphasising these values, Canadian mainstream society has encouraged, among First Nations communities and within their educational institutions, the pursuit of governance and educational goals that have institutionalised ideologies of individualism, consumerism, and the 'marketization' of citizenship. Contemporaneously, it has encouraged the fostering of leadership actions and practices that emphasise centralised authority and power differences. Ultimately, such encouragement has led to dysfunctional, unworkable, and unhealthy governance arrangements in First Nations education.

Our goal in this chapter is to engage the reader in a discussion about current and potential challenges to understanding educational leadership in a First Nations setting by addressing foundational issues of purpose and paradigm in aboriginal education and providing an alternative frame of reference to the dominant application of Euro-centric or Western-centric conceptions of educational leadership and of First Nations education. Only such grounding can provide a conceptual base for: (a) a useful and coherent critical analysis of First Nations education relevant to the enactment of educational leadership actions and practices; and (b) establishing a clear vision and purpose for aboriginal education. Such a clear vision and purpose is necessary to provide a conceptually powerful and appropriate basis for defining ways in which power within First Nations educational organisations can and should be organised, and the ends to which it should be directed and exercised within an appropriate view of educational leadership actions and practices.

The first step in constructing a coherent conceptual base is to frame discussion about the current state and possible futures of First Nations education in Canada. We do so in the first part of this chapter by positioning First Nations education within the context of competing dominant and alternative sociocultural and educational paradigms, then examining their possible implications for conceptualising educational leadership within First Nations contexts. In this first part, we seek to answer a basic conceptual-framework question: *What socio-cultural paradigm should provide the epistemological grounding (way of knowing); the view of relations among persons, society, and nature; the source of values; the ways of doing things; and the global sense of social purpose for First Nations education, and why?* Following the logic of Bertrand and Valois (1980)—who have observed how educational *paradigms* flow directly from socio-cultural ones—we further address a second logical question: *Which educational paradigm should offer the source for "general," "epistemological," cultural, political, and economic "function" of aboriginal education and conception of educational leadership, and why?* To build this foundation-level stratum of our conceptual base, we begin with the broadly integrative work of Bertrand and Valois from 1980, and update their important ideas in light of more recent work emerging from within postmodern and post-industrial schools of thought. Said another way, within this first part of the chapter, we begin with the dominant socio-cultural and educational para-digms that are generally used to frame conceptions of educational purpose for First Nations education and corresponding educational leadership actions and practices. We then turn our attention to one of the generic Bertrand-Valois socio-cultural and educational paradigms that reflect very closely holistic aboriginal ways of being in the universe and of understand-ing one's relationship to nature.

With clear ideas about both foundational issues of sociocultural and edu-cational purposes and issues related to First Nations education, as a second step in constructing our conceptual base and found in the second part of the chapter, we are in a position to engage with pivotal questions of ethical governance and leadership in the context of what we believe is a compelling argument in favour of an *ethos* of servant leadership (Crippen, 2005).

FRAMING THE DISCUSSION ABOUT CONCEPTUALISING FIRST NATIONS EDUCATION AND EDUCATIONAL LEADERSHIP

The ways education is provided and educational organisations are structured, managed, and led are based upon the choice of a socio-cultural and related educational paradigm (Bertrand & Valois, 1980; House, 2004). Therefore, the education of First Nations students, wherever it occurs, whatever its current governance arrangement and organisational structure, whatever combination of resources supports it, and whatever modes of provision, occurs within some degree of agreement about fundamental socio-cultural and educational-purpose parameters. Bertrand and Valois offer the follow-ing definition of a socio-cultural paradigm:

> The action exercised by a society, as a result of its activity, on its social and cultural practices, by the combination of five elements: a concept of knowledge, a concept of relations among persons, society, and nature, a set of values, a way of doing things, and an overarching sense of sig-nificance.
>
> (p. 69)

An "educational paradigm," according to Bertrand and Valois, consists of two parts: (a) a group of general orientations, of norms and rules that define educational reflection and action; and (b) praxis implications for "how to proceed" in terms of exemplary practices (p. 95).

Currently, increased reliance on high-stakes testing and successive waves of *performance* or *results*-based educational policy reform across

North America and beyond (*cf*. Hirschland & Steinmo, 2003), has resulted in theoretical alignment of the purposes and processes of First Nations education in general, and of educational leaderships in particular, with the assumptions, needs, values, and ways of doing things characteristic of Eurocentric or Western-centric socio-cultural and educational paradigms (Blaskesly, 2008; Paquette & Fallon, 2010; 2011). Furthermore, First Nations education in general is still confronting the requirement to conform to provincial curricula in Canada, which strongly reflects the characteristics of western industrial and post-industrial societies and their value approaches to teaching and learning along with the ways provincial and territorial educational organisations are structured, managed, and led (Paquette & Fallon, 2010, 2011).

The Industrial/Post-Industrial Paradigm

The industrial paradigm, according to Bertrand and Valois (1980), is characterised by positivist assumptions about knowledge and the relationships among persons, society, and nature. *Observer* and *subject* are separate, and knowledge is generally taken as consisting of quantitative measures of *objective variables*. Within this modern ontology, certain constructs and practices exist. Adherents believe, among other things, in (a) the primacy of humans over non-humans, and the justifiable treatment of other groups as different and inferior through knowledge-power relations; (b) the separation of nature and culture; (c) the idea of the autonomous individual separated from community; and (d) the belief in objective knowledge, reason, and science as the only valid modes of knowing. On this view, the individual person is subordinate to society as a whole as (s)he is mainly significant as a *cog* in the larger economy and competition and market values are the sole way forward for society as for the individual. Capitalist accumulation, industrialisation, and competition are the basic *modus operandi*.

Little that is fundamental needs to be changed to adjust this paradigm to the realities and *dominant* values of *post-industrialised* societies of today. Further to this view, science and technology remain the perceived way forward for economic development. Competition, accumulation, and utilitarianism are the *way we do things around here*—except that the *here* is now a global community interlocked by a global economy. Adherents of the industrial paradigm would argue that it may be true other values and potential ways of doing and understanding in the world bubble to and around the surface in a globalised and *postmodern* world, but these tend to be much more sporadic, localised, and transitory. Post-industrial societies, it has been argued by Escobar (2010), redefine the social domain in terms of the economic—arguably to a greater extent than ever occurred under classic *modernity*—where both the social and economic domains are governed by the rational choices of entrepreneurial individuals who see everything they do in terms of maximising their human and material capital. The role of the state is, on this view, simply recast, as are the actions of entrepreneurs. In the discourse of post-industrialism, society becomes synonymous with market, democracy, and individual choice; indeed, these are equated with being a consumer, and individual gain and advantage prevail over concern about the common good. At their core, post-industrial societies are characterised by the expansion of economic rationality to all spheres of human interactions[1] and reach an apogee of financial capitalism, flexible accumulation, and free-market ideology (Escobar, 2010).

Educational Paradigms Rooted in the Industrial/Post-Industrial Paradigm

Bertrand and Valois (1980) claimed that two reasonably distinct educational paradigms have emerged from the assumptions and beliefs that characterise the industrial/post-industrial socio-cultural paradigm: a *rational* and a *technological paradigm*.

Rational educational paradigm. Bertrand and Valois' (1980) rational paradigm entails the transmission of knowledge, of credible ways of thinking, and of accepted cognitive structures. Under this paradigm, teachers teach established *canons* of knowledge; learners learn them. Postivistically conceived *truths* to be transmitted are unique in their domain, regular (predictable, replicable, law-like), and take normal science as their model of what is worth knowing and how it can be known.

The cultural "function" of education is largely to "initiate the individual to the idea of progress and consumption, and to foster a vision of creativity as synonymous with economic, scientific, and technological progress" (Bertrand & Valois, 1980, p. 173). Consistent with this view of purpose, education should present human relations in terms of economic relations and foster the image of the desirable individual as one who is "opportunist, materialist, and conformist." Politically, education within the rational paradigm should "contribute to maintaining an oligarchic social structure [and] acceptance that an [elite] minority make decisions on behalf of the majority; in short, education should reflect and legitimate a hierarchical decision-making structure" (p. 173).

> In terms of the socio-economic order, such education should relativize the importance of the student as a person and a critical citizen evolving in a democracy whilst maximizing her importance as a future worker. [. . . It should] promote intellectual aptitudes, contribute to reproducing the [existing] social divisions in work, and promote the legitimacy of the established order and its values.
>
> (Bertrand & Valois, 1980, p. 173).

The overarching function of education is its contribution to maintaining the status quo of industrial and post-industrial society as a whole.

Technological educational paradigm. Also rooted in the industrial socio-cultural paradigm, Bertrand and Valois' (1980) technological paradigm of education seeks to transform education itself into a science. Its central goal is to produce the technological person, to organise efficiently the communication of knowledge, and to choose modes and strategies appropriate to such communication—in short: *to promote rational learning and knowing, and to do so with the tools and perspectives of applied science.* Within the technological paradigm, teachers again teach established canons of knowledge, but unlike in the rational paradigm every effort is made to engage the entire education enterprise in a process of ongoing systemic technical improvement and perfection.[2] The central cultural function of education within this technological paradigm is "to transmit technological development and utilization of technologies *as* [the most important] *image of creativity*" (p. 199, emphasis added).

Consistent with its overarching technological focus, the political function of education within the technological paradigm focuses on "atomizing and 'deideologizing' social debates, problems, and questions; on perpetuating an oligarchic concept of democracy; promoting 'the expert' as the foundation of all models of decision-making and problem solution" (Bertrand & Valois, 1980, p. 199). The socio-economic role of this educational paradigm is "to reflect an apparent neutrality by abstaining from all normative critique; to promote method and efficiency, control and the economy; and to transmit a 'mecanomorphic' image of the person" (p. 199). Anyone familiar with the main lines of the challenge that the late Thomas Greenfield brought to positivist ways of understanding educational administration and policy, and in particular with his eloquent and relentless insistence on the central role of human will and value-laden human choice in both, is immediately struck by how this view of the principal functions of education is diametrically opposed to Greenfield's own. Although Bertrand and Valois would not likely have known about the (then embryonic) Greenfield challenge, the purposes and methods of the technological paradigm resemble a carefully crafted recitation of all that Greenfield sought to question in education. Education for Greenfield was ineluctable and, in all its dimensions, a normative—indeed "moral"—enterprise (*cf.* Greenfield, 1986a, 1986b, 1991). Finally, as in the case of the rational paradigm, the overarching function of the technological paradigm is preservation of the status quo in society.

The New-Democratic-Society Paradigm[3]

The new-democratic-society or *symbiosynergetic* paradigm focuses on a symbiotic mode of knowing that leads to a view centred on unity between *subject* and *object*. The symbiosynergetic perspective recognises the *metaphoric* character of all explanation[4] and "the different non-contradictory levels of perception and explanation of physical, biological, and spiritual reality" (Bertrand & Valois, 1980, p. 273). Adherents to this view see reality as *unitary*.

With respect to relationships among persons, opposition among persons, society, and nature should be minimised in a comprehensive eco-system. *Community replaces society as society is transformed into community.* Persons and their society-community become one. Ironically, claim Bertrand and Valois (1980), this paradigm also leads to communities of unique and liberated persons—but this paradox is only possible where altruism and charity shape human and community development.

The *modus operandi* of this paradigm becomes a *symbiosynergy of heterogeneity*. The concept is difficult to capture in a succinct expression (Bertrand & Valois, 1980). We are reminded of a more accessible formulation set forth many years ago in a United Church of Canada publication to which we have long since lost the reference. In that article the author(s) spoke of a *cohesive diversity*.[5] Accumulation of difference within overarching and vital unity is characteristic of this concept. All contribute in different and complementary ways to community and projects. With regard to the technical and practical aspects of existence, this paradigm promotes *counter-technology* and *soft technology*, including and especially the self-production of physical elements necessary to life (in our own time this would seem to translate plausibly into discourses around *renewable resources* and *sustainable development*).

The global sense framed by the symbiosynergetic paradigm is "the symbiosynergy of persons and communities," of the "total person," in other words, because persons, as *holons*, can be whole only when fully united to society transformed into meta-community (Bertrand & Valois, 1980, p. 277). The resonances of symbiosynergetic assumptions with Bowers' (2006) critique of the malaise of contemporary industrial monoculture and its values are, by extension, similarly resonant with First Nations traditions of seeking sustainable unity with nature and guidance toward that end from a dream or vision quest to link to a guiding spirit (Denis, 1997). In fact, they could hardly be stronger. From within symbiosynergy, gone are views of nature as an *object* or *resource* to be *exploited* with scientific efficiency by humans who represent the apex of evolution. Gone too are any associated entitlements to ruthlessly and scientifically exploit the spoils of human superiority. Instead, the wholeness of the human spirit is directly dependent on symbiotic integration with nature (including all forms of life and other human beings). The perspective of symbiosynergy, in short, is completely opposed to that of modernity/coloniality.

Educational Paradigm as Rooted in the Symbiosynergetic Paradigm

The inventive paradigm. Bertrand and Valois (1980) map what they call the *inventive* educational paradigm on the principles, values, and beliefs of the symbiosynergetic socio-cultural paradigm. The general function of the inventive paradigm is to develop the capacity for "social invention" and for "creation of new social institutions" among "persons-communities" [*sic*]. Education situated within the inventive paradigm also seeks "to discover the significance and implications of intentions or projects" and to *invent* future situations and intervention modes capable of bringing about such new social institutions ("new democratic societies," otherwise stated; Bertrand & Valois, 1980, p. 295).

Epistemologically, on this view, education promotes a symbiotic mode of knowing that takes as its starting point the essential union of observer and observed as having an "identity of force" (and thus dissolving the subject-object distinction). Such education facilitates meaningful listening and develops "a critical consciousness of the situation of the person in the universe." It valorises knowledge that enables one to *situate* herself and to *become*, but to do so in the realization that no person can define herself "except by reference to the whole" (Bertrand & Valois, 1980, p. 295). Bertrand and Valois argued that *culturally*, the inventive paradigm promotes—as its model of creativity—the symbiosynergy of heterogeneity ("cohesive diversity"), differences within the essential union of the person, and the totality of the universe. (How close, we cannot resist observing again, to traditional Aboriginal views of the place of the person in the universe!)

Inventive-paradigm education, Bertrand and Valois (1980) insist, fosters the image of the person as part of a greater whole, as *holon* (ὅλον), unique but inextricably united to others in an overarching and all-encompassing *us*. Politically, such education promotes decision making based on non-hierarchical *mutualism*, which, we contend, reflects the consensus-based political decision making in traditional Aboriginal communities and societies.

Bertrand and Valois (1980) view the socio-economic role of inventive-paradigm education as one of leading persons (a) to engage themselves in all the milieus within which they work and (b) to promote conditions conducive to similar engagement on the part of all *others* in those milieus. Education constituted within inventive principles should, on Bertrand and Valois' view, "resituate personal development within community development and community development within personal development" (p. 295). In short, inventive education should promote universal but diversified participation in the symbiosynergy of the world as a whole.

Application of these principles yields an education with an exemplary dimension that develops *constituents* (in the political sense—a revealing concept of students—and, once again, one we believe not far removed from traditional First Nations teaching-learning relationships) who take charge of their own development and themselves. The educative goal for these constituents is to produce their own knowledge of how to live, think, speak, share, and act together in the daily context of their lives and in alignment with cohesive diversity. Control over the educational context properly belongs to the constituents—not to members of an educational hierarchy. Learning occurs as constituents reflect on the experience of their lives. Teachers and educational leaders assist these student-constituents and thus reconstitute the educational communication network as they work with them (Bertrand & Valois, 1980).

In accord with Bertrand and Valois (1980), it is the milieu of the community that defines the school; the community creates a local *school project*, developing the mission and broad plan. In so doing, the community sets the educational character of the school and establishes its social context. All aspects of schools and school systems, proponents of this view argue, contribute to education for a more just, more dynamic, and more fraternal society.

Critiquing and Rethinking Conceptions of First Nations Educational Leadership Within Possible Socio-Cultural Paradigms

This brief overview of the two antipodes of the Bertrand-Valois understanding of the paradigmatic foundations of societies and education contributes an important piece of the cohesive conceptual framework needed to engage in a discussion concerning conceptions of First-Nation educational leadership and organisational practices. In Table 13.1, we summarise the Bertrand-Valois framework and suggest its relevance to the *positioning* of

Table 13.1 Conceptions of First Nations educational leadership within the industrial/post-industrial paradigm.[6]

	The Industrial and Post-Industrial Paradigm	The Symbiosynergic Paradigm
paradigm base	Socio-cultural paradigm characterised by positivist and economic efficiency and assumptions about knowledge and the nature of society.	Socio-cultural paradigm characterised by sustainability of life systems, nonhierarchical complementarity of individuals, and communities as ways of being and relating in a society.
	Corresponding educational paradigms characterised by a conception of education as an efficient transmission of pre-determined knowledge designed to promote positivistic rational learning and knowing and maintain and legitimate an oligarchic socio-economic structure.	Corresponding educational paradigm is characterised by a conception of education based on a symbiotic mode of knowing in which the learners develop their capacity to create new alternatives by producing knowledge that promotes new ways of being and acting that in turn support a vision of society based on nonhierarchical and democratic decision making and a complementarity of differences.

As is the case with education in any other communities or societies, First Nations education and educational leadership practices occur within a social-cultural and a related educational paradigm. Which one(s)would be the most appropriate (and why?) to frame educational policies; educational programs; and ways educational organisations are structured, managed, and led in the future?

First Nations education and educational leadership within the most generic of possible socio-political and educational paradigms.

We are proposing an idealised conceptual model that can be used for engaging First Nations and non-First Nations policymakers, stakeholders, and educators in a dialogue leading to mutual understanding of what First Nations education *ought* to be. We are not describing what First Nations education currently is, nor how it should be translated into corresponding ways of structuring, managing, and leading First Nations educational institutions. We are here arguing that much, if not most, education proffered to First Nations students is mainly grounded in the industrial/post-industrial paradigm and its foundational assumptions. Within the industrial/post-industrial socio-cultural paradigm, one of the central purposes of First Nations education is to contribute, generally speaking, to the maintenance of an oligarchic social structure—the acceptance that a largely elite minority make decisions on behalf of the majority. In short, under this paradigm, education both reflects and legitimates a hierarchical decision-making structure. Hierarchical organisation of a community or society encourages (a) a high degree of power *distance* (the degree to which members of a community or society expect and agree that power should be shared unequally, stratified, and concentrated at higher levels of an institution or governance structure), (b) the extent to which an institution or society accepts and endorses authority, (c) great power differences, and (d) status privileges (Carl, Gupta, & Javidan, 2004). Within such a high-power-distance oligarchic social structure, the established concentration of power is expected to bring order to the community or society. Further, it allows a hierarchical allocation of decision-making roles and establishes rigid structures of power relationships between individuals. These rigid power structures are characterised by a *power over* system—explicit or implicit dominance (Hollander & Offerman, 1990). It has been recognised that high-power-distance, however, could lead to the emergence of dysfunctional organisations and abuse of power; it pre-empts members of a society or community from questioning, learning, and adapting as there is little opportunity for debate or voicing divergent views. Asking questions or advocating alternative means of decision making can be interpreted or regarded by those above as criticising and blaming. Often, difference or critique is repressed or prohibited.

Such an understanding of the political function of First Nations education within the context of the industrial/post-industrial socio-cultural paradigm has encouraged struggle over position, power, and financial rewards. This has happened in place of a political process that would enable members of Aboriginal communities to direct their own educational affairs in accordance with the aspirations, developmental goals, and purpose they accept collectively. As a result, missing is a structure that enables interested individuals to think in public and, as public beings, make public claims about educational purposes, programmes, and services. Further missing is a structure to provide reasoned argument toward the above ends in ways that balance values shared in the here-and-now of First Nations existence with traditions identified as central to Aboriginal communities. By extension, a high-*organisational*-power-distance structure in First Nations educational institutions has led to the enactment of educational leadership practices associated with conceptions of autonomous and self-protective leadership, especially but by no means exclusively, in an educational setting. *Autonomous leadership*, as we employ it here, is characterised by a high degree of social distance from *followers* or members of a community, a tendency to be aloof, and to be individualistic (House, 2004). *Self-protective leadership* focuses on ensuring the safety and security of a *ruling* minority elite through status enhancement and face-saving (House, 2004). This conception of leadership includes the following dimensions: (a) self-centred, (b) status conscious, (c) conflict inducer, (d) face saver, and (e) procedural. Given the structural and operational distance (and hence *potential* isolation from grass-roots First Nations educational activity), conceptions of educational leadership practices can provide wide opportunity for goal displacement (Carl et al., 2004). It can, moreover, provide for focusing increasingly disproportionate amounts of energy, time, and resources on goals that are different from, or even opposed to, the *formal goals* of the First Nations educational organisation.

Conceptions of First Nations educational leadership within the symbiosynergetic paradigm. Our belief is that the symbiosynergetic paradigm should provide the principal socio-cultural values and form within which First Nations education and corresponding ways of structuring, managing, and leading First Nations educational institutions should be framed. The concept of person as *holon* seems to us to have promising resonances with much First Nations teaching and understanding of the world; it reflects a unitary and integrated, rather than scientifically *atomised*, view of human nature. The emphasis Bertrand and Valois (1980) attributed to the symbiosynergetic paradigm as a teleological concept of life and evolution, and as meaningful integration of subjective experience of all sorts (intuitive, mystic, religious, and psychic) has powerful resonances with First Nations' focus on connecting with the spirit world; for example, through a vision quest (Paquette & Fallon, 2010). Furthermore, Benham and Murakami made a similar claim reflecting the main dimensions of the symbiosynergetic and inventive paradigms in 2010. They noted how several indigenous groups in North America "view life as an 'interconnected web, a 'system view of the world' that comes as a natural perspective through which to view leadership" (p. 78).

We conclude that First Nations education should occur within the assumptions of Bertrand and Valois' (1980) inventive educational paradigm. It promotes, above all, a vision of society based on non-hierarchical and democratic decision making and a complementary of differences. Such vision would nurture a sense of, and commitment to, symbiosynergy, and hence oneness with others, with the world, and with the universe. More palpably in terms of direct resonances with historic First Nations culture, the inventive paradigm would invite First Nations students, educators, and leaders to seek meaning in relationships with themselves, with nature, with the Creator, and with others, to embark on an intellectual and spiritual journey not unlike a traditional dream or vision quest. Along the same lines, Benham and Murakami's (2010) explanation of the bases of indigenous education and educational leaderships reflect the main dimensions of the symbiosynergetic and inventive paradigms. These consist of:

> (a) learning and living with integrity that sustains traditional values and principles and at the same time learns from the contemporary rivers of the current times; (b) having a primary concern for community and place (both physical and spiritual); (c) developing sensitivity and sensibility to the thoughts of other people; that is, it is not about the you or me, but it is about relationships; (d) clearly understanding and articulating individual and collective roles, responsibilities, and relationships; (e) building respectfulness, which requires a deep understanding of the complexities of social networks; and (f) being the link between the traditional and the contemporary, and between and across communities within and external to the indigenous world.
>
> (p. 82)

In terms of conceptions of educational leadership, adopting the symbiosynergetic and inventive paradigms would promote a reduced *power-distance* and, we contend, facilitate the emergence of ways of structuring, managing, and leading First Nations educational institutions.

In contrast to a high-organisational-power-distance structure, we argue that a low-organisational-power-distance structure in First Nations educational institutions would lead to the enactment of educational leadership practices associated with conceptions of *servant*/value-based leadership, team-oriented leadership, and participative leadership. Each of the preceding conceptions of leadership reflect participative approaches and flexible distribution of power. Additionally, we believe they are able to, and *perceived* as able to, minimise potential abuse of power and corruption (Carl et al., 2004).

Servant-/value-based leadership refers to the ability to inspire, to motivate, and to expect high performance outcomes from others through participative approaches. It is based on firmly held collective core values that shape and drive a culture that, in turn, binds organisational members together in pursuit of a cause greater than oneself (Glickman et al., 2004; House & Javidan, 2004). Within this conception of leadership, the following qualities are valued: vision, inspiration, self-sacrifice, integrity, decisiveness, and a performance orientation. Team-oriented leadership refers to practices that emphasise effective team building and implementation of a common educational purpose or goal among team members; ability to promote and inspire collaboration, skill, and credibility as a team integrator; and diplomacy are all qualities valued in team-oriented leaders. Participative leadership refers to the degree to which educational leaders involve others in making and implementing decisions by focusing on mutual and complementary interests (House & Javidan, 2004). Each of these conceptions of educational leadership encompass aspects of leadership and organisational practices that reflect Coyhis' (1995) and Benham and Murakami's (2010) claim that leadership in an indigenous interconnected system view of the world and society is about cooperation, relationship, humility, patience, and sharing practices that engage, ensure, and nurture an ethos of collective will and responsibility. In Table 13.2, we present a synthesis of the different conceptions

Table 13.2 Synthesis of conceptions of educational leadership within different socio-cultural and educational paradigms.

	the industrial and post-industrial paradigm	the symbiosynergic paradigm
paradigm base	Socio-cultural paradigm characterised by positivist and economic efficiency assumptions about knowledge and the nature of society.	Socio-cultural paradigm characterised by sustainability of life systems and non-hierarchical complementarity of individuals and communities as ways of being and relating in a society.
	Corresponding educational paradigms characterised by a conception of education as efficient transmission of pre-determined knowledge designed to promote positivistic rational learning and knowing and maintain and legitimate an oligarchic socio-economic structure.	Corresponding educational paradigm is characterised by a conception of education based on a symbiotic mode of knowing in which the learners develop their capacity to create new alternatives by producing knowledge that promotes new ways of being and acting that in turn support a vision of society based on non-hierarchical and democratic decision-making and a complementarity of differences.
degree of power distance	Power distance refers to the degree to which members of a shared unequally, stratified, and concentrated at higher levels community or society expect and agree that power should be of an institution or governance structure.	
conceptions of educational leadership	self-protective leadership · autonomous leadership · participative leadership · team-oriented leadership · servant leadership	
	Emphasis on hierarchical and rigid structure of power relationships with a concentration of power at higher levels in the organisational structure.	Emphasis on value-based and participative approaches that encourage questioning, learning, debate, and voicing of divergent views.

of educational leadership within different socio-cultural and educational paradigms.

Given the imperative of *Kymlicka's constraint*—the reality that *most* powerbrokers in mainstream society will be non-aboriginal for the foreseeable future (Turner, 2006)—First Nations education leaders will need not only to convince themselves of the value and worth of the identities and educational vision they seek to build, but they will also need to convince those with power over resources and opinion in mainstream Canada of their worth. We address this issue in the next section of this chapter.

ETHICS AND FIRST NATIONS EDUCATIONAL LEADERSHIP

> [T]he capacity of any single Indigenous community to shape education on its own is limited. Changes in technocratic education and the end of cultural marginalization and educational alienation confronted by us require complex approaches involving partnerships and practice that straddle Indigenous communities. This requires a different way of thinking with key roles for Indigenous educators as catalysts, brokers, coordinators, and monitors as well as Indigenous forms of leadership that support all of the people aspirations, not simply "fattens" the leader. . . . Maori views include contexts of education such as economic, social, and environmental impacts, Maori tribal distinctiveness, access to language and culture, and access to natural resources. It also addresses responsiveness of education to Maori aspirations.
>
> (Kēpa & Manu'atu, 2006, p. 26)

The ongoing colonial impositions of Western industrial and post-industrial beliefs, attitudes, and ways of acting on current First Nations education entities include material acquisition, expansion, privatization of common goods, competition, and an obsession with technology and sciences. In overemphasising these values, Canadian mainstream society has encouraged the pursuit among First Nations communities of governance goals that have, to a considerable extent, institutionalised individualism, selfishness, and greed in their ways of structuring, managing, and leading their educational organisations. At the most profound level, re-examination of current governance models in First Nations education needs to deal with the value system underlying it, and further to recognise deep ties of that value system into a long series of educational governance formulations historically proven to be unworkable and unhealthy. While such emphasis on values, moral principles, and ethics may vary or entail different nuances of meaning for each First Nations community, most Aboriginal community members would probably agree, on reflection, that each of these is an important dimension of Aboriginal self-determination and its feasibility. First Nations education exists to provide a more efficient and effective, as well as culturally and linguistically appropriate education for First Nations students than provincial or territorial school systems.

However, despite a federal Canadian investment in First Nations education that now exceeds $1 billion annually, every two to four years, an Auditor General's report deplores the of lack of accountability for that investment and the desperate educational deficit on the part of First Nations people. For those interested, the policy *space* between Auditor General's reports (*cf.* Auditor General of Canada, 2002; Auditor General of Canada, 2004) is filled with reminders, often in the form of media reports, documentaries, and parliamentary committee evidence and reports,[7] that little is changing in First Nations education as a whole. It is our view that restoration of efficiency and effectiveness to Aboriginal educational institutions will be possible only if accompanied by a profound change in value systems and ethics that will lead to mainstream Canadian investment in a collective First Nations *educational project* for the common good of First Nations students. Value systems and ethics are not peripheral to any possible conceptions of First Nations educational leadership in education; they constitute its very basis and driving force.

The Nature and Importance of Ethics in First Nations Educational Leadership

"Organizations are not objects in nature; an organization is a moral order invented and maintained by human choice and will" (Greenfield, 1993, p. 217). Ethics is a complex and contested concept and philosophical domain. The ethical issues surrounding First Nations education in our day must be critiqued carefully within a coherent position first on the nature of ethics and then on its importance, both generally within social and economic relations in society as a whole and more particularly within questions of governance and administration of First Nations education. Our main focus in this section of the chapter will be first on ethics as a theory or system of moral values and then ethics as a set of principles of conduct governing an individual or a group—as principles governing an individual in her relationship to and *roles* within a group or groups.

Ethics and moral objectivity. The historical quest for a universal code of ethics grounded in a universal moral philosophy has failed. It has failed despite a quasi-universal longing for moral objectivity that transcends time, culture, and space; a longing so intense and so widespread that Margolis (2004) has aptly labelled it the "pathos of morality" (pp. 87–88). If claims to universal moral and ethical principles have failed generally in the broader arena of moral philosophy, it is unlikely that attempts to reason to such principles in the case of First Nations peoples would have much plausibility or intellectual traction. Indeed, the pervasive claim with respect to morals and First Nations people is one of Aboriginal distinctiveness, not congruence with mainstream Canadian culture and its moral and ethical values; we will return critically to this claim later, particularly as it affects our interests in this chapter. However, we recognise that a decisive intervention into the very discursivity of the various meanings of ethics is needed to craft an alternative space for mutually acceptable and practical understanding of the concept of ethics within the context of First Nations education and its governance, and particularly in terms of ways of structuring, managing, and leading First Nations educational institutions.

In this part of the chapter, we start by providing a basic account of Margolis' (1995, 2004) reinvention of objectivity in morals and ethics. Margolis took as his starting point the position that all moral truth claims are historically and culturally situated and contexted. As humans, we can never escape the here and now of time and culture (Margolis, 2004, p. 11,); we are creatures, emergent artefacts so to speak, of our respective *sittlich*s—that is, of our particular cultural communities, with their beliefs regarding right and wrong, virtue and vice—and of how moral truth claims are to be legitimated or vested with binding moral authority. The values and belief held by members of a community or society influence the degree to which behaviours (educational leadership, in the case of this chapter) of individuals, groups, and institutions within a community or society are enacted, and the degree to which they are viewed as legitimate, acceptable, and effective. Within this perspective, ethical governance for plurality must be dynamic and needs to be approached in the context of continuously renegotiated and renewed relationships. This evolutionary dynamic should replace traditional hegemonic, hierarchical stasis as the reference form for governance of plurality away from a colonial structural pluralism designed mainly to secure normative integration of First Nations communities into Canadian mainstream society.

Our morality is constructed out of *our* particular history and culture (Margolis, 1995, 2004). That is why a single action can be assigned vastly different moral significance by two different *sittlich*s whose moral visions collide. Therefore, contests and conflict among moral visions are inevitable because of "ineliminable moral diversity" (*cf.* Margolis, 2004, pp. ix, 25, 110). Such diversity among different societies, as well as among different interests within societies, makes any broad convergence in morals highly unlikely (p. 110) and ensures both incompatibilities and "incommensurabilities" (pp. ix, 102, 119). On Margolis' view, these result in ongoing dialectical interplay (p. ix) of various sorts (from debate to all-out war) among competing moral visions.

Given the impossibility of legitimating moral truth claims in any universal way, we believe that the best one can hope to achieve is sufficient agreement on moral matters to provide a *modus vivendi* among different societies and groups with competing moral visions. Margolis (2004) calls this a "second best" morality, a *faute de mieux* (for want of anything better) morality (pp. xvii, 24, 25). But, the question may be asked, how could we agree sufficiently on such a second-best morality—allowing it to serve as a working *modus vivendi*—and why bother to do so in any case? Margolis' answer to both questions is pragmatic. We can only hope to cobble together a mutually agreeable second-best morality based on practical interests, or what he variously called "prudential needs" (Margolis, 1995, p. 15) and "prudential interests."

He argued that to find sufficient agreement among *sittlich*s with competing and colliding moral visions to provide a workable *modus vivendi*, we need to be guided, not by universal principles, but by a "compelling account of human interests . . . [centered on] our hopes and fears regarding life and death in all its forms" (p. 14).

Margolis (2004) sensed an obligation to provide some meaningful parameters around the general idea of prudential interest and did so by insisting on *humanitas*, "an unrestricted concern and respect for human life and its care: that is, the refusal to permit any part of the human race to be excluded or ignored in our moral deliberations" (p. 113). Margolis insisted that *humanitas* is a viable basis for agreement precisely because it is "vacuous," that is, because it carries with it no particular moral principles or privilege of any sort—except that no group is beneath its ultimate concern and respect for human life.

It follows that the development of the capacity "of the offspring of a society" entails development of the "moral agency" in the young. To become fully human in Margolis' (2004) sense, the young need to be nurtured as:

> (a) moral agents . . . capable of knowing the lay of the entire world, both natural and cultural, in which they act; (b) [who,] rightly informed . . . act with the knowledge that they cannot legitimate what they do, beyond the resources and limitations of one or another second-best morality; and (c) who . . . know they act under the conditions of an evolving history, their own *sittlich* formation, their partisan commitments, horizoned understanding, and the impossibility of avoiding conflict with the normative convictions and partisan commitments of other agents differently formed and informed.
>
> (p. 86)

Human agency is a process of social engagement that allows members of a community to critically shape their own responses to problematic situations or catalytic events. To act within such a process requires continual refocusing of past and future ways of acting, being, interacting, and learning. Emirbayer and Mische (1998) define human agency as the

> temporally constructed engagement of social actors of different structural environments—the temporal relational contexts of action—which, through the interplay of habit, imagination, and judgment, both reproduces and transforms those structures in interactive response to the problems posed by changing historical situations.
>
> (pp. 970–971)

We have not yet turned to the second question we posed at the beginning of our brief summary of Margolis' position on moral objectivity, that is, why bother with the strenuous work needed to find mutually acceptable moral *ententes* among divergent *sittlichs*? Margolis (2004) contended that

> we have reached a point in history at which the proliferation of contests of the 9/11 sort (just now identified) are so dangerous and destructive and so easy to match in a retaliatory way that the world cannot afford to neglect the chance to work out an answer that is at once coherent, pertinent, responsive, viable, reasonable, effective, practical, apt—and possibly even nonstandard in the way of tempering the pressure for further such confrontations.
>
> (pp. xi–xii)

Effective, efficient, and appropriate First Nations education requires moral leadership based on truthfulness, good faith, the moral commitment of conscientious stewardship focused unreservedly on "capacitation" of Aboriginal youth as responsible moral agents and on responsibility itself. The code of ethics drafted by the Assembly of Manitoba Chiefs Youth Secretariat reflects such values:

> To serve others, to be of some use to family, community, nation or the world is one of the purposes for which human beings have been created. Do not fill yourself with your own affairs and forget your most important task. True happiness comes only to those who dedicate their lives to the service of others.
>
> (Assembly of Manitoba Chiefs Youth Secretariat, 2006, n.p.)

We are encouraged by their work.

Ethical Governance and Conception of Educational Leadership

Unfortunately, the ethics role model provided by the institution at the centre of colonising First Nations people, namely the residential school, was at the antipodes of an open organisation in an open culture and society operating transparently for the benefit of those it was created to serve. Arguably the most devastatingly dysfunctional lesson it taught to its inmates was that of unquestioning service to absolute power, enforced by whatever means were necessary to impose that power. This was power imposed by fear and mistrust, nothing like the power of expertise, charisma, respect, or formal position.

> [D]o what I say, accept what I do, or I will harm you! My point of departure for everything that I will do to you, moreover, is based upon the inherent superiority of mainstream Canadian culture and hence the

inferiority of your language and culture. Underpinning my assumption of this absolute power over you is the indisputable fact that nothing aboriginal has ever been part of an 'educated person' or ever will be, so my mission is to eradicate every trace of indigeneity in you. I will use whatever tools are available to accomplish this mission and your duty is only to accept and obey.

(Paquette & Fallon, 2010, p. 312)

Given this sense of mission among those who led and worked in residential schools from those earliest experiments on the part of the Jesuits in New France, it may be more surprising that First Nations education, and particularly its administration, is not more dysfunctional than it is—especially when the debilitating diseconomies of scale under which it generally labours are taken into consideration. Not only did this sense of mission catastrophically divorce everything *Indian* from everything associated with the image of an educated person endorsed by schools and schooling, it modelled the exercise of absolute power with impunity as the *norm* in educational leadership. It is hardly surprising that, despite a great deal of lip-service paid to the contrary, a disturbing amount and degree of self-serve leadership has continued to manifest itself in First Nations education since the beginning of formal *devolution of control* a generation ago.

It is no coincidence that some of the most widely read authors in educational administration in North America have insisted in recent years on the importance of an *ethos* of stewardship, of servant leadership. As Sergiovanni noted some time ago, trust is at the very core of leader stewardship—and the *moral authority* it both requires and fosters.

Stewardship represents primarily an act of trust, whereby people and institutions entrust a leader with certain obligations and duties to fulfill and perform on their behalf. For example, the public entrusts the schools to the school board. The school board entrusts each school to its principal. Parents entrust their children to teachers. Stewardship also involves the leader's personal responsibility to manage her or his life and affairs with proper regard for the rights of other people and for the common welfare. Finally, stewardship involves placing oneself in service to ideas and ideals and to others who are committed to their fulfillment.

(Sergiovanni, 1992, p. 139)

Nor is it coincidental that this line of reasoning and argumentation has such strong resonances with our own repeated insistence on the particular importance of servant educational leadership in First Nations education as a fiduciary, indeed, a sacred trust with regard to student learning, social adjustment and integration, and intellectual and spiritual growth. Toward these ends, servant leaders nurture the trust required by servant leadership through equity of treatment, respect for others, honesty in dealing with others, openness, promise-keeping, and competence (Robbins, 2005)—and by insisting that all other members of the organisation honour these principles in word and deed.

Of course, no one, however altruistic and talented, can be a good steward of what she does not have. If good stewardship implies getting the job done, then resources adequate to the task need to be provided. Before one can decide what would constitute adequate resources for a given educational sector or enterprise, however, one must have some clarity about the vision one has for it. Clear vision, after all, shapes the purposes, mandates, and expectations that one can legitimately impose upon an organisation and those who work in it, as well as the scope of reasonable resource needs and limitations.

As a former principal of the Peguis School noted with regard to grounding trust within what amounts to a moral context of servant educational leadership:

> If we care about others, our community and the future, then we will make a difference when we join together to practice respect, truth, honesty, wisdom, humility and bravery. Making education meaningful for everyone is our goal; we need the help of everyone to make this a success.
> (Bell, 2004, pp. 207–208)

Servant leadership is about caring for students and then *doing something about it*; about putting student welfare first, not just in word, but in deed! It inverts the political-economy agenda and insists that leaders "ask not" what the organization can do for them, but what they can do for the children who are the *raison d'être* of the organization!

CONCLUDING COMMENTS

We hope that this chapter will constitute a platform for engaging in authentic dialogue with First Nations communities, as well as policy makers, scholars, and students interested in and involved with First Nations education and educational leadership. Throughout this chapter, our intention was not to present a binary or a static view of potential conceptions of educational leadership within a First Nations setting, but to provide conceptual space for engaging in a robust discussion about First Nations education and corresponding ways of structuring, managing, and leading First Nations educational institutions in Canada. Such a discussion about particularly difficult puzzles could be interpreted and translated into empowering educational policies and educational leadership practices for First Nations communities. Too often, discussions about educational leadership within the contemporary First Nations world are filled with either pity and pathos or romanticism; that is, such discussions are often focused on the social ills of poverty, not on current efforts of First Nations peoples to reclaim legitimate rights of educational self-determination and full participation in the democratic process within their communities and in the mainstream Canadian society. The very nature of our discussion should signal clearly that we do not believe that there is one, uniform, *best-practice solution* for creating and maintaining educational policy and practice for First Nations education and leadership. Rather, First Nations people themselves, in choosing, crafting, and recrafting their collective and individual identities, should shape educational programmes and services and their conception of educational leadership appropriate to their identity visions.

NOTES

1. Of course, sobering warnings of the impact of such *market fundamentalism* not only on society but, ironically, also on the market system itself have not been wanting—and sometimes from some startling sources (*cf.* Soros, 1998).
2. One is immediately reminded of various reform projects in educational policy over the last fifteen years that have ranged from various versions of total quality management to the idea, problematic in our view, of "acceptable yearly progress" built into the American *No Child Left Behind* legislation.
3. Bertrand and Valois (1980) use the terms "new-democratic-society communities," "biosynergetic," and "symbiosynergetic" interchangeably (p. 263).
4. To appreciate the significance of the claim, one needs to recall the classic distinction between inquiry as pursuit of (scientific, "causal") explanation as opposed to "understanding" in the sense of Weber (MacIntyre, 1981, see especially pp. 88–108; Schutz, 1966).
5. The expression, we realise, has since been picked up and applied in a variety of contexts including one that is, by most standards, less than edifying.
6. The concept of paradigm refers to the action exercised by a community or society on its social and cultural practices by the combination of five elements: a concept of knowledge; a concept of relations among persons, society, and nature; a set of values; a way of doing things; and an overreaching sense of significance (Bertrand & Valois, 1980). Each socio-cultural paradigm frames a specific conception of education (educational paradigm) that defines the norms and rules that determine educational reflection and action, on the one hand, and praxis that promotes particular modalities regarding teaching methodologies, on the other.
7. Parliamentary committee evidence, reports, and responses can be searched through the website of the Canadian Parliament.

REFERENCES

Auditor General of Canada (2002) Indian and Northern Affairs of Canada—Elementary and secondary education. *In Report of the Auditor General of Canada to the House of Commons*. Ottawa: Office of the Auditor General of Canada.

Auditor General of Canada. (2004). *Report of the Auditor General of Canada to the House of Commons: Indian and Northern Affairs Canada: Education program and post-secondary student support*. Ottawa, ON: the Author.

Bell, D. (Ed.). (2004). *Sharing our success: Ten cases in aboriginal schooling*. Kelowna, BC: Society for the Advancement of Excellence in Education.

Benham, M., & Murakami-Ramalho, E. (2010). Engaging in educational leadership: The generosity of spirit. *International Journal of Leadership in Education, 13*(1), 77–91.

Bertrand, Y., & Valois, P. (1980). *Les options en éducation.* Québec, PQ: Ministère de l'Éducation.

Blakesley, S. (2008). Remote and unresearched: Educational leadership in Canada's Yukon territory. *Compare, 38*(4), 441–454.

Bowers, C. A. (2006). *Revitalizing the commons: Cultural and educational sites of resistance and affirmation.* Lanham, MD: Lexington Books.

Busher, H., & Barker, B. (2003). The crux of leadership: Shaping school culture by contesting the policy contexts and practices of teaching and learning. *Educational Management & Administration, 31*(1), 51–65.

Carl, D., Gupta, V., & Javidan, M. (2004). Roots of power distance. In R. J. House, P. J. Hanges, M. Javindan, P. W. Dorfman, & V. Gupta (Eds.), *Culture, leadership, and organization: The Globe study of 62 societies* (pp. 513–559). Thousand Oaks, CA: Sage Publications.

Coyhis, D. (1995). Servant leadership: The elders have said leadership is about service. *Wind of Change, 8*(3), 23–24.

Cranston, N. C. (2002). School-based management, leaders and leadership: Change and challenges for principals. *International Studies in Educational Administration, 30*(1), 2–12.

Crippen, C. (2005). The democratic school: First to serve, then to lead. *Canadian Journal of Educational Administration and Policy, 47,* 1–17.

Danielson, C. (2007). The many faces of leadership. *Educational Leadership, 65*(1), 14–19.

Denis, C. (1997). *We are not you: First Nations and Canadian modernity.* Peterborough, ON: Broadview Press.

Emirbayer, M., & Mische, A. (1998). What is agency? *The American Journal of Sociology, 103*(4), 962–1023.

Escobar, A. (2010). Latin-America at a crossroad: Alternative modernizations, post-liberalism, or post-development? *Cultural Studies, 24*(1), 1–65.

Fullan, M. (2006). The future of educational change: Systems thinkers in action. *Journal of Educational Change, 7*(3), 113–122.

Glickman, C. D., Gordon, S. P., & Ross-Gordon, J. M. (2004). *Supervision and instructional leadership: A developmental approach* (6th. ed.). New York: Pearson.

Gonzales-Parra, C., & Simon, J. W. (2011). Globalization traditions: New styles of leadership and new organizational forms in Pehuenche communities in Chile. *Una Revista de Historia social y literatura de América Latina, 8*(2), 197–223.

Greenfield, T. (1986a). The decline and fall of science in educational administration. *Interchange, 17*(2), 57–80.

Greenfield, T. (1986b). Leaders and schools: Wilfulness and non-natural order in organizations. In T. Sergiovanni & J. Corbally (Eds.), *Leadership and organizational culture* (pp. 229–271). Chicago: University of Illinois Press.

Greenfield, T. (1991). Re-forming and re-valuing educational administration: Whence and when cometh the phoenix? *Educational Management and Administration, 19*(4), 200–217.

Greenfield, T. (1993). Science and service: The making of the profession of educational administration. In T.B. Greenfield & P. Ribbins (Eds.), *Greenfield on educational administration: Toward a humane science* (pp. 199–228). London: Routledge.

Hirschland, M. J., & Steinmo, S. (2003). Correcting the record: Understanding the history of federal intervention and failure in securing U.S. educational reform. *Educational Policy, 17*(3), 343–364.

Hollander, E. P., & Offermann, L.R. (1990). Power and leadership in organizations. *American Psychology, 45*(3), 179–189.

House, R. J. (2004). Illustrative examples of Globe findings. In R. J. House, P. J. Hanges, M. Javindan, P. W. Dorfman, & V. Gupta (Eds.), *Culture, leadership, and organization: The Globe study of 62 societies* (pp. 3–7). Thousand Oaks, CA: Sage Publications.

House, R. J., & Javidan, M. (2004). Overview of Globe. In R. J. House, P. J. Hanges, M. Javindan, P. W. Dorfman, & V. Gupta (Eds.), *Culture, leadership, and organization: The Globe study of 62 societies* (pp. 9–49). Thousand Oaks, CA: Sage Publications.

Jules, F. (1999). Native Indian leadership. *Canadian Journal of Native Education, 23*(1), 40–56.

K pa, T. M. A., & Manu'atu, L. (2006). Indigenous Maori and Tongan perspectiveson the role of Tongan language and culture in the community and in the university in Aotearoa-New Zealand. *American Indian Quarterly, 30*(1 & 2), 11–27.

Lam, Y. L. J. (2002). Defining the effects of transformational leadership on organizational learning: A cross-cultural comparison. *School Leadership and Management, 22*(4), 439–452.

MacIntyre, A. (1981). *After virtue: A study in moral theory.* Notre Dame, IN: University of Notre Dame.

Margolis, J. (1995). *Historied thought, constructed world: A conceptual primer for the turn of the millennium.* Berkely: University of California Press.

Margolis, J. (2004). *Moral philosophy after 9/11.* University Park, PA: The Pennsylvania State University Press.

Ottmann, J. (2005). *First Nations leadership development.* Banff, AB: Aboriginal Leadership and Management.

Paquette, J., & Fallon, G. (2010). *First Nations educational policy in Canada: Progress or gridlock.* Toronto, ON: The University of Toronto Press.

Paquette, J., & Fallon, G. (2011). Framing First Nations education policy: Toward constructing a coherent conceptual "place to stand." *International Journal of Interdisciplinary Social Sciences, 5*(9), 331–374.

Robbins, S. (2005). *Organizational behavior.* Upper Saddle River, NJ: Pearson Education.

Ryan, J. (1998). Critical leadership for education in a postmodern world: Emancipation, resistance and communal action. *International Journal of Leadership in Education, 1*(3), 257–278.

Turner, D. (2006). *This is not a peace pipe: Towards a critical indigenous philosophy.* Toronto: University of Toronto Press.

Schutz, A. (1966). *Collected papers III: Studies in phenomenological philosophy.* The Hague, NL: Martinus Nijhoff.

Sergiovanni, T. J. (1992). *Moral leadership: Getting to the heart of school improvement.* San Francisco: Jossey-Bass Publishers.

Soros, G. (1998). *The crisis of global capitalism: Open society endangered.* New York: Public Affairs.

14 Beginning in the Middle

Networks, Processes, and Socio-Material Relations in Educational Administration

Melody Viczko

Where should we start? As always, it is best to start in the middle of things . . .

Latour (2005, p. 27)

In this chapter, I aim to assemble an account of *actor-network theory* (ANT) in educational research in order to theorise areas in which educational administration might be informed by this approach. While I offer some historical introductions to ANT, considering its origins and ontological and episte-mological suppositions, my purpose is not to cover the breadth of studies undertaken by ANT scholars. Rather, I do as Latour suggests by beginning in the middle, by proposing what we might learn as educational administration scholars from fairly recent accounts informed by ANT and areas that show promise for our future research. In the following account, I begin with an introduction to ANT and quickly delve into examples of ANT-informed research in order to illustrate the significance of such research to recent thinking in the field of educational administration. Then, I offer some ideas for areas in which educational administration scholars have much to contribute in the field of ANT studies.

WHAT IS ACTOR-NETWORK THEORY?

The term actor-network was first developed by Michel Callon in Paris between 1978 and 1982 (Law, 2009), though John Law pointed out that the approach itself is broad and could be considered itself a network, spread over time and place, so that its particular origin seems arbitrary. Other seminal scholars of ANT include Bruno Latour (1999a, 2005) in sociology, John Law (1999, 2003, 2009) in sociology of organisations, and Annemarie Mol (1999, 2010) in public health and policy. Recently, Tara Fenwick and Richard Edwards (2010) signalled the relevance of ANT to the study of education, conducting rather large and significant reviews of what they deemed ANT and ANT-ish studies. Their contribution is significant and seminal as it ploughs a trench in the field of educational research for the legitimacy of socio-material, and particularly ANT-informed, research by demonstrating the breadth to which its socio-material concepts may be applied to educational problems.

Law (2009) characterised actor-network theory as a "disparate family of material-semiotic tools, sensibilities, and methods of analysis" (p. 141), and both he and Latour (1999a, 1999b) specifically stipulated that ANT is not a theory. Law offered that ANT's propensity towards analyses that describe, rather than explain, suggest it is not a theory. Rather, he elaborated, "it tells stories about 'how' relations assemble or don't. . . . [I]t is better understood as a toolkit for telling interesting stories about, and interfering in, those relations" (p. 142). He continued that ANT offers particular saliency as a sensibility drawn to the messy practices of materiality and relationality, describing the *how* of practices and relations. In the next section, I elaborate on two key aspects of ANT relevant for the purposes of this text: the relational ontology assumed in ANT and the importance of interactions and processes in the study of the actor-network.

ASSEMBLING THE ACTOR-NETWORK

Actor-network theory is based on an ontology of relations, a material-semiotic approach that treats "everything in the social and natural worlds as a continuously generated effect of the webs of relations within which they are located" (Law, 2009, p. 141). Given the assumption that reality emerges in the enactment of relations, Law contended ANT scholars are inherently concerned with the mechanics of power:

> How some kinds of interactions more or less succeed in stabilising and reproducing themselves: how it is that they overcome resistance and seem to become 'macrosocial'; how it is they seem to generate the effects of such power, fame, size scope or organisation which we are all familiar . . . how, in other words, size, power or organisation are generated.
>
> (p. 2)

As Law and Urry (2003), stipulated, "the move here is to say that real is a relational effect" (p. 5). The authors elaborated ANT's controversial position of the real by stating, "the 'real' is indeed *real*, it is *also* made and that it is made within relations" (p. 5). In doing so, these scholars, along with others such as Latour (2005) and Mol (1999), argued that neither relativist nor realist positions reflect the ontological position of ANT. Rather, the world as interpreted by the social sciences is both real and the product of human actions (Law & Urry, 2003).

A relational ontology suggests that entities *become* through relations, through interactions between actors, as "ANT does not only propose a new way of questioning reality; it also introduces a new way of conceptualising the understanding of reality" (Cordella & Shaikh, 2006, p. 14). Rejecting a realist position, Fenwick (2010) addressed this issue, stating, "a network in ANT *does not connect things that already exist, but actually configures ontologies*" (p. 119).

An important distinction of the nature of reality in ANT is that "entities achieve their form as a consequence of the relations in which they are located. But this means that it also tells us that they are *performed* in, by, and through those relations" (Law, 1999, p. 4). Fenwick (2010) described how such performance is the central focus of ANT studies.

> ANT-inspired studies trace the micro-interactions through which diverse elements or "actants" are performed into being: how they come together—and manage to hold together—in "networks" that can act. These networks produce force and other effects: knowledge, identities, rules, routines, behaviors, new technologies and instruments, regulatory regimes, reforms, illnesses, and so forth. No anterior distinctions such as "human being" or social "structure" are recognized—everything is performed into existence.
>
> (p. 120)

Other scholars have taken up the task of clarifying the ontology offered in ANT. Annemarie Mol (1999) focused on the ontological politics of ANT and emphasised the possibilities of multiple ontologies. That is, there is not social *order*, but rather social *orders*. She stipulated that the multiple ontologies of ANT are distinct from the pluralist sensibilities of interpretation, in which multiplicity means plural understandings. Rather she insisted that ANT regards plural ontologies of ordering. ANT scholars are interested in the notion of multiplicity of performance. That is, things are multiple in their performances. This suggests

> a reality that is *done* and *enacted* rather than observed. Rather than being seen by a diversity of watching eyes while itself remaining untouched in the centre, reality is manipulated by means of various tools in the course of a diversity of practices.
>
> (Mol, 1999, p. 77)

Mol's (1999) writing is devoted to discussing ontological politics, the "way in which the 'real' is implicated in the 'political' and *vice versa*" (p. 74). Consequently, a key concept in ANT is the actor-network. The point of ANT studies "move[s] the focus of the analysis from the actor . . . towards a more complex and less defined phenomenon that is the interaction" (Cordella & Shaikh, 2006, p. 9). The assumption here is that the focus on interactions means that actors are not seen as existing outside of their relations; actors hold a material relationality (Law, 2009). The actor-network is the process by which actors assemble into networks and this becomes the focus of study rather than individual actors themselves. An actor is anything, claimed Latour (2005), that is the source of action: "any thing that does modify a state of affairs by making a difference is an actor—or, if has no figuration yet, an actant" (p. 71). The heterogeneity of actants, both human and non-human, is essential to ANT studies. In educational contexts, objects, such as texts, playground set-ups, policy documents, strategic plans, meeting minutes, office spaces, and classrooms sites all are viewed as actants. They have agency and are influential. Given the relational materiality of ANT, actants develop as networks, to associate or disassociate with other actants to form networked associations, "which in turn define them, name them, and provide them with substance, action, intention and subjectivity" (Crawford, 2005, p. 1). Hence the hyphenated term, *actor-network*.

Latour (1999b) warned against the use of the technical meaning of network "in the sense of a sewage, or train, or subway, or telephone 'network'" (p. 1). Rather, he advocated for networks in terms of nodes with diverse dimensions and connections, adopting a network-like ontology, rather than a flat two-dimensional surface more commonly used in network conceptualisations. The consequence of such conceptualising of the actor-network requires scholars using ANT to avoid focusing on the individual as powerful actor, in isolation from the networked context in which it is located. Rather, the focus in ANT is to trace the ways in which the actors are connected, assembled, and defined in the actor-networks.

CONNECTING ANT IN EDUCATIONAL RESEARCH TO EDUCATIONAL ADMINISTRATION

The point of this section is to begin a discussion about the ways in which ANT might better inform our understandings about educational administration as both a theoretical field and a practice. To do so, I identify three themes that I believe ANT can offer to educational administration. In each theme, I begin with examples of relatively recent studies that use ANT to inform the conceptual and methodological frameworks within which the research was conducted. Further, I offer a brief discussion about how such studies might open up, shift, or revamp how some concepts, issues, and dilemmas are taken up in educational administration. From there, I elaborate on some areas that I see as possible directions for future research.

EXPLORING PROCESSES RATHER THAN OUTCOMES THROUGH SOCIO-MATERIAL NETWORKS

In a study of innovation in a programme focused on training staff for IT usage in classrooms, Mulcahy and Perillo (2011) demonstrated how socio-material practices were instrumental in the leadership of the programme.

In this research, they traced how the programme developed from an initial instrumentalist and strategic plan of seven modules. This plan was implemented through formalised learning that targeted teachers' skills towards a more open-process based set of interactions between the initial formalised plan and the teachers and material objects in the learning environment. Drawing on ANT, Mulcahy and Perillo justified an approach to the research that resisted asking why things happen but instead focused attention on "how they arrange themselves. How the materials of the world (social, technical, documentary, natural, human, animal) get themselves done in particular locations for a moment in all of their heterogeneity" (Law, 2008, as cited in Mulcahy & Perillo, 2011, p. 128). In their research, great consideration was given to the material objects in the room: paint colour on walls, furniture comfort, accessible equipment, among others. In looking at the interactions between the social and the material, Mulcahy and Perillo concluded,

> Innovation and change at Viewbank Grammar is not treated merely as the realization of pre-existent possibilities (staff training program); it is improvisatory and performative—it does not exist outside its "doing'". Practices of managing and leading change are multiple and emergent, distributed among materials, managers and staff.
>
> (p. 137)

Using ANT to highlight process rather than explanation, the scholars concluded that management and leadership emerge in the collective work of people, processes, and materials. Paying attention to such socio-material relations in leadership studies requires focusing on the "workings" rather than the outcomes of leadership, disrupting the mantra of the required traits of successful, individual leaders that permeate educational administration literature. Mulcahy and Perillo (2011) called for leadership studies to account for "what is assembled or associated when multiple and different ties (structural, cultural, material and so forth) are taken into account" (p. 123). Consequently, the authors argued for two commitments: (a) a characterisation of educational management that addresses both the sociality and the materiality of practices, given their interactions and co-productions; and (b) a shift beyond the duality created between leader and led, suggesting leadership as performative practice between people and objects. That is, the relationality of ANT demonstrates how both people and artefacts (of their creation) co-produce practices in organisations.

In a study of school reform, Nespor (2004) adopted a network approach drawing on ANT to illustrate what becomes connected in order to enact powerful forms of education change. Using a case study of two attempts at state-wide educational reform in Virginia, Nespor examined how educational change efforts can be viewed through the lens of network, arguing for an approach that "treats actors as dialectically constituted by social relations and treats network relations as the contingently stabilized connections produced by the movement of people and things" (p. 368). Instances of reform can be better understood by examining connections between different actors in each context: strategically located individuals; objects, such as influential expert writings connected to mobilised entities advocating for similar forms of reform; media; foundation reports that categorised particular models of reform as traditional (read *good*) and transformational (read *poor*); written curricula; and samples of children's work shared at home that became evidence of the quality of a school system as a whole. As Nespor explained:

> The point is that we need to understand "school change" as at least partly about the ways school practices are made mobile, and what and how they connect as they move. What are the structures of connections or linkages? What materials are they made of? How do things change as they move? How do connections change with this movement?
>
> (p. 368)

That is, we begin to see the network that is school reform and context, rather than isolating each concept as separate items for interrogation.

Fenwick (2011) examined large-scale reform through a study of the Alberta Initiative for School Improvement (AISI) to examine the local mobilisations of mandated reform. Using an ANT reading of school reform as the effect of assemblages interacting with each other, Fenwick explored how a heterogeneous network of connections emerges in various interactions with school change through AISI programmes and policy initiatives. In her account, Fenwick theorised that AISI was enacted as an extensive and robust network connecting classroom equipment, environments, and electronic technology to teachers, administrators, and university professors. Such networks allowed for the seemingly disconnected actions of people and objects throughout the network. Yet, in tracing how AISI became mobile throughout many educational jurisdictions, Fenwick illustrated how provincial priorities mandated through AISI become operationalised in their connections to the local activities of teachers, students, parents, and the various objects used in daily teaching and learning activities. As such, the AISI framework provided authority for schools in determining their own improvement initiatives while still being tightly connected to the provincial goal of student achievement. Fenwick showed how schools, universities, professional associations, and government bodies generated dynamics that allow them to interact with each other, thereby enacting policy at local and provincial levels.

Processes in Educational Administration and Leadership

Studies aimed at addressing efforts at school reform in the field of educational administration often focus on the notion of leadership. For this reason, studies and literature in educational administration have more recently focused on particular characteristic varieties of leadership: transformational

(Hallinger, 2003), inclusive (Ryan, 2006), and distributed (Spillane, 2006), to name a few. From an ANT perspective, each of these models is steeped in traditions of structural-functionalist assumptions of the individual; that decision making is located in the agency of one individual to act his/her influence on a collective of other individuals; and that purposive, action-oriented thinking, planning, and acting from one actor can be fostered, developed, and unleashed to solve educational problems. Even the more constructivist models have been critiqued for their reliance on individuality—and perhaps even *collective individuality*—whereby the power of leadership can be shared by many individuals (Mulcahy & Perillo, 2011).

While ANT also exhibits a focus on agency, its theories are suggestive that such agency is located in the actions of an assemblage of actors, both human and non-human. That is, agency does not rest in one individual alone, rather agency emerges as people interact with the material world in which they are embedded. So, from this perspective, ANT offers a shift in how we think about agency in two ways. First, the focus of agency moves away from humans alone and considers objects (things, the non-human, etc.) as sources of equal agency. Latour (2005) called this principle *symmetry* and rightly expressed,

> ANT is not the empty claim that objects do things "instead" of human actors: it simply says that no science of the social can even begin if the question of who and what participates in the action is not first of all thoroughly explored, even though it might mean letting elements in which, for a lack of a better term, we would call *non-humans*.
>
> (p. 72)

Second, ANT offers a new way of viewing organisations, moving away from a structural functionalist view of organisations, towards studying practices and processes of organising (Alcadipani & Hassard, 2010). Lawrence and Suddaby (2006) offered that ANT provides exciting opportunities for scholars concerned with institutional theories because of the focus that takes precedence in its studies. Citing Law (1992), Lawrence and Suddaby highlighted the connections between ANT and the study of organizations by illustrating the focus of ANT on process. Here, Law explained the core of the ANT approach:

> How actors and organizations mobilize, juxtapose and hold together the bits and pieces of which they are composed: how they are sometimes able to prevent those bits and pieces from following their own inclinations and making off and how they manage, as a result, to conceal for a time the process of translation itself and so turn a network from a heterogeneous set of bits and pieces each with its own inclinations, into something that passes as an actualized actor.
>
> (Law, 1992, p. 386)

Lawrence and Suddaby suggested ANT as a fresh perspective to institutional theory through its focus on the struggles and contestations that generate and reproduce institutions. In this case, the stability of institutions should be considered as *relational effects* (Law, 1992), moving the focus away from outcome of institutions, such as norm production, and instead focusing on the interactions that produce particular outcomes, such as particular policies and relational positioning of actors.

Such prospects from ANT offer opportunities for focusing on process-oriented rather than individual-centered theories in educational administration. For example, possible research may address how we understand leadership as an effect of the processes by which educational practices are carried out daily. In this way, research questions shift from an orientation towards the kinds of leadership styles that are desired to research questions that explore in what conditions leadership effects are enacted and produced, that is, as relational effects of the human and non-human actors involved in education.

ENACTING THE TEACHER

Mulcahy (2011) examined teaching standards that dominate professionalised discourses in Australia and other Western education systems to consider the notion of the *accomplished teacher*. Contrasting two idiomatic conceptualisations of standards as either representational or performative, Mulcahy set out to illustrate how the accomplished teacher is produced. Mulcahy (2011) challenged the value of teacher standards when viewed as static, representational tools focused on particular outcomes representing what "teachers know, believe and do" (p. 96). Such representations, she critiqued, serve to disconnect teachers from the material and social relations in which they are engaged and also the actions by which teaching is performed. Rather, drawing upon ANT theories of relational and multiple ontologies, Mulcahy used empirical research collected in three settings to argue that when standards are viewed through the lens of performativity, the multiplicity and complexity of ways in which the accomplished teacher is enacted comes into focus. Referencing the data collected in observing teachers in the practice of teaching, she illustrated the prolific socio-material ways in which standards emerge. Mulcahy demonstrated the ways that practice, identity, and standards are co-assembled as they contemporaneously emerge and grow. Her study radically served to shift ways in which commonly held assumptions about teacher identity, practices, and standards are conceptualised in network fashion.

Exactly What Are We Studying? Ontological Challenges to Educational Administration

While Mulcahy's (2011) study focused specifically on intersections of practice, objects, standards, and people that produce idyllic identities, such as the *accomplished*, and presumably, variations of the *unaccomplished* teacher,

ANT offers the opportunity for educational administration scholars to relinquish other pre-determined categories and assumptions in order to question what it is we assume about schools as organisations, education as an institution, and students as learners.

Lee and Hassard (1999) argued an ontological relativist position of ANT in "permitting the world to organize differently" (p. 391). These scholars argued that ANT is ontologically relativist "in that it typically embarks on research without a clear picture of what sort of entities it will discover through interaction" (p. 394). ANT informed studies search for how organisations, institutions, and entities emerge, treating the objects of research as active, "organizational participants, working and reworking not just their various descriptions of organizational form, but organizational form itself" (p. 399). Lee and Hassard criticised studies whereby existence is taken for granted, where goals, environment, and strategy are treated a priori as the foundations of organisation (Chia, 1996). These scholars contended that such treatment limits the questions that can be asked in research to those related to effectiveness of goal strategies, alignment between goal and strategy, and impact of environment on goal pursuit. However, ANT research orients to questions that probe "how do goals 'mobilize' and become 'mobilized'" (Lee & Hassard, 1999, p. 402). Such questions highlight "ANT's unwillingness to decide the shape of the world on behalf of the domains it examines" (p. 402). Such consideration allows for examining "how contemporary flexibility, responsiveness and liveliness, whatever they may consist of, are achieved" (p. 402). Indeed, ANT asks us to consider what, which, and how boundaries are being created. In terms of educational administration, we may ask, how are our schools, as organisations, created?

KNOWLEDGE AS EFFECT OF ASSEMBLING PRACTICES

Gorur (2011) examined the knowledge produced through the OECD's Programme for International Student Assessment (PISA) to critique claims of the certainty of scientific evidence upon which the PISA results are premised. She drew upon Latour's (1999c) position of truths as "being neither facts nor naïve beliefs but results of collective experimentation" (Gorur, 2011, p. 90) to highlight the conditional nature of knowledge. In this article, Gorur reported on interviews with a senior official and a data analyst from PISA to show how the assessment results come to be used as a form of knowledge that renders a certainty about the state of national education systems, and by its comparative nature, postulate directions for policy initiatives in international educational contexts that may otherwise seem disconnected. Here, Gorur highlighted Latour's (1999c) work in which he suggested provisional, messy, and controversial production of facts by looking ethnographically at how scientific knowledge is constructed in laboratories through the work of human scientists as they interact with other scientists and their tools in the production of claims of truth. Gorur took a similar approach to studying the

"PISA laboratory [to] observe how PISA scientists classify and order the outside world into definable categories" (p. 78) and collect samples of data to produce *PISA facts*. Gorur questioned the nature of these facts by examining the practices of data collection, mathematical modeling and mobilisation that work to produce them.

One aspect of Gorur's approach that is relevant to the field of educational administration is the way in which the PISA facts become mobilised to influence and direct policy initiatives in far-flung places remote from the sites in which the data were collected. That is, how is it that data collected in Finland can be universalised with other internationally collected data into league tables to effect educational policy initiatives in other national contexts, such as Japan, Canada or Chile? By tracing the processes through which PISA officials and data work to encapsulate the students and the learning into "detached, separated, preserved, classified, and tagged" (Latour, 1999c, p. 39) inscriptions so that PISA scientists can "reassemble, reunite and redistribute them" (Gorur, 2011, p. 88), Gorur illustrated the socio-material nature of such knowledge production. "Frameworks acted as gatekeepers. Mathematical models pronounced judgments. Inscriptions prescribed and controlled. Booklets represented student knowledge" (p. 90). In doing so, data as knowledge become completely detached from the students and their learning contexts.

> The teachers, the test items and the students have bowed out, no longer relevant in their particular forms. The bustle of the classroom and the fuss of real people and things have been translated into a neat-two dimensional, ordered world of logits. And because logits are standard for a given pool of test items (Wright & Stone, 1979), data from PISA tests can be compared across time and place. The various bits of data can be worked on, manipulated and combined in new and different ways to create new patterns and understandings.
>
> (Gorur, 2011, p. 86)

Other scholars have considered knowledge in professional learning contexts. In a study of teacher professional learning in one Canadian school, Riveros and Viczko (2012) questioned the nature of the relationship between knowledge and practice in teacher professional learning. Using interviews collected from teachers in a case study of one school, Riveros and Viczko examined how the ways in which teachers spoke of their professional learning reflected a spatial separation in their understandings between the contexts of practice and the context of learning. Drawing on ANT to suggest that persons, objects, knowledge, and locations are relational effects (Latour, 2005), they saw such conceptual distinctions between scenarios of learning and scenarios of practice as problematic for teacher learning. Much of the professional learning literature and policy documents position professional learning as occurring in communities whereby teachers can reflect on their practices; however, such arrangements of professional learning resulted in teachers' understanding of learning as occurring outside of their teaching practice.

> In this view, the classroom seems to be perceived as a scenario for professional practice that is *influenced* by the knowledge originated in the context of collaborative groups. One teacher was explicit in this regard when she indicated that [professional learning] was meaningful to her "because I came back and I could use it the next day. It wasn't something that I had to figure out, 'Where am I going to put this?'".
>
> (Riveros & Viczko, 2012, p. 47)

Given the proliferation of collaborative professional learning models, Riveros and Viczko (2012) viewed teacher learning as a process that spans time and space between the scenarios of collective discussion and individual teaching practice. That is, knowledge needed for improving teaching and learning in classrooms must be conceived as emerging through a variety of teacher practices, including acts of teaching and acts of participating in professional learning activities. They suggested that ANT provides a lens through which to further interrogate how viewing knowledge as emerging through practices as they are enacted might better inform our understandings of teachers' knowledge, how it is connected to classroom practices, and the ways in which professional learning models influence such enactments.

FOLLOWING ANT IN EDUCATIONAL ADMINISTRATION

There are two further areas on which I draw attention for ANT in the study of educational administration. First, while the concept of scale has been taken up by scholars in educational research, the study of global educational policy initiatives is an area of promise for ANT (Fenwick & Edwards, 2010). As we have seen earlier in this chapter (Gorur, 2011), the ways in which globalised institutions travel through localised spaces can be traced in order to understand how particular forms of knowledge are constructed as powerful in a globalising policy field (Rizvi & Lingard, 2010). Latour (1999a) articulated the significance in ANT studies of rejecting essentialist a priori orderings of the world; there is neither a local nor a global scale, only a relational one. Consequently, he rejected such dualisms of global/ local or micro/macro since "big does not mean 'really' big or 'overarching', but connected, blind, local, mediated, related" (p. 18). Law (2009) agreed, considering level as a relational effect. In what ways might this inform educational administration?

Scalar distinctions such as global and local are problematic for ANT and, therefore, abandoning such a priori divisions disrupts theories of ideational diffusion and institutional isomorphism (Lawrence & Suddaby, 2006) often used to explore policy transfer and convergence. Gorur (2011) considered PISA as a global player in educational policy spaces, yet the strength in her study was in showing how it has become so through local practices. Adopting an approach informed by actor-network theory requires breaking with understandings of a powerful *global* and a powerless, un-agential *local*. Rather, there is a need to study how educational policies are taken up across networks of relations, across political and social boundaries, to examine what actors become assembled in particular policy contexts and what emerges as powerful in such assemblages.

Recently, the work of Ball, Maguire, Braun, and Hoskins (2011) sought to address the notion of enactment to the study of secondary school policies. Departing at the premise that "policies do not normally tell you what to do, they create circumstances in which the range of options available in deciding what to do are narrowed or changed, or particular goals or outcomes are set" (Ball, 1994, p. 19), the authors challenged functionalist assumptions of linear policy processes by arguing that putting policies into practice requires creative, complex, and contentious acts of enactment. In their broad study of four secondary schools in England, they aimed to show how policies are enacted as assemblages of various national and local initiatives in secondary schools. Such research is greatly needed in developing our understanding of how policies work in schools. While Ball et al. (2011) recognised the contributions of actor-network theory to educational research, the conceptual leverage of scale offered by ANT was not taken up in their work and an exploration of how policies are enacted beyond local policy spaces might produce deeper understandings of the global-local dialectic in policy studies.

Second, power is core to ANT studies, highlighted in the focus on "analyzing the exercises of power by which cultural, social and economic capital is produced and reproduced" (Edwards, 2002, p. 355). In this way, ANT is useful at probing the way that politics work to constrain and enable certain enactments (Fenwick, 2010). The field of educational administration theory and practice is embedded in a dynamic of power relations, between struggles for power and influence in decision making, curriculum design, policy implementation and jurisdictional governance, to name a few. By considering power dynamics as emerging through the interactions of a network of heterogeneous actors, there is much to be explored in the ontological politics (Mol, 1999) of governance, policymaking, and decision making in educational administration processes and practices in school contexts.

CONCLUSION

My goal in this chapter was to examine some areas for scholars situated in educational administration to take up and engage with actor-network theory as a conceptual tool for exploring networks, processes, socio-material relations and knowledge production. ANT is not without its adversaries—those who criticise its perspectives as too realist or too relativist, or too ambiguous to offer a critical look at social science studies (Latour, 2005). However, such critiques offer opportunity for scholars to engage in the ontological politics (Mol, 1999) pertaining to questions of "what is the field of educational administration and how is it conceptualised by contemporary scholars?" As Hernes (2008) suggested, an entity *"becomes* what it is through its various encounters with other technologies, communities and actors" (p. xix). While the answers to such questions seem endless, Latour offers advice for beginning the journey by immersing oneself in the context of the problems we want to study—that is, in the middle of things.

REFERENCES

Alcadipani, R., & Hassard, J. (2010). Actor-Network Theory, organizations and critique: Towards a politics of organizing. *Organization, 17*(4), 419–435. doi:10.1177/1350508410364441

Ball, S. (1994). *Education reform: A critical and post-structural approach.* Buckingham, UK: Open University Press.

Ball, S., Maguire, M., Braun, A., & Hoskins, K. (2011). Policy subjects and policy actors in schools: Some necessary but insufficient analyses. *Discourse: Studies in the Cultural Politics of Education, 32*(4), 611–634. doi:10.1080/01596306.2011.601564

Chia, R. (1996). The problem of reflexivity in organizational research: Towards a postmodern science of organization. *Organization, 3*(1), 31–59.

Cordella, A., & Shaikh, M. (2006). *From epistemology to ontology: Challenging the constructed "truth" of ANT.* Retrieved from http://is2.lse.ac.uk/wp/pdf/WP143.PDF

Crawford, C. (2005). Actor network theory. In G. Ritzer (Ed.), *Dictionary of social theory* (pp. 1–3). London: Sage.

Edwards, R. (2002). Mobilizing lifelong learning: Governmentality in educational practices. *Journal of Education Policy, 17*(3), 353–365.

Fenwick, T. (2010). un(Doing) standards in education with actor-network theory. *Journal of Education Policy, 25*(2), 117–133. doi:10.1080/02680930903314277

Fenwick, T. (2011). Reading educational reform with actor network theory: Fluid spaces, otherings and ambivalences. *Educational Philosophy and Theory, 43*(S1), 113–144. doi:10.1111/j.1469-5812.2009.00609.x

Fenwick, T., & Edwards, R. (2010). *Actor-network theory in education.* London: Routledge.

Gorur, R. (2011). ANT on the PISA trail: Following the statistical pursuit of certainty. *Educational Philosophy and Theory, 43*(S1), 76–93. doi:10.1111/j.1469-5812.2009.00612x

Hallinger, P. (2003). Leading educational change: Reflections on the practice of instructional and transformational leadership. *Cambridge Journal of Education, 33*(3), 329–351.

Hernes, T. (2008). *Understanding organization as process: Theory for a tangled world.* New York: Routledge.

Latour, B. (1999a). On recalling ANT. In J. Law & J. Hassard (Eds.), *Actor network theory and after* (pp. 15–25). Oxford, UK: Blackwell.

Latour, B. (1999b). *The trouble with actor-network theory.* Retrieved from http://www.cours.fse.ulaval.ca/edc-65804/latour-clarifications.pdf

Latour, B. (1999c). *Pandora's hope: Essays on the reality of science studies.* Cambridge, MA: Harvard University Press.

Latour, B. (2005). *Reassembling the social: An introduction to actor-network theory.* Oxford, UK: University of Oxford Press.

Law, J. (1992). Notes on the theory of the actor network: Ordering, strategy and heterogeneity. *Systems Practice, 5*(4), 379–393.

Law, J. (1999). After ANT: Complexity, naming and topology. In J. Law & J. Hassard (Eds.), *Actor network theory and after* (pp. 1–14). Oxford, UK: Blackwell.

Law, J. (2003). *Notes on the theory of the actor network: Ordering, strategy and heterogeneity.* Retrieved from http://www.lancs.ac.uk/fass/sociology/papers/law-notes-on-ant.pdf

Law, J. (2008), Actor-Network Theory and material semiotics. In B. S. Turner (Ed.), *The new Blackwell companion to social theory* (pp. 141–158). Oxford: Blackwell.

Law, J. (2009). Actor network theory and material semiotics. In B. S. Turner (Ed.), *The new Blackwell companion to social theory* (3rd ed.; pp. 141–158). Chichester, UK: Blackwell.

Law, J., & Urry, J. (2003). *Enacting the social.* Retrieved from http://www.lancs.ac.uk/fass/sociology/papers/law-urry-enacting-the-social.pdf

Lawrence, T., & Suddaby, R. (2006). Institutions and institutional work. In S. Clegg, C. Hardy, W. R. Nord & T. Lawrence (Eds.), *Handbook of organization studies* (pp. 215–254). London: Sage.

Lee, N., & Hassard, J. (1999). Organization unbound: Actor-network theory, research strategy and institutional flexibility. *Organization, 6*(3), 391–404.

Mol, A. (1999). Ontological politics. In J. Law & J. Hassard (Eds.), *Actor network theory and after* (pp. 74–89). Oxford, UK: Blackwell.

Mol, A. (2010). Care and its values: Food food in the nursing home. In A. Mol, I. Moser, & J. Pols (Eds.), *Care in practice: On tinkering in clinics, homes and farms* (pp. 215–234). Bielefeld, Germany: Transcript.

Mulcahy, D. (2011). Assembling the 'Accomplished' teacher: The performativity and politics of professional teaching standards. *Educational Philosophy and Theory, 43*(S1), 94–113. doi:10.1111/j.1469–5812.2009.00617.x

Mulcahy, D., & Perillo, S. (2011). Thinking management and leadership within colleges and schools somewhat differently: A practice-based, Actor-Network Theory perspective. *Educational Management Administration & Leadership, 39*(1), 122–145. doi:10.1177/1741143210383895

Nespor, J. (2004). Education scale-making. *Pedagogy, Culture and Society, 12*(3), 309–326.

Riveros, A., & Viczko, M. (2012). Professional knowledge "from the field": Resituating professional learning in the contexts of practice. *McGill Journal of Education, 47*(1), 37–52.

Rizvi, F., & Lingard, B. (2010) *Globalizing education policy.* New York: Routledge.

Ryan, J. (2006). Inclusive leadership and social justice for schools. *Leadership and Policy in Schools, 5*, 3–17.

Spillane, J. (2006). *Distributed leadership.* San Francisco: Jossey Bass.

Wright, B. D., & Stone, M. H. (1979). *Best test design.* Chicago: Mesa.

15 Rethinking Schools as Living Systems

Coral Mitchell and Larry Sackney

This book contains numerous organisational theories, each with its own assumptions about the organisational world and with its own ways of thinking about complex problems. This condition of difference is typical of organisation studies in the twenty-first century. In their own recent collection of contemporary organisation studies, for example, Nord, Lawrence, Hardy, and Clegg (2006) found a multiplicity of approaches to organisational theorising, which they categorised along a continuum from traditional scientific inquiry on the one end to social constructivist discourses on the other. This plethora of approaches, coupled with the influence of root metaphors and institutional thought worlds, implies that organisational knowledge, regardless of the approach taken to create that knowledge, is always socially constructed and contextually situated.

Knowledge construction in organisation studies is further mediated by time and location. March (2007) observed this mediating process in his analysis of shifts in organisation studies since 1945, noting that both the methods of investigation and the contents of the theories changed as scholars and practitioners confronted different challenges and realities in different times and places. March claimed that "generational imprinting is a striking feature of the intellectual history of organization studies" (p. 11) and he warned that "forecasting the future is a fool's conceit" (p. 16). After delivering that warning, however, he encouraged scholars to continue the work of theorising about organisation: "[o]ur task is not to discern the future in order to join it; nor even to shape it. Our task is to make small pieces of scholarship beautiful through rigor, persistence, competence, elegance and grace" (p. 18). In this chapter, we are mindful of March's warning: We do not attempt to forecast the future of organisation theory, but rather we offer a way of thinking about organisations for the twenty-first century. We begin our analysis with a look back at traditional theories and the critiques of that tradition. We move forward from the critiques with a description of the principles and properties of living systems, we present some applications of those properties in schools and other organisations, and we conclude with some justifications for thinking of organisations as living systems.

TRADITIONAL THEORIES OF ORGANISING

Several theorists (e.g., Gergen & Thatchenkery, 2004; Reed, 2006; Tetenbaum, 1998; Wheatley, 2006) have noted that traditional theories of organisation are rooted in the view of science prevailing in the late nineteenth and early twentieth centuries, which was dominated by Newton's seventeenth-century model of physics and mathematics. A core belief of the Newtonian paradigm was that the universe is objective, stable, regular, predictable, and linear. Knowledge could be discovered through empirical observations, and rational analyses of the observed data would yield causal laws and universal principles that could be used to explain phenomena and to predict future outcomes. Any phenomenon could be understood by breaking it down into its constituent parts and analysing the parts to determine their contribution to the intended outcomes.

When applied to social realities, Tetenbaum (1998) argued, "the lens of Newtonian science led us to look at organizational success in terms of maintaining a stable system" (p. 21). Luke (2011) described a parallel influence exerted by the Royal Society of England of the eighteenth century, whose goal was "to develop universal standards of measurement and scientific procedure" (p. 369). These standards were seen as providing a "forum for the adjudication of scientific truths and findings. The assumption was that the very advancement of modernity, of civilization as it was known, depended on this approach to formal codification and authorization of method, of definition, of procedure" (pp. 369–370). Taken together, the various seventeenth- and eighteenth-century developments led to what Gergen and Thatchenkery (2004), among many others, have labelled the modernist era of the nineteenth and twentieth centuries.

For Gergen and Thatchenkery (2004), the modernist era was characterised in organisations by an array of cultural practices that revolve around (a) rational agents responding to organisational concerns in systematic ways, (b) objective knowledge gathered from careful empirical testing of scientific propositions, (c) language and discourse patterns that represent an objective reality, and (d) a general assumption of ongoing progress as rational agents make better organisational decisions based on access to better empirical knowledge. With this cultural apparatus, Wheatley (2007) noted, the dominant organisational narrative is a story of command and control that attempts to erase human interests and emotions and to offset human frailties and inconsistencies.

Although the modernist narrative has yielded a number of deeply troubling consequences, its original goal was honourable. It began, according to Wheatley (2007), "with a dream that it was within humankind's province to understand the workings of the universe and to gain complete mastery over physical matter" (p. 17). In organisation studies, Reed (2006) claimed, the traditional logic "confidently anticipated the triumph of science over politics and the victory of rationally designed collective order and progress" (p. 19).

In education, Luke (2011) explained, the generation and dissemination of standardised knowledge was intended to equip individuals to move freely across institutional and geographic boundaries. The standards were seen as "the road to the classical liberal goals of fairness and equality of access" (p. 370). In other words, the goal of the old organisational narrative was one of ongoing progress and continuous improvement based on scientifically derived and universally transferrable knowledge.

In schools, this paradigm is reflected in the clocks that start and stop classes, the operating manuals, prescribed curricula, and routines for teaching and learning. These mechanisms hold the parts together by prescribing, standardising, regulating, and controlling human behaviour (of teachers, students, and administrators, alike). According to Mitchell and Sackney (2009b), the traditional narrative provided the justification for school systems to be "structurally hierarchical, functionally task-specific and rule-bound, and relationally impersonal" (p. 8). In this way, behaviour and learning could be directed and predicted to achieve specified educational outcomes. However, Luke (2011) posed a critical question:

> [a]t what point does standardization go beyond any purported need for interoperability—and become a repressive limitation of the available, imaginable cultural tools and artifacts and, thereby, a sociogenetic limitation and constraint on what can be thought, felt, done, and created?
>
> (p. 375)

This question, broadly applied, underpinned the various and ongoing critiques of the traditional narrative.

A TIME OF TRANSITION

Early in the twentieth century, Newtonian science was found to be insufficient to explain a number of phenomena. Largely influenced by the work of Einstein and colleagues, new scientific ideas emerged to accommodate observations that "time and space are not discrete and independent, that complex systems are not predictable, and that living systems self-organize and change in response to the feedback they receive from their environments, yet retain the integrity of their purpose and meaning" (Mitchell & Sackney, 2009b, p. 8). According to Wheatley (2006), these accommodations broke through the Newtonian juggernaut and ushered in a "new science" based on quantum physics, dissipative structures, and complexity theory.

As the twentieth century moved on, the world became increasingly connected; information grew exponentially; social, physical, and geopolitical environments became increasingly fragile and unstable, and human existence became increasingly complex and unpredictable. These dynamic conditions have continued unabated in the twenty-first century. Several theorists (e.g., Bowers, 2008; Capra, 2002; Gergen & Thatchenkery, 2004) have pointed out that the challenges and opportunities of this century cannot be resolved with the cultural and organisational practices inherited from the modernist era. As Wheatley (2007) said,

> [i]t is one of the great ironies of our age that we created organizations to constrain our problematic human natures, and now the only thing that can save these organizations is a full appreciation of the expansive capacities of us humans.
>
> (p. 21)

To get to this full appreciation requires not just a different set of cultural and organisational practices but also a different set of academic practices—that is, a different theory of organising and a different way of theorising.

According to Bowers (2008), the traditional process of abstract theorising "reproduces Plato's assumption that rational thought, which only an elite can effectively engage in, is a more reliable source of knowledge than narratives, embodied experiences and the achievements of other cultures" (p. 327). His analysis pitted the theorising capacity of the elite experts against the problem-solving capacity of members of a particular cultural commons, and Bowers (2002) appeared to weigh in on the side of cultural members in his observation that "language thinks us as we think within the conceptual categories that the language of our culture makes available. As thought is inherently metaphorical, there is always the possibility of identifying more adequate analogies" (p. 23). In other words, members of the cultural commons live not only with the conceptual categories that can constrain theory but also with current realities that can catalyze the search for better categories. Therefore, their experience and knowledge are central elements in the quest for adequate theories.

The ongoing search for "more adequate analogies" led to the postmodern turn in academic discourses, which Sim (1999) described as "a gesture of dissent . . . a form of scepticism—scepticism about authority, received wisdom, cultural and political norms, etc." (p. 3). As a gesture of dissent, postmodern discourses have been primarily negative in tone as they critiqued existing taken-for-granted assumptions and linguistic categories. Corson (1996), however, offered a more positive contribution:

> [t]he postmodern condition that we now find ourselves in is emancipatory in one respect above all others: It reveals a world where orthodoxies, ideologies, disciplinary boundaries, and closed contexts exist only in the minds of those positioned by them. Awareness of this fact allows us to begin to "reclaim reality."
>
> (p. 1064)

Postmodern debates over the ontological and epistemic foundations of knowledge and knowledge creation have played out in all academic disciplines, but according to Nord et al. (2006), they have been particularly vigorous (and vicious) in organisational studies. As a consequence, Reed (2006) noted, "contemporary students of organization find themselves at a historical juncture and in a social context where all the old ideological 'certainties' and technical 'fixes' that once underpinned their 'discipline' are fundamentally being called into question" (p. 20). Unfortunately, while postmodern discourses called into question the structured and prescriptive narrative of modernist organisations, they failed to explain the underlying character of a new narrative, other than that it was not modern in nature. In short, as a disruptive or transition term, postmodernism worked well, but as an explanatory or descriptive term, it lacked form and character, causing Gergen and Thatchenkery (2004) to complain that, "although critique is pervasive and catalytic, it has not yet been restorative. While faulting existing traditions, it has left the future in question. How do we proceed?" (p. 234).

Although the intellectual and methodological pluralism of postmodern discourses has continued into the twenty-first century, a way to proceed is coming into focus. For Bowers (2002), ecology is emerging as the new root metaphor for understanding and dealing effectively with current realities. This root metaphor, he says, "foregrounds the relational and interdependent nature of our existence as cultural and biological beings. This includes our participation in a highly complex web of symbolic relationships deeply rooted in the past" (p. 29). This root metaphor is also evident in organisation studies, where Tsoukas (2008) identified two emerging trends: "an ecological view . . . whose main feature is the acceptance of complexity" and "the view that organizations are constituted by knowledge" (p. 195). Both of these trends, he says, acknowledge "the centrality of human agency in the constitution and functioning of organizations" (p. 195). Wheatley (2007) and Capra (2002) took the root metaphor to a practical level through the frame of organisations as living systems, wherein the study of organisational variables is replaced by a consideration of how the "organization arises from the interaction and needs of individuals who have decided to come together" (Wheatley, 2007, p. 26). In short, thinking of organisations as living systems means being centrally interested in the actions and relationships of people as they construct their organisational world.

During the past two decades, the question of constructing a sustainable educational world has underpinned our investigations into schools as learning communities. In high-capacity learning communities, we noticed that the ways of acting and interacting throughout the schools breathed life and energy into teaching and learning (Mitchell & Sackney, 2009a). Yet, in practice, many so-called learning communities fail to deliver the promised results because they have been constructed from the premises and with the characteristics of modernist systems (Sackney & Mitchell, 2008). We propose, with Luke (2011), that "other pathways, other pedagogic/curricular traditions, other forms of knowledge, other forms of childhood and child rearing, other forms of school leadership and institutional organization are possible and necessary, and may offer sustainable ways forward" (p. 369). Our argument is that learning communities flourish if educational institutions are reconstituted to reflect the principles and properties of living systems. In the remainder of the chapter, we describe the defining features of living systems and examine the way forward for schools and education on the basis of this theory.

PROPERTIES OF LIVING SYSTEMS

To think of organisations as living systems is to understand that the construction of organisation is a complex process of individual action, social interaction, and collective negotiation, at both the practical and linguistic levels. As Corson (1996) put it,

> mental activity is not tied to some internal set of processes; it is a range of moves set against a background of human activity governed by informal conventions or rules, especially rules to do with the ways in which words and other symbols are used within the structures of a language. . . . Getting inside those structures means getting inside the forms of life, norms, conventions, and rules, and seeing them as the subject does.
>
> (p. 1044)

Gergen and Thatchenkery (2004) further articulated the social character of human rationality: "viable language depends on communal cooperation . . . [and] making sense is a communal achievement" (p. 235). Within the community, "language gains its meaning not from its mental or subjective underpinnings but from its use in action" (p. 236); as such, language "is not a reflection of a world but is world-constituting" (p. 236). The work of language in the constitution of a world means that people, and their lived experiences, are always at the centre of any theory of organisation and in any process of theorising about organisations.

The world-constituting role of language defines living systems as dialogic, communicative, and learning-oriented in character. Knowledge creation is a generative process that emerges as people make sense of their world and move forward into novelty in personally meaningful ways. According to Capra (2002), the process begins as people pay attention to the disturbances in their world that are both meaningful and compelling:

> [a] living network responds to disturbances with structural changes, and it chooses both which disturbances to notice and how to respond. . . . A message will get through to [people] not only because of its volume or frequency, but because it is meaningful to them.
>
> (pp. 111–112)

As Wheatley (2007) pointed out, this characteristic means "that we can never direct a living system—we can only hope to get its attention" (p. 46). This feature of living systems positions meaning and attention as key elements in the processes of knowledge creation, learning, and development for people and organisations.

As people respond to disturbances in their environment, they build systems that help them to act meaningfully. This process of self-generation and self-organisation is, according to Wheatley (2007), a key feature of living systems: "[o]rganization is a naturally occurring phenomenon. Self-organization is a powerful force that creates the systems we observe and testifies to a world that knows how to organize from the inside out" (p. 25). For Capra (2002), the mechanism of self-generation is communication grounded in meaning and purpose: "[e]ach communication creates thoughts and meaning, which give rise to further communication. In this way, the entire network generates itself, producing a common context of meaning, shared knowledge, rules of conduct, a boundary, and a collective identity for its members" (p. 108). The common context of meaning and the collective identity of members set the standards by which people assess the relevance of new ideas, monitor the effectiveness of current practices and structures, and make changes that accommodate novelty without harming the integrity of the system or undermining the purpose of the work. In this way, form and function follow from meaning and purpose as people rely on the collective wisdom not only to align activities and cohere practices, but also to "move toward greater complexity and order as needed" (Wheatley, 2007, p. 33).

This purposeful approach to organising holds change and stability in dynamic balance, with some parts of the system changing to accommodate novelty and other elements staying the same. Bowers (2002) described the pattern this way: "[l]iving systems involve both the replication (conservation) of patterns of organization as well as changes introduced by internal and external perturbations" (p. 29). For Bowers (2008), conservation is an often undervalued or overlooked aspect of human systems, but he sees it as an essential component of the cultural commons. He explained, "[c]onserving involves, among other things, an awareness of the ecological importance of the many forms of intergenerational knowledge, skills, and patterns of interdependence and support" (p. 328). With this awareness, members of a living system can respond to changing realities and new opportunities in ways that respect the wisdom of the past and that protect their environment, including, as far as possible, the local and global physical environment.

In living systems, the dynamic relationship between conservation and novelty supports a naturally unfolding change process. According to Capra (2002), "the spontaneous emergence of new order . . . takes place at critical points of instability that arise from fluctuations in the environment, amplified by feedback loops" (p. 116). The context-specific character of this process makes it impossible to control the flow of the process or to determine the outcomes in advance. As Wheatley (2007) put it, "[t]he freedom to experiment, to tinker oneself into a form of being that can live and reproduce, leads to diversity that has no bounds" (p. 25). Diversity has long been understood as an essential feature of a healthy biosphere that is evolving naturally. Hargreaves and Fink (2006) observed, "[i]n ecological and evolutionary terms, biodiversity performs two functions; *resilience* and *flexibility*" (p. 160). In living systems, the resilience and flexibility afforded by diversity suggest that the meaningful end points of any change initiative will be determined by the people living through and living with the change.

In the midst of diversity, living systems hold together because of their inherent interdependence. This feature constitutes the world not as a collection of disconnected parts but rather as a complex integrated system in which all aspects are interconnected, reciprocal, and relational. To understand how patterns emerge from apparent randomness so as to form dynamic integrated systems, Hatch (2006) turned to complexity theory. She explained:

- Each complex system is unique because it consists of many different elements with multiple interaction and feedback loops between elements.
- Each element of the complex system responds only to local information and not to the broader information. Feedback loops facilitate the movement of local information through the system.
- Interactions are non-linear and reciprocal. As a result, small changes in one part of the complex system can have major effects in other parts.
- Complex systems evolve and change in unpredictable ways because of their nonlinearity.
- Order emerges through the process of self-organization.

(p. 331)

In short, events happening at one level of a system are profoundly connected to, influenced by, and mutually influencing what takes place at other levels. The feature of interdependence, as played out through the processes of complex systems, shifts the focus from looking at distinct parts of a system to examining the relationships, interactions, and mutual influences that emerge among and between people and their environments.

To understand how the various components and functions of a system are integrated is to recognise that living systems operate as interlinked networks. Capra (2002) explained that the network "is one of the very basic patterns of organization in all living systems" (p. 81). He contends that social networks function not just through a set of linked practices but also, and more importantly, within a context of shared meaning:

Through this shared context of meaning individuals acquire identities as members of the social network, and in this way the network generates its own boundary. It is not a physical boundary but a boundary of

expectations, of confidentiality and loyalty, which is continually maintained and renegotiated by the network itself.

(p. 83)

Wheatley (2007) concurred that the key issue for a community in a living
system is not one of common social practices but one of shared purposes.
As language patterns, shared purposes and meanings, and boundaries of
expectation shape individual action, social interaction, and social practices,
the living system forms and evolves. It is "not a representation of an independently existing world, but rather a 'bringing forth' of a world through
the process of living" (Capra, 2002, p. 42).

PRACTICES IN LIVING SYSTEMS

The properties of living systems indicate that organisations (such as educational systems) are not naturally occurring entities but emerge out of the
challenges that individuals and groups confront as they do their work. As
people map out the solutions, practices, and processes of their lives, they
generate a set of mental and practical frameworks that constitute the scripts
of the organisational narrative. These scripts represent the preferred ways
of solving problems, doing daily work, and relating to one another. In the
interconnected, relational, and knowledge-driven world of the twenty-first
century, a new organisational narrative, one in harmony with an ecological
view of nature and based on living systems principles, is emerging.

Although the tendency is to think of living systems as a metaphor for
framing organisational realities, Capra (2002) intended "to go beyond the
metaphoric level and see to what extent human organizations can literally
be understood as living systems" (p. 102). Gergen and Thatchenkery (2004)
provided a pathway for moving Capra's intention forward in their shift
from seeking out universal organisational truths to investigating and understanding local and practical concerns. They saw this as a fluid and dynamic
process: "with each fresh current of understanding, the phenomenon is
altered. In this sense, we find organization science as a generative source of
meaning in cultural life . . . . [that can] furnish people with implements for
action" (p. 240). The point is not to identify the best way of organising and
administering, but "to inquire into the process of 'organization' as a form
of cultural life" (p. 241).

When organisation and administration are viewed as forms of cultural
life, leaders give up command and control in favour of facilitation, negotiation, and communication. Although Reed (2006) warned that "new
network-based organizational forms and cultures remain embedded in
power structures and control regimes that are there to protect and legitimate
the material, social and political interests of dominant classes and elites"

(p. 39), his warning should be read as generative rather than cautionary. In living systems, people can resist the authoritative power of vested interests by reclaiming the meaning of authority. Capra (2002) explained:

> The original meaning of "authority" is not "power to command," but "a firm basis for knowing and acting." . . . The origin of power, then, lies in culturally defined positions of authority on which the community relies for the resolution of conflicts and for decisions about how to act wisely and effectively. In other words, true authority consists in empowering others to act.
>
> (p. 89)

Capra's definition of authority underpins Wheatley's (2007) reconstituted role for leaders:

> People need a great deal from their leaders. They need information, access to one another, resources, thrust, and follow-through. Leaders are necessary to foster experimentation, to help create connections across the organization, to feed the system with information from multiple sources—all while helping everyone stay clear on what we agreed we wanted to accomplish and who we wanted to be.
>
> (p. 70)

Capra's and Wheatley's conceptions positioned leadership as both an emergent and a designed process. Leaders emerge naturally when they have the capacity and interest to act in specific situations, but designated leaders are still required to bring in resources, disturb the status quo, connect the dots, and remind people of the purposes for which they came together. In schools, this kind of leadership empowers and equips educators to transform teaching activities into authentic learning for students, for colleagues, and for themselves.

Leadership of this character is best supported by a combination of designed and emergent structures. Capra (2002) explained, "[d]esigned structures provide the rules and routines that are necessary for the effective functioning of the organization . . . . Emergent structures, on the other hand, provide novelty, creativity, and flexibility" (p. 121). The two types of structure are held in dynamic tension, with specific structures being added, modified, or dismantled as required to sustain "the right balance between the creativity of emergence and the stability of design" (p. 121). This balance provides the structural support for people to experiment with new practices without the threat of forced compliance. In living systems, the appropriate balance of emergence and design happens naturally as the system reaches out to novelty in ways that protect the integrity of the system. In social systems, like schools and other organisations, keeping the emergent and designed structures in dynamic balance is a critical leadership task.

Balancing emergent and designed structures is especially important in schools, where the heavy hand of the modernist era continues to drive teaching and learning activities in tightly specified directions and toward externally imposed outcomes. However, as Wheatley (2007) observed, "[f]reedom and creativity always create diverse responses. If conformity is the goal, it will kill local initiative" (p. 69). Walker and Quong (1998) pointed out that "diversity holds the key to learning and continuous improvement" (p. 93), with the tensions aroused by difference serving as catalysts for critical reflection and as sources of novelty. When the structures respect and accommodate diversity, educators can direct change efforts in ways that support teaching and learning appropriately and authentically. This approach is confirmed by what Hargreaves and Fink (2006) discovered in a study of 50 teachers' responses to educational change:

> Positive change for these teachers was self-driven, flexibly developed, connected to teaching and learning, and professionally current. Negative change was seen as driven by governments and bureaucracies that failed to understand classroom practice and even withdrew support from it so they could implement other, noneducational agendas.
>
> (p. 167)

The findings from Hargreaves and Fink's study demonstrated that educators can and will make meaningful changes if they are in control of the process, but they will resist imposed or meaningless initiatives. Senge (1990) pointed out that "[r]esistance to change is neither capricious nor mysterious. It almost always arises from threats to traditional norms and ways of doing things" (p. 88). Consequently, to design schools that support diversity and creativity is to recognise "the interaction between structure and agency in particular contexts and how this is mediated by individuals' values, personality and personal history" (Simkins, 2005, p. 19).

In living systems, the mechanism for regeneration is attention and sense-making. Wheatley (2007) noted, "[l]iving systems give form to their organization and evolve those forms into new ones because of exquisite capacities to create meaning together, to communicate, and to notice what's going on in the moment" (p. 27). Activating this feature requires the free flow of information and conversation throughout the organisation, facilitated by strong communication networks and collaborative work patterns. With frank and frequent discussions about issues, successes, and challenges, the members' relationships and interactions become "the pathway to the intelligence of the system. The more access people have to one another, the more possibilities there are" (p. 40). As people move out of their offices (or classrooms) to share knowledge and to address compelling disturbances with colleagues, the intelligence of the system enables them not only to broaden and inform their practices, but also to see different things and to see things differently. Through collaborative work and common understandings, members build a community of practice that guides subsequent individual and collective action. In education discourses, a school with these features is called a *learning community.*

Gaining access to the stocks of knowledge embedded in the community requires a specific kind of interaction. At the outset, it depends on a shared sense of the common good (Tsoukas, 2008) and of the overarching purpose of the work (Wheatley, 2007). When individuals realise that they stand on common ground, they "discover one another as colleagues" (Wheatley, 2007, p. 109). With this shared understanding in place, colleagues gain access to the stock of knowledge through a process of thick description (Bowers, 2008). Thick description opens to view the broad set of work activities and practices that take place on the ground and in the moment. For Bowers, however, thick description was not merely concerned with technical knowledge (such as teaching practices) but also included

> giving voice to the differences in relationships, patterns of moral reciprocity, feelings, patterns of thinking, what cannot be made explicit in [oral and print-based] modes of communication and so forth. In effect, it leads to making explicit what may otherwise be taken for granted and thus not recognized as either problematic or as a life-and community-enhancing pattern.
>
> (p. 333)

From this perspective, the embedded knowledge extends beyond the professional "tools of the trade" (although these are important pieces in the stock of knowledge) to include the social practices that define who gets to speak and who stays silent, what knowledge is legitimated and what knowledge is devalued, and what practices are preferred and what practices are questioned. Uncovering the social practices that shape and limit the intelligence of the system can be disruptive because it exposes the underlying power dynamics of the group. To work through the emotions and tensions that are likely to emerge, leaders turn the attention of the members back to the shared purposes and the shared sense of the common good.

Personal emotions and agendas can be further offset when differences and issues are viewed through a systemic lens. Senge (1990) defines systems thinking as "a discipline for seeing wholes. It is a framework for seeing interrelationships rather than things, for seeing patterns of change rather than static 'snapshots'" (p. 68). For Senge, this view required "understanding dynamic complexity, not detail complexity" (p. 72), with dynamic complexity becoming visible as feedback processes show "how actions can reinforce or counteract (balance) one another" (p. 73). According to Senge, "[i]n mastering systems thinking, we give up the assumption that there must be an individual, or individual agent, responsible. The feedback perspective suggests that everyone shares responsibility for problems generated by a system" (p. 78). Understanding responsibility as a collective feature enables people to move past their personal agendas and to work with colleagues on solutions and practices that can improve the system as a whole.

A systemic view is not limited to local conditions but invites engagement in a broader context. For Senge, Scharmer, Jaworski, and Flowers (2005), connections between local and global conditions can be made through what they called *presencing*: the ability to see an emerging whole and to penetrate deeply into the patterns of relationship, influence, and reciprocity that move between, across, and within systems. As Senge et al. put it,

> If our awareness never reaches beyond superficial events and current circumstances, actions will be reactive. If, on the other hand, we penetrate more deeply to see the larger wholes . . . the source and effectiveness of our actions can change dramatically.
>
> (pp. 13–14)

Participating consciously in a larger field gives people a sense of emerging trends, and enables them to shift their responses from recreating the past to bringing forth a meaningful future. Leaders play a key role in the process by helping people to see beyond the horizon and to work across boundaries. To engage meaningfully in this process requires leaders, and others, to listen deeply, to move beyond their own perceptions and typical ways of making sense, to understand the impact of their own presence, and to resist the urge to control.

In summary, practices in living systems turn on two sets of characteristics:

> One is a strong sense of community and collective identity around a set of common values; a community in which all members know that they will be supported in their endeavours to achieve their goals. The other set of characteristics is openness to the outside world, tolerance for the entry of new individuals and ideas, and consequently a manifest ability to learn and adapt to new circumstance.
>
> (Capra, 2002, p. 105)

Capra argued that these characteristics keep organisational processes dynamic and outcomes unpredictable even with a common goal in place, and they explain why theories, policies, and practices do not travel well:

> In human organizations, emergent solutions are created within the context of a particular organizational culture, and generally cannot be transferred to another organization with a different culture. . . . What [leaders] tend to do is replicate a new structure that has been successful without transferring the tacit knowledge and context of meaning from which the new structures emerged.
>
> (Capra, 2002, p. 119)

For Tsoukas (2008), "[a]ppreciating the emergent texture of organizations—namely treating them not so much as collections of routines, structures and rules but as interactive accomplishments—leads us to appreciate also the inherently creative role individuals play" (p. 196). In essence, organisation and administration are forms of cultural life that are brought forth as people build an organisational world through the process of living.

RATIONALE FOR A NEW THEORY OF ORGANISING

From an ecological perspective, the various elements of a school (events, experiences, activities, structures, materials, networks, knowledge, people, artefacts, understandings, commitments, and so forth) constitute an institutional ecology that "exerts a particular mediating influence on the character of teaching and learning in the school" (Mitchell & Sackney, 2009b, p. 6). In our research, we have found that, when the ecology of a school reflects the characteristics of the managed system, teaching and learning are unnatural, forced, and often difficult. In the real world, however, learning unfolds spontaneously and autonomously as people make sense of the "teaching moments" (the compelling disturbances) that capture their attention. We have found schools that support this natural learning process, but they are rare (Mitchell & Sackney, 2009a). Unfortunately, the tensions, constraints, and confusions that are the legacy of the modernist era continue to haunt schools in the twenty-first century.

A prime example of the modernist legacy in contemporary educational systems is the privileged place of standardised practices, learning outcomes, and evaluation measures. In each case, Luke (2011) argued, "standardization of educational practices has the potential to flatten out cultural, linguistic, intellectual, and educational diversity, with potentially deleterious effects on residual and emergent educational traditions" (p. 372). He was concerned that "the new common sense of accountability" (p. 368) has silenced critiques of the standards and has erased matters of culture, ethics, or value from policy discussions. He pointed out, however, that "[m]atters of culture, ideology, and political economy are not incidental burrs in the making and implementation of policy. They are essential, square one considerations" (pp. 367–368). In his view, "[a] principled policy borrowing depends upon an interpretive analysis of a whole educational system in operation: an understanding of everyday cultural practices, of diverse communities and demographics, of contending ideologies and relations of power, and of the human beings who make that system what it is" (p. 374). Yet under modernist assumptions of standardisation, these human and cultural elements would be considered problematic rather than generative.

A second example of the modernist legacy is the relations of power that play out in the normative structures and socialisation practices in education. Corson (1996), for example, described the structures of power and relations of dominance inherent in most schools: "[t]he non-dominant adhere to the norms created by the dominant groups, while not recognizing that they are being 'voluntarily coerced'" (p. 1048). The traditional power relations are then replicated in the relations between teachers and students: "The concentration of control and passive student activities in classrooms reflects the ethos of control that is still an outstanding feature of most school organizations" (p. 1059). As children (and teachers) are normalised and socialised at school, Corson claimed,

> they are prepared for uncritical admission into hierarchical sociocultural conditions discursively constructed well in advance of that admission. Rather than preparing children for 'initiation into a worthwhile form of life', schools offer them filtered immersion in the discursive practices in which schools themselves are positioned.
>
> (p. 1063)

According to Bowers (2008), modernist relations of power can also be seen in educational reform discourses. He explained that many of the authors who propose a transformative agenda of critical pedagogy continue to rely "on an abstract Western epistemology that carries forward a number of misconceptions and prejudices" (p. 327). That is, they assume that change, as framed in their rational analyses, is inherently progressive; they fail to acknowledge the cultural conventions and ethnocentrism that frame their own thinking; and they either do not notice or they ignore the contributions and value of local cultural traditions and embedded knowledge. For Bowers, the voices of the powerful experts drown out the members of the cultural commons, and the wisdom of culturally relevant knowledge is lost. He was not optimistic about breaking through "the silence about the need to acquire a deep knowledge of culture, that of the teacher as well as the culture of others that are to be decolonized" (p. 334). Thus, through the structural dominance of the leadership elite and the discursive dominance of the academic elite, modernist relations of power trap less powerful members within a set of cultural and organisational practices that they have had little say in creating and over which they have little control.

The presence and tacit acceptance of modernist relations of power bring the discussion back to Gergen and Thatchenkery's (2004) question: "How do we proceed?" (p. 234). According to Capra (2002),

> The problem is that human organizations are not only living communities but are also social institutions designed for specific purposes and functioning in a specific economic environment. Today that environment is not life-enhancing but is increasingly life-destroying. The more we understand the nature of life and become aware of how alive an organization can be, the more painfully we notice the life-draining nature of our current economic system.
>
> (pp. 125–126)

Capra positions the quest for life-enhancing organisations as a global economic issue, but individuals can choose to reject life-draining conditions in their own local contexts. This choice can be supported by a new set of images and root metaphors for organisations—that is, a new theory of organising. The root metaphors emerging from the lessons of living systems replace the language of command and control with a language of meaning, purpose, patterns, connections, and relationships. People can turn to these new images to guide their search for processes and practices that reflect and accommodate the structural, environmental, and relational conditions that support and sustain life.

For new root metaphors and images to take hold requires a radical shift in the epistemic and ontological assumptions that undergird the processes of theorising. Reed (2006) distinguished between philosophical assumptions that treat organisations as entities existing independent of the people working within them versus assumptions that treat organisations as socially constructed artefacts that depend on organisational members for form, functionality, and viability. When organisations are theorised under the first set of assumptions, the emphasis is on organisational variables, and the constructs emerge as abstract and lifeless, as in Baum and Shipilov's (2006) description of organisational ecology. By contrast, Wheatley's (2007) treatment of the same topic was full of life, energy, enthusiasm, and interest because she focuses squarely on the activities and purposes of the people who populate the organisations. The first consideration, therefore, is not what constitutes the contents and topics of organisation theories, nor even which theory is correct and which is wrong. It is, rather, what philosophy frames specific moments of theorising. As Wheatley pointed out, "self-organization is not a new phenomenon. It has been difficult to observe only because we weren't interested in observing it. But as we describe organizations as living systems rather than as machines, self-organization becomes a primary concept, easily visible" (p. 34). If theories of organising are "grounded in an open-world ontology, an enactivist epistemology, and a poetic praxeology" (Tsoukas, 2008, p. 197), then the properties and practices of living systems might become more easily visible.

The question of epistemic anchors is as relevant for educational institutions as for any other organisation. As an example, distributed leadership has been suggested as a strategy for moving teaching and learning forward in meaningful and contextually relevant ways. However, Simkins (2005) warned that "it is important to be clear about what the term means. In some forms it may indeed be a key component in the emerging model of leadership described earlier. In others, however, it may just be the traditional model in a new guise" (p. 16). In education, Simkins noted, "the argument has typically set what are often termed 'managerialist' values and processes against . . . the 'bureau-professional' settlement, within which professionals are free to exercise power in the bests interests of their clients" (p. 13). However, a philosophy consistent with living systems would not privilege the professionals any more than the managers. Luke (2011), for example, sidelined both managers and professionals by pointing directly at the lives and experiences of the people who are affected by any educational policy:

> Courageous policy makers lead by building public understandings, engaging with complexity across real and imagined boundaries, moving toward durable educational settlements around shared values and social contracts. This requires a close eye on the local articulation and recontextualization of policy: a kind of narrative scenario planning and public explication based on rich interpretive historical, cultural, and political understandings. A narrow managerial science cannot suffice for such a task.
>
> (p. 368)

For the twenty-first century, Simkins said, "[i]t is more helpful to see our current public sector—and educational—world as one in which discourses are in contention, different accommodations are being reached in different contexts, and these accommodations are changing over time in a very dynamic way" (p. 14). In organisation theory, Tsoukas (2008) argued,

> the ecological ideal, with its emphasis on inter-connectedness, situatedness and creative action, helps generate knowledge that is more organic, notices the emergent properties of organizations and the processes through which they are generated and views human agency in poetic (making/creative) terms.
>
> (pp. 197–198)

Positioning organisation theories and processes of theorising in ways suggested by Simkins and Tsoukas focuses attention squarely on the lived experiences of people as they work out and work through their individual and collective challenges and as they construct, individually and collectively, their social and organisational practices.

CONCLUSION

Thinking of educational organisations as living systems brings forth an image of teaching and learning as gardening and teachers and students as gardeners. Planting gardens involves a process of death and rebirth as the seed *dies* in the ground and the new plant is born. A substantive transformation of matter takes place as the raw materials undergo a change of state and emerge with new properties, functions, and name. Similar transformations occur in teaching and learning. As students and teachers engage with material, information, and activities, they transform the raw materials into something new. At each stage of the process, learning regenerates the transformative process and changes the organisation.

To think of teachers and students as gardeners is to see a different set of power relations. Each activity, regardless of whether it is conducted by a student, a teacher, or an administrator, influences the ultimate transformation. The more integrated the work of all participants and the closer the match of activities to the desired transformation, the more likely it is that the outcome will be achieved. In this way, the purposes of all work in a school are tightly and causally linked to the practices of teaching and learning. That is, all activities are highly interdependent and reciprocal, and ultimate transformation relies on *whole work* in practice. It requires the involvement, effort, and support of the total group, and structures are needed to support the free and autonomous contribution of each person and to open spaces for relationships to grow. As the school is transformed to accommodate the shared work, hierarchical power relations become meaningless, unproductive, and unsustainable. In an educational system like this, traditional theories of organising and abstract processes of theorising make little sense.

In general terms, Gergen and Thatchenkery (2004) positioned the role of theory as opening spaces for dialogues that broaden the conversational options and knowledge resources for members of an organisation. They saw theory as attempting not to define or solve a problem but to facilitate a continuous exchange and assessment of knowledge among the people living in a particular system. Consequently,

> each of the existing theories represents a discourse potentially available for purposes in a variety of contexts. Generative efforts may include, then, reinvigorating the theories of the past, redefining or recontextualizing their meanings so not to be lost from the repository of potentials.
> (p. 243)

As research and theorising about organisations continue, Gergen and Thatchenkery argue, "we are not moving ineluctably forward on the road to truth; we are—as many would say—simply replacing one way of putting things with another" (p. 237).

We agree that theory should open spaces for generative dialogue, and we concur that the living systems construct is not an ineluctable move forward on the road to truth. However, we see this construct as a radical break from the past rather than just a new way of putting things. Although traditional theories of organising might continue to describe and explain many organisational realities, they no longer make sense as the epistemic and ontological foundations on which organisations are built. From an epistemological perspective, Capra (2002) explained,

> Living beings . . . act autonomously. They can never be controlled like machines. To try to do so is to deprive them of their aliveness. . . . To

see the company as a living being . . . is to realize that it is capable of regenerating itself and that it will naturally change and evolve.

(p. 104)

Wheatley (2007) moved the discussion to the ontological level:

Some people still wonder if organizations *are* living systems. I don't engage in that question anymore, ever since I realized that the people working in organizations are alive. Therefore, they must respond to the same needs and conditions as any other living system.

(pp. 76–77)

Thinking of organisations as living systems at both the epistemological and ontological levels brings into sharp relief the lack of vitality and responsiveness in modernist theories of organising and abstract processes of theorising. To generate organisational knowledge that is recognisable and meaningful to the people working in an organisation is to put those people directly in the spotlight at centre stage.

The properties of living systems offer not just a different way of theorising about organisations, but also a different way of living in them. They bring into view the relational and interconnected nature of organisational life. They signal that people affect one another and their environment whether they want to or not, and whether they realise it or not. This deep interdependence and reciprocity calls people to consider the consequences of their actions, to collaborate effectively, to share knowledge and ideas broadly, to discuss issues and challenges openly, and to move forward from a place of deep respect—not only for all members of the community but also for broader institutional, social, cultural, and physical environments. Awareness of one's inescapable presence in the making of a world paves the way for people to take collective and personal responsibility for constructing a system that supports and sustains the natural processes of life.

REFERENCES

Baum, J. A. C., & Shipilov, A. V. (2006). Ecological approaches to organizations. In W. R. Nord, T. B. Lawrence, C. Hardy, & S. R Clegg (Eds.), *The Sage handbook of organization studies* (2nd ed.; pp. 55–110). London, UK: Sage.

Bowers, C. A. (2002). Toward an eco-justice pedagogy. *Environmental Education Research, 8*(1), 21–34.

Bowers, C. A. (2008). Why a critical pedagogy of place is an oxymoron. *Environmental Education Research, 14*(3), 325–335.

Capra, F. (2002). *The hidden connections: Integrating the biological, cognitive, and social dimensions of life into a science of sustainability.* New York: Doubleday.

Corson, D. (1996). Emancipatory discursive practices. In K. Leithwood, J. Chapman, D. Corson, P. Hallinger, & A. Hart (Eds.), *International handbook of educational leadership and administration* (pp. 1043–1067). Dodrecht, Netherlands: Kluwer.

Gergen, K. J., & Thatchenkery, T. J. (2004). Organization science as social construction. *Journal of Applied Behavioral Science, 40*(2), 228–249.

Hargreaves, A., & Fink, D. (2006). *Sustainable leadership*. San Francisco: Jossey-Bass.

Hatch, M. J. (2006). *Organization theory: Modern, symbolic and postmodern perspectives* (2nd ed.). New York: Oxford University Press.

Luke, A. (2011). Generalizing across borders: Policy and the limits of educational science. *Educational Researcher, 40*(8), 367–377.

March, J. G. (2007). The study of organizations since 1945. *Organization Studies, 28*(1), 9–19.

Mitchell, C., & Sackney, L. (2009a). *Sustainable improvement: Building learning communities that endure*. Rotterdam, Netherlands: Sense.

Mitchell, C., & Sackney, L. (2009b). *Sustainable improvement: From managed systems to living systems*. Paper presented at the annual conference of the International Congress of School Effectiveness and Improvement, Vancouver, BC.

Nord, W. R., Lawrence, T. B., Hardy, C., & Clegg, S. R. (2006). Introduction. In W. R. Nord, T. B. Lawrence, C. Hardy, & S. R Clegg (Eds.), *The Sage handbook of organization studies* (2nd ed.; pp. 1–15). London, UK: Sage.

Reed, M. (2006). Organizational theorizing: A historically contested terrain. In W. R. Nord, T. B. Lawrence, C. Hardy, & S. R Clegg (Eds.), *The Sage handbook of organization studies* (2nd ed.; pp. 19–54). London, UK: Sage.

Sackney, L., & Mitchell, C. (2008). Leadership for learning: A Canadian perspective. In J. MacBeath & Y. C. Cheng (Eds.), *Leadership for learning: International perspective* (pp. 123–136). Rotterdam, Netherlands: Sense.

Senge, P. (1990). *The fifth discipline: The art and practice of the learning organization*. New York: Doubleday.

Senge, P., Scharmer, C. O., Jaworski, J., & Flowers, B. S. (2005). *Presence: Exploring profound change in people, organizations and society*. London, UK: Nicholas Brealey.

Sim, S. (1999). Postmodernism and philosophy. In S. Sim (Ed.), *The Routledge critical dictionary of postmodern thought* (pp. 3–14). New York: Routledge.

Simkins, T. (2005). Leadership in education: "What works" or "what makes sense"? *Educational Management, Administration & Leadership, 33*(1), 9–26.

Tetenbaum, T. J. (1998). Shifting paradigms: From Newton to chaos. *Organizational Dynamics, 26*(4), 21–32.

Tsoukas, H. (2008). Toward the ecological ideal: Notes for a complex understanding of complex organizations. In D. Barry & H. Hansen (Eds.), *The Sage handbook of new approaches in management and organization* (pp. 195–198). Los Angeles, CA: Sage.

Walker, A., & Quong, T. (1998). Valuing differences: Strategies for dealing with the tensions of educational leadership in a global society. *Peabody Journal of Education, 73*(2), 81–105.

Wheatley, M. J. (2006). *Leadership and the new science: Discovering order in a chaotic world* (3rd ed.). San Francisco: Berrett-Koehler.

Wheatley, M. J. (2007). *Finding our way: Leadership for an uncertain time*. San Francisco: Berrett-Koehler.

Epilogue

Engaged Scholarship, Epistemic Cultures, and the Worlds of Practitioner and Scholar

Pat Renihan and Fred Renihan

In this chapter, we will return to Allison's eloquent *tour de force* through 'moments' in the history of academic study of educational administration found in chapter two of this volume: a tour that is both edifying and grounding. It proves an excellent contextual backdrop to the discussions presented in successive chapters of this text. The product is reminiscent of the comments made by Wren and Bedeian (2009) at the outset of the 6th edition of his work on the *Evolution of Management Thought,* where he stated:

> The study of management, like the study of people and their cultures, is an unfolding story of changing ideas about the nature of work, the nature of human beings, and the functioning of organizations. The methodology of this study of management will be *analytic, synthetic and interdisciplinary: analytic* in examining the people who made significant contributions, their backgrounds, their ideas and their influence; *synthetic* in examining trends, movements and environmental forces that furnish a conceptual framework for understanding individuals and their approaches to the solution of management problems; *Interdisciplinary* in the sense that it includes-but moves beyond-traditional management writings to draw on economic history sociology, psychology, social history, political science, and cultural anthropology to place management thought in cultural and historical perspective.
>
> (p. 3)

Allison moves us through four stages in the history of the scholarly study of educational administration: *inception*; the *rise of practical science*; the *development of theoretical science*; and the *current context of conceptual complexity* (reflective of the variety and nature of the conceptualisations presented in this very text), each of them significantly subjected to the influence of the analytic, synthetic, and interdisciplinary forces described above. In delimiting the arena for discussion, Allison (understandably) devotes some considerable attention to making clear the relative worlds of the practitioner and the academic, worlds where, he notes, academics and practitioners view things of common interest in characteristically different ways.

A RETROSPECTIVE ON THE NATURE OF THIS TEXT

Educational administration is the underlying focus of this collection, and, as such, it is, and it represents, a field of study. Indeed it is represented thus by many of the contributors to this collection, and we would certainly concur with that designation. As such, educational administration has drawn from the variety of disciplines that comprise the social sciences, and even a few disciplines beyond those bounds—as described by Wren and Bedeian (2009). Their attractiveness to those of us involved in our various sub-communities and activities within the educational administration *field* lies not so much in the pure conceptualisation and insights that they have to offer *as* theory or *as* perspective, as for their value to our continuing sense-making in this particular field of study: elucidating research problems, research approaches, contextual realities, organisational dynamics, and organisational actions that become apparent within it.

Thus we would agree with the editors in their view of *context* as integral to the broader conversation. How has the evolving environment of this field of study influenced the structure and dynamics—the past, present, and future—of the field? How do the broad functions of *theorising, researching,* and *practicing* interact in these changing environments? The context in which knowledge is generated, justified, and assessed has undergone some significant change over the period covered by the discussions contained herein. Indeed, the initial hope expressed by the editors of this book—that the importance of *context* in the development of new perspectives will become evident—is to a fairly significant extent realised. It is the nature of the change that has influenced the shape of the field that concerns us most in this chapter.

This text is about the multidimensionality of sense-making. It directs attention to four areas of representation that run the gamut from the paradigmatic and the meta-theoretical to the strategic and the practical—along the sphere of activity represented by Aristotle from *theoria* to *technē*. In the early chapters it directs attention to the grand tour *epistemological and ontological questions;* through the chapters on Daoism and First Nations conceptions of leadership, it explores the promise underlying the consideration of *ideological-perspectives;* in its examination of the feminist perspective, critical theory, critical realism, sociological perspectives, and the cognitive study of educational administration, it provides perspective on a variety of emerging traditions in the analysis of *organisational action;* in its explication of schools as living systems, actor network theory and school system transformation in context, it uncovers some of the complexity and richness lying within the culture metaphor, constructs that continue to find great resonance with practitioners; namely *schools as living systems, actor network theory,* and *school system transformation in context.* Though not exhaustive, the final product covers significant territory and it raises the opportunity for insight across the spectrum of educational administration scholarship.

The above contributions, and the perspectives they evoke, are profound, and they are rich in their possibilities to inform and guide original research and reflection *on* and *in* practice. With this in mind, we need to take a step back and interrogate the nature of the broader epistemological context that constitutes *the field*: Who are the actors, communities and sub-communities that comprise the *field* of educational administration? Who are privy to our conversations about conceptualisations and related activity when we attempt to make meaning about the 'field'? What are the sub-communities that constitute the field? What are their arenas of action and the knowledge cultures that have evolved around them? What has changed over time that might have changed the responses to these questions?

We will define the arena for our discussion here, though we take a somewhat broader view of the relevant community than did Allison. Our focus is on the scholarship of educational administration, its functions, and relevant communities. As such, its *functions* include teaching, research, knowledge generation, and administrative/leadership practice. It follows that the *relevant communities* include *academics*, academic sub-communities of teaching professors, research professors, graduate students, and practitioners representing a variety of roles and situated within a multiplicity of contexts throughout the educational administration world. Their common denominator is (and has always been, throughout the various stages of the field's history) their actual or potential interest in the scholarship of educational administration. Their points of difference stem from their occupational interests and varying epistemic views regarding the ideas discussed herein. However, as we will argue in this chapter, the levels and nature of the engagement of these various sets of communities *across the functions of the field* have changed and are changing drastically (in true postmodern fashion).

In this chapter, we examine the broader consideration of coherence across the field, through an exploration of how **conceptualisations** of educational administration such as those we have read in this text relate to the **study** of educational administration and, in turn, to the **practice** of educational administration. Specifically, we interrogate the epistemological contexts of the *field of educational administration* through four areas of attention:

1. Continuing perspectives on the theory/practice *conversation*;
2. Epistemic limits to views of the theory/practice gap;
3. A view of the educational administration field as an intricate web of epistemic cultures; and
4. A repositioning of the theory/practice debate as an argument for integrative mechanisms across a complex network of epistemic communities.

THE THEORY/PRACTICE CONVERSATION

We believe that a logical point of departure for a discussion of coherence across a field of study and what this has to say about the interface between communities of thinkers, researchers, and practitioners, is the nature of the relationship between theory and practice across the field. The folklore has been that there is a smooth and seamless progression from fundamental research and theory to practice: from thoughts to ideas to application.

The prevailing and likely most common image conveyed in discussions about theory and practice is that of a gap, a gap that represents an undesirable rift in need of repair. This in turn creates a popular image of communities of theorists, researchers, and practitioners engaged in their own epistemic parallel play, each driven more by the cultures, reward systems, and conventions of their own arenas of activity than by significant developments and conversations across the field of study. From a social work background, Fook (2001) described the phenomenon in the following terms:

> Take some of the common experiences with which most of us are familiar. Practitioners complain that the idea of research intimidates them. Researchers complain that practice is not evidence-based. Students complain that textbook theory is too abstract, and that they learn most from field practice. Educators complain that students are more interested in being lectured to by current practitioners, rather than academics whose knowledge is seen to derive from books or research. We all have beefs against each other, in a profession in which it seems as if separate worlds vie for privilege and recognition.
>
> (p. 1)

This represents the conventional image of the phenomenon. From our experiences, the *gap* has been expressed in a variety of forms: as a problem of repressed praxis and reflection; as a divide between university-based and profession-based activity; as an inability on the part of researchers to pursue, disseminate, and translate research findings; as an abdication of the responsibility among researchers to follow up on findings with field-based practitioners; as an ignored element of (leadership) preparation programmes; as the product of the priority attached to fundamental research over outreach programmes and community-based activities in the planning and reward systems of universities; and further as a rift exacerbated by field-based practitioner preferences for course-based and project-based, rather than research-based, Masters' and doctoral programmes.

Van de Ven and Johnson (2006) viewed the phenomenon from the perspective of how we view knowledge. They differentiated between *scholarly knowledge* (seeing specific situations as instances of a more general case as a means of explanation) and *practical knowledge* (knowing how to deal with specific situations encountered in a particular case). Indeed, this distinction seemed to be at the heart of Allison's distinction between the worlds of the academic and the practitioner. Van de Ven and Johnson examined, in the context of management, three interconnected ways in which the gap between theory and practice has been typically framed. The first, is as a *knowledge transfer problem*, based on the assumption that practical knowledge in a professional domain (such as educational administration) is largely a product of scholarship-based research knowledge. Hence the problem is one of translating and diffusing research knowledge into practice. The second *frame* for the gap is one that views *theory and practice as distinct forms of knowledge*, each reflecting a different ontology (truth claim) and epistemology (method for answering different questions). The third view is that the theory-practice gap is a *knowledge production problem*. In response to which Van de Ven and Johnson proposed a method of engaged scholarship in which researchers and practitioners co-produce knowledge in a given domain that can advance theory and practice.

Many contributors to the dialogue around the theory/practice gap, in the fields of nursing and management, address mismatches between *research* and practice. Viviane Robinson (1998) suggested that a much-neglected reason for the limited contribution of research to the understanding and improvement of educational practice is the mismatch between educational research methodologies and the generic features of practice.

According to Robinson (1998), increasing the match requires an account of practice that clarifies its methodological implications. She proposed a problem-based methodology (PBM) in which practices are treated as solutions to practical problems and explained by inquiry into the problem-solving processes that gave rise to them. Searching for epistemological compatibility, Porter and Ryan (1996) argued that one methodology that could facilitate this broadening of nursing's epistemological boundaries is critical realist ethnography, which works under the assumption that the relationship between social structures and individual actors involves a two-way process, in that while the enablements and constraints imposed by structures influence individual actions, those actions in turn either maintain or transform social structures.

In short, much of the commentary and research on the theory/practice debate focuses on *functional* disjunctions (knowledge transfer issues, knowledge production issues, absence of practitioner-based research, finance and support issues, and concerns with research methodology). However, we believe that deeper cultural and change forces are at play that challenge the unity of the field of educational administration and professional fields of study, more generally. With this in mind, we turn to an examination of the concept of epistemic cultures as a viable explanation of theory/practice tensions in a knowledge environment that is rapidly and inexorably changing.

EPISTEMIC CULTURES IN THE EDUCATIONAL ADMINISTRATION ECOSYSTEM

Drawing upon the groundbreaking work of Karin Knorr Cetina (1999), numerous researchers have examined the notion of epistemic cultures as a focus of research, and as a *community* phenomenon. Cetina defined epistemic cultures as follows:

> It refers to those sets of practices, arrangements and mechanisms bound together by necessity, affinity and historical coincidence which, in a given area of expertise, make up how we know what we know. Epistemic cultures are cultures of creating and warranting knowledge.
>
> (p. 364)

Dobusch and Quack (2008) examined the key internal features of epistemic cultures, characterising them as having a *common project, shared interests,* and *shared principled beliefs.* They further identified them as having: (a) limited size, (b) relatively clear boundaries, (c) low heterogeneity, (d) consensus around their causal beliefs, (e) a shared knowledge base, and (f) a self-understanding of their own *project* as a means of changing the world.

We believe that this provides a valuable vantage point from which to view the broad culture of the field of educational administration. Cetina (1999) elaborated on a property of epistemic cultures that sheds some light upon the centrifugal forces at play within a field of study. Her analysis is insightful:

> Cultural specificities arise, one assumes, when domains of social life become separated from one another—when they curl up on themselves and become self-referential systems that orient more to internal and previous system states than to the outside environment. . . . [Epistemic culture] brings into focus the content of the different knowledge-oriented lifeworlds, the different meanings of the empirical, specific constructions of the referent, particular ontologies of instruments, specific models of epistemic subjects. Epistemic unity, then, is a casualty of the cultural approach to knowledge production.
>
> (p. 364)

We would suggest that, in the not too distant past, such separation did not bring with it this type of epistemic disunity. However, the knowledge context has drastically changed and, concomitantly, the lines of distinction between the locus of knowledge *generation*, the locus of knowledge *consumption*, and the locus of *responsibility for both* have, across contexts, become virtually indistinguishable.

The function of knowledge generation, once the virtual monopoly of the university, has become demystified, democratised, widened, and proliferated. Thus the university is no longer the sole research initiator and knowledge generator. Individual agencies—particularly those with the resources at hand—develop their own epistemic cultures; governments, through the creation of research laboratories, the initiation of regional initiatives, the specification and mandate of broad priorities for action, create across professional fields a plethora of knowledge cultures—an epistemic jungle that defies navigation. The age-old tradition of the ivory tower speaking truth to the practitioner is an anachronism. The direction of attention for conversation about the field has taken an inward turn. The simple notion of a *theory/practice gap* is rendered irrelevant: a modernist explanation for what is essentially a postmodern problem.

The disunity that accompanies this phenomenon has assumed various forms. Some researchers have found that different expert cultures can have negative impacts across a broader field. Mork, Aanestadt, Hanseth, and Grisot (2008) examined interprofessional knowledge production in a medical research and development department comprising different expert cultures (doctors, nurses, radiologists, and engineers) and found that epistemic cultures in this context were divergent and conflicting in a manner that created obstacles for learning across communities of practice. Mork et al. concluded that such obstacles are rooted in different epistemologies, and that new knowledge which challenges practices in individual communities is more likely to become marginalised.

Researchers have studied the impact of this phenomenon on the theory/ practice relationship. Moisander and Stenfors (2009), for example, studied knowledge production in strategic management research and demonstrated how epistemic cultures may complicate, rather than facilitate, the communication between academics and corporate practitioners. They argued that differences in epistemic culture may also result in management scholars producing knowledge and strategy tools that lack pertinence for corporate actors.

Jones (2007) investigated ways in which critical thinking is understood in two related but distinct disciplines (history and economics). She found the epistemic culture of the discipline appears to influence conceptions of critical thinking. This has implications for the ways in which generic skills are framed within the broader university community, and has implications for policy at both the university and political levels, and applications across what Jones referred to as the *skills landscape*.

More broadly, Cronin (2003) employed the concept of *epistemic cultures* as a vehicle for describing cultures of scholarly writing and dissemination in universities and disciplines. Mork et al. (2008) noted that, while the concept of epistemic cultures has gained a significant foothold in science studies (it has also been utilised in political sciences, feminist epistemologies, and organisational studies), it is hardly used in studies of education and learning in higher education. They suggested that this is remarkable, given that teaching and learning in higher education tend to be research based, and many educational programmes (at least at graduate levels) aim to introduce students to a field of research-based knowledge. In light of the above argument, and given the power and potential underlying the phenomenon at all levels, we would argue (as an aside) that the concept of epistemic cultures has merit in studies of the field of educational administration.

RETHINKING THE TRANSLATIONAL FUNCTION

In the foregoing sections, we have discussed the nature of the theory/practice conversation—initially characterised as a *gap*—and have explored its analysis in fields other than educational administration, determining in the process that perhaps research can be either the problem or the solution, depending upon the spirit with which such research is engaged, and the success with which it is translated into administrative/leadership practice.

Across the globe each year, billions of dollars are invested in research, professional training, and continuing professional development in the field of educational administration and leadership. Despite this, the *translation* of research findings into practice and policy has fallen far short of its potential. Helping professionals to make sense of new perspectives is a continuing need in organisations, and the locus of the challenge continues to be in *completing the process loop* from theory/research to *informed interpretation* to experimentation and trial to practice.

The translational role of research has been a source of considerable attention in the health field in recent years, and it has been a source of some considerable attention in health-related literature. Grimshaw et al. (2012) noted that one of the most consistent findings from clinical and health services research is the failure to translate research into practice and policy. They note that, as a result of these evidence-practice-and-policy gaps, patients fail to benefit optimally from advances in healthcare. Those writers structured their discussion of the issue around five key questions: What should be transferred? To whom should research knowledge be transferred? By whom should research knowledge be transferred? How should research knowledge be transferred? And with what effect should research knowledge be transferred?

A University of Iowa initiative combined the work of practitioners and researchers on the basis of a knowledge transfer framework (Titler, 2007) that encompasses sets of focused activities around three major stages: (a) *knowledge creation and distillation*, (b) *diffusion, dissemination, and adoption*, and (c) *implementation and institutionalisation*. The focus on the translational function in bringing research to practice has undoubtedly gained a foothold in that field.

The resonance of this development for research findings within the educational administration field should be self-evident. It prompts serious attention to concepts and processes that guide knowledge translation activities. Though the topography of the fields of educational administration and medicine are undoubtedly very different, problems related to knowledge transfer and implementation are very similar. However, *knowledge creation* is not the major issue in the field of Educational Administration, and most other professional fields for that matter. The existing methods for *generating* theoretical and research knowledge are working relatively well. It is at the stages of *distillation, diffusion, dissemination, adoption, implementation*, and *institutionalisation* that the disjunctions appear.

While it might be argued that the literature and research on change, implementation, and adoption have served us well in the field of educational administration, their application has tended to be in the adoption of mandated change and in broader (often government initiated) innovations. We suggest that the dissemination of research findings and theoretical conceptualisations is organised and expedited rather well *within* epistemic communities, through academic conferences and the refereed journals of the scholarly field. The introduction of research findings into the arenas of policy-making and management, however, remains sporadic, and one wonders at the amount of research findings with the potential to inform the practice and scholarship of educational administration that has found a permanent home on the shelves and computer files of offices in universities, school systems, and educational agencies. Levesque (2011) put the point well:

> Today's researchers understand that it is no longer enough to do research, write up the results and present them at a conference to like-minded peers. The work has to be mobilized out of the ivory tower and into the hands and minds of those who will use it to shape emerging policies and practices.
>
> (p. 1)

Translational efforts are vital to the task of getting ideas and practices into the schools, institutions, offices, and teams where it can be brought to bear on policy and practice.

The important question, however, relates to how the translational function might best be facilitated. One mechanism by which this has found some leverage in the educational administration field has been the leadership centre, a function based upon basic principles of outreach with the clear objective of connecting the university-based activities to field-based groups, agencies, and institutions, translating the products of fundamental research, new perspectives, models, theories, and paradigms to the realities of professional contexts, and as a catalyst for reciprocity: an institutional transfer station, linking knowledge and research of communities of practitioners, theorists and researchers at all levels.

A second mechanism lies in challenging the assumption that the flow of academic knowledge passes from university-based scholarship to contexts of practice. There is no reason to doubt that there is, and likely always will be a strong tradition of university-based research. However, to assume that the translational function is unidirectional—given the contemporary environment we have discussed—would constitute an oversimplification in any contemporary field of interest. We have argued that research activity is becoming democratised and dispersed across professional fields. University researchers and field-based researchers in this view are, simultaneously, designers, creators, translators, and consumers of research, and the translational function is essentially a reciprocal relationship.

Third, there is a need for the continuing realisation of the power of graduate programmes in the field of educational administration at the Masters' and doctoral levels as a powerful conduit for the translational function. The activities within university seminar rooms are essentially translational, and the conversations within those areas are continuing arenas for the translation of theories and research findings to multiple practical contexts of administration and leadership. At a deeper level, they can be models of praxis, exemplars of reflection that can lend action and policy a critical eye, while creating the predisposition for (and cultures *of*) praxis among school and system leaders.

A relatively recent phenomenon across the global landscape of educational administration is the introduction and proliferation of education doctorate (EdD) programmes. Such programmes come in many forms, but their purpose is uniform in that their focus leans more toward a theory-into-practice orientation. These programmes are normally cohort-driven and problem-based, designed to respond to the needs of those educators who are already in, or aspiring to the upper reaches of, administrative work. The research they pursue is intended to inform and improve administrative practice. In most instances, faculty for courses in these programmes are populated with experts in the field educational administration. These experts, designated as clinical or adjunct professors, work alongside regular faculty in the delivery of teaching and research supervision. The idea of a leadership programme where practitioners and academics work side by side in grounded research endeavours is a compelling one and, while it is relatively early in the institutional life of such doctoral programmes, their possibilities for making inroads into the theory-practice gap appear to hold promise.

Toward Epistemic Unity in a Fractured Field: Essential Conversations

We have reflected, in this text, across the spectrum from the meta-theoretical and paradigmatic, through the theoretical, to action and practice-based perspectives. We have examined a variety of viewpoints on the theory/practice *gap*, and have repositioned this debate in terms of the proliferation of *epistemic cultures* in an increasingly complex knowledge environment. We examined the need in the field of educational administration for an enhancement of *the translational function* in bringing educational administration research findings (from across its communities) to policy and practice.

Finally, we turn our attention to the identification of five sets of conversations that we believe to be essential for the variety of epistemic communities and the variety of arenas of action that exist within the field of educational administration to cohere: conversations about *knowledge generation and dissemination*; *engaged scholarship*; the *leadership centre as an integrative mechanism*; *broadening the arena for reflection*; and (returning to Allison's opening discussion) conversations about what we would suggest, from this discussion, as constituting *defining elements of the emerging* fifth age *in the scholarship of educational administration.*

CONVERSATION #1: KNOWLEDGE GENERATION AND DISSEMINATION

There is an urgent need to revisit the flow of knowledge, and to challenge the traditional assumption that knowledge emanates from theory through research to practice. How might a critical theory orientation such as that explicated in this text address this issue? What does the *grand narrative* in the field of educational administration say regarding the nature of the relationship among theory, practice, and research in the field? What interests are our current approaches to knowledge creation, dissemination, and use privileging? What advantages might be gained from challenging the view of *scholarly knowledge* as the domain of university-based scholars, and *practical knowledge* as the domain of school-and system-based practitioners?

Across professional fields, the study and practice of dissemination remains, to a great extent, neglected (Johnson et al., 1996; Schwartz & Capwell, 1995). Literature on organisational change is replete with discussions of the more common organisational issues that serve as blocks to dissemination of critical research findings. King et al. (1998) noted that the dominant view is of dissemination as a one-way process—a downstream transfer from a group who produce the knowledge to a group who implements programmes. They recommended a two-way process, suggesting:

> There is considerable theoretical and practical evidence that linkage systems between researcher and implementer groups can foster more effective transfer of programs. . . . It appears that dissemination is most likely to be influential if it is based on a two-way process of exchanging knowledge between researcher and implementer groups.
>
> (p. 237)

One of the major barriers to the generation of useful knowledge is the lack of authentic sharing of information. Key conversations on this topic can emerge from such question as:

- *How do we address the apparent disconnect among policy makers, school and system professionals, and university-based academics on the constraints that administrators face?*
- *How can we open up arenas for discussion on issues such as the diversity, changing community contexts, over-regulation of school systems, union relationships, and political environments?*

- *What structures and cultures of engagement can best enable practitioners of leadership and administration to participate in structuring the content and processes of educational administration programmes—what is taught and what is researched? How do we open access to the findings of university-based research?*
- *In what fora should knowledge be weighed, assessed, and tried? Who gets to kick the tires? What opportunities are available for new knowledge to be tried on the anvil of community opinion?*

CONVERSATION #2: TOWARD ENGAGED SCHOLARSHIP

Van de Ven and Johnson (2006) proposed the practice of *engaged scholarship* as a collaborative form of research that implies a fundamental shift in how scholars define their relationships with the communities in which they are located, including other disciplines in the university and practitioners in relevant professional domains. They point out:

> Engaged scholarship is a relationship between researchers and practitioners in a learning community. . . . Instead of viewing organizations as data collection sites, and funding sources, an engaged scholar views them as a learning workplace (idea factory) where practitioners and scholars produce knowledge on solely important questions and issues by testing alternative ideas and different views of a common problem.
>
> (p. 810)

This line of thinking presupposes an orientation on the part of the membership of epistemic communities to embrace external perspectives and to hold their own practices and processes up to scrutiny and the possibility of change: to break away the protective boundaries and the mystique, and to welcome ideas and dialogue. We would argue that the environment of contemporary educational organisations—schools, school systems, and related agencies—is such that cultures of research and scholarship are in the ascendancy. This is due, in part to the increased emphasis on research activity in educational organisations, the phenomenon of communities of practice in their various forms, the broadened research experience among practitioners as part of their professional work, and the increasing numbers of administrative professionals with Masters' and doctoral degrees. Fook (2001) noted:

> This kind of conceptualization opens the way for reformulating the research role as one of assisting in the building of theoretical knowledge directly from practice, so that the knowledge created is contextually relevant and flexible. . . . This reformulation questions fundamental assumptions about appropriate ways of knowing, and the types of

knowledge which are valued or discounted. In this way it opens up possibilities for legitimating knowledges and perspectives which have previously been ignored, trivialized or disallowed, and in this sense, has the potential to change and transform currently acceptable ways of operating. This reconceptualization of the integration of research, practice and theory thus has emancipatory possibilities.

(p. 3)

On the basis of the above developments, we argue that the practice-based scholarship of educational administration is growing in its levels of sophistication. In the scholarly study of educational administration, the argument for *engaged scholarship*—formalised relationships between researchers and practitioners—as put forth by Van de Ven and Johnson has considerable merit. This initiative gives rise to such questions as:

- *What structures and processes might be put in place for the relationships suggested by Van de Ven and Johnson to occur?*
- *Who needs to be part of these discussions?*
- *How might "engaged scholarship communities" frame themselves as epistemic cultures with those three qualities identified by Dobusch and Quack—that is, having a common project, shared interests, and shared principled beliefs?*

CONVERSATION #3: THE LEADERSHIP CENTRE AS AN INTEGRATIVE MECHANISM

We hope that we have made the point that there is a dire need for an integrative function that nurtures interaction across epistemic cultures, one that might serve as the major broker of translational activity, that fosters the type of praxis that makes reflection an outward as well as an inward activity, that identifies and recruits the boundary-spanners and individuals who possess the *heteroglossia* that enables them to relate across epistemic cultures: across communities of theoreticians, researchers, policymakers, practitioners, and, indeed, the laity.

One phenomenon that has made inroads in this respect has been the escalating investment by governments in the creation of leadership centres. These have proliferated, in most instances through a widespread belief in the leadership centre as a vehicle for translating and structuring the implementation of government-driven educational initiatives. Were their function to stop there, they would simply represent another arm of government. However, we believe that (in many cases serendipitously) they have developed an identity as an integrative mechanism for the field as a whole, serving as *responders* to the emergent needs of systems and educational agencies; as *matchmakers* between ideas and people, and between researchers and practitioners; as *distributors*, disseminating leadership, management, and policy knowledge to their broader professional communities; and as *catalysts* for the pursuit and identification of new research and practice initiatives, and for dialogue within communities and among communities.

Leadership centres have emerged as a vehicle for creating, accessing, and disseminating knowledge outside of the constraints of the traditional knowledge *system*. They can in many respects represent a healthy challenge to the grand narratives that have driven the traditions of the field of educational administration throughout its history.

Key conversations on this topic relate to such questions as:

- *How can universities nurture the creation of educational leadership centres?*
- *In what ways might such centres inform knowledge development?*
- *How can school system and university scholars and practitioners collaborate in centre development and operation?*

CONVERSATION #4: BROADENING THE ARENA OF REFLECTION: A PHRONETIC VIEW ACROSS EPISTEMIC CULTURES

Breaking through traditional university/field boundaries represents a culture change that in many contexts represents a complex and daunting prospect. Yet cultures of research, reflection, collaboration, and change involving academics and school system practitioners flourish in more than a few settings. They are by no means figments of the imagination. We believe that perspectives on organisational culture, as explicated earlier in this text, can bring a great deal to the conversation:

- *Within an environment of engaged scholarship, as we have discussed, what would cultures of collaborative, critical, creative, and objective analysis of our work look like?*
- *How can we promote the inherent interdependence among theory, research, and practice?*

It is this reasoning that led Kavanagh (2013), in her discussion of business as practice, to frame her work around what she referred to as a phronetic paradigm. Aristotle (2004) pointed out that *phronesis* is not simply a skill (*technē*) because it involves not only the ability to decide how to achieve a certain end, but also the ability to reflect upon and determine good ends consistent with the aim of what he termed *living well*.

- *In educational administration: How can we nurture cultures of reflection in a broadened, distributed epistemic community?*

CONVERSATION #5: THE SCHOLARLY STUDY OF EDUCATIONAL ADMINISTRATION IN THE FIFTH AGE

One additional and inescapable point concerning context must be made. Unlike university colleges in the *pure* social sciences and natural sciences, university-based professional colleges and schools have their real and present professional communities that, for better or worse, are their lifeblood. Indeed, university-based scholars should be mindful that the professional communities also serve as powerful arbiters of their relevance. If there is credence to Allison's comment that the evolution of academic administration appears to have progressively distanced and isolated the work of university departments from immediate concerns and interests of school administrators, the argument for engaged scholarship assumes even greater urgency.

And so to the question: Whither educational administration in the fifth age? There can be little doubt that the forces we have identified above, and alluded to throughout this discussion, have powerful implications for the scholarly study of the field, and for the structures and processes by which its actors will ply their trades. In light of these implications, we can identify some prognostications about the scholarly study of educational administration, and some of their more significant potential influences. We frame these as *enduring influences* and *emergent realities*.

ENDURING INFLUENCES

Professional community. There will always be a community of professional practitioners, and there will always exist significant potential for productive and innovative relationships that can enhance the transfer of knowledge, the relevance of research, and the quality of graduate scholarship and learning.

University norms. University traditions and modes of operation undoubtedly influence the predisposition among scholars for engagement in professional communities. There is little question that this will be influenced by the reward system and related university traditions. To a great extent, scholarly and teaching pursuits have been *independent* activities. Making the switch to predominantly *interdependent* relationships can be a tough sell internally; it will take some additional commitment and perseverance when it comes to collaboration with school practitioners. Nonetheless, we consider it critical that departments of educational administration and leadership, in conjunction with school systems, explore and implement ways of building engaged scholarship and communities of practice across traditional boundaries.

Paradigmatic and theoretical guideposts. With reference to Wren's notion of *the past as prologue*, there will always be presence of theoretical perspectives by which we can engage our collective sense-making and research about the workings of schools and their people. Such theoretical perspectives and related debates as captured in this text are more varied, and the debates more common than ever before—providing tools for the study and analysis of educational administration at deeper and richer levels of insight.

EMERGENT REALITIES

Reflecting once more on our quote from Daniel Wren, our discussion has been synthetic in examining trends, movements, and environmental forces that have provided a basis for our examination of approaches to the functions of research, theorising, and teaching in educational administration. Those forces have included *sophistication* of practitioner communities in on-site research, knowledge generation, reflection, and application in communities of practice; the increasing *heterogeneity* of educational populations, bringing diversity of ideology and cultural perspective; *technological leaps* that continuously confound our efforts to keep pace; and the *blurring of functional boundaries* that throughout the prior stages of development of educational administration have been sharply delineated. We believe those forces are playing a major role in shaping the ways in which we are engaging the scholarship of educational administration. More critically, they are changing the criteria by which the sub-communities of the educational administration field remain relevant.

In light of these forces, we envision the fifth age in the scholarly study of educational administration to be characterized by:

- distribution of the locus of responsibility for teaching and research;
- dispersal of venues for knowledge creation;
- democratisation of research across communities of the field;
- blurring of the distinction between the locus of knowledge *generation*, the locus of knowledge *consumption*, and the locus of *responsibility for both* across contexts;
- dissemination as a continuing, multi-instrumental, reciprocal phenomenon;
- transformation of the roles of researcher, teacher, learner, and relationships among them;
- growth of professional doctorates in an increasingly sophisticated professional population;
- diversification of educational populations, with escalating demands on support and curriculum design functions; and
- formalisation of linkages between communities of scholarship and practice within the field of educational administration.

CONCLUSION

Will the above discussion inform a positive direction for educational administration's fifth age? Or will its sub-communities curl up on themselves as self-referential systems increasingly separated from each other, and from reality? Our intent in suggesting these five areas of conversation was to have them take place across communities of scholarship and practice, rather than purely within them. Kuhn (2002) addressed the strategy in terms of networks consisting not merely of individuals but also concepts, traversing, but not dissolving, boundaries between communities of practice. To achieve this requires mechanisms that are much more formal, much more tangible and systemic than they are informal and sporadic. It requires a philosophical transformation from the view that scholarship and practice are independent activities, to one that sees them and their constituencies as irrevocably interdependent. For scholars, this entails making the language of their thinking and research accessible; it involves decoding, translating, and discussing, so that the inherent power of the ideas strips away their mystique and widens the arena for conversations about the broader possibilities. For those epistemic cultures that coalesce around areas of knowledge within organisations, this requires a perpetual interaction with their broader contexts and an ever-present reflexivity as to their own continuing relevance.

> Today is not like yesterday, nor will tomorrow be like today:
> Yet today is a synergism of all our yesterdays, and tomorrow will be
> the same.
>
> —*Daniel Wren*

REFERENCES

Aristotle. (2004). *Nicomachean ethics* (J. A. K. Thomson, Trans.). London: Penguin.

Grimshaw, J. M., Eccles, M .P., Lavis, J. N., Hill, S. J., & Squires, J. E. (2012). Knowledge translation of research findings. *Implementation Science, 7*(50), 21–36.

Cetina, K. K. (1999). *Epistemic cultures: How the sciences make knowledge.* Boston, MA: Harvard University.

Cronin, B. (2003). Scholarly communication and epistemic cultures. Keynote address to *Scholarly Tribes and Tribulations: How Tradition and Technology Are Driving Disciplinary Change.* Washington, D.C.: Association of Research Libraries.

Dobusch, L., & Quack, S. (2008). *Epistemic communities and social movements: Transnational dynamics in the case of creative commons.* Discussion Paper: Max Planck Institute for the Study of Societies.

Fook, J. (2001). Linking theory, practice and research. *Critical Social Work, 2*(1), 1–4.

Jones, A. (2007). Multiplicities or manna from heaven? Critical thinking and the disciplinary context. *Australian Journal of Education, 51*(1), 84–103.

Johnson, J., Green, L., Frankish, C. J., MacLean, D., & Stachenko, S. (1996). A dissemination research agenda to strengthen health promotion and Disease prevention. *Canadian Journal of Public Health, 87*(2), 5–11.

Kavanagh, D. (2013). Problematizing practice: MacIntyre and management. *Organization, 20*(1), 103–115.

King, L., Hawe, P., & Wise, M. (1998). Making dissemination a two-way process. *Health Promotion Journal, 13*(3), 237–244.

Kuhn, T. (2002). Negotiating boundaries between scholars and practitioners. *Management Communication Quarterly, 16*(1), 106–112.

Levesque, P. (2011). *Translating research into policy and practice.* Ottawa, ON: University of Ottawa, Centre for Continuing Education.

Moisander, J., & Stenfors, S. (2009). Exploring the edges of theory-practice gap: Epistemic cultures in strategy-tool development and use. *Organization, 16*(2), 227–247.

Mork, B. E., Aanestadt, M., Hanseth, O., & Grisot, M. (2008). Conflicting epistemic cultures and obstacles for learning across communities of practice. *Knowledge and Process Management, 15*(1), 12–23.

Porter, S., & Ryan, S. (1996). Breaking the boundaries between nursing and sociology: A critical realist ethnography of the theory-practice gap. *Journal of Advanced Nursing, 24*(2), 413–420.

Robinson, V. (1998). Methodology and the research-practice gap. *Educational Researcher, 27*(1), 17–26.

Schwartz, R., & Capwell, E. (1995). Advancing the link between health promotion researchers and practitioners: A commentary. *Health Education Research, 10*(3), i–vi.

Titler, M. (2007). Translating research into practice. *American Journal of Nursing, 107*(6), 26–33.

Van De Ven, A. H., & Johnson, P. E. (2006). Knowledge for theory and practice. *Academy of Management Review, 31*(4), 802–821.

Wren, D., & Bedeian, A. (2009). *The evolution of management thought* (6th ed.). New York: John Wiley & Sons.

Contributors

Derek J. Allison is Professor Emeritus at Western University in London, Canada. Career research interests revolve around education as an organised activity, administration as a cultural activity, and associated epistemological challenges.

David Burgess is Head, Graduate Chair, and Associate Professor in the Department of Educational Administration at the University of Saskatchewan in Saskatoon, Canada. His research interests include philosophy of organization, organizational theory, educational law, methods in legal instruction and research, comparative educational administration, and critical realism. Burgess holds university teaching concentrations in history of organizational theory, philosophy of organization, and educational law.

José da Costa is a professor of Educational Administration and Leadership. He joined the Faculty of Education at the University of Alberta in 1993. His research focus is centred on how educational programming and administrative structures impact student success in school.

Scott Eacott is Associate Professor and Leader of the Contemporary Thought and Analysis in Educational Leadership, Management and Administration (ELMA) research group at Australian Catholic University in Sydney, Australia. His contributions to and interest in educational leadership fall into three main areas: theorising leadership, management, and administration; leadership preparation and development; and re-conceptualising strategy in educational administration.

Gerald Fallon is a former teacher, school principal, director of instruction, and senior district-based administrator in human resource and labour relation. Currently, he is an Assistant Professor of Educational Administration and Leadership at the Faculty of Education of the University of British Columbia. His research interests include indigenous education, international and comparative education, leadership and organizations, and educational policy. Dr Fallon teaches courses related to leadership, aims of education, school law, economics of education, and educational policy.

Deborah Hicks is a doctoral candidate with the Department of Education Policy Studies at the University of Alberta, Edmonton, Canada. Her research interests are focused on the construction of librarians' professional identities, the impact of technological change on the professional identities of librarians, and representations of information seeking practices in popular culture. She is the author of *Technology and Professional Identity of Librarians: The Making of the Cybrarian,* published with IGI Global.

Renate Kahlke is a PhD candidate in the Faculty of Education, Department of Educational Policy Studies at the University of Alberta. Her work examines how health science educators understand critical thinking, and how that understanding relates to educational policy in the health sciences. This current follows from a career as an academic administrator developing curriculum and implementing policy in the field of interprofessional health science education. In her Master's work at McMaster University, she studied in the Department of English, Cultural Studies and Critical Theory, with an emphases in Marxism, Critical Theory, and Postcolonial theory.

Coral Mitchell is a Professor in the Faculty of Education at Brock University, where she teaches undergraduate and graduate courses in educational administration, school organizations, and leadership practices, and supervises master's and doctoral students' research. Her educational career has also included classroom teaching and system consulting in elementary and secondary schools. Her research agenda addresses the development of learning communities, capacity-building for improved professional practice, and the educational role of school leaders, with a focus on how to construct life-enhancing educational organizations and administrative practices.

Robin Mueller is an Educational Development Consultant at the Taylor Institute for Teaching and Learning at the University of Calgary in Calgary, Canada. Dr Mueller is a parent, scholar, educator, educational developer, and organizational consultant. Her research interests include higher education teaching and learning, organizational theory, critical realism, and educational leadership.

Paul Newton is an Associate Professor in the Department of Educational Administration at the University of Saskatchewan. His research interests are school improvement, the principalship, staff development, and teacher professional learning.

Trâm Trương Anh Nguyễn is a PhD candidate in the Department of Educational Policy Studies, University of Alberta in Edmonton, Canada. Her research interests include global citizenship education, internationalization of higher education, theories of educational administration and leadership, and Asian wisdom traditions.

Jerald Paquette is a Professor Emeritus at the Faculty of Education at the University of Western Ontario. His main research interests are in education finance, minority education policy, First Nations education, research theory and methods, educational policy and related issues of social purpose, and equity and public funding of private education in the Canadian context.

Madeline M. Press is a faculty member in the School of Nursing at Saskatchewan Polytechnic (SaskPolytech) in Saskatoon, Canada. She is an Adjunct Professor with the Faculty of Nursing at the University of Regina and is currently completing her PhD in Educational Administration at the University of Saskatchewan, Press is engaged in a number of collaborative research projects with colleagues at institutions in Western Canada. Her research focus is community wellness and nursing education.

Fred Renihan is currently research associate and adjunct professor in the Doctoral program in Educational Leadership at Simon Fraser University in Vancouver, Canada. He was, until 2005, Superintendent of Schools in Surrey British Columbia. He has been a Dean of Education, a teacher, a principal, Director of Education, Executive Director of Curriculum and Instruction, and Assistant Deputy Minister of Education with the Government of Saskatchewan.

Pat Renihan is a Professor Emeritus in Educational Administration at the University of Saskatchewan in Saskatoon, Canada. In addition to service on a variety of local, provincial, and national boards and committees concerned with educational leadership, his professional career has offered experience as teacher, superintendent, department head, chair of graduate programmes, and founding Director of the Saskatchewan Educational Leadership Unit. Renihan's scholarly contributions are pronounced in areas related to the principalship, supervision, organizational theory, effective teaching, effective schools, and Board/CEO self-assessment.

Augusto Riveros is Assistant Professor in critical policy, equity, and leadership studies at Western University in London, Canada. His research explores the intersections between philosophy, educational leadership, and educational policy analysis. His areas of inquiry are teacher learning, professional identities, leadership discourses in education, and the history of educational administration.

Larry Sackney is Professor Emeritus in the Department of Educational Administration at the University of Saskatchewan. His area of teaching expertise is school improvement, educational change, and professional learning. His career has included classroom teaching, school administration, school and system consulting, and teaching and administration at the university level. His research agenda addresses the development of learning communities, capacity-building for improved professional practice, and the educational role of school leaders, with a focus on developing school systems and structures that support authentic teaching and learning.

Pamela Timanson is a PhD candidate in the Educational Administration and Leadership stream of the Department of Educational Policy Studies at the University of Alberta. She completed her BEd and MEd (Workplace and Adult Learning) through the University of Calgary. Her doctoral research is focused on the examination of how teachers learn informally within the knowledge culture of their workplace.

Melody Viczko is an Assistant Professor at Western University in the area of Critical Policy Studies, Equity, and Leadership Studies in the Faculty of Education. Her recent research involves a relational approach to studying multi-scalar governance in the internationalization of higher education, examining how policy enrolls different actors and knowledges in the enactment of internationalization. Other interests include exploring the knowledge contributions of female scholars in educational administration research and teaching in Canadian universities.

Dawn Wallin is a Professor in the Department of Educational Administration, Foundations, and Psychology; and Associate Dean, Graduate and Professional Programs, and Research, Faculty of Education, at the University of Manitoba in Winnipeg, Canada. Her areas of scholarship include educational leadership, rural education and governance, and gender issues in leadership.

Index

CPSIA information can be obtained
at www.ICGtesting.com
Printed in the USA
LVOW13*1007260218
567885LV00009B/72/P